RESEARCH PROJECTS FOR BUSINESS & MANAGEMENT STUDENTS

Sara Miller McCune founded SAGE Publishing in 1965 to support the dissemination of usable knowledge and educate a global community. SAGE publishes more than 1000 journals and over 800 new books each year, spanning a wide range of subject areas. Our growing selection of library products includes archives, data, case studies and video. SAGE remains majority owned by our founder and after her lifetime will become owned by a charitable trust that secures the company's continued independence.

Los Angeles | London | New Delhi | Singapore | Washington DC | Melbourne

RESEARCH PROJECTS FOR BUSINESS & MANAGEMENT STUDENTS

2ND EDITION

SIAH HWEE ANG

Los Angeles | London | New Delhi
Singapore | Washington DC | Melbourne

Los Angeles | London | New Delhi
Singapore | Washington DC | Melbourne

SAGE Publications Ltd
1 Oliver's Yard
55 City Road
London EC1Y 1SP

SAGE Publications Inc.
2455 Teller Road
Thousand Oaks, California 91320

SAGE Publications India Pvt Ltd
B 1/I 1 Mohan Cooperative Industrial Area
Mathura Road
New Delhi 110 044

SAGE Publications Asia-Pacific Pte Ltd
3 Church Street
#10-04 Samsung Hub
Singapore 049483

Editor: Matthew Waters
Assistant editor: Jasleen Kaur
Assistant editor, digital: Sunita Patel
Production editor: Tanya Szwarnowska
Copyeditor: Catja Pafort
Proofreader: Sarah Cooke
Indexer: Judith Lavender
Marketing manager: Abigail Sparks
Cover design: Francis Kenney
Typeset by: C&M Digitals (P) Ltd, Chennai, India
Printed in the UK

Library of Congress Control Number: 2020949367

British Library Cataloguing in Publication data

A catalogue record for this book is available from the British Library

ISBN 978-1-5297-0947-6
ISBN 978-1-5297-0946-9 (pbk)

At SAGE we take sustainability seriously. Most of our products are printed in the UK using responsibly sourced papers and boards. When we print overseas we ensure sustainable papers are used as measured by the PREPS grading system. We undertake an annual audit to monitor our sustainability.

For Xiaochen

Contents

About the author

Professor Siah Hwee Ang is Professor of International Business and Strategy, inaugural Chair in Business in Asia and Director of the New Zealand's Southeast Asia Centre of Asia-Pacific Excellence at Victoria University of Wellington in New Zealand. He has published in international top-tier journals such as the *Strategic Management Journal*, *Journal of Management*, *Journal of Management Studies* and *Journal of World Business*. He is also Senior Editor at the *Journal of World Business*, a leading international business journal, and has sat on the editorial boards of various international top-tier journals over the years. For the last twenty years, he has been teaching research design and methods to research students.

Before joining Victoria University of Wellington, Professor Ang was Professor in Strategy and Associate Dean Postgraduate and International (Asia) at the University of Auckland Business School. He has also held appointments at the Cass Business School of the City University of London and the National University of Singapore, where he completed his PhD in Management. Professor Ang is Visiting Professor to several Asian universities. He writes frequently in the media.

Preface

Business and management research is fast becoming an important element of business organizations. In many countries, research has some bearing on the extent of government education funding. Universities that seek domestic and foreign students use research ranking as one of their key attraction points. Organizations, recognizing that learning from other organizations' mistakes is less painful than learning from their own mistakes, are increasingly engaged in research-informed decision making.

Research is the systematic inquiry or investigation into a subject in order to discover or revise facts, theories and applications. Research allows us to generate more awareness of human behaviours, organizations and society. Research also allows organizations to reduce uncertainty as due diligence is done before any new ventures are implemented. Over the last three decades, as tertiary institutions and organizations have come to recognize the importance of business and management research, we see that research capabilities and research programmes have started to take centre stage. This in turn generates significant interests in research design and methods, which involve the fundamental skills required to conduct any form of research.

The number of books on research design and methods that are on the market are increasing by the day. We see mainly two types of books. First is the type that deals with mainly design, and like this book, is concerned with how a researcher or student goes about conducting research, right from the inception of ideas to the published outputs. Second, which is what this book is not, is the type that is more tailored to specific research methods. For example, there are books that cater broadly to quantitative research methods or qualitative research methods. There are also books that deal with more specific methods such as case studies, multivariate analysis, content analysis, etc. You are unlikely to run out of options in terms of finding a book that fits with your needs.

Yet, despite the abundance of research books on research design and methods, two observations have to be made. First, most research design books are structured in a way that pitch the process of conducting research as a linear one that involves sequentially structured components. Whilst there is no doubt that the components of the research are generally structured in a certain way to allow more clarity, the actual process of research is far from linear. A linear structure will allow for more systematic learning – but is definitely not a good reflection of the reality of research.

Second, and I would say more critical than the first observation, most books are pitched in a way that suggest that, somehow, the research process itself is a prescriptive one. In other words, for each phase of a research, so long as you handle the expectations of what are required, you will be fine in your research work. Of course, it is easier for systematic learning if a textbook is prescriptive. Nonetheless, it is more likely that a student or researcher will hit a hurdle in the research process and will struggle to find help. Normally, this help involves the implicit tacit knowledge that is usually not well-documented. The only available sources of advice in such instances are often a research supervisor or mentor.

It is these two observations which I have repeatedly experienced in my time teaching research design and methods, supervising students and researching, that gave rise to the idea for this book. While it will not cover all the various tacit research processes that are not covered in other books, it is a good step towards providing a more realistic view of the actual research process. While I seek to decode some of the more commonly understood tacit knowledge of research in this book, clearly the content of this book – especially in terms of research reminders – should not be treated as being prescriptive. Rather, these reminders should just be treated as a guide, not to mention that the actual research process (in the cognitive sense) is in fact much more complicated than it is pitched in this book.

The picture is further complicated by the fact that the expectations of the rigour differ across international, regional and national journals, as well as across research degrees and tertiary institutions. Researchers from different areas in business and management also do not possess the same research skills. As such, the training of their students and the students' exposure to research follow paths that actually result in differences in research students' perception of what research exactly is when they graduate.

This book aims to provide an introductory to intermediate level (depending on the level to which it is utilized) guide to the research process and research method approaches in business and management. It provides extensive discussions of both the explicit and tacit knowledge embedded in research. The textbook is ideal for both senior undergraduate and graduate students undertaking research dissertations, theses and projects. It can also work as a textbook for research-oriented courses. As the book also includes practical aspects of research, it is also suitable for managers who want to undertake research-informed projects for their decision-making.

The standard features of the chapters in this textbook include conversation boxes, end-of-chapter summaries, end-of-chapter questions, key terms, illustrations and figures, references, and additional readings. Throughout the text, key terms have been bolded. This book has incorporated a feature called conservation box, which provides some highlights of the issue to be discussed in the text, simultaneously bringing to your attention some of the dilemmas that will surface in the research process.

Online resources

Research Projects for Business & Management Students, 2nd edition is supported by online resources for lecturers to help support teaching. These resources are available at: **https://study.sagepub.com/ang2e**

For Lecturers

- **Easily integrate the chapters** into your weekly lectures by using the **PowerPoint slides** created by the author.

1
FUNDAMENTALS OF RESEARCH

1.1 INTRODUCTION

> ### Conversation box
>
> Professor Richardson, as the Dean of Research, makes routine presentations in under-graduate classes to encourage the students to engage in the Masters programme. Below is an encounter after one of the Professor's presentations.
>
> *Josephine [student]:*   Hi, Professor, I'm Jo, I'm now in the third year of my undergrad-uate studies. Before your talk today, the whole notion of doing postgraduate studies hadn't crossed my mind. For me, it has always been about getting a tertiary education and then a good job and career progression etc. But given how businesses work, is there some value for me to engage in graduate studies that involve some research before going into the job market?
>
> *Professor:*   Jo, it's great that the talk has got you thinking. One should not assume that our knowledge comes out of nowhere. What you have learned from textbooks throughout your undergraduate studies – those facts, concepts and even examples – are out-comes derived from research conducted by researchers or the authors of the textbooks. Without research, generic knowledge will become stagnant, though contextual knowledge will continue to accumulate. A graduate degree will bring you closer to poten-tially linking your study to business realities.

Research is an important part of our accumulation of knowledge in business and management. Without research, understanding of the business world and the behaviours of organizations within it will be restricted. It is restricted in the sense that **learning** can still happen and will reside within individuals and within a single organization, and around the shared linkages between individuals across organizations and between sets of organizations, but not beyond. Learning is thus confined to our own experience and individual case exposure to the business environment. But as a society, our collective knowledge will make marginal progress. Research and its documentation allow wider learning to occur as research outcomes are disseminated, resulting in a better understanding of human behaviour, organizations and society, beyond individual experiences.

Nevertheless, while the research processes and outputs can take various forms, the expectations and challenges of conducting research are fundamentally similar. This chapter covers what is involved in business and management research – including basic terminologies and types of research and their dissemination. This will be followed by some fundamental expectations about conducting research. A discussion of ethical research behaviours and the consequences of not adhering to ethical standards when doing research follows, before typical research processes are presented. The chapter rounds off with an overview of the rest of the book.

1.2 BASIC TERMINOLOGIES

Before we proceed to discuss the types of research and the research process, it is essential to know the basic terminologies that are being used in research.

Any research typically starts with an issue. This research issue can arise from your experience as you encounter or observe a certain **phenomenon**. For example, you might like to understand if becoming an organizational citizen can enhance career prospects within your organization. You will then undertake a study on the linkage between being an organizational citizen and career progression of a sample of other individuals. As another example, you are interested in the phenomenon of the sharing economy, in particular around how individuals and organizations can benefit from such a logistic phenomenon. You will study whether companies who have embraced the sharing economy are doing better than their competitors who have not. These inquiries will constitute the **research question** for your **research project**.

A **research topic** usually consists of investigating issues around a concept or the relationships between two or more concepts. A **concept** is a bundle of meanings or characteristics associated with certain events, objects, conditions, situations and behaviours. Concepts are often developed over time through shared usage by researchers. Hence, there is always some degree of consensus as to what a particular concept constitutes. This common understanding also allows you to have a base to which you can relate all the developments surrounding the research topic. In every piece of research work, it is important that concepts and their links are well articulated. The applicability of research hinges on how clearly you conceptualize and how well others understand the concepts you use. Becker (1998) extensively discusses some of the characteristics of concepts.

A research issue can arise as a result of a request to either conduct an exploratory study or derive a solution. For example, let's say you are working in a bank as an analyst. Your manager has just asked you to conduct some research into the extent to which logistics companies such as Grab or DiDi have started to build payment platforms for their clients. This will require you to work on a research project that assesses logistic companies' engagement in this space. Further, your manager may also expect you to come up with a solution around how the bank can work with these logistics companies. To provide this deeper recommendation, more research into what other banks are doing will be necessary, resulting in a bigger **research scope**.

A research issue can also be established from a research gap in our general understanding of a particular concept or a business area. For example, the notion of the importance of having a good reputation is widely agreed. However, the extent of how fast and effective a company can build its reputation is less understood. You are interested to understand more on how companies go about generating reputation in order to fill this research gap and will undertake a research project as a result.

The sources of a research question or topic mentioned above are indeed not mutually exclusive. In the example on the research gap in reputation building, it is also possible that your company may ask you to examine the same research topic for the purpose of finding ways to bolster its reputation. Both motivations, i.e. your company's (recommendations) and yours (gap) can converge. In other words, the same research topic can be derived from different avenues.

Even if you do not have a specific research topic in mind at the start of your research project, it will be necessary to have a broad research area of interest, to help provide a direction in which to start your **research process**. In essence, you will need the help of some keywords to set up the search process. A **literature search** can then help you shape your general area of interest into a more manageable research topic. The scope of a research topic usually involves a **judgement call**.

A **literature review** involves going through all the previous research related to your research topic. It covers both theoretical and empirical works. Theoretical works typically involve conceptual discussions of a research topic, and sometimes may involve a current stock-take of a particular research area. Empirical works include the examination of a research topic typically with the help of **data** points. The literature review can also cover anecdotal evidence, defined as testimony that something is true, false, related, or unrelated based on isolated examples of someone's personal experience. This is extremely useful in the context of the specialized knowledge of a particular individual or a specific group of individuals.

The outcome from a literature review usually involves a corroboration of past research as well as some areas that can be considered for further research.

A research project can also be labelled as being generic or context-specific. Testing the direct and indirect contributions a group of industries make to an economy using data across multiple countries in Asia and Europe is a generic research project. Testing these effects only in the context of the United States constitutes a country-specific issue. The same relationship testing using data in the biotechnology industry results in an industry-specific study. An examination that includes a single or limited number of years of data is a cross-sectional project, while testing the relationships over time will lead to a longitudinal study.

Next, you will have to work on the research design that best addresses your research topic. There are mainly three types of design – **quantitative, qualitative** and mixed methods. Quantitative research usually involves large quantities of data whereby the researcher looks for patterns across the data points. It usually starts from logically driven **propositions** or **hypotheses**, which are then empirically tested. Propositions are over-arching statements that provide a general direction for the study. Hypotheses are statements that elaborate on your research question – making it testable. Qualitative research is more exploratory. A researcher using this method explores research issues by observing behavioural patterns and seeks to find theories to explain the observed patterns. Mixed methods involve a mixture of quantitative and qualitative methods and are often used to add **rigour** to a research study if the use of either quantitative or qualitative methods is deemed to be inadequate for the research purpose. Basically, mixed methods combine the strengths of both quantitative and qualitative methods. An example would be using qualitative data to provide supplementary information for understanding an aspect of a research topic to which quantitative data are not readily available.

Once the research design is set, the next step is to work out the data and variables needed to investigate your research question. Data availability often helps inform the feasibility of the research topic and the use of research design. Variables are easily derived from the research topic itself, although you also have to take care of other extraneous factors that may have an impact on the relationships you are examining. The choice of variables is also contingent on your ability to observe them, or at least to be able to proxy them through indirect ways. Measurements of these variables can be in the form of direct or indirect observations. Direct observations can involve inter-views, focus groups and participant observations. Indirect observations usually involve surveys or archival data.

Having collected your data, you will then need to analyze them using statistical and interpretative methods. There are many variations within these methods so it will be important to make the right choices here. This is selected mostly based on the data that you are analyzing, i.e. the assumptions, boundaries, scope and scale of the data.

Writing up the findings is the final step in the research process. In general, you will have to report the findings, and discuss and conclude your research. The contribution of a new piece of research will come from making incremental or substantive contributions using existing theories, or applying a theoretical lens that has not been used in previous studies in the area. Recommendations and solutions are increasingly expected as outcomes of research projects. The writing up process often involves writing and rewriting of the research output as you piece together all parts of your research project.

1.3 TYPES OF RESEARCH

There are many ways to classify research. This section will illustrate three common ways of segregating research: **concept-driven** vs. **solution-driven** (based on research outcome), **inductive** vs. **deductive** (based on research process) and **quantitative** vs. **qualitative** vs. **mixed** (based on research methods).

1.3.1 Concept-driven vs solution-driven

Research can be classified based on the demand side – what drives the research? Broadly speaking, there are two classifications: concept-driven and solution-driven. Concept-driven research usually starts with a research gap at hand. Researchers then seek to address this gap by conducting a study. The quality of work is often assessed based on how much contribution the study has advanced addressing this gap. This contribution in turn determines the grade outcome of a research project or the quality of the journal in which the research output can be published. This can take either the inductive or deductive approach (Section 1.3.2) and can adopt quantitative, qualitative or mixed methods (Section 1.3.3). Building on the example in Section 1.2, conducting research on how companies such as Grab and DiDi have built payment platforms and how these have impacts on their performance is an example of a concept-driven research.

Solution-driven research is research conducted to assist with making better-informed decisions. **Market research** that seeks to address a market need, for example to assess consumer perceptions and market potential of a particular product or service offering, is often considered to be solution-driven. Likewise, to work towards recommendations for a bank for potential collaborations with Grab or DiDi is a solution-driven research project.

It is important to note that concept-driven and solution-driven research can inform each other. For example using theoretical underpinning and prior empirical findings for **organizational research** can result in an appropriate solution-driven piece of research well grounded in conceptual standing. Increasingly, research projects are conducted using this combinative model.

Very often, concept-driven research has been labelled as 'in a black box' research and thus does not have any practical value, even though some of these studies still find their way into high quality journals in the field. Increasingly, however, business and management fields are more demanding in terms of 'why we care about the outcomes of this research project'. Thus, it is getting rarer to encounter good research that has no relevance, albeit the impact or span of influence may be smaller in some cases. Nonetheless, researchers continue to think that more can be done to translate research outcomes into actionable practices for businesses and managers (Pearce and Huang, 2012). Part of this perceived weak link between research and practice can be attributed to the complexity of research in business and management, which tends to utilize theories from other social science disciplines such as psychology, sociology, economics and political science (Devinney and Siegel, 2012).

Vermeulen (2005) makes good arguments for the fact that a piece of research cannot be relevant without research rigour even if it claims to be so, as what is being discussed does not have any scientific backing. Any work or any claim that is believable should be well grounded in research. The same will apply to solution-driven research projects. It is possible for research rigour and relevance to be more balanced in some sense. While this bridging is never easy, it is important to take note of the remarks Vermeulen (2005), and, earlier, Staw (1995) have made. This is also by no means different from trying to bridge the academic–practitioner divide (Rynes et al., 2001).

1.3.2 Inductive vs. deductive

Research can also be classified based on the approach used – whether it is inductive or deductive. The inductive approach is grounded in observations – seeking to explain what was observed. Figure 1.1 shows a simple diagrammatic representation of the inductive approach.

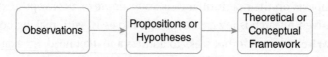

Figure 1.1   An inductive approach to research

The inductive approach is one whereby a researcher makes observations and attempts to link these observations using common threads, i.e. finding some relationships or patterns among the observations. They formulate propositions or hypotheses that help explain the observed patterns or relationships. From this, they establish conclusions and a theoretical or conceptual framework.

A research project with limited observations typically adopts this approach. Phenomenon-based research (Doh, 2015; Von Krogh et al., 2012) will also tend to start with this approach. As the inductive approach seeks to make a broader conclusion based on only a part of the premise, the strength of the generalization from indicative reasoning will be dependent on the extent of representation of observations. The strength of the inductive reasoning increases as the number, scope and diversity of observations increases.

The opposite of the inductive approach is the deductive approach. Research adopting the deductive approach is more theoretically or conceptually driven. That is, a researcher first establishes some relationships between concepts. This is then narrowed down to more specific hypotheses. These hypotheses are then tested using a relatively large number of observations. The analysis will determine if the hypotheses are supported or not. Conclusions and implications are then derived from these results. Figure 1.2 presents a simple diagrammatic representation of the deductive approach.

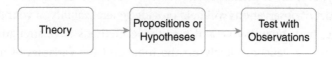

Figure 1.2 A deductive approach to research

The inductive approach is more exploratory – as it relies on observations as a starting point to address the research question. The deductive approach is more funnelled and focuses on testing various facets of the research question. It is important to note that the inductive and deductive approaches, while mutually exclusive, are often being used simultaneously by researchers. This is especially evident in the business and management field. As you can see from the figures, the two approaches can be easily integrated to form a cyclical process involving feedback loops – an important element of research that will be highlighted throughout this book.

1.3.3 Quantitative vs. qualitative vs. mixed methods

Quantitative researchers stress the positivist approach to research: they emphasize the importance of formulating propositions and hypotheses through logical arguments from well-supported theories and literature. This form of research often involves substantial data points for statistical analysis. This is commonly associated with the deductive approach as discussed in Section 1.3.2. Qualitative researchers adopt mostly the inductive approach, using observations as a starting point, and seek explanations for the observed behaviours. Compared to quantitative research, this form of research tends to be grounded in fewer observations. While quantitative methods have their origins in physical science research, which tends to be more deterministic, qualitative methods have only become more common since the 1970s, when concerns were raised on the limitations of quantitative methods in general to deal with the complexity of social science research (Morgan and Smircich, 1980).

Due to the differences in the two methods, research design and methods books often position the quantitative and qualitative methods as mutually exclusive and sometimes as competing methods. However, while each of these methods has its strong points, they also have weaknesses. Interestingly, some of the weaknesses of one method can be partially addressed by using the other method. For example, you are interested in studying if employee incentives such as bonuses affect performance. Anecdotal evidence may suggest that this is true within your department. As the conclusion is only based on your department size of eight people, it is hard to ascertain if this applies to other departments, limiting **generalizability**. Different departments have different work-flow and expectations so some incentives may not work equally well in other contexts. Broadening your study to include observations in other departments, i.e. increasing the overall number of observations will help provide generalizability of your prediction.

In essence, both quantitative and qualitative methods have strengths and weaknesses. The choice depends largely on the topic and the variables of interest. Even within the same research area, one method might fit better than the other depending on the relationships you are examining. Edmondson and McManus (2007) provide some guidelines on how to make this choice. For example, in research areas that are more mature, i.e. variables are better understood, quantitative methods are useful to enhance knowledge through greater generalizability.

Over time, researchers start to realize the potential of using these methods in complementary ways, hence the advent of *mixed methods*. Mixed methods essentially involve the use of both quantitative and qualitative methods of investigation within a single research project. The concurrent use of the two methods allows the strengths of both to be combined, while at the same time addressing the shortcomings of each (Molina-Azorin, 2017; Turner et al., 2017). Using the above example on employee incentives, let us say in the process of analysis, it was discovered that data for one of the variables of interest – retention allowance – is not readily available due to its sensitivity. As a result, this could no longer be included in the analysis. In this case, a couple of case studies on retention allowance using qualitative methods may be used to supplement the research results.

1.4 FUNDAMENTAL RESEARCH EXPECTATIONS

At different levels in the research community there are different expectations of research. For research projects, the theoretical contribution is less important than the practicality of the topic for the audience. For graduate research degrees, both the theoretical contributions and practical implications are expected to be increased. For PhD candidates, the expectations for both contributions and implications are relatively higher. For research bound for publications, a reasonable level of originality is expected. For the best journals in a field, high levels of originality will be expected. Nonetheless, despite all these differences in expectations, there are some fundamental expectations good research must fulfill at all levels.

1.4.1 Objectivity

Research has significant influence on both knowledge and practice. In order to pass on the right knowledge, from both the epistemological and managerial viewpoints, maintaining **objectivity** in research is essential. Objectivity is the extent to which the researcher's methods are free of prejudice (Armstrong, 1979). Researchers have documented the risk with having subjectivity in our research process (e.g. Ford, 2004). For example, untentionally influencing subjects while conducting experiments through additional communications and cues.

Maintaining objectivity is by no means easy, though. We have interests in the topic that we research, which conditions us to have a perspective that is formed from our own experience and exposure. As a result, we tend to be advocates of our research, proposing ideas that we hope would advance the field. However, as a researcher advocates for their hypothesis, there is a chance they can become biased (Armstrong, 1979).

Researchers have long recognized that the objectivity of scientific discovery can become difficult to disentangle from our engagement (Mitroff, 1972). Along this line, there have been anti-objectivism movements and cases have in fact been made against potential objectivity in social science research (Cunningham, 1973). Nevertheless, striving for objectivity in research ensures that the research process and findings are not tainted by subjective biases or that these are reduced to a minimum, making our research findings more convincing and useful. For example, Armstrong (1979) recommends that multiple hypotheses should be proposed to enable the reduction of bias associated with advocating a dominant hypothesis. Hunt (1993) provides a good discussion of maintaining objectivity in the field of marketing, suggesting that it is neither impossible or undesirable to pursue objectivity in marketing research. In their analysis of objectivity and reliability of executing content analysis research, Kolbe and Burnett (1991) finds that most factors pertaining to objectivity assessment are either unreported or unattended by authors, suggesting the need to be more transparent in reporting processes and procedures in research to ensure objectivity is demonstrated.

1.4.2 Rigour

All research is expected to be conducted with rigour. By rigour, we mean that the researcher does his utmost to ensure that the research process is appropriate and well carried out. The boundary of the research needs to be set. A study on larger firms need to be recognized and stated explicitly as there may be little implications for small and medium-sized enterprises (SMEs). What was or was not carried out in the process of research should all be well documented. A quantitative study that looks at how SMEs expand into international markets should ideally take into account both home and host country contexts. If, due to limitations in accessing some data on entry into Latin American markets, the analysis does not include that particular region, an explanation needs to be put forth to account for this omission. Literature search and analysis must be thorough. Various forms of search process may be needed to ensure that there is no omission of key literature. Analysis needs to account for potential contingency effects through additional tests for rigour.

Research findings resulting from a rigorous research process allows us to draw better conclusions from our research. Without rigour, findings are suspect. It is important to note that reporting everything does not constitute rigour; rigour has got more to do with the process of conducting research. Applied work that may sometimes be interesting does not always enforce rigour in the process. A research project needs to enforce rigour to ensure the quality of the work that supports recommendations and solutions.

Conversation box

Stephanie [Masters student]:   Professor, I'm working on making sure that my research project is as rigorous as possible. How can I achieve that?

Professor: There's no answer to what maximum rigour in research contexts means. I'm afraid it's a combination of many factors, such as those we discussed in class, for example appropriate research process and methods, very well-crafted research design, thorough data collection process, strong analysis, ruling out alternative explanations, etc.

1.4.3 Parsimony

Business and management research needs to be **parsimonious**, i.e. the need to find a model with the best explanatory power yet not over-fitting the number of factors to make it impossible to execute in real life. At times, we can be overwhelmed with data and information and it becomes difficult to disentangle the important aspect of a research project. In such circumstances, we will have to balance the marginal contribution of having each extra little piece of information. It is easy to be bogged down by excessive information in business and management research when there are a lot of factors that can lead to any behaviour of managers and organizations. Take, for example, a quantitative study, where introducing an additional explanatory variable only leads to a small percentage improvement in the model for explaining the outcome variable. Here it is not economical to include this explanatory variable. Such a decision is an act of being parsimonious.

Widening the context, most of our research tends to address a tiny piece of organizational reality (Daft, 1983). Thus, we should not have the mentality that we are going to solve all issues within a single study. Being parsimonious will simplify, while not over-simplifying the context of investigation, in some ways making it easier to enhance the rigour and **replicability** of a research. In reality – and if we are to act on the advice of any research implication – being parsimonious allows easier implementation of the recommendation put forth in the research project.

Conversation box

Professor: Class, please try to be parsimonious in the analytical model that you propose in your assignment.

Margaret [Honours student]: Professor, how many factors should we include in our model?

Professor: Margaret, there is no specific number for this. You have to make a judgement call on this. Once newly added factors provide only marginal contributions, you may have arrived at a parsimonious model. In the conceptualization of your assignment, you can rely on the literature review for assessing the relative importance of factors.

1.4.4 Generalizability

Research emphasizes originality. But originality needs to be framed within a research topic and cannot be proven without recognition of the background literature. Part of the purpose of this is to see how your research is positioned alongside prior works and provides us with new knowledge moving forward. To get more mileage for learning, the findings of your study are encouraged to be as generalizable as possible. If your research is too narrowly focused, such as only applies to the consumption patterns within a small population pool in your neighbourhood, restricted to policies within a city or province, or very time-sensitive and specific to one particular ad hoc or rare event, then it is likely that the contribution will be perceived as less significant. This degree of significance is largely based on an assessment of how wide the audience of your research will be. If the audience is confined to a small group, it is likely that the research is deemed to be less generalizable. Research that has greater generalizability tends to draw the attention of a wider audience.

However, it is important to note that you should not broaden your research scope just for the sake of reaching out to a wider audience. For example, an attempt to conduct a study on what factors affect company performance is likely to bring in hundreds of factors to consider. This gives the appearance of solving all problems and issues on company performance in one swoop, using one study. But in reality, conducting a study that involves a hundred factors is unlikely to add much value to our existing knowledge base on this topic. The widening of this scope does come with costs, such as lower feasibility to collect a large sample of data points; data availability; and subsequent issues with analysis, as many factors are highly correlated or spuriously related. Balancing this generalizability issue is thus a key judgement call.

1.4.5 Replicability

For research to be deemed credible, it must pass the test of replicability. A study is replicable if it can be conducted again using another sample within the sample frame with comparable results. If your research is context-specific, then there will always be doubts about the applicability of your findings in other contexts. Replication is essential to ensure that our knowledge is accumulated in a way that is not dependent on choice of sample or methods (Singh et al., 2003). In order to ensure that replication is possible, it is important that your research process is well documented so that another researcher can potentially use the same procedure to conduct a study using another sample or with the addition of new variables and factors. To yield consistent results, drawing on another sample will deepen our knowledge of the topic.

Replication studies, however, have been argued to provide limited value, as there are many unexplored or underexplored issues in the business and management field that require attention. Replication of existing work is deemed less of a priority.

Nevertheless, Singh et al. (2003) highlights examples that reiterate the importance of replication, and also recommends the use of good-enough replication in the context of business and management. In essence, the authors propose the relaxation of strict forms of replication that is only possible in hard science, and to adapt replication definition such as 'good-enough replication', that is more applicable for business and management research.

1.5 RESEARCH INTEGRITY AND ETHICS

There are certain legal and moral responsibilities and requirements that a researcher must fulfil in order to maintain their reputation in the research community. Many business and management research projects are conducted with the permission of commercial organizations. Some studies are conducted with the consent of individuals. Either way, it is important that although the research outcome will probably end up being a public document, the confidentiality of the participants should be protected. Besides confidentiality, other factors a researcher needs to take into consideration are various rights, including intellectual property rights and copyright. Central to any research is research integrity and ethics. Any research should be carried out with high ethical standards to maintain strong research integrity. For example, if a study relies on privileged access to company records and files, the researcher needs to ensure that all information is protected. If consent is needed, then the researcher needs to make sure that the person giving the consent is fully informed of what they have agreed to.

Many of the ethical issues that arise in the act of conducting research are often not explicit. If a research process breaches ethical standards, the research outcomes are deemed void. It is essential that good ethical standards are maintained, as otherwise scholarship will turn into chaos. A key reason for this is that while the process of awarding degrees involving research projects and the journal publication process are both managed to minimize issues with unethical behaviours, a seamless monitoring system for ethical behaviours is impossible to organize. As such, we rely on researchers to document what actually happened in the research process rather than shadowing them every day to document this process. Likewise, any shortcoming and limitation of the research or research process should be explicitly recognized by the researcher, as opposed to a system that allows tracking of what these are from a third-party perspective. If a researcher intentionally misrepresents the actual conduct of the research, erroneous knowledge will be passed on.

To highlight what ethical standards might mean, here is a scenario:

Scenario 1

A researcher is working on a very large research project. He identifies three potential research publications coming out of it. The general directions of the papers are identical. He decides to include paragraphs from the first paper in the second and third papers without changes.

The researcher was making life easier for himself by using materials from one paper for another. Surely this should not be an issue, as he has the intellectual property rights to the first paper and thus the right to use the same materials for subsequent publications. This assumption is now debatable. In the code of ethics of research, this behaviour – labelled as self-plagiarism and double-dipping – is not desirable. The consequences of **self-plagiarism** behaviour will be discussed more extensively in Section 1.5.2. Moreover, some publishers share the copyrights to the articles that are published in their journals. In this case, the researcher may also be violating this copyright arrangement.

Here is another scenario:

Scenario 2

In the midst of conducting a study, a researcher found another study that is identical to the conceptual relationships she is examining in her work. She chooses to ignore the existence of this discovery as incorporating it would mean that she has to significantly change the approach adopted in her own study, resulting in a delay in the work being sent for publication.

Understandably, no one can read all there is to read in her field. However, in the code of ethics of research, the researcher here has violated two fundamental ethical expectations. First, in research, it is expected of a researcher to identify and read all previous related literature in order to justify the originality of her work. Second, research also emphasizes transparent reporting – in that a researcher needs to report what has happened in the actual research process without concealing any information. In fact, in this example, by ignoring this discovery the research will probably end up with less significance when it finally reaches the audience, as the audience would by then have read a similar article (the one that she has just discovered). Failure to recognize a significant work that overlaps with your research is a bad sign for the reader on how professionally you have treated the research process.

The two scenarios above clearly highlight issues pertaining to ethical standards expected in research. Good research must be conducted within the boundaries of ethical behaviours, hence providing the necessary integrity and validity to the findings. Mirvis and Seashore (1979) raise some ethical considerations in organizational research. Tymchuk (1982) provides a framework to consider when confronted with the dilemma of how to behave in the face of an ethical issue in research. The following sub-sections highlight some of the more common research ethical expectations.

1.5.1 Accurate reporting of research findings

Researchers are expected to truthfully and accurately report their research findings when disseminating their work. This involves not fabricating the data, not omitting data that are relevant to their work and not falsifying results. Research findings should be reported whether they confirm or contradict the expectations of the researcher, and whether they support or contradict previous literature in the field. All underlying assumptions, theories and concepts, research design and methods, measurements and analyses adopted in their work should be clearly specified in the output. Due to the space and length limitations in some outlets, such as for journal publication and for research projects and dissertations that have word limits, not all results will eventually fit into the reporting. But the main findings should be part of the main text and supplementary findings should be listed as appendices. If space limits persist, then it is sometimes valid to list additional analysis and testing as available upon request.

Humans err, and honest mistakes should be rectified. A researcher should not feel embarrassed about the error and thus leave it as it is. If a researcher discovers that there are errors in their publication, presentation of data, or if any parts are misrepresented, they need to take appropriate steps to correct such errors in the form of a correction, retraction or published erratum. It should be noted here that more and more journals are explicitly reminding authors that their data are subject to assessment by the editor in order to verify the findings presented. It is thus in the best interest of a researcher at any level to ensure the accuracy of information provided in any research output.

1.5.2 Referencing and plagiarism

It is important that all information used from other sources is properly cited. Complete citation and **referencing** are expected in any form of research outputs. These will be discussed in detail in Chapter 4, when we touch on how to conduct a good literature review. When you use materials from any other sources, not citing these sources will constitute non-recognition of their contributions to your work and at the same time could be considered as stealing the intellectual property rights of the source material. The theft of ideas is a difficult area to prevent as it is hard for any researcher to have control over ideas and the thinking around these ideas. Hence, being cited is a form of protection that is the least an author should expect from other researchers.

To plagiarize is to take from someone else's writing without referencing. It is essential for researchers to explicitly identify, credit and reference the author of any source material. This is regardless of whether the work is published, unpublished, or electronically available. Citation is necessary even if the materials have been reorganized or paraphrased. Some research has suggested that there might be a cultural issue associated with referencing and **plagiarism** issues, especially around researchers who have English as second language (Angelova and Riazantseva, 1999; Ashworth et al., 1997). Further research has suggested that plagiarism can happen in any cultural context (Hayes and Introna, 2005). It should also be noted that plagiarism is not always related to cheating (Hayes and Introna, 2005; Howard, 1995), as there is potentially unintended copying of materials. Unintended copying is always tempting as we often find that the materials we read are so well written that it is hard even to paraphrase them. Chen and Van Ullen (2011) find that workshops around plagiarism and research processes improve international students' understanding of these practices in a Western university context. Howard (1995) provides some good guidelines on gauging plagiarism. If you are studying in a foreign country for the first time, it will be good for you to become accustomed to the different education system context, to ensure that you avoid situations associated with plagiarism.

In recent years, **research ethics** codes have also included circumstances whereby a researcher should avoid using materials from his previous works without making substantial changes. This violation constitutes self-plagiarism (Collberg and Kobourov, 2005; Samuelson, 1994). Cases of both plagiarism and self-plagiarism are on the rise in recent years, and are found not just among younger, or junior researchers, nor researchers outside North America and Europe (Martin, 2013). Both incentives and pressures to publish well have led to proliferation of these behaviours even within North American and European regions that house the majority of the best journals in the world.

Nonetheless, the extent of how serious academic integrity has been breached in the case of self-plagiarism is still debatable (Bruton, 2014; Robinson, 2014). Bruton (2014) provides a discussion of the different forms of self-plagiarism. It is good for us to take note of what self-plagiarism entails and check in with the relevant education system context to avoid self-plagiarism. These days, more journals are requiring authors at the submission process to declare the extent their paper submission is similar to any of their prior works and ask for explanations to which similarities occur to justify originality in the new submission. This process is there to ensure adequate originality and to help track potential self-plagiarism.

1.5.3 Authorship order and credit

Authorships of any publication should be treated seriously. Order of authorships and authorship credits in a paper should be based on scientific or professional contributions of the individuals involved (Clement, 2014; Fine and Kurdek, 1993). A researcher should only take authorship credit for work she has actually performed or to which she has contributed substantially. A student will have full authorship credit for her research project. The author of a single-authored journal publication will have full credit of the authorship of the paper.

Conversation box

A discussion at a conference ...

Li [student from one university]: Is it not common for a student to let the senior person in the research collaboration take the lead and be the first author of the work, though the chances are that the student may do most of the work for the paper?

Chen [student from another university]: In our university we have co-authorship rules that govern this. It is not a given that the senior person should always be the lead author in a collaboration. It really depends on the amount of contribution that each author makes. This is especially so when it comes to research papers coming out of our degree research project as we have full authorship credit for the work.

Li: That's good to know.

Relating to authorship, researchers should not exploit persons whom they have evaluative or other authorities over (Fine and Kurdek, 1993). While junior faculty members and research students represent new blood to the research community, it does not necessarily mean that they cannot take the lead in a research collaboration. For example, they should not be deprived of being the lead author of a paper just because there are senior faculty members onboard. While there are grounds for justification for research students having hands-on exposure in working on research papers and hence doing more of the leg work, they should not be treated unequally when it comes to authorship credit.

With the increasing extent of collaboration in research activities, the level of contribution of each author in a large team tends to be become less transparent (Borenstein and Shamoo, 2015). In many cases, the use of alphabetical order of the last names of authors is used as a way to list authorship. While this is a potential practice, it does not recognize the level of contribution provided by each author. It is also important to note that authorship credit does not always mean the amount of work done or the hours clocked; rather credit should be assessed by the contribution of each author to the work. Clement (2014) and Geelhoed et al. (2007) provide scientific methodologies which researchers should consider when assessing authors' contributions. These are applicable when deciding the order of authorship in a publication as well.

On the flip side, questions often arise as to what extent a supervisor should help a student in the research process leading to a gradable project or programme degree (Fine and Kurdek, 1993). Students engaging in a research project will have to ensure that the content of the work is to a large extent their own work in order to earn their programme degree. Areas in which ethical issues can arise include amongst others the writing process (how much should the supervisor be involved in editing the student's drafts?), the data collection process (how much of the data needs to be collected solely by the student as appropriate for what is necessary for the research output?), the data analysis process (can the student engage help from others to analyze the data?), and the originality aspect of the research (to what extent should the supervisor help with the crafting of the research direction?). There are clearly ethical challenges in the research supervision process and both students and supervisors need to have a common and mutual understanding of research ethics in the relationship.

1.5.4 Preparation of submission of manuscripts for publication

There are some rules that researchers need to adhere to when they submit their manuscript for consideration for publication. For example, when a paper is submitted for consideration for publication in a journal, this paper should not concurrently be in consideration for publication in another journal, i.e. a piece of research should not be under review by multiple journals at one single point in time (e.g. Feldman, 2003). The researcher can only submit the work to a second journal after receiving an editorial decision of rejection from the first journal or after retracting the submission from the journal where the work is currently under review.

In terms of the expectations of journals on submissions, a researcher should locate a page titled 'author guidelines' or similar on the website of the journal. This page often details the expectations that the journal has of authors. Following the expectations closely is my best advice, as most journals do not appreciate too much deviation from what they expect to see in submissions. For example, most journals are very particular about the length and format of the manuscripts they receive.

1.5.5 Conflict of interest

Conflicts of interest or the appearance of conflicts should be avoided. Researchers should refrain from assuming roles that will impair their objectivity, competence or effectiveness in their research work. It is thus important to disclose relevant information and personal or professional relationships that may have the appearance of or potential for a conflict of interest. Conflict of interest may often happen in the review process, where a researcher may be asked to review and find that they may know the authors as an earlier version of the manuscript may have been sighted. Failure to disclose this information to the editor can result in potential bias in assessing the research, while disclosure will be deemed ethical. In this example, it is likely that the editor will request another reviewer to assess the paper.

Role of editors

An editor of journals, books or other publications should always be fair in the process of applying research publishing standards. A high level of objectivity is required in terms of making judgements with regard to the quality of the submissions. Confidentiality during the review process should be well protected to ensure conformity with the double-blind review process, where reviewers and authors do not know each other's identity. In assessing the reviewers' comments, not being swayed by reviewers' academic status and mainly relying on their comments, is essential for editorial work.

Role of reviewers of articles and examiners of projects

Reviewers of submitted work to journals often run into various forms of conflict of interest. The reviewers of a paper are charged with the responsibility for quality control of the manuscripts under submission. It is important to note that research that undergoes the peer review process is more credible or perceived to be so. Thus, the onus will be on the reviewers to ensure that a high standard is applied when they are reviewing the papers. The reviewer has the responsibility to disclose any conflict of interest or decline requests to review a paper when any potential conflict of interest may exist. For example, researchers have their own networks. Even though journal review follows a double-blind process, a researcher may still be able to identify the author of a paper that they were asked to review because the dataset allows them to recognize that the work comes from another author in the same network group. The editor who assigned the reviewers for the paper may not be aware of this network tie. In such a situation, it will be appropriate for the reviewer to highlight this connection to the editor and request the paper to be reassigned to another reviewer.

Examiners of research projects will know the student author of the research work that they are examining. A conflict of interest can arise when an examiner is a close collaborator with the supervisor of the student's project. This essentially means that the author of the work and the examiner are somewhat connected to the same network. Likewise, if a researcher has at any point advised on a research project, they should try to avoid being the examiner of it eventually. Because of this, it is essential to be conscious of this limitation when reaching out for advice. Likewise, in arranging for a friendly reviewer for a draft of a paper, the author needs to be careful with restricting who might be eligible to review a subsequent submission to a journal.

1.6 CONSEQUENCES OF BREACH OF ETHICAL RESEARCH BEHAVIOUR

As highlighted in the last section, it is essential that ethical standards are maintained in the act of conducting research. Failure to cover these ethical grounds will result in various forms of consequences – some of which will be discussed in this section.

1.6.1 Consequences of erroneous research findings

Many scholars read journals to update themselves on the latest thinking in their field. Their assumption when they first pick up a **journal article** is that there were some prior quality control processes leading to this publication. The quality control process includes quality of the author's submission, the reviewers' comments and advice, as well as the editor's view of the relevance and the quality of the submission. Any eye-catching error should have been singled out before the paper was published subsequently. Time, however, is not on the side of these actors. For example, there is often not enough time for reviewers to request the raw data to conduct a check on the credibility of the findings as reported in the submission. Reviewers must opt to give authors the benefit of the doubt in almost all cases.

When there are erroneous findings, this will result in the audience reading material that is not accurate – misleading them as they utilize these findings in their own work. This becomes more serious when these erroneous findings are used to motivate subsequent studies – resulting in a spiral chain of honest mistakes. Under pressure to publish, some researchers often commit errors pertaining to reporting research findings, albeit unintentional. These actions have consequences for the knowledge that is being passed on in the field. Thus, it is essential that high ethical standards are maintained when research findings are presented.

1.6.2 Consequences of inaccurate referencing

Referencing is an essential element of research. However, very often we encounter referencing that is not accurate. This often happens when researchers start citing references from the reference list of another paper without actually going back to the original source. This second-hand citation behaviour in conducting a literature search can often lead to erroneous references, be it the names of the authors, the date of publication, the title of the article, the name of the journal, the volume and issue, or page numbers. Inaccurate referencing can result in a reader getting incorrect information about the academic contribution of the journal article they are reading, as well as about the reference articles that the focal article has cited.

1.6.3 Consequences of plagiarism

Plagiarism is an act of not respecting the intellectual property rights of authors. Research takes significant time to craft. Failure to cite while utilizing published materials discredits the creativity and time spent by researchers on their work. Copying several paragraphs of another article, even with citation, is unwarranted. In other words, plagiarism can be seen as robbing another researcher of their work, making it uneconomical for any researcher to expend their efforts. Systems such as turnitin. com allow us to check on potential overlap with other articles; the level of detail they pick up is amazing. Researchers who have been found to plagiarize will have their work retracted and will likely be blacklisted in the research community. Research students are likely to be penalized with a failing grade for their work if they are found to plagiarize substantially.

Section 1.5.2 also discussed self-plagiarism. While textual recycling is not necessarily an issue in some disciplines, it is essential that you as a researcher check on current practices that are allowed in your field. In some fields, self-plagiarism can have the same negative connotation as plagiarism, leading to undesirable outcomes. It is important to note that if you are working on a research project, copying paragraphs from a previous assignment in the same topic can also constitute self-plagiarism. Even though the latter might not be a publicly available document, it has been used to obtain another assignment grade making the re-use of its parts a double-dipping issue.

1.6.4 Consequences of a breached review process

As mentioned above, the review process is the gatekeeping mechanism of the journal publication world. In this world, editors and reviewers are the gatekeepers. The review process can be breached in many ways though, one of which is when the reviewer knows who the author of the submitted paper is based on their familiarity with the research. Two issues might arise here. The first issue is when the reviewer does not like the author or their work in general, owing to conflicting views. With this starting point, the reviewer may be biased towards identifying problematic issues from the paper to find a way to reject the submission. The second issue, which surprisingly is a more serious one, is when the reviewer knows the author or likes their work in general. This opens the door for the author. The reviewer is more likely to find merits in the submission and this increases the probability of the paper being accepted for publication, even when there are issues with the submission.

The issues presented above have different consequences. In the first case, a good piece of work may not be exposed to scholars as a result of the compromised process. This is likely to be a short-term problem: a rejected paper can be resubmitted to another journal and it is difficult to imagine that all journals will reject a publishable piece of work. Good papers will always find a home. The second case is more peculiar. If a decent paper is accepted even though the reviewer is biased, the outcome is not a bad one though the process should have been better. However, if the paper is flawed and it was accepted as a result of reviewer bias, this has dire consequences. Papers falling through the cracks will not be subjected to be reviewed again. This can be detrimental to scholarship as junior researchers and research students may be exposed to these publications with the assumption that these have passed the quality control tests and hence are credible sources for guiding their own research. Notwithstanding such potential issues in the review process, you are always advised to read any work, including those published in top journals, with a critical lens regarding the extent to which they are convincing.

1.7 THE RESEARCH PROCESS

This section provides an overview of the research process – which will be discussed in more detail throughout the rest of the book. Knowing what is expected in the research process is an essential first step towards the successful completion of a research project.

The research process that is often depicted in research books tends to over-simplify the reality of research undertaking, and in some cases misrepresents what actually happens in the process. A typical research process that you often come across for a quantitative study is depicted in Figure 1.3, while that for a qualitative study is shown in Figure 1.4.

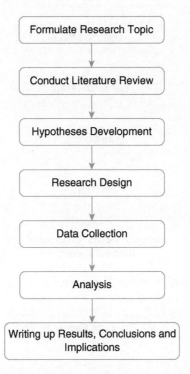

Figure 1.3   A typical quantitative research process

Implicit in these models is that the research process follows a particular linear sequence and that the components of the research process are clearly defined. However, anyone who has been involved in any research work would argue that the research process is never this straightforward. For example, you might find yourself needing to adjust your propositions as you collect your data because you could not gain access to the desired participants or some variables as planned. Relatedly, you will need to adjust your literature review accordingly to align with this change of plan to your propositions. This leads the direction of change backward to where you started, i.e. the research topic and question.

A more realistic research process is relatively more complicated than the linear research processes illustrated in Figures 1.3 and 1.4. More realistic quantitative research and qualitative reseach processes are shown in Figures 1.5 and 1.6 respectively.

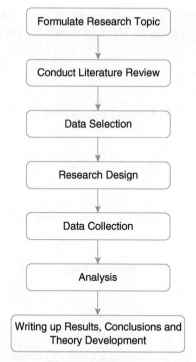

Figure 1.4   A typical qualitative research process

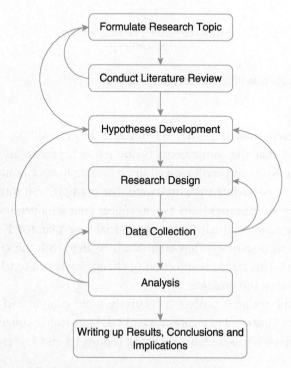

Figure 1.5   A more realistic quantitative research process

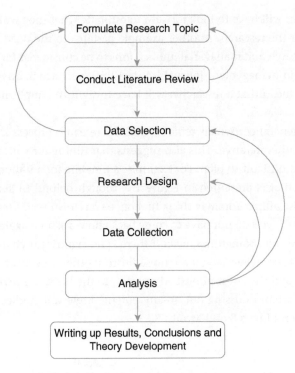

Figure 1.6   A more realistic qualitative research process

It is likely that the number of backwards steps (represented by the arrows) is more than what are shown in Figures 1.5 and 1.6, but these are the typical ones you would expect. For example, it is common practice to have a feedback loop from analysis straight back to hypotheses development in a quantitative research process in order to make the research more coherent. In the case of a qualitative research process, analysis might lead to data re-selection.

There are some discussions as to whether feedback loops are always necessary. Feyerabend (1993) suggests that to always link from results to theory would require the preconditioning of the data to fit the theory. In reality, there are many alternative explanations for observed behaviours in addition to the theoretical perspectives adopted. Recognizing these alternative explanations is crucial as loopholes in old theories can be identified and new ones may emerge (Feyerabend, 1993). A garbage-can model of research suggests mixing the research components together when making decisions (Martin, 1982). Thus, decisions pertaining to methods are decided at the same time as the decision with respect to the research topic is being made. It is almost implicit in this model that a researcher would be able to see the outcome before the research starts. It is not surprising to see the garbage-can model in action when it comes to research. For example, most research funding applications expect the applicant to provide some potential outcomes from an application. This necessarily means that the applicant will have to look forward to estimate what they will undertake during the course of the research. Another example pertains to the need for submissions to have both research and managerial implications to be considered for publications by most business and management journals. A decision to engage in any research that is publishable will mean that a researcher will have to sight the implications first before engaging in the research.

Overall, the general consensus remains that the research process is by no means a linear one, but rather iterative. This also suggests that timing for your research project can be somewhat difficult to plan. For example, a timeline for a 9-month quantitative research project that is presented in Figure 1.7, though helpful to keep your pace in check, can be misleading. You may think that once you finish your literature review by the end of Month 3, you do not have to come back and work on it again. However, that is usually not the case. Sometimes, even if there is no significant change in the direction of the literature review as you are not adjusting other aspects of your study, you will still need to add the latest published research to the literature review by Month 7 or 8 so that you are not missing out on any potential relevant studies that have been published between Month 3 and Month 8.

Components	Month								
	1	2	3	4	5	6	7	8	9
Introduction	▓								
Literature review		▓	▓						
Hypotheses development				▓					
Data collection					▓				
Data analysis						▓	▓		
Results and Conclusions								▓	▓

Figure 1.7   Sequential timeline for a research project

What all this means is that you are unlikely to be able to incorporate this added required time (from having to move back and forth between components) within a linear research process. As a result, the process will not be as smooth and there are likely to be delays. A more realistic timeline to cater to the cyclical nature of the research process is presented in Figure 1.8. The timeline in Figure 1.8 shows the need for you to go back and update the literature review in Month 7 or 8. More importantly, it also suggests that the research components are interconnected and in many of the cases, you need to work on more than one research component concurrently. In summary, the research process is cyclical and definitely not linear.

Components	Month								
	1	2	3	4	5	6	7	8	9
Introduction	■	■							
Literature review	■	■	■				■		
Hypotheses development		■	■	■		■			
Data collection				■	■	■			
Data analysis						■	■		
Results and Conclusions								■	■

Figure 1.8   A more realistic timeline for a research project

It should be noted here that the amount of time available for a research project to be completed will directly influence both the research time schedule and its level of complexity. The time frame for different research projects varies according to what sort of programme degree you are pursuing, ranging from 3 months to a few years. It is recommended that you make a detailed plan or timeline for your study in order to make sure that milestones are met. This should include how many hours you are planning to dedicate to the project after taking into account other commitments. Your supervisor can advise you on realistic time estimates to complete each task or you can swap notes with other students who are doing or have done a similar project in the past. The schedule should aim to incorporate a degree of flexibility. For example, the schedule should end a couple of weeks before the actual deadline to allow for any task that might take longer than expected. After developing a time schedule, you need to check whether the resource implications of what needs to be done are reasonable, in particular funding for the project if required, training for the research methodology and access to resources such as library databases.

1.8 OVERVIEW OF THE REST OF THE BOOK

There are two key elements of this book which differentiate it from many other research project books. First, is the recognition that the research process is not linear. Unfortunately, the book in itself cannot be structured in the same way. Thus, you will still see the sequence of chapters aligned with what we expect of a typical research process. Nonetheless, the cyclical nature of the research process will be reflected within each chapter as appropriate – exemplified by how they are linked to other preceding and succeeding research components. For example, data availability (Chapter 6) may impede the execution of a research hypothesis, leading to changes in the research topic (Chapter 3), literature review (Chapter 4) and research design (Chapter 5).

Second, the book contains a lot of what we consider as tacit knowledge in research. These are normally not well documented in research books as researchers themselves will have to make some judgement calls in reality when executing a research project; they can also be specific to each research project. Judgement calls are made with experience. This is like the saying of experts – 'I don't know how I know but I just know'. As a research student or a new researcher, if you reach a juncture where you cannot decide what to do and there is no documented guidance on what the potential solutions are, you will have encountered a situation needing to make a judgement call.

Some of these judgement calls are aided by prevalent practices. Nonetheless, they can be subjected to various interpretations. Among those discussed by McGrath et al. (1982) in their book devoted to judgement calls, many are not specific to business and management research. It is important to recognize that we are all creating knowledge, in some cases in research areas that are relatively unchartered. On that point, the more I can highlight some of these judgement calls in research, the better this book will be in helping with researchers working on research projects who have doubts about their research process. They might realize then that looking for research boundaries such as what constitutes adequate scope for a research project or the number of variables needed in a quantitative study will not bring definite answers. But it is at least good for them to know there are no definitive answers to these questions either, as they will not go on a search in vain.

The rest of the book will be structured as follows. Chapter 2 builds on this chapter to discuss misperceptions and challenges during the research process. It is important for you to understand the broad context to which research projects are situated. And as much as the research process can be challenging, there are some excitements that come with it. Chapter 3 covers the search for research topic and will include the different types of search that you can use in a rigorous search process, and the various sources of information from which you can get ideas for your research. Somewhat related to Chapter 3, Chapter 4 shows how to conduct a good literature review, which can help one to crystallize the research topic and make adjustments if needed. An initial literature review may always be necessary for arrival at a broad research topic. Chapter 4 also covers referencing formats and expectations, as mentioned in this chapter on the importance of referencing and how to avoid plagiarism and self-plagiarism.

Chapter 5 highlights the factors that will lead to research design decisions. It also includes some discussion on the temporal aspects of research design in business and management, especially around causality of factors that a study might involve. Chapter 6 includes various data, sampling and measurements useful in the business and management context, while Chapter 7 highlights the various data collection methods. Chapters 8, 9 and 10 cover descriptive and exploratory analysis, qualitative analysis and quantitative analysis respectively. As the book is not focused on methods alone, the demonstration of how analyses are conducted and how some software is used are not part of the scope of this book. There are many methods books out there that either have a more hands-on approach to analysis or the use of a particular software and those will supplement this book well. Finally, Chapter 11 provides advice on writing up a research project.

KEY TERMS

- Authorship
- Concept
- Concept-driven research
- Conflict of interest
- Data
- Deductive
- Generalizability
- Hypothesis
- Inductive
- Journal article
- Judgement call
- Learning
- Literature review
- Literaure search process
- Market research
- Objectivity
- Organizational research
- Parsimony
- Phenomenon
- Plagiarism
- Proposition
- Qualitative
- Quantitative
- Referencing
- Replicability
- Research ethics
- Research process
- Research project
- Research question
- Research scope
- Research topic
- Rigour
- Self-plagiarism
- Solution-driven research

SUMMARY

- Research is important to the accumulation of knowledge.
- Various comparisons of research exist, for example induction versus deduction, quantitative versus qualitative versus mixed methods, and concept-driven versus solution-driven.
- The fundamental research expectations can be viewed in terms of objectivity, rigour, parsimony, generalizability and replicability. These research expectations are generic to all research projects.
- Maintaining high research ethical standards is essential to keep the research integrity of all the works that we read and cite. There are consequences when research ethics are breached.
- There are various ethical aspects of research that a researcher needs to be aware of, for example reporting of research findings and rectifying error reporting, referencing and plagiarism, authorship credit and order, preparation for submission of manuscripts for publication and conflicts of interest.

- The research process should be viewed as cyclical as opposed to linear.
- Judgement calls reside in all components of the research process. These are normally made with experience.

QUESTIONS

1. What are the differences between inductive and deductive approaches to research? How are these related to the research methods used?
2. In which situations is concept-driven research likely to be appropriate? How is that different from solution-driven research?
3. Briefly discuss the fundamental research expectations of research objectivity, rigour, parsimony, generalizability and replicability.
4. Why is research ethics important in the conduct of research activities? What are some of the consequences of breaches of ethical research behaviour? Briefly discuss.
5. What are some of the issues with plagiarism and self-plagiarism? What are the consequences of these violations?
6. Briefly describe a cyclical quantitative research process.
7. Briefly describe a cyclical qualitative research process.

ADDITIONAL READINGS

Aguinis, H. and Henle, C.A. (2002) 'Ethics in research', in S.G. Rogelberg (ed.), *Handbook of Research Methods in Industrial and Organizational Psychology*. Malden, MA: Blackwell. pp. 34–56.

Barzun, J. and Graff, H.F. (2003) *The Modern Researcher*, (6th edition). Belmont, CA: Cengage Learning.

Booth, W.C., Colomb, G.G., Williams, J.M., Bizup, J. and Fitgerald, W.T. (2016) *The Craft of Research*, (4th edition). Chicago, IL: University of Chicago Press.

Burke, L.A. and Rau, B. (2010) 'The research-teaching gap in management', *Academy of Management Learning and Education*, 9 (1): 132–43.

Crane, A. (1999) 'Are you ethical? Please tick yes or no on researching ethics in business organizations', *Journal of Business Ethics*, 20 (3): 237–48.

Floyd, S.W., Schroeder, D.M. and Finn, D.M. (1994) '"Only if I'm first author": Conflict over credit in management scholarship', *Academy of Management Journal*, 37 (3): 734–47.

Goodyear, R.K., Crego, C.A. and Johnston, M.W. (1992) 'Ethical issues in the supervision of student research: A study of critical incidents', *Professional Psychology: Research and Practice*, 23 (3): 203–10.

Ireland, R.D. (2012) 'Management research and managerial practice: A complex and controversial relationship', *Academy of Management Learning and Education*, 11 (2): 263–71.

Lowman, R.L. (ed.) (2006) *The Ethical Practice of Psychology in Organizations*, (2nd edition). Washington, DC: American Psychological Association.

Lundberg, C.C. and Young, C.A. (2005) *Foundations for Inquiry: Choices and Tradeoffs in the Organizational Sciences.* Stanford, CA: Stanford Business Books.

Office of Research Integrity (ORI) (2013) 'Avoiding plagiarism, self-plagiarism, and other questionable writing practices: A guide to ethical writing', US Department of Health and Human Services. Available at: http://ori.hhs.gov/avoiding-plagiarism-self-plagiarism-and-other-questionable-writing-practices-guide-ethical-writing (accessed July 27, 2020).

Podsakoff, P.M., MacKenzie, S.B., Podsakoff, N.P. and Bachrach, D.G. (2008) 'Scholarly influence in the field of management: A bibliometric analysis of the determinants of university and author impact in the management literature in the past quarter century', *Journal of Management*, 34 (4): 641–720.

Popper, K. (1982) *The Open Universe.* New York: Routledge.

Popper, K. (2002) *The Logic of Scientific Discovery.* New York: Routledge.

Remenyi, D., Williams, B., Money, A. and Swartz, E. (1998) *Doing Research in Business and Management.* Thousand Oaks, CA: Sage.

Rosenzweig, P. (2007) *The Halo Effect ... and the Eight Other Business Delusions that Deceive Managers.* New York: The Free Press.

Sandler, J.C. and Russell, B.L. (2005) 'Faculty-student collaborations: Ethics and satisfaction in authorship credit', *Ethics and Behavior*, 15 (1): 65–80.

Scandura, T.A. and Williams, E.A. (2000) 'Research methodology in management: Current practices, trends, and implications for future research', *Academy of Management Journal*, 43 (6): 1248–64.

Seeman, J.I. and House, M.C. (2010) 'Influences on authorship issues: An evaluation of receiving, not receiving, and rejecting credit', *Accountability in Research*, 17 (4): 176–97.

Singleton, R.A. Jr. and Straits, B.C. (2009) *Approaches to Social Research* (5th edition). New York: Oxford University Press.

Thomas, A.B. (2004) *Research Skills for Management Studies.* London: Routledge.

Waltman, L. (2012) 'An empirical analysis of the use of alphabetical authorship in scientific publishing', *Journal of Informetrics*, 6 (4): 700–11.

REFERENCES

Angelova, M. and Riazantseva, A. (1999) '"If you don't tell me, how can I know?": A case study of four international students learning to write the U.S. way', *Written Communication*, 16 (4): 491–525.

Armstrong, J.S. (1979) 'Advocacy and objectivity in science', *Management Science*, 25 (5): 423–8.

Ashworth, P., Bannister, P. and Thorne, P. (1997) 'Guilty in whose eyes? University students' perceptions of cheating and plagiarism in academic work and assessment', *Studies in Higher Education*, 22 (2): 187–203.

Becker, H.S. (1998) *Tricks of the Trade: How to Think About Your Research While You're Doing It.* London: University of Chicago Press.

Borenstein, J. and Shamoo, A.E. (2015) 'Rethinking authorship in the era of collaborative research', *Accountability in Research*, 22 (5): 267–83.

Bruton, S.V. (2014) 'Self-plagiarism and textual recycling: Legitimate forms of research misconduct', *Accountability in Research*, 21 (3): 176–97.

Chen, Y.-H. and Van Ullen, M.K. (2011) 'Helping international students succeed academically through research process and plagiarism workshops', *College and Research Libraries*, 72 (3): 209–35.

Clement, T. P. (2014) 'Authorship matrix: A rational approach to quantify individual contributions and responsibilities in multi-author scientific articles', *Science and Engineering Ethics*, 20 (2): 345–61.

Collberg, C. and Kobourov, S. (2005) 'Self-plagiarism in computer science', *Communications of the ACM*, 48 (4): 88–94.

Cunningham, F. (1973) *Objectivity in Social Science*. Toronto: University of Toronto Press.

Daft, R.L. (1983) 'Learning the craft of organizational research', *Academy of Management Review*, 8 (4): 539–46.

Devinney, T.M. and Siegel, D.S. (2012) 'Perspectives on the art and science of management scholarship', *Academy of Management Perspectives*, 26 (1): 6–11.

Doh, J.P. (2015) 'From the editor: Why we need phenomenon-based research in international business', *Journal of World Business*, 50 (4): 609–11.

Edmondson, A.C. and McManus, S.E. (2007) 'Methodological fit in management field research', *Academy of Management Review*, 32 (4): 1155–79.

Feldman, D.C. (2003) 'When is a new submission "new"?', *Journal of Management*, 29 (2): 139–40.

Feyerabend, P. (1993) *Against Method*. London: Humanities Press.

Fine, M.A. and Kurdek, L.A. (1993) 'Reflections on determining authorship credit and authorship order on faculty-student collaborations', *American Psychologist*, 48 (11): 1141–47.

Ford, N. (2004) 'Creativity and convergence in information science research: The roles of objectivity and subjectivity, constraint, and control', *Journal of the American Society for Information Science & Technology*, 55 (13): 1169–82.

Geelhoed, R.J., Phillips, J.C., Fischer, A.R., Shpungin, E. and Gong, Y. (2007) 'Authorship decision making: An empirical investigation', *Ethics and Behavior*, 17 (2): 95–115.

Hayes, N. and Introna, L.D. (2005) 'Cultural values, plagiarism, and fairness: When plagiarism gets in the way of learning,' *Ethics and Behavior*, 15 (3): 213–31.

Howard, R.M. (1995) 'Plagiarisms, authorships, and the academic death penalty', *College English*, 57 (7): 788–806.

Hunt, S.D. (1993) 'Objectivity in marketing theory and research', *Journal of Marketing*, 57 (2): 76–91.

Kolbe, R.H. and Burnett, M.S. (1991) 'Content-analysis research: An examination of applications with directives for improving research reliability and objectivity', *Journal of Consumer Research*, 18 (2): 243–50.

Martin, B.R. (2013) 'Whither research integrity? Plagiarism, self-plagiarism and coercive citation in an age of research assessment', *Research Policy*, 42 (5): 1005–14.

Martin, J. (1982) 'A garbage can model of the research process', in J.E. McGrath, J. Martin and R.A. Kulka (eds), *Judgement Calls in Research*. Beverly Hills, CA: Sage. pp. 17–39.

McGrath, J.E., Martin, J. and Kulka, R.A. (1982) *Judgement Calls in Research*. Beverly Hills, CA: Sage Publications.

Mirvis, P.H. and Seashore, S.E. (1979) 'Being ethical in organizational research', *American Psychologist*, 34 (9): 766–80.

Mitroff, I.I. (1972) 'The myth of objectivity or why science needs a new psychology of science', *Management Science*, 18 (10): B613–B618.

Molina-Azorin, J.F., Bergh, D.D., Corley, K.G. and Ketchen, D.J. Jr. (2017) 'Mixed methods in the organizational sciences: Taking stock and moving forward', *Organizational Research Methods*, 20 (2): 179–92.

Morgan, G. and Smircich, L. (1980) 'The case for qualitative research', *Academy of Management Review*, 5 (4): 491–500.

Pearce, J.L. and Huang, L. (2012) 'The decreasing value of our research to management education', *Academy of Management Learning and Education*, 11 (2): 247–62.

Robinson, S.R. (2014) 'Self-plagiarism and unfortunate publication: An essay on academic values', *Studies in Higher Education*, 39 (2): 265–77.

Rynes, S.L., Bartunek, J.M. and Daft, R.L. (2001) 'Across the great divide: knowledge creation and transfer between practitioners and academics', *Academy of Management Journal*, 44 (2): 340–55.

Samuelson, P. (1994) 'Self-plagiarism or fair use?', *Communications of the ACM*, 37 (8): 21–5.

Singh, K., Ang, S.H. and Leong, S.M. (2003) 'Increasing replication for knowledge accumulation in strategy research', *Journal of Management*, 29 (4): 533–49.

Staw, B.M. (1995) 'Repairs on the road to relevance and rigor: Some unexplored issues in publishing organizational research'. in L.L. Cummings and P.J. Frost (eds), *Publishing in the Organizational Sciences*. London: Sage Publishing. pp. 85–97.

Turner, S.F., Cardinal, L.B. and Burton, R.M. (2017) 'Research design for mixed methods: A triangulation-based framework and roadmap', *Organizational Research Methods*, 20 (2): 243–67.

Tymchuk, A.J. (1982) 'Strategies for resolving value dilemmas', *American Behavioral Scientist*, 26 (2): 159–75.

Vermeulen, F. (2005) 'On rigor and relevance: fostering dialectic progress in management research), *Academy of Management Journal*, 48 (6): 978–82.

Von Krogh, G., Rossi-Lamastra, C. and Haefliger, S. (2012) 'Phenomenon-based research in management and organisation science: When is it rigorous and does it matter?', *Long Range Planning*, 45 (4): 277–98.

2

MISPERCEPTIONS AND CHALLENGES IN RESEARCH

2.1 INTRODUCTION

Despite the importance of research, the question why research is necessary always arises. For example, why would history matter enough that we have to do a background literature search each time we conduct a new research project? How are these past research findings applicable to the current context? Are they still relevant given the passage of time? Undergraduate students always wonder why they would engage in postgraduate research studies. What is the value of having another (research) qualification? Does a postgraduate degree enhance their job prospects? Does having a research Masters degree make any difference to the opinion of a potential employer? The list of questions goes on and on. Yet many of these questions are often left unanswered. While there may be answers to some of the above questions for some, for others the uncertainty surrounding these issues generates some degree of misunderstanding about what research means. This also leads to misperceptions of research, some of which will be covered in this chapter.

Chapter 1 has highlighted the research process in reality. The cyclical nature of the research process creates additional complexity. In the process of engaging in research, there are some challenges that are generic to all research processes. While there are specific individual challenges within each component of the research process that will be covered in subsequent chapters, this chapter will cover the more generic challenges that business and management researchers commonly face. First, there is the challenge of choosing a research topic area to work in. This is followed by the challenge of ensuring there are substantive theoretical developments and the use of hypotheses and their developments. Then there are challenges relating to uncertain research outcomes and time constraints that we often face in our research activities. Finally, the chapter covers aspects of the research supervisory process and **journal review process** which students and researchers should learn to navigate.

2.2 MISPERCEPTIONS OF RESEARCH

2.2.1 Research is only for people who want to become academics and has little significance for practice

With the business community pushing for more **research-informed** managerial decisions, the statement that research is only for people who want to become academics must be a significant **misperception**. Research is certainly at the core of someone pursuing an academic career. While most universities also push for teaching excellence as part of the performance expectations of faculty members, research remains a key performance criterion for academics.

However, in the current business climate, companies have to constantly generate competitive advantages, and wish to make decisions in a more organized and scientific way. This is especially imperative for larger organizations. As such, executives often turn to making research-informed recommendations by engaging in research projects that entail proper **due diligence processes**. Many organizations even set up in-house research teams. Moreover, market research and consulting companies, and more recently banks, also hire employees with research skills. Their investments in such human capital are also a reflection of their clients' – the business community's – desire for research-informed decision-making. Hence, over time, people with research skills are in high demand in the market.

Conversation box

Company manager A:	Academics think differently from us [managers]. I'm not sure if the kind of problem that we are facing will make sense for them to work on.
Company manager B:	I've attended some courses within the university and the academic who was teaching us seemed to relate well to our type of thinking. He has also done extensive consulting work, even though I heard he is also a well-known theorist.
Company manager A:	This is news to me.
Company manager B:	Yes, apparently some university professors do connect their research to practice, and so they can provide some different yet good perspectives for us in the classroom.

There is a perception that research is 'in here' and practice is 'out there'. How can one apply what is 'in here' to a context 'out there'? It is indeed true that there is a gap between research and practice (Ireland, 2012; Rynes et al., 2001). 'Gap' implies some misconnections between the two modes. However, this does not mean what is being examined by researchers is more advanced than what is being practised by managers and vice versa. Such stereotyping can actually reinforce the gap, making it seemingly difficult to bridge research and practice.

In reality, given that more executives are returning to business schools to engage in advanced learning and that many more are working on research-informed projects, this gap is likely to be bridged gradually. This is helped by academics' increasing participation in research-led teaching and consulting projects. The onus is on the academics to bring the latest thinking in business and management research to the business community and for managers to apply what they learn in the classroom to their work environment.

2.2.2 Projects related to practice do not need research rigour

The section above suggests that good research should have relevance to practice. Now, should good practice be grounded in research? For any good practice to be trustworthy, it has to be appealing. How do one's ideas appeal to a particular audience? This leads us back to the ability of an idea to be *convincing*. Part of the reason for organizations to increasingly engage in research-informed decision-making is to enhance the convincing power of an argument or a proposal. This also means that any practice-oriented project will need to have some degree of research **rigour** to be more convincing. In this vein, Staw (1995) and Vermeulen (2005) put forth strong arguments for the need for research rigour in practice-oriented projects. Journal articles published in good managerial type journals that you will encounter in your research process are also likely to contain a fair amount of research rigour.

2.2.3 Research is isolating and frustrating

When you attend a taught course, you are surrounded by your fellow classmates who will move through the learning process together with you. However, as you reach the research phase of your study, very often you start to feel isolated. This could mainly be due to the fact that none of your peers are working on a research topic related to yours. As a result, discussion of your research topic can hardly occur as everyone is busy with their own research work. Moreover, it is also difficult to expect others to learn about your work in order to provide constructive comments. It is either too difficult for you to explain everything (including the literature) from scratch or too difficult for them to absorb your materials, not to say there is likely to be little incentive for them to do so. As a result, you might find yourself feeling the boredom of the research process.

Conversation box

Professor: Diane, come and present your research ideas to my second-year undergraduate class. It will be useful practice.

Diane [PhD student]: I'm happy to do that, Professor. But do you think they will appreciate what I'm doing given that this is a very specialized area and they have not progressed into specialization in their curriculum yet?

Professor: The presentation, even without specific feedback, will help you work out how clear your ideas are. So just come and enjoy the process and show how a new research is incepted.

Nowadays, business schools have larger cohorts of students doing research projects. A cohort allows a student to meet other students engaging in research. While it is often not easy to find many peers who work on the same area of research, discussions about the research process and talking to others about your research is a practice that is encouraged. Discussing your ideas with others will help you crystallize your thoughts. As a rule of thumb, when your listener does not seem to grasp your broad research idea, there is cause for concern. It could either be the case that your explanation of your idea is unclear or that there are loopholes in your thinking. One would hope that the former is the case. Very often, discussions can also lead to new ideas that eventually result in collaborative research. The bottom line is that there is always room to create your own active research environment so that you can avoid feeling isolated.

As explained in Chapter 1, the execution of the components in research is far from a linear process and it often takes longer than you expected. Every step of the process is filled with hurdles, some predictable and others less so. You spend time trying to find a workable research topic – bouncing off many ideas that are found not to be feasible. You spend time on crafting your hypotheses and propositions, yet they do not seem to be flowing smoothly. You try to collect the data and find that gaining access to organizations and individuals is harder than you expected. Even archival data are not available for your chosen sample. Worse still, the results from your analysis do not support your hypotheses and you wonder what went wrong. For the paper that you crafted for a journal, the reviewers came back with lots of comments that disagreed with your conclusions and rejected your paper. Every one of these hurdles can cause frustrations in the research process.

All the above issues are part and parcel of the research process. There is no intention to discourage you from engaging in research activities. You just have to dig in further in the hope of a good outcome after more work. You might find some of these challenges to be mountainous and become demoralized. But do not feel that way. Under most circumstances, there is always a way out. Try to work yourself out of the situation with the advice and help of others in your research environment. Facing up to such challenges will only make your research better, and at the end of the process you will really find doing research to be more satisfying and enriching rather than frustrating. Figure 2.1 provides some tips for dealing with frustrations in research.

Areas of frustration	Tips on how to counter frustration
No one in my school conducts research similar to mine – no one to bounce ideas off	Have broad conversations with peers within the business and management field about your topic. If a topic is well articulated, it should be easy to understand. Deep feedback may be unlikely, but people outside your black box may be able to contribute good points.
I don't seem to be able to narrow down my research topic	If this is due to reading too broadly, maybe it is time to narrow down to a specific few articles and draw some connections as a starting point. Chapter 3 will cover this mapping process.
I don't seem to be able to understand some aspects of the articles that I read	It may be due to the fact that you have not yet got full command of the literature in your field. Some articles are more difficult to comprehend if your knowledge of the research area is not yet holistic. The more you read, the less this will become a problem.
I don't seem to be able to understand the design or the statistical methods used in the articles I read	This is also common. Some designs and statistical methods are sophisticated and thus require specific reading or training to understand. Knowing the fundamental reason for the choice of design and statistical methods would be good for a start. Learning the actual use is not required in the first instance and may never be necessary. However, if any of the articles are a core reading, then it is wise to try to learn the design and statistical methods used.
I don't seem to be able to understand what theoretical developments mean	It might be useful to draw a diagram showing how A leads to B. Then ask the questions: why and how are these linked? By answering these questions you will have the structure of the theoretical development in place. Writing out the details will lead you to have a theoretical development. Rewriting many times helps to crystallize the link. Use this practice and you are one step closer towards better theoretical development.
I don't seem to be able to stop reading as articles in the literature are plenty	At some point the reading has to slow down and writing has to start. More often than not after an adequate quantity of articles have been read, insights from further articles become marginal (provided they are not classics and from eminent scholars in the field), as the full picture of the linkages would have more or less surfaced.

Areas of frustration	Tips on how to counter frustration
I don't seem to be able to understand some of the things my supervisor says	Return to ask for clarity. Supervisors do not have problems in repeating themselves for clarity. It is always good for both parties to be on the same page.
I don't seem to know where to start looking for data	Talk to a librarian, or to a more experienced researcher in the field.
I don't seem to know how to find out what methods would be best for my research	Use articles in the literature to help you locate this, especially relying on those that are closely aligned with your work.
My peers do not seem to be able to understand what I write	If this happens more than once, then your writing needs to improve. It is likely you are not writing for your audience. You might want to avoid jargon. Further, try to write from your audience's perspective.

Figure 2.1 Tips on How to Deal with Frustrations in Research

Research supervisor

At the university, you are paired with a **research supervisor** when you work on a research project. Sometimes, your university will organize this supervisory arrangement. Other times, you will be asked to locate a potential supervisor with whom you will work on your research project. Research supervisors are knowledgeable people in your field of work who are able to provide you with input and guidance to both research content and processes. It is common that a potential research supervisor will help shape your research study, sometimes refining it and sometimes providing the appropriate guidance and direction. You are likely to be negotiating the topic as well if your potential research supervisor's thinking deviates from yours.

Moving into the supervision process after supervisory arrangements are confirmed, there are also other challenges relating to the process in which the research supervisor plays a key role. For example, a research supervisor may help open doors for access to an organization to study or allow the student to be exposed to the academic world through their networks. Of course, personality clashes can potentially happen, which does not bode well for any supervisory arrangement.

Due to their roles, research supervisors often have a lasting impact on your research and your personal and career development. You don't know what you don't know. It is these people who are the ones to expose you to the 'don't knows' so that you can make sense of your research environment and how you deal with some of the unknowns in your research process.

Peers

It is easy to appreciate why your research supervisor is a critical element of your research environment. But why are **peers** important as well? Peers can be a crucial part of your research journey. Simply put, they can exert influence on you and your research in at least two ways.

First, peers create a sense of belonging and provide group support. Peers may or may not be researchers who are working in your field. But the common language is research. Consider two scenarios. You and your peers are new researchers and are always feeling that you are bumping around in the research process without a clear direction as to what you are looking for or what is in place for you. In this situation, you can share your frustrations. Venting your frustrations about research can help clear your mind. Or, you and your peers are researchers with some experience. Now, other than sharing frustrations, which incidentally applies to senior researchers as well, you can share experience. As discussed earlier in this book, there is a lot of tacit knowledge involved in the research process. Everyone is unlikely to run into all possible difficulties within the research space. Wouldn't it be nice to already know some of these potential hindrances before you actually encounter them yourself? Wouldn't it be even better if you can avoid some of these before they arrive at your doorstep? Without openly discussing these experiences, no one would have imagined that everyone else is in fact facing potentially the same issues and challenges in research. Sometimes a listening ear helps to relieve the pressures when we encounter research hurdles.

Peers also help provide an independent perspective of your work and can even be informal reviewers. When we write, we are always encapsulated in a black box. When we read what we have just written, we are always influenced by the fact that we know what will turn up in the next line or paragraph, which generally makes us poor reviewers of our own work. Peers provide a fresh pair of eyes on your work – language or clarity or content. In this way, reviewers or examiners will not be the first readers to run into the mistakes that you may have made, hence not affecting your chance of publication or a better grade for your research project. In fact, sometimes it is good to have a peer who is less versed with your research area test your ideas. To be able to articulate to someone who is less versed in your research will help to crystallize your thoughts.

Research collaborators

Beyond the research project that you do as part of your degree, there are times when a research opportunity arises. This is where a **research collaborator** comes into play. Research collaboration is easy to establish but good research collaborators are difficult to come by. The best research teams always contain members with good complementary skills. This is especially important when it comes to publishing. The review process of most business and management journals takes you through an average of three rounds of reviews by three reviewers. These reviewers are well versed in your area of work and often approach your submission from different perspectives. To have research collaborators will ease the pressure on you to be able to handle reviewer comments coming from multiple perspectives.

Conversation box

Juliana [PhD student]:   Professor, would it be wise to work with a peer on a research project?

Professor: Juliana, everything starts from somewhere. Working with a peer allows you to learn from each other and share new ideas.

Juliana: But isn't it better to work with someone more senior in research so that there's more guidance?

Professor: Of course, potentially you can learn even more from a senior researcher. But sometimes some of them are not available to work with you while others may not have the time to focus on the research work with you even after they have agreed to be on the project. Having the ability to put in adequate efforts in the research project is a bonus to having a peer as a research collaborator.

Beyond the supporting role described above, peers are often a good resource as research collaborators. Peers are likely to be in the same stage of development in their research career trajectory. As such, their pressures and desire to do research can be quite similar. Having senior researchers as collaborators has its benefits but also pitfalls, as highlighted in the conversation box above. Peers, on the other hand, have similar incentives to publish well.

Finding research collaborators is the easy part, making the collaboration work is the hard part. If your potential collaborator is busy, you may want to consider carefully how much time they can devote to your collaboration. Every researcher also has different working styles, such as how much work they will do while travelling and during weekends when deadlines are near. These different working styles need to be aligned and respected. If it is not possible to align them, then you should avoid working on a project together. More often than not, collaborators bring different sets of skills to a research project. For example, one of the researchers may be good at conceptual work while another may be stronger on the empirical part. Likewise, each of the two researchers in a project may be good at different perspectives that are adopted in the research project. As most research projects last for a couple of years or longer, collaborators have to work in tandem for a research project to be successful. So, do not be surprised if a couple of collaborative research projects do not work out. Sometimes research collaboration may also not work out because of power differences in the team. The complexity of collaboration rises as the number of research collaborators increases. Figure 2.2 provides some tips in handling research collaboration.

If you are the lead researcher in the team
1. Keep abreast on the timeline of what needs to be achieved and by whom
2. Constantly keep in touch with co-researchers
3. Be the main connector to the journal after submission
4. Try to be understanding in terms of what to expect from co-researchers as they will have other workflows to manage – rework timeline accordingly
If you are not the lead researcher in the team
1. Try to stick to the schedule as agreed with the lead researcher
2. Constantly keep in touch with lead researcher and co-researchers
3. Try to be understanding in terms of what to expect from co-researchers as they will have other workflows to manage

Figure 2.2   Tips on How to be Collegial in Research

2.2.4 Research is subjective

Conversation box

Professor: Class, when you do your background literature work, please apply a critical lens to it.

Joan [Honours student]:   Professor, what do you mean by applying a critical lens?

Professor: While we know that most studies have undergone a good quality control process, the bottom line is that some research is better and more objective than others. To have a critical lens is to adopt a perspective that you will need to be convinced by what you are reading and citing, rather than taking the work at face value simply because it has been published.

Research students usually do not challenge what is in print – be it in journals or magazines. They assume some sort of checks have been in place and thus anything that goes to print has a certain quality attached to it. However, even reliable, print-published research papers may have some **subjective** opinions attached to them. For example, some journals will publish opinion pieces that incorporate an expert's view on a particular topic. Nonetheless, most journals are peer-reviewed – a paper submission to one of these journals has to be reviewed by two or more persons who are specialized in the topic area of the paper and are able to assess its quality. In this way, subjectivity of research is checked and hence kept to a minimum. It is not easy for subjective views of individual authors to pass through such a rigorous process of quality control. Therefore, to a large extent, peer-reviewed research outputs that you commonly see do have a more limited degree of subjectivity. Nonetheless, it is critical to adopt a critical lens as demonstrated in the conversation box above to further reduce the likelihood of encountering a paper that falls through the cracks in the review process. The critical lens will also help guide the extent to which you should rely on a paper while conducting your own research.

2.2.5 The more coverage the study, the better it should be

Wouldn't there be a chance of better contribution if the scope of a research project proposed is larger? Moreover, would it not be fair to say that in business and management research (and in social science for that matter) the complexity of phenomena would suggest that many factors need to be taken into account in our research to rule out alternative explanations?

These are all valid points in favour of a wider scope of coverage for any research project. But in reality, these are only theoretically right. Take for example, in a test of how a firm's strategy can affect its performance, one could easily propose a list of 20 factors that can be used for testing this relationship, for example a firm's domestic and international strategies, competitor strategies, and all its functional strategies. Having 20 factors certainly provides good coverage. But imagine trying to collect data for all of these factors in the same research project! In a world of research without other forms of constraint, such as time and resources, this might be possible. Nevertheless, it is unlikely to be feasible in practice.

When a sizeable number of factors are introduced, it begs the question as to which one(s) might provide the key contribution. It is unlikely that all 20 of these factors will contribute equally to firm performance. This means that you will still have to sort out what the key factors are. This assessment will also allow you to know which factors are peripheral to the research. It is these factors you should consider eliminating when the time comes for narrowing the focus of the research. If a research topic sits within a broad research area where our understanding is relatively advanced, the desired form of research work is always about *deepening* our understanding rather than *broadening* our understanding. Proposing broad topics in this case is likely to lead to research with marginal contribution.

The key point here is that more coverage does not necessarily mean better. In fact, 'less is more' will prevail in most areas of research in business and management. The value of more marginal work has been questioned (e.g. Shaver, 2013). Studies with broad coverage will fall into that category. As Chapter 1 has highlighted, we should seek parsimony in our work, and thus more work that deepens our understanding in our field will be desirable. More detail on honing ideas into research topics will be discussed in Chapter 3.

2.2.6 The research process will be linear and prescriptive

Conversation box

Professor:	Neil, can you look into how to measure these constructs that you're proposing in your research?
Neil [graduate student]:	I'm still doing my literature search. Once I finish this off, together with hypotheses development, then I'll look into the constructs. This might take me another three weeks. Will this be alright, Professor?
Professor:	You should work on some of these research components concurrently.
Neil:	But I thought this process should follow a sequence.
Professor:	In practice, your process will evolve as your understanding deepens. It is ideal to ensure that constructs are possible to make your project feasible. If you proceed with your sequence of research, you might form ideas that will turn out to be challenging when it comes to constructs. Therefore, I would advise that you think about these components concurrently.

Partly as a means to deal with uncertainty and unknowns when they are exposed to research, students frequently desire a step-by-step approach. How many times have research project supervisors been asked by their students to provide them with specific itemized schedules to allow them to complete their research on time? As briefly considered in Chapter 1, the research process is by no means a linear one. Research always follows a cyclical process, where feedback loops link the components.

Not only will there be no answer to a request for a step-by-step approach to research, there are also many tacit practices in the research process. These are often referred to as **judgement calls**. While some rules of thumb exist in the research world, we will still have to make judgement calls all the time. While there is certainly codified knowledge in research, there are also many grey areas in the research process where there are no specific answers to questions such as 'am I right to do this?' and 'is this OK?' More often, it is about having an answer that is right for 80% of the time. Figure 2.3 highlights some suggestions on the mindset needed for dealing with misperceptions in research.

---

1. Research is only for people who want to become academics and has little significance for practice; and projects related to practice do not need research rigour.

   a. Research allows anyone to be better informed, so it should not always be just for academics. Think in terms of the ability to convince when it comes to a conversation about management practice.
   b. There is nothing wrong in engaging in a programme that is more research-oriented. In reality, this frequently complements well for students who are already working or have some work experience.
   c. For managers looking to put forth recommendations, think of the value of research when it provides backing to the analysis and recommendations being put forward.
   d. Think of how you can make your arguments and proposals different and superior with the help of research.

2. Research is isolating and frustrating.

   a. Realise that everyone is facing the same challenges.
   b. Find someone to talk to about your research or have broad discussions about research. It will remind you that you are still passionate about research.
   c. Join groups that share challenges and solutions – you will find some help there.
   d. Do not give up easily; nobody says research is easy.

3. Research is subjective; and the more coverage the study, the better it should be.

   a. Always keep an eye out for research that you deem may be subjective. Seek to understand biases so that you can avoid the traps.
   b. As far as possible, make sure your own research is objective.
   c. Try not to be greedy – you cannot solve an issue with just one piece of work. An issue may need to be addressed with the triangulation of multiple studies to present a holistic picture. Remember: Less is more, but be careful of being too unambitious and mediocre.

4. The research process will be linear and prescriptive.

   a. The research process is never linear. Make sure that you are thinking and dealing with more than one component of your research at all times.
   b. As you deal with one component of your research, always look backward and forward to ensure the links are still intact.
   c. There is always more than one way to conduct a study, so be flexible and adapt when needed throughout the research process.

Figure 2.3   Mindset for Dealing with Misperceptions in Research

2.3 SOME CHALLENGES IN THE RESEARCH PROCESS
2.3.1 The choice of research areas and settings

While there seems to be an abundance of research areas that a business and management researcher can work on, and researchers have freedom of choice of research interests, there are some extraneous factors that often shape our interests in one direction or another. For students, the choice of research area can be constrained by the research expertise of the faculty members. As a research student, you will be allocated to a faculty member who will provide expert advice on your research topic. Supervision is easier when your research topic is well aligned with the research area of the faculty member. In some schools, whether a student can proceed with a particular research direction or not actually depends on the availability of faculty member to supervise. As the business and management field is diverse, many of the research areas become interdisciplinary. It is not uncommon to find that some research areas are not represented in the business school you are enrolled at. This might influence your decision in choosing a research area of interest or might influence your decision to enrol in a particular university.

Some research settings are chosen by design – the research topic requires the choice of certain types of organizations or groups for observations. Others are chosen for convenience. Take for example a researcher who wants to study empirically the dynamics of group behaviour. While groups exist in most organizations, over-sampling of organizations for the study of groups within them introduces a lot of 'noise' due to differences across the organizations. In such cases, it will be appropriate to choose organizations that usually operate with groups, such as consulting companies. The selection process will create another query regarding the extent to which findings from this research can be applicable to organizations that usually do not operate in groups. When a research design is chosen for convenience, it is common for a researcher to adjust the research issue depending on the organizations they are able to access. This is necessary as this convenience selection is likely to be scrutinized for **objectivity** and validity when it is mapped to a broader research question that covers a wider set of organizations.

The familiarity with particular methods is another factor that usually influences the research topic choice and setting. Researchers have a tendency to choose their most familiar methods for research instead of exploring alternative new methods to investigate the research topic (Kaplan, 1964: 28). In fact, Trow (1957: 35) suggests that researchers even choose research issues that are easiest to resolve using the methods they are familiar with. This would be an extreme case, but not entirely impossible to envisage happening in reality. The ability to execute a research study requires multiple sets of skills that can stretch what most individuals are capable of. In a research project, as a student is the sole author, the research topic and scope will be shaped by what they are capable of. In research undertaken for publication, researchers overcome this hurdle by collaborating with others who possess complementary skillsets.

2.3.2 Theory and hypotheses development

When attending any research-related course, you will often run into the word **theory**. We often associate theory with ground-breaking understanding in science, such as Einstein's Theory of Relativity. In our research, we also run into various theories such as transaction cost economics (Williamson, 1975), agency theory (Jensen and Meckling, 1976) (both borrowed from economics), resource-based theory (Barney, 1991), knowledge-based theory (Grant, 1996), etc. There are many more micro theories relating to business and management.

When you are doing your research project, you are often asked 'what is your theoretical contribution?' This question often immediately creates stress for you: what is theoretical enough? You will wonder why you are being asked this question, as you are definitely not in the business of generating 'new' theories. You also hear about 'theory building'. What does that mean? What constitutes the process of theory building? How does a researcher know when he has a theoretical contribution? These are some of the issues that will be discussed in this subsection. In addition, some of the implicit rules of theorizing that make some research more rigorous than others will also be highlighted.

Paradigm development

Paradigm development refers to the technological uncertainty associated with the production of knowledge in a given scientific field or subspecialty (Lodahl and Gordon, 1972). Every research field and subfield go through different stages in their development; some fields are more developed than others. The degree of paradigm development also differs across subfields within business and management (Pfeffer, 1993). Accumulation of knowledge depends largely on the progress of research in the field, which is reflected in the extent of theoretical and methodological understanding within a field (Edmondson and McManus, 2007). Normally, this requires some level of consensus among researchers within the field or subfield. Consensus refers to the common understanding of theories and methodologies judged to be suitable and fit for a field by researchers within the field. Webster and Starbuck (1988) argue for the need for theories to drive towards more consensus in management research. To gain consensus, Pfeffer (1993) suggests that minimizing the disagreements over key research questions, the ways relevant variables are measured and modelled, methodologies, theoretical models and the rules of determining how to approach these four domains are critical to the progress of a field.

Failure to have consensus will lead to fragmentation of a particular field and will slow down progress. Zammuto and Connelly (1984) have argued that the fragmentation of the field of organizational science has obstructed its scientific progress. Social science, unlike physical science, often requires more time to be spent in explaining complex concepts and it is often difficult for researchers to come to a consensus. Highly developed paradigms have fewer such issues and thus allow easier communication and consensus (Salancik et al., 1980). This in essence has many implications for the business and management field. For example, it takes a longer time for research to be published in good management journals as compared to journals from the more paradigmatically developed scientific fields (Beyer, 1978; Hargens, 1988).

As relatively new and complex disciplines, business and management research areas face significant challenges in obtaining consensus on various aspects of research. The lack of consensus in business and management also makes training in the field difficult. We often run into multiple theories to explain a particular phenomenon. The research findings we gather from our literature review process often show a lot of inconsistencies within a research area. These complexities make it difficult for students to distinguish between good and not-so-good application of theories and can lead to a longer time period needed to complete their research degrees (Zammuto and Connelly, 1984).

As the business and management field also has a liking for novelty, there are always efforts to seek new ways of looking at phenomena or new areas of research. That is, there are proactive efforts to detract from mainstream thoughts in the field. This tendency can also divert research time and effort from deepening our understanding in the mainstream areas of the field. To advance the field as a whole, it is imperative to recognize instances of good **theory development** when that happens.

But what exactly is theory in business and management? Theory can be briefly defined as the branch of a science or art that deals with its principles or methods, as distinguished from its practice. Thus, theory deals with the underlying logic of phenomena. Given its complexity, however, it is never clear what a theory is (e.g. Bacharach, 1989). In essence, theory takes various forms and actually differs across fields. While it is difficult to define exactly what a theory is in business and management, Sutton and Staw (1995) provide a good overview of what theory is not.

Referencing is not theory

Chapter 1 has briefly highlighted the ethical behaviour of accurate referencing. More will be discussed about referencing in the context of conducting a good literature review in Chapter 4. Good references are commonly used to justify the links between constructs as a researcher attempts to convince the reader that the relationships he proposed are grounded in support from prior research works. Articles published in highly selective, peer-reviewed journals and articles by eminent authors are especially good references for this purpose.

Just as an example, let us say that we are interested to test the effect of top management diversity on firm performance. The concept of top management diversity in itself does not have any positive or negative meaning attached to it. It merely reflects a static structure of organizing executives. However, we also know that some degrees of top management diversity can lead to learning and debates that enhance decision-making and ultimately better firm performance. With this in mind, the tendency is to find evidence from previous research to support the relationship between top management diversity and learning and debates, and between learning and debates and enhanced decision-making.

Finding support and citing references on both these relationships, however, does not constitute theory. Theory involves the articulation of the actual relationships as a whole. One needs to articulate the flow of logic from top management diversity through learning and debates to enhanced decision-making and eventually better firm performance. Merely citing previous works on these linkages does not constitute theory development.

Data and findings are not theory

Related to referencing articles, arguments merely based on prior findings do not constitute theory. For example, if we theorize based on prior findings, we can find ourselves able to link 'a need to access resources' with 'better firm performance' through prior findings on the link, for example, between the need to access resources and the conduct of acquisitions and the positive effect of acquisition on firm performance.

There are two issues here. First, while the two linkages are well established individually, the logic supporting the conclusion is less appealing. Acquisition in this case is just an en-route. There is a question about what the implication is of finding the linkage between 'a need to access resources' and 'better firm performance'. That is, 'a need to access resources' needs to be translated to action that can then lead to 'better firm performance'. And acquisition is just one type of such actions. If acquisition is used as an en-route in this study, then the focus of the work has to surround its use. Second, these two linkages are supported in different studies, probably in different study periods across different industries and companies and maybe even different country contexts. Are we able to connect and assume that the second linkage works for the data used in the first linkage without actually testing that? The answer is a definite no.

Thus, prior findings and data cannot substitute for causal reasoning. For every research study, the linkages must be well articulated and grounded in theory and not based on bits and pieces of empirical findings derived from different studies that are likely to use different contexts.

Listing of variables or constructs is not theory

In many circumstances, we are faced with the situation of introducing some new variables to explain a certain phenomenon. Many a time, we feel that we have addressed a gap in the literature by introducing this variable and observing an effect on the outcome variable. This new finding can then add to a more theoretical understanding of the phenomenon being examined.

However, in actual fact, adding a new variable or list of variables to test the effect on an outcome variable does not constitute theory or theory development. You need to justify why adding such a variable actually furthers our understanding of the phenomenon under investigation. You also need to argue how this new variable can fit in with existing frameworks and other variables in this literature. Essentially, addressing the question 'why do we care about this variable?'

In addition, just stating that there is a relationship between two constructs does not contribute to theory. Ex-post observation of a relationship does not in itself contribute to our understanding. In fact, finding a relationship without justifying the linkages makes it a 'data mining' exercise. Likewise, testing and concluding that some variables have bigger impacts on the outcome variable than other variables also does not constitute any theory development. A comparative test of variables is not the same as a comparative test of theory. In order to contribute to theory, these variables must be connected by logical arguments and articulated as such. Comparative empirical tests of variables need to be accompanied by compelling arguments.

Hypotheses (or predictions) are not theory

The deductive approach to research emphasizes the need to have some hypotheses or predictions. Hypotheses may also be formulated in the course of an inductive approach to research. A hypothesis is a tentative explanation for an observation, phenomenon, or scientific problem that can be tested by further investigation. The number of hypotheses expected in any study varies and is not an indicator of the degree of intellectual contribution of the study. Nor is it necessary to have a pre-determined number of hypotheses in a study. Sometimes you may come across a published paper with only one or two hypotheses, while other times you may run into a published paper with a dozen hypotheses.

Again, having a good list of testable hypotheses does not constitute theoretical contribution. Hypothesis statements only show the 'what' and not the 'why' of the relationship between constructs. They are just statements without leading arguments. In order to meaningfully contribute to theory development, these statements must be well grounded in logical arguments. Chapter 5 will include a discussion of how to craft good and testable hypotheses.

What then might be a theory? What constitutes good theoretical development?

According to Sutton and Staw (1995), a good theory is often representational (graphical) and verbal (rich process to be described). It must be simple and show some interconnectedness, and it normally starts with one or two conceptual statements that serve as a stepping-stone for building logical arguments. Whetten (1989) proposes that a theoretical contribution (of a study) needs to have four elements: (1) *what* factors logically should be considered for the study; (2) *how* are the factors interrelated; (3) *why* are they interrelated; and (4) *who, where* and *when* these interrelations will hold. In this framework, the first two elements provide the structure of the study. The third element is the one that spells out the linkages proposed, which in essence is where the theoretical contribution lies. The last element sets the boundary conditions to which the structure applies.

The relationship between theory and data is always complicated. The key question has been 'which precedes the other?' How does one construct a research study that starts off with a theory? This is by no means easy. Thus, it is not surprising to find that observation is always the easier and more common way to motivate a research study. After all, the entire consulting industry is built around problem-solving research – that theory is very much driven by observations. In recent years, there has also been rising phenomenon-based research that emphasizes the need for theory development to explain various phenomena. Many researchers have also started to highlight the potential intertwining relationships between theory and data (e.g. van Maanen et al., 2007). Nonetheless, there have been warnings around the risk of focusing too much on data and methods which can cause theoretical development to be weakened (Davis, 2010). In fact, theoretical development in business and management has been suffering from a lack of focus on specificity in the predictions (Edwards and Berry, 2010).

Our research work tends to be shaped by the methodologies that we are familiar with. Our methodological knowledge further tends to be affected by what we are exposed to in our postgraduate and PhD studies. As a result, in our subsequent work, sometimes we just hope that we can use the methodologies that we are familiar with. This is a common observation, but it is not the optimal way of going about doing research, as also mentioned earlier in Section 2.3.1. This mentality can reach the level that might make you believe if you do not use the most complicated and complex methodologies, it is unlikely your research work will get noticed. Theories and methods evolve almost simultaneously (Maanen et al., 2007). Fields which are relatively new or emerging tend to be more receptive towards exploratory methods where these serve a purpose for our careful exploration. Fields that are more advanced or phenomena that have been extensively investigated are more likely to demand methods of greater complexity in order to further the development in that area. So, one can argue that theoretical development determines the methodology needed (Edmondson and McManus, 2007). If so, then methodology might indeed be a tool, and theoretical development and rigour are the real keys to good research.

There are three main forms of research papers, namely pure theoretical, pure empirical and mixed approach papers. Pure theoretical papers are always more difficult to write. The contribution has to be substantial. Thus, it is seen as a dangerous route to adopt for less established researchers. Research students are generally ill-advised to engage in theoretical studies for their first piece of research work. As fewer researchers work on pure theoretical papers, the readership of journals focusing on pure theoretical papers is limited. Thus, it is not commercially viable for many publishers to engage in publishing theoretically focused journals. Note that the *Academy of Management Review* is one of the few top business and management journals with a special focus on publishing theoretical papers. Pure empirical journal outlets are plenty. However, many also tend to be journals of lower quality. The top journals tend to publish articles that have both theoretical and empirical contributions. A mixed focus also ensures greater readership. Chapter 4 will provide a listing of top journals in the business and management field.

The requirements for both theoretical and methodological rigour have escalated in recent years. To advance theory incrementally, it is possible just to build on existing methods in the literature. Investigations that can lead to substantial contribution to theory often face observation limitations. Sutton and Staw (1995) suggest a need to rebalance the theory–method selection process. An important element is to relax conditions on new or provocative ideas to encourage advancements. In such cases, illustrative data, rather than definitive data, may be deemed adequate. Hambrick (2007) further suggests that some business research areas are more pragmatic than others when it comes to the expectations of theoretical contribution. In particular, he cites published examples from both the marketing and finance disciplines on their practice to relax demands of strong theoretical development in favour of the use of good data.

The ability to write theory can only come with practice and is thus considered by many researchers as a by-product of the system. Even for seasoned researchers, this part of the research process is the most challenging and difficult. However, this is also a main component of differentiating a lacklustre paper from a good paper, and a good paper from an excellent one.

2.3.3 Highly uncertain research outcomes

If there is something that cannot be avoided in research, it is that research always involves high uncertainty, especially with respect to the outcome. While this book discusses a lot of tacit issues you will run into when you actually conduct your research, many of these issues do not have a definite answer. In other words, it is possible that some of these will not be resolved in your specific research situation – making it necessary for you to alter your research plans. Seasoned researchers are better at avoiding some of these potential stumbling blocks and are generally more able to anticipate these problems. Such anticipation comes with experience. If you are a research student, you will have to slowly learn the trade, both through the hard way of encountering and countering unexpected hurdles and the easier way of seeking advice from your supervisor or senior researchers when you cannot resolve the issue by yourself after several attempts. Over time, you will find yourself better able to cope with the highly uncertain nature of research activities and better able to anticipate potential hurdles.

2.3.4 Time constraints

Different programme degrees have different time specifications within which to carry out the research activities. Small research projects are usually done within three to four months, Honours dissertations are usually done within six months and Masters theses usually within a year. PhD studies usually take three to five years. At times, trying to fit all the components of the research process into a short timeframe feels like an onerous task on its own. Given these time constraints, as a student you may start to envy faculty staff members as you probably think they do not face similar restrictions in their research work. However, that is not true. Faculty members are expected to produce research outputs and the expectations of these outputs are higher than for the research project that you are working on. This expectation can come from their university but will mainly be derived from the journal that the faculty member is targeting to publish their work. Getting published in a good journal is becoming increasingly demanding. As such, the necessary research process is increasingly time consuming. In addition, in order to get greater mileage from research efforts, faculty members often engage in larger projects that take a longer time to produce results. While these projects may eventually materialize as top journal outputs which justify the time needed, faculty members also need to have frequent research outputs to show for their work (and employment basically). Some journals have special calls for papers, which have deadlines. Likewise, conferences and grant funding applications all have deadlines. Hence, faculty members are also facing time constraints in many of their research activities.

Time consumption and time constraints represent significant challenges to all researchers, whether you are a research student, a new researcher or a more seasoned researcher. Elizondo-Schmelkes (2011) has found that competing attention for time has led many students to abandon their research degrees during the research phase. This adds to the complexity to manage the cyclical research process that was discussed in Section 1.7. Putting these into perspective, it is not surprising to observe that research processes in tertiary institutions mimic those in consulting companies, where time availability plays a big role in the **research scope**, process and outcomes. Unfortunately, this may also mean that sometimes time constraints can limit our ability to perform our research with the maximum rigour possible.

2.3.5 Navigating the research supervision process

As a research student, one of the key aspects of your research environment is your relationship with your supervisor. Sometimes this additional element can make your research life easier as you are being shepherded through the process of research, while other times managing this relationship itself can be challenging. As such, it is important to understand how this process works and managing this process in tandem with your supervisor will ensure that your experience of the research process is a good one.

Various research studies have been done on the supervisory relationship and what potentially constitutes successful determinants of the outcomes from this research arrangement. Yet, the nature of the work has been scattered across disciplines and across various degrees that require different levels of supervision. Moreover, the very nature of this one-on-one teaching mode means that there is a high degree of flexibility in the interactions, making our learning further segregated. Thus, our understanding is far from complete. Nonetheless, the literature does provide some guidelines.

Different supervisory styles have been proposed and discussed. For example, Vilkinas (2008) proposes six roles that supervisors can assume: developer, deliverer, monitor, broker, innovator and integrator. Kam (1997) summarizes the potential tasks that characterize the relationship between the supervisor and the student, namely topic selection, work planning, defining research scope, literature search, research proposal preparation, establishing research methodology, work monitoring, concern about research progress, ensuring work quality and standard, submitting drafts for review, acquiring thesis writing skills, problem anticipation and interaction. These studies however conclude that there is no prescription as to which supervisory style is the best.

Given that the interaction between the supervisor and the student is key to the outcome of a postgraduate degree, there have been some studies that seek to investigate the potential overlapping and varying expectations. For example, Styles and Radloff (2001) reflect on the authors' experience as supervisor and student, and how they have established the research collaboration that led to publications. Their reflections suggest the importance of the self-regulatory model of supervision, whereby the student is given the autonomy of thought and drives the interactions and research process while the supervisor takes the role of the facilitator of learning. This is in alignment with Delamont et al.'s (1998) study that suggests the importance of balancing the autonomy of a novice researcher and the need for the senior researcher to control the process to ensure its smooth path to success. Success in this context can mean the timely completion of the research project or a publication deriving from the research.

Woolhouse (2002) also conducts a similar study about expectations. The study puts forth some recommendations that are worth highlighting here, including the discussion of expectations between supervisor and student, not focusing on the time schedule too early in the process and emphasizing the importance of the research instead, structuring more tutorial meetings, and introducing strategies that encourage more independence on the part of the student. Fraser and Mathews (1999) find that students generally view non-expertise-related characteristics of the supervisors as a more important element in the supervisory process than expertise-related characteristics. In particular, they find that supportive supervisors are highly desirable, as these supervisors are able to balance the need to be critical and the need to provide directions for the student as and when necessary. Nonetheless, the supervision process is always going to be one that has to be carefully managed. To that end, Acker et al. (1994) find that while the supervision process tends to go through stages, it usually goes by the negotiated order process. This means that every stage in the supervision process contains negotiations between the research supervisor and the student and each will have to manage the other's expectations along the way.

Overall, it is clear that the self-regulatory model tends to be encouraged in the supervision process. The model encourages shared interests, shared beliefs in the work, shared commitment to the process and shared responsibilities in working out the procedures, strategies and actions, especially when facing difficulties. The research student is expected to have some autonomy of thought and action, and an awareness of being in control of the supervision process (Schunk, 1994). Negotiating regular meetings can in many cases help as well (e.g. Heath, 2002). Armstrong et al. (2004) further advise that different cognitive styles of supervisor and student will lead to different outcomes. One might also argue that ultimately supervision success can only be assessed long after it has ended, for example, if the student chooses to continue to stay in touch with the supervisor after the completion of the research process (Moriarty et al., 2008).

Research supervision that involves more than one supervisor is more complex than supervision involving only one supervisor, even though both arrangements have advantages and disadvantages. Having more than one supervisor provides the following advantages: First, a supervisory team might provide a more balanced view of the research topic than a single supervisor. As most academics are versed in a limited set of perspectives, the approach to research topics can be biased towards prior training. A multi-supervisor team will provide a more holistic picture of the student's research topic in hand. Second, and related to the first point, a multi-supervisor team is likely to provide a greater breadth of knowledge. Third, a multi-supervisor team will allow the supervision to continue should the main supervisor be unavailable due to other commitments or illness. Fourth, beyond the content of the supervision process, more supervisors will provide more access to networks for the student. Some of these advantages, of course, naturally become the potential disadvantages of having a multi-supervisor team. For example, supervisors coming from different perspectives might provide conflicting views on aspects of the research topic, potentially resulting in the student's confusion as to which way they should lean.

Power dynamics exist in research collaborative work between supervisor and student (Styles and Radloff, 2001). Recall in Section 1.5.3 where we discussed authorship and ownership of research work dilemmas involved in the extent of participation of the supervisor in the research work of the student. In terms of collaborative research for publication, the issue of authorship was also raised. A junior researcher in any research collaboration should not be deprived of being the lead author. However, given that the senior researcher in the collaboration is also the supervisor, it is hard to imagine that the junior researcher will negotiate to be the first author of their paper. Some like to call this the 'apprenticeship' where such collaboration is part of the learning process for the student to learn how to publish. This is probably true to some extent as the challenge of publication can be a tall order compared to writing up a research project. Nonetheless, this 'apprenticeship' should also be viewed as a temporary arrangement that is subject to negotiation between the supervisor and student with each subsequent work. Authorship credit should always as far as possible be judged by the contribution of each author as opposed to the seniority of the authors.

2.3.6 Navigating the journal review process

Beyond negotiating a smooth research supervision process that will help with the completion of the programme degree, another challenge facing a junior researcher would be that of navigating through the journal review process. As an Honours or Masters student, you may not have to go through this process unless you choose to work on a publication, either on your own or with research collaborators. As a PhD student, you may have already been encouraged to embark on a publication journey.

There are two characteristics of the journal review process that make it significantly different from the research supervision process. First, the journal review process is conducted with a **double-blind** approach. The authors do not know who the reviewers are and vice versa. Only the editor will know the identities of both parties. In the research supervision process, at least you know who your supervisor is, and they know it is your work they are reading. The journal review process will be closer to the stage where your thesis or dissertation gets examined – your examiner will be aware of whose research project they are examining, but you would normally not know the identity of the examiner. Second, in the journal review process, you will have review comments from two or more reviewers to deal with and will not have the benefit of being able to explain and clarify with them in person – everything is done through writing. You will probably have conversations with your supervisor during the research supervision process to seek some feedback. In instances where your research project involves an **oral examination**, you will also get the opportunity to clarify issues with the examiner that will help with the revision of the research project. It should be noted that normally smaller research projects do not have this oral examination component at the end.

These differences lead to a whole new set of challenges for a researcher, whether junior or not. Fundamentally, it means that whenever you write an article, you will have to consider where potential reviewers may have concerns around your research and try to address these before you actually submit the article for review. In particular, top journals have high rejection rates and rejections are largely based on the editor's and reviewers' assessments. Therefore, it is important to ensure that reviewers appreciate the potential of your work the first time they read it.

Content and rigour aside, it is crucial that an author takes care of some aspects of the paper submission to ensure that the process does not frustrate both editor and reviewers. Feldman (2005) provides a good checklist of items.

In terms of things for authors to be cautious about or avoid, the following items come to mind. The non-content-related items include: submitting an excessively long article, picking the wrong journal, having grammatical and spelling mistakes, and formatting which doesn't conform to journal requirements. These are generally easy to fix and should be rectified or avoided as far as possible so that the paper submission has a better chance of getting to the review stage. Content-related items can include: a bad abstract and introduction that do not entice the editor or reviewer to read further, a less than adequate literature review that demonstrates a lack of complete understanding of the topic, a lack of hypotheses development, a research methodology description that is not transparent enough for demonstrating rigour, and a discussion that does not accurately reflect the findings. Some of these are relatively easy to fix as well and ensuring that these are taken care of before submission will be the difference between an outright rejection and an opportunity to revise and resubmit the paper.

On the other hand, while authors seek to do their best to ensure the quality of their submissions, the reviewers themselves need to regulate their behaviour in important ways. If good articles can only get through with the help of reviewers, good reviews become an essential element of getting good research published.

A reviewer's role is one mainly of development – in other words, helping the author understand how their work can be improved (Feldman, 2004). However, in recent years there have been concerns with regard to the degree of intervention that reviewers have over the authors' submissions (e.g. Bedeian, 1996; Tsang and Frey, 2007). The key concern is that reviewers impose greatly on the author to adjust the paper to their liking, to the extent that the idea in the final article is not a true reflection of the idea in the original submission.

Beyond influencing the ideas, various other undesirable behaviours of reviewers have also been identified, for example, by Feldman (2005). These include providing general comments and feedback without supporting justifications, spelling and grammatical mistakes in the review, being late in providing the review, failure to provide guidance on how problems and issues identified can possibly be fixed, not distinguishing the difference between major and minor concerns, insisting on the author citing the reviewer's own work, providing mixed signals in the review by being positive to authors yet advising the editor for a rejection, and using language that talks down to the author.

A good review always includes but is not limited to evaluating the importance of the research question raised, the appropriateness of the methodology used, the clarity of arguments, and the quality of communication of ideas. The review should cover both the major strengths and weaknesses of the article. Ideally, these are listed in order of importance and seriousness. Major concerns and minor concerns should also be separated. Such organization of the review will not only allow the author to understand the thinking behind the reviewer's concerns but also allow the editor to make a well-informed decision about the article to either be further considered for publication or be rejected.

A good review does not have to comment on every aspect of the submission. In addition, a reviewer should also avoid expecting the author to write in the same style as they would. The reviewer also has to be considerate in providing comments and raising issues that are unimportant is not desirable. In terms of assessing rigour and methodology, a reviewer should be open-minded regarding the diversity of approaches out there, rather than expecting the author to use a particular methodology. In other words, a reviewer should not dictate which of a number of acceptable alternatives an author should choose. It is fine to note that a particular method is inappropriate in the particular situation and why, but it is the author's choice which of several competing methods was chosen, as long as it is appropriate. This applies to both design and methods used. It is, however, appropriate for a reviewer to make a friendly suggestion that in the future the author should consider (i.e. using a particular design or methods as it is superior).

Reviewers should give reasons for why something is inappropriate, and they should be as specific as possible. General reasons will not be informative. For example, if all data are collected in a single questionnaire, to merely say that the study might have common method variance is not helpful. It should be stated why this is a problem. A constructive reviewer might even suggest how this can be addressed. Every study has flaws, so reviewers should also avoid making comments about limitations that are true of virtually any study. If a scale used or a procedure is a widely accepted practice, then a reviewer should not argue against it unless they can provide a better alternative, and this alternative should also not be based on personal preference.

The peer review process is an invaluable procedure that is essential for maintaining quality control in any discipline. Its main purpose is to assure that each published article meets rigorous standards and is published on its merits. In this process, authors can get feedback and suggestions from colleagues, which can help improve not only the present work, but future work as well. Nonetheless, the role of a developmental reviewer is not an easy one (Feldman, 2004). Even authors can become cynical of the review process as a result (Bedeian, 2003). In as much as we are trying to educate reviewers (e.g. Lepak, 2009), we must know that reviewers themselves are authors and hence as authors we should try to appreciate the value that reviewers provide and adapt accordingly while relying on our own judgement on what is right (Starbuck, 2003). And even for students, going through a similar process of receiving and giving critiques has been found to be useful for their own writing skills (Caffarella and Barnett, 2000).

KEY TERMS

- Double-blind review
- Due diligence process
- Journal review process
- Judgement call
- Misperception
- Objectivity
- Oral examination
- Paradigm development
- Peer

- Research-informed decision-making
- Research collaborator
- Research scope
- Research supervisor
- Rigour
- Subjective
- Theory
- Theory development

SUMMARY

- The claims that: research is conducted by people who wish to become academics and has little relevance for practice; projects related to practice do not need research rigour; research is isolating and frustrating; research is subjective; the more coverage the study has the better it should be; and that there is always a correct way to conduct each of the steps in research and so the research process can be linear, are all exaggerated misperceptions of what the research process is.

- Business and management research are relatively new fields, making consensus hard and paradigm development difficult.
- Referencing, data and findings, listing of variables or constructs and hypotheses are not substitutes for theoretical development.
- Hypotheses are formulated from research questions, and good practice should be exercised to ensure the hypotheses are formulated and tested in ways that allow you to address the research question.
- Research supervision involves a lot of interaction between supervisor and student. The expectations of both should be negotiated throughout the process of the supervision.
- The journal review process is different from the research supervision process in that it is conducted through a blind review process and the whole process is done through writing.
- The role of reviewers is a developmental one that helps the author understand how a research work can be improved.
- Time constraints can affect the level of rigour expected and achievable in research.
- The ability to make good judgement calls comes with experience.

QUESTIONS

1. Research has little relevance on practice – what are your views? Why?
2. The more variables that are covered in a single study, the higher the level of rigour it should have. Do you agree with this statement? Why or why not?
3. Why is theory development in business and management difficult?
4. Based on your understanding of theory development and theorizing, what is theory in your view?
5. What are the two main differences between the journal review process and the research supervision process?
6. What are some things that an author should avoid when submitting an article for a journal to review?
7. What are some of the judgement calls in the research process? Briefly discuss.

ADDITIONAL READINGS

Aguinis, H. and Henle, C.A. (2002) 'Ethics in research', in S.G. Rogelberg (ed.), *Handbook of Research Methods in Industrial and Organizational Psychology*. Malden, MA: Blackwell. pp. 34–56.

Barzun, J. and Graff, H.F. (2003) *The Modern Researcher*, (6th edition). Belmont, CA: Cengage Learning.

Booth, W.C., Colomb, G.G., Williams, J.M., Bizup, J. and Fitgerald, W.T. (2016) *The Craft of Research*, (4th edition). Chicago, IL: University of Chicago Press.

Busse, C., Kach, A.P. and Wagner, S.M. (2017) 'Boundary conditions: What they are, how to explore them, why we need them, and when to consider them', *Organizational Research Methods*, 20 (4): 574–609.

Cascio, W.F. (2008) 'To prosper, organizational psychology should... bridge application and scholarship', *Journal of Organizational Behavior*, 29 (4): 455–68.

Colquitt, J.A. and Zapata-Phelan, C.P. (2007) 'Trends in theory building and theory testing: A five-decade study of the *Academy of Management Journal*', *Academy of Management Journal*, 50 (6): 1281–303.

Daft, R.L. (1983) 'Learning the craft of organizational research', *Academy of Management Review*, 8 (4): 539–46.

Edwards, J.R. (2010) 'Reconsidering theoretical progress in organizational and management research', *Organizational Research Methods*, 13 (4): 615–19.

Feldman, D.C. (2003) 'When is a new submission "new"?', *Journal of Management*, 29 (2): 139–40.

Fisher, G. and Aguinis, H. (2017) 'Using theory elaboration to make theoretical advancements', *Organizational Research Methods*, 20 (3): 438–64.

Klein, K.J., Dansereau, F. and Hall, R.I. (1994) 'Levels issues in theory development, data collection, and analysis', *Academy of Management Review*, 19 (2): 195–229.

Leavitt, K., Mitchell, T.R. and Peterson, J. (2010) 'Theory pruning: Strategies to reduce our dense theoretical landscape', *Organizational Research Methods*, 13 (4): 644–67.

Locke, E.A. (2007) 'The case for inductive theory building.' *Journal of Management*, 33 (6): 867–90.

Lundberg, C.C. (1976) 'Hypotheses creation in organizational behavior research. *Academy of Management Review*, 1 (2): 5–12.

Lundberg, C.C. and Young, C.A. (2005) *Foundations for Inquiry: Choices and Tradeoffs in the Organizational Sciences*. Stanford, CA: Stanford Business Books.

McKinley, W. (2010) 'Organizational theory development: Displacement of ends? *Organization Studies*, 31 (1): 47–68.

Mithaug, D.E. (2000) *Learning to Theorize: A Four-step Strategy*. Thousand Oaks, CA: Sage Publishing.

REFERENCES

Acker, S., Hill, T. and Black, E. (1994) 'Thesis supervision in the social sciences: Managed or negotiated?', *Higher Education*, 28 (4): 483–98.

Armstrong, S.J., Allinson, C.W. and Hayes, J. (2004) 'The effects of cognitive style on research supervision: A study of student–supervisor dyads in management education', *Academy of Management Learning and Education*, 3 (1): 41–63.

Bacharach, S.B. (1989) 'Organizational theories: Some criteria for evaluation', *Academy of Management Review*, 14 (4): 496–515.

Barney, J. (1991) 'Firm resources and sustained competitive advantage', *Journal of Management*, 17 (1): 99–120.

Bedeian, A.G. (1996) Improving the journal review process: the question of ghostwriting. *American Psychologist, 51* (11): 1189.

Bedeian, A.G. (2003) 'The manuscript review process: The proper roles of authors, referees, and editors', *Journal of Management Inquiry*, 12 (4): 331–8.

Beyer, J.M. (1978) 'Editorial policies and practices among leading journals in four scientific fields', *Sociological Quarterly*, 19 (1): 68–88.

Caffarella, R.S. and Barnett, B.G. (2000) 'Teaching doctoral students to become scholarly writers: The importance of giving and receiving critiques', *Studies in Higher Education*, 25 (1): 39–51.

Davis, G.F. (2010) 'Do theories of organizations progress?', *Organizational Research Methods*, 13 (4): 690–709.

Delamont, S., Parry, O. and Atkinson, P. (1998) 'Creating a delicate balance: The doctoral supervisor's dilemmas', *Teaching in Higher Education*, 3 (2): 157–72.

Edmondson, A.C. and McManus, S.E. (2007) 'Methodological fit in management field research', *Academy of Management Review*, 32 (4): 1155–79.

Edwards, J.R. and Berry, J.W. (2010) 'The presence of something or the absence of nothing: Increasing theoretical precision in management research', *Organizational Research Methods*, 13 (4): 668–89.

Elizondo-Schmelkes, N. (2011) 'Authenticizing the research process', *The Grounded Theory Review*, 10 (2): 1–20.

Feldman, D.C. (2004) 'Being a developmental reviewer: Easier said than done', *Journal of Management*, 30 (2): 161–4.

Feldman, D.C. (2005) 'Writing and reviewing as sadomasochistic rituals', *Journal of Management*, 31 (3): 325–9.

Fraser, R. and Mathews, A. (1999) 'An evaluation of the desirable characteristics of a supervisor', *Australian Universities' Review*, 41 (1): 5–7.

Grant, R.M. (1996) 'Toward a knowledge-based theory of the firm', *Strategic Management Journal*, 17 (S2): 109–22.

Hambrick, D.C. (2007) 'The field of management's devotion to theory: Too much of a good thing?', *Academy of Management Journal*, 50 (6): 1346–52.

Hargens, L.L. (1988) 'Scholarly consensus and journal rejection rates: Comment-reply', *American Sociological Review*, 53 (1): 139–51.

Heath, T. (2002) 'A quantitative analysis of PhD students' views of supervision,' *Higher Education Research and Development*, 21 (1): 41–53.

Ireland, R.D. (2012) 'Management research and managerial practice: A complex and controversial relationship', *Academy of Management Learning and Education*, 11 (2): 263–71.

Jensen, M.C. and Meckling, W.H. (1976) 'Theory of the firm: Managerial behavior, agency costs and ownership structure', *Journal of Financial Economics*, 3 (4): 305–60.

Kam, B.H. (1997) 'Style and quality in research supervision: The supervisor dependency factor', *Higher Education*, 34 (1): 81–103.

Kaplan, A. (1964) *The Conduct of Inquiry*. San Francisco, CA: Chandler.

Lepak, D.P. (2009) 'Editor's comments: What is good reviewing?', *Academy of Management Review*, 34 (3): 375–81.

Lodahl, J.B. and Gordon, G. (1972) 'The structure of scientific fields and the functioning of university graduate departments', *American Sociological Review*, 37 (1): 57–72.

Moriarty, B., Danaher, P.A. and Danaher, G. (2008) 'Freire and dialogical pedagogy: A means for interrogating opportunities and challenges in Australian postgraduate supervision', *International Journal of Lifelong Education*, 27 (4): 431–42.

Pfeffer, J. (1993) 'Barriers to the advance of organizational science: Paradigm development as a dependent variable', *Academy of Management Review*, 18 (4): 599–620.

Rynes, S.L., Bartunek, J.M. and Daft, R.L. (2001) 'Across the great divide: knowledge creation and transfer between practitioners and academics', *Academy of Management Journal*, 44 (2): 340–55.

Salancik, G.R., Staw, B.M. and Pondy, L.R. (1980) 'Administrative turnover as a response to unmanaged organizational interdependence', *Academy of Management Journal*, 23 (3): 422–37.

Schunk, D.H. (1994) 'Self-regulation of self-efficacy and attributions in academic settings', in D.H. Schunk and B.J. Zimmerman (eds), *Self-regulation of Learning and Performance*. Hillsdale, NJ: Lawrence Erlbaum Associates. pp. 75–99.

Shaver, J.M. (2013) 'Do we really need more entry mode studies?' *Journal of International Business Studies*, 44 (1): 23–7.

Starbuck, W.H. (2003) 'Turning lemons into lemonade: Where is the value in peer reviews?', *Journal of Management Inquiry*, 12 (4): 344–51.

Staw, B.M. (1995) 'Repairs on the road to relevance and rigor: Some unexplored issues in publishing organizational research', in L.L. Cummings and P.J. Frost (eds), *Publishing in the Organizational Sciences*. London: Sage Publishing. pp. 85–97.

Styles, I. and Radloff, A. (2001) 'The synergistic thesis: Student and supervisor perspectives', *Journal of Further and Higher Education*, 25 (1): 97–106.

Sutton, R.I. and Staw, B.M. (1995) 'What theory is not', *Administrative Science Quarterly*, 40 (3): 371–84.

Trow, M. (1957) 'Comment on "participant observation and interviewing: A comparison"'. *Human Organization*, 16 (3): 33–5.

Tsang, E.W.K. and Frey, B.S. (2007) 'The as-is journal review process: Let authors own their ideas', *Academy of Management Learning and Education*, 6 (1): 128–36.

van Maanen, J., Sørensen, J.B. and Mitchell, T.R. (2007) 'The interplay between theory and method', *Academy of Management Review*, 32 (4): 1145–54.

Vermeulen, F. (2005) 'On rigor and relevance: Fostering dialectic progress in management research', *Academy of Management Journal*, 48 (6): 978–82.

Vilkinas, T. (2008) 'An exploratory study of the supervision of Ph.D./research students' theses', *Innovative Higher Education*, 32 (5): 297–311.

Webster, J. and Starbuck, W.H. (1988) 'Theory building in industrial and organizational psychology', in C.L. Cooper and I.T. Robertson (eds), *International Review of Industrial and Organizational Psychology*. London: John Wiley & Sons. pp. 93–138.

Whetten, D.A. (1989) 'What constitutes a theoretical contribution?', *Academy of Management Review*, 14 (4): 490–95.

Williamson, O.E. (1975) *Markets and Hierarchies: Analysis and Antitrust Implications*. New York: The Free Press.

Woolhouse, M. (2002) 'Supervising dissertation projects: Expectations of supervisors and students', *Innovations in Education and Teaching International*, 39 (2): 137–44.

Zammuto, R.F. and Connelly, T. (1984) 'Coping with disciplinary fragmentation', *Organizational Behavior Teaching Review*, 9 (2): 30–7.

3

IN SEARCH OF A RESEARCH TOPIC

3.1 INTRODUCTION

How does a research topic come about? Will an extensive literature search always lead to a good research topic? Or is it better to be opportunistic when seeking a research topic? What sources of information are reliable for this purpose? And are there systematic processes for this search? These are just some of the questions raised surrounding the search for a research topic.

As highlighted in earlier chapters, a simple classification of approaches to search for a research topic would be to ask whether we are looking for an issue to be investigated for which findings will have research and managerial implications, or whether we are trying to resolve an issue that we have been confronted with. Regardless of which type of research project you are doing, some background concepts and conceptual frameworks will probably be required, and the research is expected to possess a degree of **(contextualized)** originality. Due to these needs, proper search processes need to be in place when one is searching for a research topic.

In a research project oriented towards academic contributions, the process of research often involves conducting an extensive literature review, which will be the focus of Chapter 4 of this book. This traditional way of generating research topics has been challenged in recent times, as it is deemed not always the most fruitful way to engage in cutting-edge work (e.g. Sandberg and Alvesson, 2011). In a different work, Alvesson and Sandberg (2011) propose the method of problematization for generating questions. In essence, problematization involves the scrutiny of existing assumptions that are embedded within a particular disciplinary domain. While this method of generating a research topic may be used to help balance the tendencies to use research gap-spotting, the authors recognize that there are challenges to its adoption. For example, researchers may find it easier to get their papers accepted for publication if they follow previous works closely (Starbuck, 2003).

A research project that is more practice-oriented often originates from issues that organizations or an organization faces. It may also be one that is related to a phemonenon, which will be highlighted in Section 3.5.4. Sometimes, companies also engage analysts to work on this type of research. This is usually done on the basis that the organization is at a juncture that needs some rethinking of its positioning, or a plan to look towards in anticipation of changes. In any case, research topics in this category are often clearer at the outset than those that are academic-oriented. The issue and question addressed in this category also tend to be more organization-specific and thus in some cases less generalizable.

The common perception maintained by research students and even junior researchers is that academic-oriented research is not consistently aligned with practice-oriented research. This perception however is mistaken (as discussed in Chapter 2) and should be recalibrated. The bottom line is that aligning research rigour and practice relevance is crucial in both types of research work. Hence, regardless of the origin of the topic, there should always be a systematic and proper search process involved, one which can be replicated.

This chapter will first highlight the starting points for searching for a research topic. It will then discuss the various systematic search processes that one can use. This is followed by the various sources of information that you can utilize in search of a research topic, including how to use them. Finally, the chapter provides some guidelines on gauging what would constitute a good research topic.

3.2 STARTING POINTS OF A SEARCH PROCESS

Researchers conduct a literature search in order to hone in on a research topic. However, given the increasing number of journals and periodicals, and many other sources, the process of searching becomes complicated. It is not the intention of this book to provide an extensive discussion of research philosophies. Nonetheless, it is important to recognize the two key approaches here: positivist and interpretivist. Most research tends to adopt one or the other, though we see an increasing number of research studies using both approaches (Lee, 1991).

The **positivist approach** to research emphasizes that social science research, including business and management research, should as far as possible seek to achieve the same level of explanation and prediction as natural sciences. This approach focuses on using rules of formal logic and hypothetico-deductive logic, so that theoretical propositions can survive multiple tests of falsifiability, logical consistency and relative explanatory power. In the positivist approach, propositions must be logically articulated, and connections must be made as to where these propositions are placed in the framework. Thus, all propositions must be well grounded, and any proposition not properly connected to other propositions is deemed irrelevant. This logical deduction process allows a researcher to rule out propositions that are subjective or biased. In addition, many facets of business and management research cannot be directly observed, making some propositions more hypothetico-deductive. The main idea behind hypothetico-deductive logic is that theorized entities have actions or outcomes that are observable, even if the entities themselves are not. The theorizing proposed from a positivist approach is then tested using facts. If we find that the theory does not fit well with the facts, we then look for alternative explanations in order to further refine our propositions.

The **interpretivist approach** (sometimes also referred to as the constructivist approach) is viewed as the approach to address the inadequacy of the positivist approach. The intrepretivist approach is more exploratory than the positivist approach. It emphasizes the interactions of multiple actors, factors and contexts. Hence, observations are manifested from complex relationships between these elements. The interpretivist approach looks at research issues as a whole, emphasizing individual differences in the interpretation of observations. In this view, each individual constructs their view of the world based on their background, culture, experience and personal views. As perception is fallible, these constructions may thus be imperfect. Triangulation becomes essential to allow some degree of objectivity. Objectivity is thus less reliant on individual researchers' interpretations and is rather more socially constructed.

In essence, both these approaches can be applied to both academic- and practice-oriented research projects. The adoption of either approach may mean different starting points in search of a research topic. This is dependent on factors such as the area of interest of the researcher, the state of development of the sub-field in general, the extent to which a researcher is comfortable with one approach more than the other, etc. Nonetheless, overall, journals tend to be a main source of information on which a research project should depend. At this level, relying on Google or other search engines is inadequate, as journal articles tend not to be freely accessible (though they are becoming increasingly so).

There are a lot of well-established journals, with many more seeking to achieve similar status. Every journal has a mission; this is often found on the website of that journal. It is up to the editor, editorial board members and reviewers to carry out this mission to identify what types of research should be published in the journal. Journals are also ranked on the quality of their outputs. There are journals that are commonly referred to as top journals or top-tier journals or simply A-journals. These are followed by second tier or B-journals, which are then followed by third tier or C-journals. There are also journals that are not ranked. Journals not ranked usually have outputs that are not well cited, or they are simply newly created. Each category of journals has different expectations – not just in terms of journal focus as described above, but also in terms of the level of rigour of the research published, which of course in turn contributes to the journal's status.

In order to assist with the process of recognizing good journals or journal articles, researchers engage in exercises that seek to rank journals based on the levels of research rigour and quality. The common element in various ranking exercises is the citation of articles within those journals. That is, journals with articles cited most often are the ones that are highly rated. Top journals have the highest expectations in terms of the originality of ideas and the rigour of the research processes in the papers they publish. Partly as a result of having a stringent screening process, these journals also publish the best research work. Research outputs published in these journals represent the frontiers of knowledge in their respective areas. These journals then become the best sources for

Business area	Top journals
Management	*Academy of Management Annals*
	Academy of Management Journal [R]
	Academy of Management Review [R]
	Administrative Science Quarterly
	Entrepreneurship Theory and Practice
	International Journal of Management Reviews [R]
	Journal of Business Ethics
	Journal of Business Venturing
	Journal of Management [R]
	Journal of Management Studies [R]
	Organization Science
	Organizational Research Methods [R]
	Strategic Management Journal [R]
International business	*Journal of International Business Studies* [R]
	Journal of World Business [R]
	Management International Review
Human resource management and organizational behaviour	*Human Resource Management*
	Journal of Applied Psychology [R]
	Journal of Organizational Behaviour
	Organizational Behaviour and Human Decision Processes
Marketing	*International Journal of Research in Marketing*
	Journal of Consumer Research
	Journal of Marketing
	Journal of Marketing Research [R]
	Journal of the Academy of Marketing Science [R]
	Marketing Science
Operations management and information systems	*Information Systems Research*
	Journal of Technology Transfer
	Management Science
	MIS Quarterly
Academic–Practitioner	*California Management Review*
	Harvard Business Review
	Long Range Planning
	Sloan Management Review

Figure 3.1   Some top journals in key business and management areas

[R] Indicates that journal also often includes articles that discuss methodological issues.

Note: For a good overview of the ranking of journals, please refer to https://harzing.com/resources/journal-quality-list.

research ideas. Figure 3.1 lists some of the top journals in key business and management areas. Some journals also publish articles that highlight the latest methodologies, and assessments and issues around the use of some methodologies in certain research areas. These are also shown in the figure. It must also be added here that not all papers published in top journals are necessarily the very best studies (Starbuck, 2005). This goes back to our point about the need for us to have a critical lens when we read, even with regard to outputs in good journals.

The Social Science Citation Index (SSCI) and Harzing.com represent the two ways that one can locate the rankings of journals. The SSCI database provides a comprehensive coverage of the impact of articles within journals, while Harzing.com for many years has compiled various rankings of journals which allows comparisons at a glance. Norris and Oppenheim (2007) find that as compared to CSA Illumina and Google Scholar, Scopus would be a stronger alternative to the SSCI when a researcher wants to evaluate research impact in the social sciences. As different ranking systems use slightly different rules, the advice is always not to rely on one single source of ranking system when assessing journal quality.

Upon finding the best journals in your field, one way to move forward with the literature search using these journals is to read the latest issues of the journals. Normally, this requires you to read at least a few years of back issues before you start to have a picture of what areas of research are common and perhaps trending, what aspects of these research areas are attracting the most attention, and what might be a potential research topic that you can work on. If you have a narrower research area, the process will be easier. For example, you can also go for a search within these journals for specific articles, or even particular keywords within a particular set of journals.

However, this process does not automatically result in the identification of a research topic. In fact, this process would be considered ad hoc and is a fast yet incomplete way to engage in the search for a research topic. With time and various other constraints, sometimes having this process will suffice. Given ample time and resources though, upon finding out what is current and what may be worth researching, it is essential for you to engage in a more systematic search in order to narrow down the research topic and ascertain if the potential research topic or specific area of focus offers new insights.

The search through journals is simplified by having access to major search engines of academic and magazine articles such as ABI/INFORM Global, EBSCOhost and JSTOR. A discussion of such article search databases can be found in Section 3.4. These databases span thousands of publications, with the majority of articles available for download in full, if your institution has access. The wide-range coverage allows a complete systematic search of articles related to the research area you are working on. The more extensive the search process, the more rigorous it will be. However, in order to fully exploit these search databases, you will need to be systematic about your searches. The next section will provide detailed information about this process.

3.3 SYSTEMATIC SEARCH PROCESSES

While searching the literature seems like a simple task, the process itself is often time-consuming and requires a lot of careful planning. The key question here is 'Do you know what you are searching for?' This sounds like an awkward question to ask – as researchers are supposed to be creative and full of ideas and initiative. Yet this question remains reasonable and in fact a challenging one to answer. After all, if you are engaging in a search for a potential research topic, how would you know what potential topics are out there? While a researcher would hope that the search process would help them zoom in on a good research topic, it turns out that the search process requires their inputs in the first place!

Let's say you are searching for a potential research topic related to collaboration between companies, i.e. whether independent companies engage in some form of cooperation with other companies to enhance their competitiveness. However, you are not aware what specific research can be conducted in order to contribute to this area of work. A systematic search will help. But where should you begin your search? Specifically, what are the keywords that you need to use in order to narrow the search results down to a reasonable initial reading list?

No doubt based on your initial research path 'collaboration' will certainly be the first keyword that you will tackle. If you access ABI/INFORM Global database and search using 'collaboration' as a keyword to appear in the abstract of paper articles and limit the search to articles written in English appearing in peer-reviewed scholarly journals with full text availability (note how these options help you to narrow down search results to more relevant articles), the search will return 118,959 articles (as of February 2020). This is definitely not a small number of articles. But does this look like a reasonable start? Yes, only if time permits. But even going through 100 articles a day will take you more than a year to read. The reality is that most of the research that we do does have time constraints, as discussed in Chapter 2. So, coming up against 118,959 articles is the last thing that you need.

At this stage, there are several options. One option is to narrow down the search to 'collaboration' found only in the title of articles. This reduces the search result to 2,027 articles, which is only about 1.7% of the previous search outcome of 118,959 articles. Another option is to introduce another keyword to narrow down our search, for example, introducing another keyword such as 'competitiveness'. Adding 'competitiveness' as an additional keyword immediately reduces the search outcomes from 118,959 to 20,871 articles. Searching the keyword 'collaboration' in the abstract and 'competitiveness' in text would generate 1,772 results and futher searching the keyword 'collaboration' in the title and 'competitiveness' in text would fetch 379 articles. With both 'collaboration' and 'competitiveness' in the abstract would return 19 articles. Finally, there is only 1 hit when one searches both 'collaboration' and 'competitiveness' in the document title.

Several issues arise from this illustration of the search process. Which one of the search results should we use? Realistically, we should rule out the '118,959' option. The 1-hit option does not really allow you to have a proper start to the literature stocktake process, so that is out of the question as well. Surely, the outcome of 379 articles looks reasonable. But would a drop to the next level of detail that led to 19 articles be justifiable for missing out on the 360 articles in this initial search process? Conversely, how would we know if the 19 articles are adequate for this purpose without the benefit of doubt from hindsight? The 19-hits option is tempting, and it may well form a good basis from which the search can branch out. But the issue is whether we can be sure that we have covered all bases of prior research that links collaboration to competitiveness using this option. It seems that we are faced with yet another judgement call at this juncture.

The answers to these questions are complicated by three aspects. First, these search article databases are rigid systems to say the least. They follow blindly the characters that you have entered. For example, wrong spelling on your part will not be picked up. In other words, the systems will not go beyond the keyword you have entered, hence a difference in the search outcomes. Second, researchers, whether or not they come from the same specialization, have a tendency to use terminologies loosely. That is the reality. Sometimes, there is no intention on the part of the researcher to differentiate between, for example, collaboration and alliance. In fact, a search shows that entering the two keywords of 'collaboration' and 'alliance' for an abstract search results in 313 articles. It means that 313 articles have used these two words concurrently in the summary of an article. The chances are that the authors of some of these articles may have used these terms interchangeably. If we go for the concurrent use of these keywords in the text of source articles, we find that 25,461 articles have these two words in their articles! The unintentional use of these two words simultaneously in the same article may complicate some of our searches.

Third, some authors, in an attempt to differentiate their work from others in the field, intentionally use different terms. For example, an article that discusses 'alliances' may actually be referring to the same form of cooperative agreements among firms as another article that uses 'collaboration'. What this means is that whenever we do a literature search, it will be necessary to use multiple keywords with the same meaning for the search to be more complete. Otherwise, we run the risk of missing areas of the literature where different keywords are used, even when the actual content referred to is similar. Therefore, we are really talking about the need to have various permutations of search keywords when we are running a literature search process.

In the above example, 'collaboration' is not the only word that researchers or authors use when they discuss cooperation among independent companies. Some other words that are used in this context include alliance, joint venture, pact and cooperation to name a few. Going back to ABI/INFORM Global database, a search on both 'alliance' and 'competitiveness' in the abstract of journal articles yields 86 hits (as compared to collaboration's 19 hits), the case for 'joint venture' has 9 hits, 'pact' has 13 hits and 'cooperation' brings us up to 289 hits! It can be seen here that there are substantial differences in search outcomes when different keywords are used. It is therefore important that the keyword search process is rigorous and does not rule out potentially important articles with the wrong judgement calls.

In the systematic search these are some of the issues you will encounter that suggest hard work is a *sine qua non*. Clearly the various permutations that you will use are going to come back with overlapping search outcomes. Going through these outcomes alone will require some degree of patience. But patience, not to be misinterpreted as procrastination, is a virtue in research. Should some of the permutations become too large to handle, it is often also necessary to use more keywords or conditions to narrow down the scope of search to avoid information overload, as illustrated earlier. This is called **convergence search** and is discussed in the next section.

3.3.1 Convergence search

The process of narrowing down the search by setting conditions or introducing an additional keyword can be broadly classified as convergence search. The process of narrowing down in the collaboration–competitiveness example shows that there are quite a few ways of conducting convergence searches. There is no straightforward answer as to which is the most appropriate way of narrowing down a search. As mentioned, this process constitutes a judgement call. In the example, the question is whether the 19 hits that were generated when the second keyword 'competitiveness' was also introduced in searching the article abstract is sufficient. Is the scope of this search overly filtered? It is important to note that while some students may feel relieved that they have only very few documents to get through to have an understanding of the collaboration–competitiveness linkage, there are also significant risks associated with gaining insufficient coverage from the literature search.

A literature search emphasizes that a researcher should be aware of all the issues and relevant articles that have been published in the research area prior to their own work. In this case, the researcher would have to make sense of the search by asking the question 'would this area of research have only 19 prior research outputs?' If you are new to this research area, one suggestion is to have a conversation with someone who might know the area better than you do, such as your project supervisor. This will immediately give you an idea whether or not you are heading in the right direction. It might even be better if that person is helpful enough to give you the names of a couple of authors who are experts in that area. That will allow you to verify if your search has included the right authorities in the field.

Convergence simplifies the process of literature search. However, there are risks involved with overdoing it, i.e. using keywords that are so limiting that you arrive at a small number of articles in your search outcome. The danger of over-convergence in your search is twofold. First, the literature review that you will include in your research work will not be representative. Inadequacy in a literature review will result in a substandard output. This is the last thing that you need when a literature review is arguably the easiest part of the project as you are largely in control of the proceedings. Second, and more seriously, by reading lesser papers with over-convergence in your search, you may be misled (by yourself!) into believing that there are potentially many research issues left unexplored in the area. As a result, your research project topic may overlap with other existing studies that you have excluded in your search as a result of your overly convergent search process. This will potentially create issues with respect to the final contribution of your research.

So can over-convergence be avoided, and if so, how can we do that? Yes, the risk of over-convergence search can be minimized to say the least. There are mainly two ways: one is to use the method of snowballing; the other is to increase the number of key-word searches – a **divergence search** after the convergence search. These methods will be discussed in the following two sections.

3.3.2 Snowballing search

Snowballing is the process of research where you start with a small number of articles and use these articles as a starting point to expand your search further. The snowballing approach is extremely useful when there could be too many articles in your initial wider search process or when you are not clear about the boundaries of your search. Not being clear about the boundaries of your search is not uncommon. This occurs when you have only rough ideas of what you are looking for but have no idea how far you should go. Snowballing allows you to start with a few good articles and in this way avoid this confusion. By following the trails of key articles, you are actually following the path of scholarship in the area.

The onus in snowballing is on you to find the best articles to start with. You can engage the help of a more senior researcher or someone whom you think will be more knowledgeable in the research area. They will perhaps be able to provide some initial starting points for the snowballing process. Another way is to start off with only articles from the top journals in your field. Regardless of which approach you choose, the most important thing in this step is to make sure that you are using good – ideally recent – articles to start the process. These initial articles should cover a wide range of themes so that you are not leaning towards particular directions in your prescribed readings, for example only using articles from a single journal. These articles can be

Conversation box

Steve [PhD student]: Professor, I am going to start my literature review process next week. Would you be kind enough to offer me some guidance in giving me some relevant articles?

Professor: Steve, I would be happy to give you some titles. But at this stage, given that you have ample time to work on your literature review, my advice is for you to avoid snowballing and use a more systematic search for your literature. While snowballing is faster, it requires significant judgements throughout the process, creating potential problems in the scope of the coverage of your reading list.

related, but you should avoid walking into a closed loop of readings in the early stages of your literature search process. Yet a third way is to find the most cited papers in the research area that you are working in and start from there. This can be done with the help of Scopus or SSCI mentioned in Section 3.2.

In the process of reading the few selected articles, pay attention to the other articles that these articles cite, and start reading those articles in the reference list that you deem relevant to your research. This selection requires some judgement calls. But I would also advise reading even those that you are not sure about, i.e. those which you cannot judge at the outset from the title and abstract of the articles. The process should continue with these new additional articles found – hence the snowballing process. The literature search process will end once you exhaust all the potentially relevant articles from subsequent readings and their reference lists. A check on the level of relevance will be how an article is related to the topic of your project. This is by no means easy, but you need to be both open-minded and critical about how relevant these potential new articles might be. As the whole process involves significant judgements throughout, subjectivity can result in a biased set of readings in your literature search.

The snowballing process can balloon into a potentially large set of readings. For example, with 10 initial readings and 10 references picked from each of these readings, the process will explode into 1,000 articles to be read within two rounds of the snowballing process. This ballooning effect suggests that you need to be somewhat strict when it comes to selecting references from subsequent rounds of readings, i.e. selection at the later stages should be stricter. It is important to note in later rounds – although it is possible that the number of references considered to be relevant might be reduced due to exhaustion – the fact that the topic may have gone deeper than previous rounds may also in some cases lead to a longer list of relevant references.

It is also possible that as you go through further in the rounds, the readings can become peripheral to the core of your research topic.

Another way to use the snowballing approach as mentioned above is to rely on citation databases in your search process. Using this search mode, you start off with a few articles and use citation databases such as the SSCI database to trace the subsequent articles that have cited this initial set of articles. This mode is extremely useful if your research work is grounded in a few well-established articles.

Article search using the starting point of other well-cited articles can be less time-consuming. The SSCI by ISI Web of Science makes it possible to rank-order articles for specific journals and years by number of citations. It only provides information on the impact of these journals and the specific list of articles that cite each paper. In addition to SSCI, 'Publish or Perish', which uses the Google Scholar database and can be accessed via www.harzing.com, is another good source. This same website includes a detailed analysis of advantages and disadvantages of using Google Scholar versus SSCI.

It has been noted that Google Scholar may be a better source of citation as it captures international impact better than SSCI due to a wider coverage of citations in publications in languages other than English. Google Scholar is also broader in terms of the operationalization of article impact because it includes citations in dissertations, Masters theses and other non-ISI sources which are nevertheless scholarly in nature and certainly indicate whether a particular source is being read and whether it is influencing subsequent research work. According to Norris and Oppenheim (2007), which compares SSCI, Google Scholar, Scopus and CSA Illumina across various dimensions, SSCI and Scopus offer the best coverage of citations.

3.3.3 Divergence search

We have discussed earlier the need to conduct a convergence search. But why do we need to even consider divergence search as a legitimate form of literature search process? It may sound ironic – why would a researcher wish to expand their search scope if they know what they are looking for? Don't we encourage convergence to arrive at a good and manageable set of articles? The answer for the need to have divergence search in place sometimes lies with the possibility of a 'dead-end' search outcome.

A 'dead-end' search outcome occurs when you cannot find enough decent journal articles through your search process. For example, in the case of an elaborated exercise like searching on 'collaboration' and 'competitiveness' concurrently, you ended up with 19 articles, which arguably is not really sufficient. When that happens, it is important not to immediately rule out the possibility that you have excluded some relevant articles and concluded that there is a lack of studies in the topic area. While the latter is a possibility, the advice will be to conduct a divergence search in order to ascertain if that is the case. One good reason for this is that, as mentioned before, many researchers use different words to discuss the same phenomenon. This leads to extra burden placed on the search process as failure to cover as much ground will make your literature search less rigorous and incomplete. Though we can then use the snowballing process from there, as shown above, the snowballing process requires many judgements on relevance. The divergence search process provides a more systematic approach.

A typical divergence search will include relaxing search conditions and perhaps broadening the search terms, for example losing one keyword and replacing it with another. If this still does not work, the chance is that you may have restricted your search too narrowly, which led to a small set of search outcomes. Generally, there is no guideline as to how broad this should be – yet another judgement call. But it will be enough to conduct this broadening sensibly until there are deemed enough representations of journal articles in the broadened search process that you are comfortable with.

In this section, we have highlighted the various search processes that allow one to hone in on a relevant set of readings. Each of these processes has strengths as well as weaknesses. In practice, you are encouraged to use more than one of these processes in your literature research to ensure rigour. If time permits, rotating between the three processes for a couple of rounds of search will ensure the most stringent search process. Figure 3.2 illustrates their concurrent use in your search.

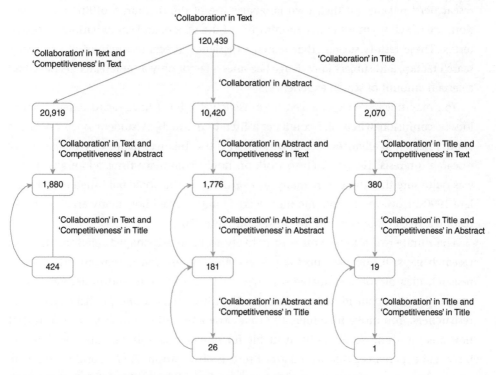

Figure 3.2   Relationships between search processes

Note: Straight arrows represent convergence search and curved arrows represent divergence search. The snowballing search can be initiated from the reference lists of the 26 articles (with 'collaboration' in abstract and 'competitiveness' in title) or 19 articles (with 'collaboration' in title and 'competitiveness' in abstract).

Research work on the topic of the search process has suggested that a researcher's appreciation of the topic does influence their search tactics, process and outcomes generated (Pennanen and Vakkari, 2003). In their research, Pennanen and Vakkari (2003) also find that the number of concepts and the proportion of subconcepts related to a construct contribute indirectly via search tactics to locate some references, and the use of additional query terms will improve the search results. Further, a researcher's knowledge of the domain does to a large extent determine the search outcomes, regardless of the search tactics used (Vakkari et al., 2003).

Particularly interesting is the study conducted by Hsieh-Yee (1993) on the interaction of a researcher's knowledge and their search experience. The author observes four behaviours from this interaction. First, when familiar research topics are searched, experience affects a researcher's use of synonymous terms, monitoring of the search process, and combinations of search terms. Second, when unfamiliar research topics are searched, search experience affects a researcher's reliance on their own terminology, use of the thesaurus, offline term selection, use of synonymous terms, and combinations of search terms. Third, within the same experience group, subject knowledge has no effect on novice researchers. Fourth, subject knowledge affects experienced researchers' reliance on their own language, use of the thesaurus, offline term selection, use of synonymous terms, monitoring of the search, and combinations of search terms. These results suggest that search experience affects researchers' use of many search tactics, and subject knowledge becomes a factor only after researchers have had a certain amount of search experience.

You may not have experienced it yourself (yet!), but I have heard remarks about lots of confusion when one conducts a literature search. A student once asked me about research in alliances back in London in 2004. Alliances happens to be one of my research interests. He was keen to work on how e-commerce firms adopt alliances. I was quite sure that there were many good articles on this topic published even in the late 1990s. However, he told me there weren't any! I asked how many articles he had read to arrive at that conclusion. His response was '20'.

The number of articles you read is likely to have a U-shaped relationship with research gaps. If you read nothing, every area of research is new and thus every research idea of yours is doable research. As you read more and more, very often you realize that your ideas have actually been investigated and published by other researchers. You move incrementally to a close alternative, but as you read in that new area, nothing seems to be available for research as well. Perhaps some of you have had experiences that would attest to this observation. Finally, and I can assure you of this, as you read a significant number of articles (and I'm talking in the high hundreds), everything will be crystal clear at that point. You will also learn how to differentiate the origins of cross-over literature, such as that on the areas of market entry modes and internationalization (market entry mode research largely comes from the perspective of host market while internationalization research is mainly driven from the perspective of home country). What this also means is that the number of articles you read has an inverted-U shaped relationship with the level of confusion you will have. The more you read, the more confused you might become. But don't panic. Stay calm, continue to read in an organized way and be patient. I'm sure at some point everything will be clearer. No time spent on pursuing a research topic is ever a waste.

3.4 SOURCES OF INFORMATION

This section provides a list of some of the main sources of information for your literature search, and discusses some issues with using each of these sources.

3.4.1 Article search databases

Your institution is likely to have subscribed to many article search databases. These are generally available through the library system. Article search databases compile materials from many sources of publications and serve as a one-stop search engine for articles. The search engines provide convenience for researchers as they do not have to go through a search on individual journal or publication sites. In addition, the search engines also allow you to set conditions in your search, thereby helping you to provide a more relevant set of outcomes from your search.

As demonstrated in the search processes above, different article search engines work differently in terms of their search algorithms. This means that you will need to spend some time to learn how these work in order to decide which ones will suit you best. You will find a wealth of knowledge out there which you never will have imagined before. Having access to the major search engines such as ABI/INFORM Global, EBSCOhost or JSTOR is essential. If you find that some periodicals in your area of research are not accessible, it may be advisable to talk to your librarian to potentially request a subscription to these or access through another affiliated institution. A description of some article search databases is shown in Figure 3.3.

Database	Content
ABI/INFORM Global	The ABI/INFORM Global is one of the most comprehensive business databases on the market, offering the latest business and financial information for researchers at all levels. It includes in-depth coverage from thousands of publications, most of them in full text. The database also includes ABI/INFORM Archive, which offers a deep backlist of many of the most important business journals of the last century. Key ongoing full-text periodicals include: *Wall Street Journal*, *Financial Times*, *The Economist*, *Barron's*, *Canadian Business* and *Foreign Affairs*. Key ongoing full-text analyses include market and industry reports from: Economist Intelligence Unit, Global Data and Aroq. Other key full-text non-journal content includes: Working papers, dissertations, business cases and conference proceedings.
ABI/INFORM Trade & Industry	The ABI/INFORM Trade & Industry contains in-depth coverage of companies, products, executives, trends and other topics. With ABI/INFORM Trade & Industry users can study and compare specific trades and industries, including telecommunications, computing, transportation, construction, petrochemicals and many others. Key market research reports are available from publishers and analysts including: Economist Intelligence Unit, Dun & Bradstreet, Business Monitor International, Plunkett, Barnes reports, Experian, Organization for Economic Cooperation and Development (OECD), Progressive Digital Media/Global Data, Acquisdata, Oxford Economics and Chart Marker.
Business e-Books Online	Business e-books Online is an online database that gathers 500 of the best-known textbooks and reference materials in business education in convenient digital format. Included e-books come from the most recognized names in business education, including David Cooperrider, Edgar Schein, Charles Manz, and Kim Cameron. The majority of works were published in 2011 or later, so you can rely on their quality and relevance to today's ever-changing business landscape.
Business Market Research Collection	The Business Market Research Collection allows users to conduct company, industry, economic and geopolitical market research with information from these three sources: (1) Hoover's Company Profiles – information about more than 40,000 global public and non-public companies including location, financials, competitors, officers, and more; (2) OxResearch – succinct articles covering regional economic and political developments of significance from a network of 1,000 faculty members at Oxford, other leading universities, and think-tanks; (3) Snapshots – market research overviews on 40+ industries and 40 countries.
Business Source Premier	Provides full text for nearly 7,800 scholarly business journals and other sources, including full text for more than 1,125 peer-reviewed business publications. This database offers information in nearly every area of business, including management, economics, finance, accounting and international business. It also includes Country Monitor and Industry Yearbook Reports from WEFA and country reports from the Economist Intelligence Unit (EIU), the Wall Street Words dictionary and a Dun & Bradstreet company directory.
EBSCOhost	Contains a set of databases from EBSCO Publishing – mostly full-text periodical collections, with an emphasis on peer-reviewed journals. Major components are Academic Search Premier and Business Source Premier. Smaller, more specialized full-text databases include Computer Source, Health Business Elite, Health Source Consumer Edition, Health Source Nursing/Academic Edition, the Psychology and Behavioral Sciences Collection, the Religion and Philosophy Collection and the Sociological Collection.

Database	Content
EconLit	EconLit, published by the American Economic Association, provides bibliographic coverage of a wide range of economics-related literature. An expanded version of the *Journal of Economic Literature* (JEL) indexes of journals, books, and dissertations, EconLit covers both economic theory and application.
	Literature covered is of interest to researchers, academics, product managers, advertisers, product development specialists, and public policy professionals. EconLit includes information that is of prime relevance to many industries and research establishments world-wide.
Factiva	Factiva is a current international news database produced by Dow Jones, one of the leading global providers of economic and financial information. Factiva.com, from Dow Jones, combines over 32,000 sources to give students, faculty, and librarians access to premium content from 200 countries, in 28 languages.
	Users have access to a wide range of information from newspapers, newswires, industry publications, websites, company reports, and more. The broad range of content provides both local insight and global perspective on business issues and current events – especially with regard to research requiring current information on companies, industries, and financial markets.
	The database includes: national, international and regional newspapers – current content and archives (e.g., *The New York Times*, *The Washington Post*, *The Times*, *The Wall Street Journal*, *El Pais*, *The Financial Times*, *The Guardian*, etc.); magazines, journals and trade publications (e.g., *Forbes*, *Newsweek*, etc.); newswires (e.g., AFP, Reuters, Dow Jones, etc.); TV or radio podcasts (e.g., BBC, CNN, ABC, CBS, NBC, Fox, etc.); company reports.
JSTOR	JSTOR is a highly selective digital library of academic content in many formats and disciplines. The collections include top peer-reviewed scholarly journals as well as respected literary journals, academic monographs, research reports from trusted institutes, and primary sources.
	Full runs of more than 2,600 top scholarly journals in the humanities, social sciences, and sciences. JSTOR works with a diverse group of nearly 1,200 publishers from more than 57 countries to preserve and make their content digitally available.
	70,000 DRM-free eBooks from scholarly publishers, integrated with journals and primary sources are available on JSTOR. The collection includes both backlist and frontlist titles, and there are no limitations on the number of uses or downloads.

Figure 3.3   Some article search databases

3.4.2 Working papers

In your literature search, you are likely to encounter working papers. These are not found in article search databases but usually are available from individual researchers' webpages for download or available directly from the researchers themselves. Working papers are versions of articles the authors have written but which are not yet subjected to journal reviews. In other words, these are articles that are usually not classified as being peer-reviewed. As such, by definition, working papers should not be cited as they usually have not gone through a rigorous review process, though some informal feedback may have been incorporated in the current version of the working paper. In fact, authors of working papers usually have a clause stating that you should not cite the paper without their permission.

Conversation box

Professor:	Wilson, the reference list in your submitted assignment contains five working papers that are dated well before the year 2016.
Wilson [Honours student]:	But Professor, these are working papers from established researchers in the field. I assume then that it is appropriate to cite their working papers.
Professor:	There is nothing wrong in citing working papers, especially those by established researchers. But have you checked that these working papers were not subsequently published more recently?
Wilson:	No.
Professor:	If these are good working papers, chances are that some of them could have been published since the date of working paper version that you are holding. Check that before you cite them.

Working papers are sometimes subsequently published in journals. Hence, if you come across a working paper that is dated from a couple of years ago or so, always search for that article through a search for the author's name in article search databases to check if the paper has a later version that is published, or simply google broadly in case it has been accepted by a journal but not yet published. Be aware that the subsequent version of the working paper may have a different article title. Alternatively, you can also email the author to check if a later version of the paper is available. All this notwithstanding, a general rule is to always cite a working paper with care and, as far as possible, to avoid citing them at all.

3.4.3 Conference papers

Conference papers are also largely working versions of a paper. Many authors will present a paper at a conference in order to test their ideas and get feedback from colleagues in order to improve a paper that they may be preparing for submission to a journal. When a manuscript is submitted to a journal for consideration, the editors and reviewers will make decisions based on the quality and relevance of the paper. Thus, there is no incentive for an author to submit a paper that is still a work in progress, and so as part of the preparation process for publication many authors present their working papers at conferences to get additional comments.

Conversation box

Vivian [student]:   Professor, how much should I trust conference papers in terms of incorporating them in my literature review? The reason I ask is because there are so many conferences out there and I have no idea which conferences would be considered high enough quality for me to consider using the articles presented there.

Professor: You may have to check the quality of the conferences you are referring to, using either the acceptance rate of papers or broadly the identities and affiliations of the conference organizers. Ideally, only those papers published in the conference proceedings should be considered for citation. It is becoming common for new, short-lived conferences to arise, which may mean some dilution of quality. Thus, you should be cautious in using conference papers in your literature review.

While conference papers should not normally be cited, most researchers will agree that conference papers that are published in conference proceedings can be cited as they are in print form. This is particularly applicable for top conferences in each field. Papers that appear in the conference proceedings are normally the top 15–30% of all the papers to be presented at that conference. As with working papers, before you cite any conference papers, ensure that they have not been subsequently published in a journal. If they have, you should cite the version published in the journal.

3.4.4 Business magazine articles

Conversation box

Darcy [Honours student]:   Professor, in my search for ethics articles I have come across business magazine articles on ethics. Can I include these in my literature review? How about an article that discusses the growing trends of managerial awareness of ethical behaviour in organizations?

Professor: By all means, all those that you have described constitute part of your literature review. But be cautious of relying too heavily on business magazine articles for your arguments.

Unlike journal articles and sometimes articles in conference proceedings, business magazine articles do not go through an equivalent extensive review process. Thus, you must take extra caution when citing such articles. You will also notice that business magazine articles are often filled with subjective opinions, whereas in research we try to be as objective as possible. When considering citing business magazine articles, you will have to assess how objective or well-supported the claims being made are. Ideally, you should not rely on business magazine articles for anything beyond simple facts and information.

3.4.5 Reports and websites

Websites do not generally go through any moderation process. As such their citation should be avoided, except for reports from some reliable sources. Reports on the websites of public and government institutions tend to be cautious in their approach to publicizing data and information, thus there is some level of trust in these sources.

Some of the more reliable sources whose reports can be cited include:

- Public service organizations, such as the World Bank, WTO (World Trade Organization), OECD (Organization for Economic Co-operation and Development), UNIDO (United Nations Industrial Development Organization), UNESCO (United Nations Educational, Scientific and Cultural Organization) and IMF (International Monetary Fund).
- Major consulting companies like McKinsey, Ernst & Young, Boston Consulting Group and PricewaterhouseCoopers.

- National research institutions for economic, trade, technological and social development, such as Ministries of Economic Development and Trade.

Reports produced by government institutions need to be treated with caution as sometimes they tend to be agenda-driven and thus the conclusions can sometimes be directed in such a way that a desired message is conveyed through a report. Likewise, consulting companies produce reports for their clients and the content of some of these documents is pitched to encourage more participation of their clients as well as to attract new ones. As such, these documents tend to contain subtle messages that seek to target their customers. This means that caution must be exercised when you cite reports from consulting companies, however, using reports from these sources is still encouraged in light of the information they contain. Nonetheless, interpretation of the conclusions contained in such reports should be considered carefully.

3.4.6 Seminars and conferences

There are bound to be seminars going on at your institution in any given week, whether it is within your department or faculty or the wider university. Seminars are avenues that researchers and practitioners use to disseminate their knowledge. They are part and parcel of a researcher's research environment. For the presenter, a seminar provides a platform from which ideas can be presented and feedback can be sought. It is also a place where researchers with similar interests meet, thereby generating discussions and potentially leading to future research collaborations.

Attendance at seminars is mostly free, and we can see an increase in their numbers. Nonetheless, while some generate strong interest, others attract only limited attendance. Likewise, while some researchers continue to go to as many seminars as humanly possible, others find themselves suffering from information overload and decide they will avoid seminars altogether. Either extreme is not ideal. There are yet others who choose only seminars that relate to a particular niche research area that they are working on at that point in time. This may not be optimal either. Barring constraints, it is advisable to go to seminars that seem to have some interesting findings, which may or may not be in the exact research area that you are working on. By broadening your selection criteria, you will definitely be able to increase your exposure to potentially relevant research materials and perspectives. With cross-disciplinary studies becoming more popular, such a strategy can lead to more cross-disciplinary research opportunities.

Conferences are another similar source of information. I go to conferences for three reasons: (1) to catch up with friends and colleagues in other universities; (2) to find new potential research collaborators; and (3) to know more about the latest issues other researchers are working on. The last one on that list is always a priority for me.

The main reason is that papers presented at good conferences are the ones that are likely to appear in journals in the next few years (the 'few' to reflect the rigorous and tedious review process of good journals). In other words, conferences give a snapshot of future research outputs that your online searches are unlikely to provide.

It is good to attend both international and regional conferences to get yourself up to date. Both types of conference provide some overlapping and different benefits. In terms of focus, try to ensure that you are attending the good ones. Such conferences usually have about a 40 per cent acceptance rate or less – a stringent selection process for a conference. If you are not sure about the good conferences in your specific research area, it will be wise to consult with more senior researchers. Good conferences usually provide their acceptance rate data to demonstrate their quality.

3.4.7 The Internet

Nowadays we also have the luxury of the Internet. I recall the time when I started doing research work: there was no Internet! Just imagine that information did not come at the click of a mouse. These days if you want to know more about something, all it takes is to 'google it' or 'Baidu Yixia'. How convenient. Of course, as will be discussed in Chapter 4 on performing a literature review, not all information generated from an Internet search can and should be relied upon. Nonetheless, the Internet provides a whole new way that information not available via other forms of dissemination of research can be shared.

3.5 WHAT CONSTITUTES A GOOD RESEARCH TOPIC?

Conversation box

At the start of a research methods class, the Professor has just announced that the major assessment for the course will be a research proposal involving a good research topic.

Joey [Honours student]:   How do we know if a research topic is a good one?

Professor: It's a good one when your research topic makes a good contribution to the field.

Joey: How do I know if a contribution is a good one?

Professor:	It should have influences on theory and practice. And you will have to know your field decently well.
Joey:	I may not be able to find such a topic within such a short time!
Professor:	Don't worry, Joey, I will assist with this assessment for this assignment. At this stage you are not expected to always be able to recognize a topic with great contribution potential even if you come across one.

When I teach research design and methods courses, I often come across questions from students asking: 'is this a good enough research topic?' This question is often a tough one to answer, unless if you are already an expert in the area. It is difficult for new researchers or research students to work out what constitutes a mediocre, workable, good or excellent research topic. This is probably due to their relative lack of experience in the research area they are working in. This judgement is better made with the help of a more senior researcher specializing in the area. Over time, with increased experience, new researchers and research students can slowly recognize the difference between a mediocre and a workable research topic. A good versus excellent research topic will remain as a major challenge for any researcher throughout his career. Chapter 4 of Campbell et al.'s book *What to Study* (1982) provides an interesting comparison between significant and not-so-significant research. The level of judgement for what is original differs across research areas. For example, it will take a more significant effort to find what is new in the area of organizational behaviour, which has a long history, than to find a relatively new topic in strategic management, which is a relatively 'younger' area of research. Still, despite this difference, you will often be confronted with how original 'original' really is.

Research is conducted at different levels, with researchers going for different outputs: Honours dissertation, Masters thesis, PhD dissertation, non-peer reviewed journal article, average peer-reviewed journal article and top peer-reviewed journal article. Each of these outputs has different expectations. For example, the expectation of the contribution of an Honours dissertation is lower than that of a Masters thesis, which is in turn lower than that of a PhD dissertation. Even within each level, there can be differences. For example, among top peer-reviewed journals there are some that have more theoretical focus while others have more empirical focus. Yet while we know this difference in general, it will be judgemental to address a question like 'does a Masters thesis have to have twice the impact as an Honours dissertation?' The nature of research is such that it is the researchers who judge the contributions. Thus, while the general expectation of the differences is commonly understood, specific differences will be at the discretion of the individual institutions, journals and gate-keeping researchers – a judgement call in itself!

In general judgement on the quality of a research topic will rely on a few yardsticks. First, how much influence will the findings of your study have in your subfield and in the broader management or business context? Second, what are the likely influences on managerial practices? Third, are the contributions event-specific or time-sensitive? Fourth, are the contributions generic or specific to a particular context? These yardsticks will be touched on in this section.

3.5.1 Influence on specific field and broader business and management

A new research student in business and management is likely to think along the lines of making as much contribution as possible in her research work. The general misperception is that the broader the contribution, the more useful the research work will be to both the academic field and practice, whereas the more specific the contribution, the less it will affect either sphere as fewer people will care. This misperception is highlighted in Chapter 2.

In the business and management field, there is a vast knowledge base that a new research student can draw upon. It becomes difficult to bring a totally new perspective or new line of inquiry to generate a contribution with a very high degree of originality. In fact, these days the broader the discussion, the less informed the findings of the research will be, as neither academics nor practitioners can make good use of the research outcomes. As Daft notes, good research does not pretend to answer all the questions relating to an issue. He further adds, 'one goal of research is simply to understand a tiny piece of organizational reality' (1983: 542).

How specific and narrow can or should your research topic be? This is also a judgement call in research. Good researchers often work to inform seemingly very small parts of a broad research area and multiple research works seek to inform a more general storyline. That is, normally an article published in a journal (even a good journal) can have a good yet very minute contribution on its own based on a face value judgement. Yet, when it is connected to various other previous research works, whether conducted by the same researchers or not, an illuminated understanding of a particular research area will surface.

Thus, when making a decision to be very specific or not about your research topic, you will have to possess an awareness of the state of research within your field. That is, you need to know what research has been done in your area of work. The earlier sections in this chapter have provided you with the process and some tips for doing that. A small contribution in one area of research is not the same in another area of research, in absolute terms. Hence, much care has to be taken to avoid trying to be specific yet resulting in a meaningless research exercise. Likewise, blue-sky research that does not translate into operational knowledge is often considered a waste of precious research time.

So, who can help if you are struggling with this assessment? The best researchers in your area should be good assessors for that. But they are not always accessible, for example they may be in an overseas institution that you have little chance of coming into contact with. This means that you always have to go down the list and try to get the best possible persons that you can access. This could be someone in an institution in a neighbouring country, in another institution within your country, or in another faculty or department within your institution. Importantly, don't forget your research supervisor if that is also an option. This practice would be the same as the research review process. In the review process, an editor of the journal will find two to three researchers in your area of research to review your submission. These other researchers are deemed to be qualified persons to comment on and review the submission. Likewise, qualified examiners will be asked to examine a project and these examiners are deemed to be the best judges of whether the topic of the research project is a good one.

3.5.2 Influence on management practice

We hear remarks from students like 'this course is more practical than the other one, which has a more theoretical focus'. While this sort of remark tends to come from students, it is not uncommon for professors to recognize this as well. One of the key functions of any business school is to inform existing business leaders and provide management education to future business leaders. In fact, the business community expects the business schools to help churn enough managerial talents for its consumption.

With this pressure, it is increasingly hard to envisage that a course can be purely theoretical without taking managerial practice into consideration. The same applies to all research work, as discussed in Chapter 2. Researchers have to balance theory and practice in their work – theory to ensure that arguments are logical and well grounded and practice to ensure that theory is in check and is of relevance to the business world. Hence, whether explicitly or subtly, all research in business and management will need to have some managerial relevance. Depending on your audience, you can adjust the relative weights of these two components accordingly.

3.5.3 Event-specific and time-sensitive influence

> **Conversation box**
>
> *Dianne [student]:* Professor, a lot of research papers that I read involve data dating back to the 1980s. Some of these only included data until the mid-2010s. Does that mean the research could be out of date? Why is it that the authors didn't try to analyze more recent data?
>
> *Professor:* You raise a couple of important points here, Dianne. First, some of these studies could be longitudinal, so they cover many years of data. This can be good in terms of research rigour despite the actual date range of the data. Simply put, good theories never run out of date. Second, very often data are hard to come by, especially large datasets. It is possible that some of these studies have been crafted and went under review since the mid-2010s and the research process took longer than anticipated. That could be a reason why the data have not been updated recently. Access to data may also have been limited beyond mid-2010s; it may not be available to the researchers any longer.

Some research topics are event-specific, for example, research on the aftermath of the Asian Financial Crisis in 1997, or the more recent cases of Global Financial Crisis in 2008 and the Novel Coronavirus (COVID-19) in 2020. By event-specific, we mean research related to the occurrence of a specific event. The research projects using this kind of research are only largely relevant to that event or related forms of events. For example, the Asian Financial Crisis is one of many currency crises, and thus some implications from that specific event can be potentially be applied to the subsequent Global Financial Crisis in 2008.

Other research topics are time sensitive. These are often related to management fads due to a rush of blood from investors or consumers. A good example is the e-commerce boom in the late 1990s and early 2000s. During that period, many journal articles were written about the importance of e-commerce and how e-commerce can be managed for generating competitive advantages for firms. Since then, however, the e-commerce boom has died off and interest in e-commerce research has petered out as well. Time-sensitive research, as the name suggests, is vulnerable to change of interest in the market. Thus, a time-sensitive research study can lose significant value overnight should the tide change. Of course, that does not rule out the possibility that over time there will be a renewal of interest in the same topic. In fact, since about 2017, interest in e-commerce has picked up again, yet the nature of interest is more concerned with digital and logistics e-commerce, different forms from those focused on back in the early 2000s.

Research topics that are not event-specific and time-sensitive can be generally placed under another umbrella. Research topics that are generic are always relevant over time and probably across contexts, as the conversation box above suggests. Thus, regardless of the range of data points that were used to illustrate the phenomenon under investigation or when it finally gets published (after going through an extensive review process), such research topics are of value to their audience. The extent of this value depends on how much contextualization is needed when trying to apply the findings.

3.5.4 Generic vs. context-specific influence

There is another differentiation among research topics. While some researches are deemed generic, others make contributions that are contextualized in that the findings will only hold under certain conditions or in certain environments. This differentiation, however, is often very subtle. Thus, this may not be obvious for new researchers. In order to identify such contextualized studies, the reader needs to look into some of the assumptions made by the authors. Specifically, if part of the research design is context-specific, such as adjusting measurements to fit a local context, then such a study is contextualized and thus should be evaluated and cited with more care. For example, Roth and Kostova (2003) discuss how multinational corporations can be used as a context for research investigation.

Context can be important for understanding some phenomena of interest (Bamberger and Pratt, 2010). Some researchers indicate this contingency in their discussion of limitations in their work, thus providing their audience with some measure of the level of caution needed when utilizing the results of their studies. Bamberger (2008) labels this as context theory, suggesting that contextualization narrows the gap between the micro–macro divide in management research.

Two questions arise here. First, how much do context contributions count? To most new researchers and research students, these are indeed original. But it can be argued that unless your research topic needs to be contextualized, it is irrelevant to label a topic original by simply applying it in a different context from previously published work. The contribution is too marginal. Secondly, if no one has done it before, can it be deemed original? This is probably somewhat true for half of the time. A research topic that has not been addressed previously may have inherent problems, like difficulty in obtaining data for investigation – for example, studies related to ethical practices in organizations. A topic may also not have been investigated before due to its relatively weak appeal to researchers – for example, there has been extensive research on cross-functional teams and how these generate innovations. While this research has largely been conducted in organizations in more advanced economies, there is little reason to believe that conducting similar research in Asia Pacific will yield insightful results unless the attributes under investigation relate to cultural or national differences. Originality in a research topic should also encompass being interesting and making contributions to the research and business communities.

For a younger field, knowledge is relatively new and researchers in the area are more likely to be open-minded towards exploratory research (Sutton and Staw, 1995). For example, Singh et al. (2003) argue that strategy is a younger field and concepts are relatively harder to measure and observe. Thus, it is necessary to allow more leeway when trying to replicate strategy studies for validity purposes. They further propose a loosening of the replication definition of natural sciences to allow 'good-enough' replications to be conducted in the strategy field. Due to the uneven evolution of various fields (Nelson, 2003), it then makes sense to bear in mind that researchers have different levels of opinion regarding what is original in their field.

In recent years, researchers have started to avocate for phenomenon-based research (Chen et al., 2017; Doh, 2015; Von Krogh et al., 2012). For example, it is argued that various issues and challenges that China is facing is unique due to its position and influence on the world economy and studying it as a new phenomenon would help advance our understanding of management theories (Chen et al., 2017). Existing theories focusing on international business also do not equip us with all the explanations regarding challenges that foreign firms face in China (Doh, 2015; Li, 2019). There is certainly merit in this strand of thought, though a lot of research involving China simply treats China as a context and thus does not incorporate this uniqueness in the theorizing and design of their work, making these contributions marginal. Von Krogh et al. (2012, Table 2) propose a strategy for using phenomenon-based research to make contributions to our knowledge accumulation.

KEY TERMS

- Convergence search
- Divergence search
- Interpretivist approach
- Positivist approach
- Snowballing search
- Systematic search processes

SUMMARY

- Positivist and interpretivist are the two key approaches to a research problem.
- The key starting point for any literature search is journals.

- Convergence, divergence and snowballing are three ways of conducting systematic search processes.
- Article search databases are search engines that provide one-stop access to many journal articles and periodicals.
- Beyond article search databases, other sources of information include working papers, conference papers, business magazine articles, and reports and Webpages.
- Care should be taken when using sources other than articles from good journals. Sometimes this involves judgement calls.
- A good research question is assessed based on its influence on a specific field or broader business, its influence on management practice, whether it is event-specific and time-sensitive, and whether the contribution is generic or context-specific.

QUESTIONS

1. Discuss the differences between academic-oriented and practice-oriented research questions.
2. Briefly discuss a systematic approach to literature search.
3. What is convergence literature search?
4. What is the snowballing approach to literature search?
5. What is divergence literature search?
6. What constitutes a good research topic?
7. What are the challenges of event-specific, context-specific and time-sensitive research?

ADDITIONAL READINGS

Abbott, A. (2004) *Methods of Discovery: Heuristics for the Social Sciences.* New York: W.W. Norton & Co.

Aguinis, H., Boyd, B.K., Pierce, C.A. and Short, J.C. (2011) 'Walking new avenues in management research methods and theories: Bridging micro and macro domains', *Journal of Management*, 37 (2): 395–403.

Coates, J. (1996) *The Claims of Common Sense.* New York: Cambridge University Press.

Cornelissen, J.P. and Durand, R. (2014) 'Moving forward: Developing theoretical contributions in management studies', *Journal of Management Studies*, 51 (6): 995–1022.

Davis, G.F. (2010) 'Do theories of organizations progress?', *Organizational Research Methods*, 13 (4): 690–709.

Davis, M.S. (1971) 'That's interesting! Towards a phenomenology of sociology and a sociology of phenomenology', *Philosophy of the Social Sciences*, 1 (4): 309–44.

Gray, P.H. and Cooper, W.H. (2010) 'Pursuing failure', *Organizational Research Methods*, 13 (4): 620–43.

Hambrick, D.C. (2007) 'The field of management's devotion to theory: Too much of a good thing?', *Academy of Management Journal*, 50 (6): 1346–52.

Mathieu, J.E. and Chen, G. (2011) 'The etiology of the multilevel paradigm in management research', *Journal of Management*, 37 (2): 610–41.

Pfeffer, J. (1993) 'Barriers to the advance of organizational science: Paradigm development as a dependent variable', *Academy of Management Review*, 18 (4): 599–620.

Zammuto, R.F. and Connolly, T. (1984) 'Coping with disciplinary fragmentation', *Journal of Management Education*, 9 (2): 30–7.

REFERENCES

Alvesson, M. and Sandberg, J. (2011) 'Generating research questions through problematization', *Academy of Management Review*, 36 (2): 247–71.

Bamberger, P.A. (2008) 'Beyond contextualization: Using context theories to narrow the micro–macro gap in management research', *Academy of Management Journal*, 51 (5): 839–46.

Bamberger, P.A. and Pratt, M.G. (2010) 'Moving forward by looking back: Reclaiming unconventional research contexts and samples in organizational scholarship', *Academy of Management Journal*, 53 (4): 665–71.

Campbell, J.P., Daft, R.L. and Hulin, C.L. (1982) *What to Study: Generating and Developing Research Questions*. Beverly Hills, CA: Sage Publishing.

Chen, C.C., Friedman, R. and McAllister, D.J. (2017) 'Seeing and studying China: Leveraging phenomenon-based research in China for theory advancement', *Organizational Behavior and Human Decision Processes*, 143: 1–7.

Daft, R.L. (1983) 'Learning the craft of organizational research', *Academy of Management Review*, 8 (4): 539–46.

Doh, J.P. (2015) 'From the editor: Why we need phenomenon-based research in international business', *Journal of World Business*, 50 (4): 609–11.

Hsieh-Yee, I. (1993) 'Effects of search experience and subject knowledge on the search tactics of novice and experienced searchers', *Journal of the American Society for Information Science*, 44 (3): 161–74.

Lee, A.S. (1991) 'Integrating positivist and interpretive approaches to organizational research', *Organization Science*, 2 (4): 342–65.

Li, F. (2019) Why have all Western internet firms failed in China? A phenomenon-based study. *Academy of Management Discoveries*, 5(1): 13–37.

Nelson, R.R. (2003) 'On the uneven evolution of human know-how', *Research Policy*, 32 (6): 909–22.

Norris, M. and Oppenheim, C. (2007) 'Comparing alternatives to the *Web of Science* for coverage of the social sciences' literature', *Journal of Infometrics*, 1 (2): 161–9.

Pennanen, M. and Vakkari, P. (2003) 'Students' conceptual structure, search process, and outcome while preparing a research proposal: A longitudinal case study', *Journal of the American Society for Information Science and Technology*, 54 (8): 759–70.

Roth, K. and Kostova, T. (2003) 'The use of the multinational corporation as a research context', *Journal of Management*, 29 (6): 883–902.

Sandberg, J. and Alvesson, M. (2011) 'Ways of constructing research questions: Gap-spotting or problematization?', *Organization*, 18 (1): 23–44.

Singh, K., Ang, S.H. and Leong, S.M. (2003) 'Increasing replication for knowledge accumulation in strategy research', *Journal of Management*, 29 (4): 533–49.

Starbuck, W.H. (2003) 'Turning lemons to lemonade: Where is the value in peer reviews?', *Journal of Management Inquiry*, 12 (4): 344–51.

Starbuck, W.H. (2005) 'How much better are the most-prestigious journals? The statistics of academic publication', *Organization Science*, 16 (2): 180–200.

Sutton, R.I. and Staw, B.M. (1995) 'What theory is not', *Administrative Science Quarterly*, 40 (3): 371–84.

Vakkari, P., Pennanen, M. and Serola, S. (2003) 'Changes of search terms and tactics while writing a research proposal: A longitudinal case study', *Information Processing and Management*, 39 (3): 445–63.

Von Krogh, G., Rossi-Lamastra, C. and Haefliger, S. (2012) 'Phenomenon-based research in management and organisation science: When is it rigorous and does it matter?' *Long Range Planning*, 45 (4): 277–98.

4
CONDUCTING A LITERATURE REVIEW

4.1 INTRODUCTION

The degree of originality in research determines what is to be recognized and what is to be cited. That is, only interesting and good work will eventually be quoted and remembered. In order to recognize what is interesting and what is good about a new research project, it is essential for a researcher to understand what previous works have been done and what the current state of the field is. Who has done work previously in the field? Who are the key authors? Where are the main sources of materials published? What are the latest trends? These are the major questions that arise in your search of the literature. So how do researchers go about finding out the answers to these questions?

In order to track these, a researcher needs to go about conducting a proper **literature review**. A literature review is a summary of what is currently known about a field on the basis of research evidence and lines of argument in relation to a particular issue in that field. While this sounds straightforward, conducting a literature review can often become the most time-consuming component of a research project.

In order to fulfil the criteria of good research of objectivity, rigour and replicability, it is important to have a systematic and reproducible process in place when conducting a literature review. Systematic means justifying and documenting the selection of appropriate search criteria. Different search procedures, and even using different search engines as illustrated in the conversation box above, are likely to result in different search outputs. As such, if the process is not well documented, two persons working in the same area might end up with different paths to their research. Having different paths is not necessarily a bad outcome, but if a poor search process ends in a wrong path, it will become a problem. Having this documentation would also enable

Conversation box

The first assignment in a business ethics course involves a proposal on identifying three areas of investigation that are currently hot topics in the area of ethics. The assignment first involves a literature review in this area before the students identify their topics. Two weeks into the course ...

Alicia [in class]:   Professor, I have a question about the assignment. I have run a literature search using the research article search engine EBSCOhost, using the two key words of 'ethics' and 'strategy'. But I realized that Bruce, who is interested in the same area, has different search outcomes from his search using the key words of 'ethics' and 'strategic management'. Charlene got totally different search outcomes from search engine ABI Inform using the same key words as me. I am confused. Who is right and who is wrong?

Professor: None of you are wrong. And what you have experienced, Alicia, shows why it is important for us to document our search process so that it is clear why we might have arrived at different search outcomes.

the search process to be reproducible, whether by the same or a different researcher. Without a systematic approach, it will also be hard to tell if a literature review process is complete.

4.2 WHAT DOES A LITERATURE REVIEW INCLUDE?

In order to conduct a literature review, various steps and tools are necessary. New researchers and research students are bound to have different perceptions of what a literature review constitutes. This is especially so when a topic entails a phenomenon that leans toward an in-trend investigation rather than a more generic research topic. As a result of the varieties of research outputs, the forms and expectations of the literature review conducted will also vary. Upon performing the literature search, which was covered extensively in Chapter 3, there is also a standard expectation of what needs to be included when it comes to reporting on the outcomes of that search.

4.2.1 Steps and tools for literature review

First and foremost, you need to have a general, if not specific research topic. It must be noted here again that usually specific research topics are not derived until after a substantial literature review has been done, unless the topic is given by someone else, such as the supervisor of your research project or the company that is related to the project you are working on. If not, this would mean it will be hard for you to have a specific topic at the start, without making an arbitrary choice. Nevertheless, a general direction of what you are interested in will be sufficient to get the literature search process going. This research question will allow you to undergo a more efficient process of literature search. If you do not have a fixed direction of research guided by a research question, you may find yourself changing the search criteria from time to time, resulting in information overload and a lot of confusion as to which search outcome is appropriate. It will also be hard for you to figure out what is useful (and what is not) in your search outcomes.

The first point of contact with regard to the literature is always the search databases. These were highlighted in Chapter 3. As recently as the early 1990s we did not have the Internet – not to say that accessing information electronically these days is not always going to bring its own challenges. The old method of literature review for me was to search hard copies of academic journals and other periodicals available in the physical library in order to find relevant information. These were the times when information overload was less of an issue, but nonetheless, my eyeball search process was a strenuous one. Search outcomes were not at the disposal of our fingertips.

These days the word 'search' will bring us straight to Google. But many sources that you can trace from the Internet are not reliable, as they do not go through an objective review and quality control process. In other words, the contents of what you read are not moderated and can be overly subjective. Unless you know the nature of the sources well, these require some validation before you can use them. Yet, this validation process is difficult, as you will still rely on other Internet sources for this. Hence, the key sources that researchers should use for research projects will tend to be article search engines.

With a broad research question, you will be able to have a decent list of search terms. Search terms are terminologies that you will use in your search process and these are often the keywords related to your research question. A rule of thumb is that these are the most commonly used terms in your study. Recall the first conversation box in this chapter where Alicia experienced different search outcomes from Charlene as she used another search database and Bruce as he used a different combination of words. These two cases of arriving at different search outcomes are the reality, as discussed in Chapter 3. In the case of using different search terms, it is possible to avoid missing out on some search outputs if you adopt an exhaustive search process that involves all related keywords. For example, if you search for ethics and strategy articles like Alicia did, you might include variations such as 'strategies' and 'strategic management' for strategy and 'ethical' and 'moral' for ethics and use various combinations of these terms in your search process.

Some of these search terms would seem obvious enough – but why would you search for 'strategies' when you have searched for 'strategy'? No doubt it is likely that an article that involves the use of a keyword in 'strategy' is likely to include the word 'strategies' at some point, these are nonetheless treated as two independent words in search article engines. Search systems are not artificial intelligence machines that interpret for you. It means the onus is on you to engage in a more exhaustive search process in order to avoid missing potentially relevant materials. For this purpose, it may be wise to familiarize youself with the syntax of the search engine that you use, for example searching using wildcards that will economize on the search process. The bottom line is that a couple of search terms are always going to be too broad and limiting. But just look on the bright side, while you may end up with an extensive search process, it does ensure that you are not missing any potentially key articles, provides rigour to your research process, and you will ultimately arrive at an even better research topic.

4.2.2 What should be included in a literature review?

Upon finding the relevant articles, you will need to do a **synthesis** of those articles. Synthesizing is combining the constituent elements of separate materials into a single coherent section or document. As you read articles, you try to summarize them in paragraphs. In a literature review, it is not good enough to combine these summaries by reiterating the key elements of each of the articles read. You need to put the essence of all the articles together and provide a holistic view of the literature to the reader, linking them through common threads or themes. The literature review needs to cover the issues of how previous works are connected and how your work is going to fit alongside these previous works, often with the use of good headings that connect them.

In terms of content, what should a literature review contain? A typical literature review includes a discussion of the trends and observations of the phenomenon and context of interest in your study, the relevant theories, concepts and perspectives being used to test aspects of your research topic (including any new conceptual approach you are introducing to the research area if this is not represented in the literature so far), prior findings related to the issues you are investigating, and the variables and measurements used in these other relevant previous studies.

A lot of the research being conducted these days is phenomenon-based, briefly highlighted in Chapter 3. The context can be a country, an industry, a region, or a particular group of companies or individuals. A discussion of the trends and observations of the phenomenon and context of interest in your study is important as it gives the background to what motivates you to conduct the current study. Importantly, it gives a good introduction to the boundaries of what your research involves (and the extent that your implications cover), and perhaps provides more information as to the contribution of your work. It further gives the reader some indication of your grasp of the fundamentals of the phenomenon you are investigating. For example, if your research project involves the investigation of the economic impact of the Novel Coronavirus in 2020 on Asian economies, it will be good to draw on the literature on similar events in recent history such as Swine Flu and SARS. A broader literature can also involve how other forms of disaster may have impacted on the economic growth of Asia, shedding some light on the factors that might need to be considered generically in regard to disasters and zooming into factors specifically around health-related disasters.

Most if not all research requires some conceptual backing. Here, the word 'conceptual' rather than 'theoretical' is used. As there are really very few theories in business and management, it is less restrictive to use the word 'concepts' instead, as they cover theories as well as commonly adopted frameworks and constructs. It is not surprising to see that many phenomena in business and management can simultaneously be explained by several theoretical or conceptual perspectives. In fact, the truth is that many phenomena in the business and management context cannot be explained from the viewpoint of a single perspective! Hence, it is important that when you conduct a literature review, all the theoretical or conceptual perspectives that have previously been used to investigate an aspect of your research topic should be covered. Note that an aspect of a research topic refers to a micro level of investigation: for example, organizational change can be a research area while employee motivation in the aftermath of organizational change is an aspect of organizational change.

If you are applying a new theoretical and conceptual perspective that has not been used previously in your research area, then a good overview of this perspective will be critical. It is crucial that readers understand why the application of this new perspective will add value to the research area and they will only grasp the essence of its relevance through your literature review. Your literature review for this study will thus have to include the basic elements and assumptions of this perspective, how it has been applied in related contexts and the reasons why it is relevant for you to apply it to examine your phenomenon of interest.

Prior findings from other research outputs are important when it comes to motivating your study. It is important to synthesize prior findings that support some of your viewpoints. However, extra care must be taken in looking at how these prior findings were derived. In particular, if a study has contextualized the phenomenon in its examination – for example, the relationships only hold in the European context – this has to be reflected in your synthesis. If you are working on Asian data, the reliance on prior findings based on contextualization in Europe may need to be treated with caution, especially for context-specific phenomena. It is also crucial to note that prior findings that do not support your viewpoint should be considered seriously, if not more seriously. The reason is that more often than not contexts shape what we observe and thus we might end up with different conclusions when we investigate the same phenomenon using different contexts. Such contingencies need to be identified and recognized so that your own examination can be viewed and aligned in light of these differences.

Conversation box

Alex [student]: Professor, I have identified from the literature that there are many ways to measure the performance of an organization. I had some discussions with other Masters students but we did not manage to arrive at a conclusion of which is the most appropriate measurement to use. Some say return on assets, others say return on invested capital, yet others say market share. What might be the best measure for organizational performance then?

Professor: There is no definite answer for your question, Alex. It depends on what you are measuring organizational performance against. For example, employee turnover rate can be an organizational performance measure for implementing human resource policies. Market share change can be an organizational performance measure for a major marketing campaign, and definitely does not make sense to be linked to the implementation of human resource policies, at least not directly. In any case, you need to justify the use of measurement that you have chosen, whether this has been adopted in previous works or not.

Keeping track of the variables and measurements used in these other relevant studies is essential when it comes to backing up your own choice of variables and measurements. Take for example, if you are using a variable that is the same as that used in another study and you also wish to use the same measurement for that variable, then this other study will serve to provide you with support for your choice of variable and measurement. If you are using the same variable but trying to use a different measure, you will also need this synthesis to justify how and why you are deviating from existing practices, and whether this newly introduced measurement adds value to the literature. Essentially, you will have to justify that your choice of new variable or measurement is appropriate, and in some circumstance even deemed to be superior.

4.2.3 Using existing review articles

Conversation box

June [Masters student]:   Professor, I have found a review article on managerial ethics, my research area. I find it extremely useful. Should I be relying mainly on that article for my own literature review?

Professor: It's good that you have found a review article in this space, but you should only rely on this article for a good overview, rather than using it prescriptively. For example, your literature review should not only contain what this article says about where the literature gaps are, but also your own discovery and interpretation of the literature from other readings. In this regard, you have to go beyond what is covered in the review article. But the review article nonetheless will provide you with good references to help you conduct your own review.

As a research field evolves, researchers find a need to consolidate ideas so that it becomes more explicit what fundamental issues remain unanswered to date and where the field should be heading. As a result, in recent years, we see the publication of more and more review papers as some fields start to get more mature. For example, the *Journal of Management* explicitly publishes an annual review special issue with articles focused solely on reviews of particular research areas. Other journals are less explicit but are generally open to publishing reviews that take stock of the current state and future directions of a research field. **Review articles** provide a good overview of the field and are welcomed by both research students and researchers. They help to consolidate and guide the path of scholarship and inquiry. Post et al. (2020) provide a good discussion on the importance of having review articles for advancing theory development.

It is likely that, if you search widely, there is bound to be a review of some sort in your area of research – unless your field has only been around for a very short period of time. Review papers are often well cited. However, using them is a different matter. As these articles provide a good overview, you might find yourself over-citing the article. There will also be a temptation to try to fit your contribution to what the article deems as a research opportunity. But as the Professor cautioned in the conversation box above, you can do this only with an open mind.

4.3 HOW BEST TO UTILIZE THE SOURCE ARTICLES

Conversation box

Sally [Honours student]:   Professor, there is an abundance of research articles that I found in the ABI Inform article search engine. So now I'm finding it difficult to read and absorb them. I've heard that the fastest way to do this is to look at the abstract of the paper. Is that OK?

Professor: There's no doubt that reading the abstract of the paper is the fastest way to get an understanding of what to expect in the paper. However, it is important that when the contribution of the paper is not obvious from reading the abstract, you have to use the introduction section and perhaps the conclusion section to help you make an assessment of whether to do an in-depth reading of the article.

It takes time for you to single out good articles to read further. However, after picking the relevant and good ones, there are mainly four things to concentrate on in reading them. In particular, look out for the research issues and contributions, the research arguments, data and samples, and research findings. It is important in the process of conducting the literature review that you make good judgement calls on how much you can trust each of these elements in any particular article.

4.3.1 Research issue and contributions

The selection of a source article to read using article search engines is mostly based on the title and abstract of the paper, as demonstrated in Chapter 3. However, the importance and relevance of an article to your research are derived from its contributions to the field, and how close your specific focus is to the main message in the source article. It is often difficult to assess this contribution just by reading the abstract of the paper. The contributions are often better articulated in the introduction and conclusion sections. Thus, it is advisable to read these sections to be clearer about the contributions of the paper, whether they come in the form of theoretical advancements or empirical advancements or both.

4.3.2 Research arguments

Conversation box

Professor: Warren, you need to ensure that you have corroborated all the arguments in the literature so that your contribution can be distinguished from those in the literature.

Warren [PhD student]:   I have consolidated the hypotheses of the various empirical studies and so I understand the degree of originality my proposed set of hypotheses offers.

Professor: But the hypotheses are only a reflection of the arguments and not the arguments themselves. The arguments lead to your hypothesis statements. They contain theoretical and conceptual grounding as well as logic linkages. These are essential for understanding how the contributions of the study were derived, and the reason why I had asked you to do some corroboration.

Central to any journal article, especially those that are published in top journals, is the fluency of the research arguments leading to the research propositions and hypotheses (for quantitative research) or arising from data observations (for qualitative research). This part is normally referred to as theorizing or theory building. Theory building narrates the path leading from the predictor construct to the outcome construct. An article with weak theory building has merely gone through a mechanical exercise and hence contributes little to our understanding of the linkages between the constructs in the study. As illustrated in the conversation box above, the arguments go beyond stating the hypotheses and propositions. Hypotheses and propositions are derived from arguments. Understanding the arguments is thus the essence of recognizing the value of your readings.

4.3.3 Data and sample

It may seem that the data and sample utilized in your readings are usually less important than other elements of the research such as **research contributions** and arguments. This is by no means always true. Data and samples provide the context of investigation and in fact define the boundaries of the implication of any research study. For example, investigation of the role of unionization on human resource practices across countries has to somehow involve countries with and without unionization as part of their employment agreements. Likewise, implications from a market-oriented economy are somewhat different from those derived from a more regulated market. Thus, the utilization of the research contributions, arguments and research findings of a study have to be viewed in light of the data and sample that the researchers employed for that particular study. Understanding the data and sample will provide a lot more insights into various other aspects covered in a research work.

4.3.4 Research findings

In order to link some of your own arguments, there are times when you need to cite studies that support some of the linkages you are proposing. The research findings of the source articles are a key aspect that you should read in order to get hold of the supporting evidence. However, when you are citing these findings, you need to take extra care regarding the context in which the results were derived. For example, you are interested in the issue of how the reputation of small firms will assist them in achieving growth. You find a couple of studies that have empirically linked reputation of a firm to its ability to form alliances that may lead to growth. On first sight, it looks like you have found some empirical support to back up your study. However, on checking the dataset for the studies, you discover they have used large multinational firms as their sample. Thus, what they found will be less relevant empirical support for your purpose, even though some of their arguments may still be applicable in your small firm context. This is another illustration of how you should adopt research findings to your purposes only cautiously in light of the data and sample used, as discussed in the previous section.

Figure 4.1 shows a checklist for the use of source articles. If none of the listed areas of assessments apply to your research, it may be the case that the source article that you are looking at is not really relevant to your own research and not worth a **citation**. The extent of the relevance of a source article to your research depends on how much overlap it has with your research topic and content. However, it should be noted that if a source article is found to have research elements such as the arguments, conclusions, data, and findings very similar to your proposed research, then it is probably time to consider an alternative research topic, as making an original contribution to the field would be near impossible.

1. How is the topic of the source article relevant to your research topic?
a. If related to your dependent variable, then relevance is very high.
b. If related to your independent variable(s), the level of relevance depends on how this has been used. For example, is this also being used an independent variable in the source article? If so, then how would that be connected back to your research topic given the different dependent variables. If this variable is being used as peripheral to the source article, again, how close would its use be able to tie back to your research topic?
c. If related to your theoretical or conceptual perspectives, the level of relevance depends on how close the topic of the source article is to your research topic.
2. Are the arguments used in the source article the same or similar to your own research?
a. If they are the same, then it will be worth learning from them and adapting them to your own research.
b. If they are similar, then it is necessary to ensure that comparisons are being made to provide support for your adaptation of these arguments.
3. Is the data used in the source article the same or similar to your research?
a. If it is the same, then it will provide some legitimacy to its use as a trustable source of data for your research.
b. If it is similar, then it is necessary to ensure that comparisons are being made to provide support for your own use of data.
4. Are any of the research findings in the source article relevant to your research?
a. If yes, then it will provide some legitimacy to your research. It is also important to ensure that the arguments used are reflected upon than just merely citing the results.

Figure 4.1   Checklist for the use of source articles

4.4 SYNTHESIZING THE SEARCH RESULTS

4.4.1 Collate, don't summarize

One mistake commonly made by research students is in the way they present the literature review. There is a tendency to interpret a literature review as an awareness test – a recognition of what research is out there. But a proper literature review goes way beyond this. A literature review should show the grasp the student has of their area of work; its purpose is to show that essential readings have been read and understood. It is an illustration of the ability of the researcher to understand the area and to integrate related studies – like putting the pieces together in a jigsaw puzzle.

Merely summarizing the findings of articles is not enough. You need to collate the findings of all the previous studies and integrate them into cohesive sections. Collating will include all aspects of the research, namely theoretical perspectives that have been used in the research area, methodologies that have been used, variables and measurements, and empirical findings. Only collation will demonstrate your grasp of the research area and at the same time justify your choice of research topic. Further, in this exercise of collation, it is important to incorporate the temporal aspect of the materials being utilized. A literature evolves over time, and our understanding of a particular research area can become more sophisticated as well. For example, the initial literature on firm diversification and performance generally tests how firms diversify their product portfolios to improve their performance. Over time, there is recognition that there are pitfalls to diversification, hence the relationship may be negative and curvilinear. Conducting a study in this area would require a researcher to recognize our current state of understanding is curvilinear, as opposed to being positive. Such a recognition should be explicit in any literature review.

4.4.2 Theoretical underpinnings

Many areas of research involve the application of multiple theories and concepts. In fact, as mentioned earlier, most phenomena in business and management cannot be explained by a single theory or concept. This is due partly to the fact that theories or concepts tend to be focused and incorporate assumptions while phenomena tend to span a wider spectrum. Businesses are embedded within the social environment and present many elements that are often impossible to be explained by a single perspective. As such, even understanding a single phenomenon is often better addressed with the help of multiple theories. However, it is also very common to see contravening forces of arguments between different theories attempting to explain a single phenomenon, especially since organizations involve paradoxical tensions. Thus, it becomes very important to be precise in highlighting the nature of the opposing forces of arguments. This differentiation is highly critical in the conceptual positioning of your research. Equally critical is to recognize that more often than not theories tend to complement each other instead of directly contradicting each other.

4.4.3 Empirical underpinnings

While theoretical underpinnings of phenomenon are easily identified in readings, as authors have to explicitly articulate the contribution of their work and how it fits alongside existing literature, empirical corroboration of the results tends to be more complicated. Take for example, a research project into the governance of collaborations established by firms from emerging economies. As studies in this area start to differentiate from each other in order to justify their individual contributions, they also attempt to collect different sets of data as one of the differentiating factors, for example instead of covering only the major emerging economies, more and more studies start to focus on the smaller emerging economies. This complicates the collation process. Are data collected from two groups comparable? If they are, do they produce the same outcomes? If the results are different, which study should you believe and why? If the results across the two groups are not comparable, how can one reconcile this literature? Challenges thus arise as empirical contexts differ. Many a time the dispersion of results of empirical findings actually hinders the collation process, leading to a scattered literature review.

The complications described above can happen in your research project. So how can they be reconciled? For the sake of your own literature review and understanding of the field, it makes sense for you to try to link studies together. For your role of researcher seeking to help accumulate knowledge in a particular field of study, linking studies together helps to create value. There is, however, no standard way to do this. The most common way we see this being done is that you align the results so that it is clear from the collation that there is some consistent relationship found between two constructs, while at the same time recognizing that this pattern is derived from different samples. Likewise, when the result is different, it should be articulated clearly why this is the case. Recognizing the differences in the findings is as important as identifying the similarities. Some studies in fact conduct **meta-analysis** for the purpose of aggregating the results from previous studies.

4.4.4 Meta-analysis

Meta-analysis involves consolidating findings from previous studies in the literature with the use of statistics to find a pattern for the relationships between two or more constructs. As shown in most parts of this chapter, the literature review is often a descriptive exercise. You will have to collate the findings to provide a complete picture of the state of the field to date. However, it is not uncommon to find the existence of multiple relationships between two constructs. Take for example, the relationship between product diversification and firm performance, an example used earlier in this chapter. A firm that engages in product diversification starts conducting business in related and unrelated product areas. According to Palich et al. (2000), product diversification can have three main types of relationship with firm performance – linear, inverted-U and intermediate (where the positive effect tapers off). They then conduct a meta-analysis on previous studies and conclude that inverted-U is the dominant relationship.

Meta-analysis is useful when the literature in a research area is vast yet appears to be inconclusive. Note that it only applies to research areas that have extensive quantitative research findings. Meta-analysis has become more common in management research in the last two decades (Geyskens et al., 2009) and has been found to have effects on an article being cited (Judge et al., 2007).

4.5 ADEQUACY AND RELEVANCE OF A LITERATURE REVIEW

There are several forms of literature review that one can conduct. An extensive review of literature reviews led Grant and Booth (2009) to distinguish 14 broad literature review types and their associated methodologies. Systematic literature review is one of them, and meta-analysis, as discussed in the last section, is yet another. These are none-theless not standalone as the different forms can be combined. Verlegh and Steenkamp (1999) provide a good example of how to combine various literature review approaches to provide rigour to a literature review in country-of-origin research. Specifically, they conduct an initial narrative literature review on the research area followed by a meta-analysis on the effects of country-of-origin.

Badger et al. (2000) have highlighted various circumstances in which systematic literature reviews can become difficult and suggest a more flexible approach to sys-tematic literature reviews. For example, it can take substantial time to locate the relevant papers as shown in Chapter 3 and other time constraints will be imposed on the research project that you are working on. This may require the reconsideration of several areas relating to the scope of the research project. Badger et al. (2000) focus on four areas: defining a research question with inclusion and exclusion criteria, a focused search strategy, some fixed criteria for evaluation of studies, and a data extraction strategy.

Some characteristics in the business and management field also lead to challenges in conducting systematic literature reviews (Tranfield et al., 2003). Specifically, the diversity within each component of the research process, e.g. research question, data, sampling, etc. will make collation a difficult exercise when one conducts a literature review. Nonetheless, the authors call for more rigour and relevance in the business and management field to allow for more systematic literature reviews. Another impediment to the literature review process is the lack of transparency and systematic procedures documented in some research areas. For example, studies in supply chain management literature have made proper literature review difficult due to the complex streams of work (Seuring and Gold, 2012). In such cases, a content-analysis based literature review may be needed, as demonstrated in Seuring and Gold (2012).

4.5.1 Adequacy of a literature review

> ## Conversation box
>
> *Billy [Honours student]:*   Professor, for this assignment of a research proposal of 4,000 words, how much should be allocated to the literature review section?
>
> *Professor:*   There's no specific ratio for that. It depends on the topic and in particular the complexity of the linkages that you are trying to establish in your study. But I would advise not going above a third of the full proposal in this case as I'm interested to see more discussion in the data and methodology section.
>
> *Billy:*   Thanks. What about the depth of the literature coverage that is required?
>
> *Professor:*   Again, Billy, that depends on your topic. But given the nature of the assignment and the word limit, you have to be succinct rather than being broad and covering too much of the basics.

What is considered to be adequate coverage in a literature review? How does a student know when they have provided enough background in a literature review? These are key questions that often arise, as shown in the conversation box above. While there are no fixed answers to these questions, making a wrong judgement call on the adequacy of your literature review has implications. If you overdo it, then you will end up with a literature review that contains more confusion than clarity. There is also likely to be a lot of superfluous material. While excessive literature may mean a potentially easy task of trimming down the scope of the literature, this task is by no means straightforward. For example, it may be ambiguous to gauge what is highly relevant versus what is less relevant. For a research student or a new researcher this assessment is often difficult, as we tend to find all the readings well crafted and almost everything seems to be important! This clouds our thinking and results in a tendency to include as much as possible in the literature review. The information overload that results from this process in fact reflects a lack of good grasp of the literature and hence should be avoided. Sometimes it is advisable to engage the help of a more senior researcher to shape the boundary of the literature review.

On the flip side, if you under-do your literature review, it represents a major flaw that calls into question other aspects of your research. Critically, for example, if the literature is under-reviewed, how can you be sure that your research question has not been addressed previously? Owing to the dire consequences of under-covering a literature review – which can result in a piece of research work being declared void – it is more common to observe an excessively detailed literature review than one with limited coverage.

Figure 4.2 presents a checklist on conducting a literature review. When you are conducting a literature review or writing it up, the checklist provides some areas to consider and to look out for.

1. Given the research topic, what will the literature review cover?
   a. What is the phenomenon? Is this contextualized?
   b. What are the dependent variables?
   c. What are the independent variables?
   d. What is the theoretical literature to which the study seeks to contribute?

2. What are the subsections of the literature?
   a. A section on phenomenon? What are the trends and observations?
   b. A section on the dependent variables? And on potential measurements?
   c. A section on the independent variables? And on potential measurements?
   d. A section that links the dependent and independent variables?
   e. What are other factors in play in this research topic?
   f. A section on the theoretical literature? Is a new theoretical perspective being applied such that a deeper discussion is needed?
   g. What other sections would be appropriate?

3. Why did you adopt the perspective amongst the options available in the literature? Are the logic and conceptual reasoning explicitly demonstrated?
4. What is the best way to organize the literature review to allow a seamless flow?
5. Has the literature review synthesized knowledge from the literature into a significant, value-added contribution to new knowledge on the topic? And how have you built in the evolution of knowledge through the introduction of the literature using a chronological order?
6. Does the literature review critically analyze existing literature on the topic beyond the listing of facts? Does it lay the foundation leading to the research topic and other future research?

Figure 4.2   Checklist for conducting a literature review

4.5.2 Relevance of a literature review

Whatever research topic you choose to work on, there is likely to be substantial related research in the area. However, while it is important that your literature review is complete, what is required in the final output is often constrained by space – be it a research project or a journal article. It is then important to start thinking about what will be included and excluded in the final output. In order to do that, you need to narrow down the level of relevancy.

Let's take a look at an example. For his Masters project, Joe is interested in conducting a study of the effect of communication processes within alliances on alliance performance. An extensive literature on alliances will include the following aspects: motivation to form alliances, types and forms of alliances, partner selection criteria, governance structure of alliances, communications within alliances and alliance performance. If Joe is to include all these in his literature review, it will come to a few hundred pages, given the extensive research that has been done on these different aspects of alliances. The appropriate thing for him to do is to narrow down the literature to the two specific areas of alliances that he is interested in – communication processes (in alliance) and alliance performance. The relevant literature review in this case will be (1) communication processes of partners in alliances, (2) alliance performance and (3) all discussions relating communication process to alliance performance. This narrowing of the level of relevancy will ensure that the scope of the literature review is manageable and at the same time does not compromise the depth of knowledge within the literature review as a result of going for a larger breadth of coverage.

4.5.3 Mapping out the literature review scope

When a study has only a few key variables, it will be easier to map out what is relevant for a literature review. But for a research topic that involves many concepts, variables and perspectives, it will become harder to assess the relevance of each of the possible concepts, variables and perspectives. As mentioned above, the choices here also need to be balanced with the time and space made available by the output requirements.

Researchers have suggested the importance of using visual tools to help guide the conduct of a literature review (Nesbit and Adesope, 2006; Renfro, 2017). Notable tools are concept maps (Novak and Gowin, 1984) and knowledge maps (O'Donnell et al., 2002) which are diagrams that represent ideas as node-link assemblies. In their meta-analysis, Nesbit and Adesope (2006) find that in comparison with activities such as reading text passages, attending lectures, and participating in class discussions, concept mapping activities are more effective for attaining knowledge retention and transfer. Further, across educational levels, subject areas, and settings, it is found that studying concept or knowledge maps is somewhat more effective for retaining knowledge than studying text passages, lists, and outlines. Wheeldon and Faubert (2009) illustrate the use of concept maps.

Below I provide an illustration of how a map might help with your decisions on the relevance of a literature review. Figure 4.3 shows an illustration of the literature review process for a research project on 'alliances as market entry mode and their performance'. The research itself is a tightly coupled topic involving two variables – alliances and their performance. However, when alliances are introduced as part of being a type of market entry mode, complications arise. This suggests that the intention of the study is to treat the context of this study as consisting of only cross-border alliances for market entry purposes. Introducing alliances as entry modes also means that there needs to be some background literature on market entry modes (Link 1). But as the figure shows, it should include only that part of the market entry mode literature that compares cross-border alliances with other modes of market entry (Link 2). Would it be relevant to compare the performance of cross-border alliances with other market entry modes in your literature review?

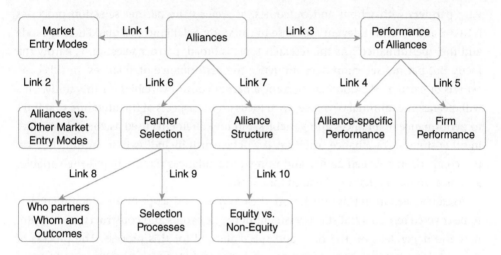

Figure 4.3   The literature review process for a study on 'Alliances as market entry mode and their performance'

The answer to the above question is dependent on what you may want to achieve by testing the performance of alliances (Link 3). Performance of alliances can broadly be assessed in two ways, one regarding the performance of an alliance itself (Link 4), for example how well the alliance is functioning and how many milestones have been made, and the other regarding its effect on firm performance (Link 5), for example how a firm's sales improve as a result of having that alliance. If performance of an alliance itself is the outcome that you are after, then comparing the performance of alliances with other market entry modes is not relevant to this study. On the other hand, if the outcome is about how an alliance affects firm performance, then it may make sense to compare different market entry modes. In doing so, you are making a case that alliance affect firm performance positively when compared to other forms of market entry modes, and hence your focus on alliances in this study. Any literature on market entry modes that you include that goes beyond this comparison can be argued to be less relevant, especially if there are space and time limitations. Now, as you can see, there is a judgement call going on with this decision. But the degree of relevance needs to be considered properly before the literature review that you perform becomes too broad.

Next to be considered are aspects of cross-border alliances that are instrumental in the performance of alliances. I have listed two here for illustration purposes. One is alliance partner selection (Link 6) and the other is alliance structure (Link 7). As the topic concerns market entry modes, the decision to use alliance as a mechanism is likely to be dependent on the ability to find partners, while the structure of the alliance is dependent on who the company partners with and how a particular structure might impact performance outcomes. For partner selection, there will be literature around who partners with whom and outcomes, as well as the partner selection processes (Links 8 and 9). How relevant are these in the study of 'alliances as market entry mode and their performance'? As the research topic is broad, partner selection is hardly the focus, but partner selection does influence the performance of alliances. In this case, aspects of partner selection may become a part of control variables for this study. This will mean some minimal coverage, with focus on the aspects of the literature that links to performance of alliances and variables and measurements used as control variables in other studies. For alliance structure, it will be worth including basic information on the comparison between equity and non-equity alliances (Link 10) and the variables and measurements that can be used for control.

As can be seen from this illustration, the relevance and scope of the literature review to be covered rest on a holistic assessment of the keywords and constructs used. Again, it is also dependent on the time and space allowed for this process. The process of determining what is to be included and excluded includes a fair number of judgement calls, which come with experience.

4.6 REFERENCING

Referencing is one of the nitty-gritty aspects of research. Probably for the same reason, you will sometimes encounter referencing errors, especially in projects, theses and working papers. However, proper and accurate referencing is important for crediting the authors for their contribution. It is crucial that the referencing format for any output is consistent throughout the document when producing a project, thesis, or paper.

Referencing a source involves mainly two separate steps. First, you need to indicate in the body of the text when materials are taken from a source article to ensure there is an identifier for the source. This is called a 'citation'. Then, you need to list this source in its entirety in a separate section of the work, normally called the 'References' or 'Bibliography'.

There are several methods of referencing articles in journal and book publications. In business and management, the most common ones are the **Harvard** (author–date), the American Psychological Association (APA) (author–date) and to a lesser extent the

Vancouver (numbered) referencing styles. The citation styles expected by journals and various outlets may differ, but most are likely to be a variation of one of these three key referencing formats. Whichever you use, the most important thing is to make sure that you are consistent in using the same format in a single research output.

4.6.1 Harvard referencing style

This system uses the author's name and the date of publication for the citation in the body of the text. Names and dates are enclosed in parentheses unless the author's name is part of a sentence. The references in the References section are listed alphabetically by authors' last names. It is important to note that there are multiple variations of the Harvard referencing style. Thus, the illustrations here will be broad and it is advisable that you check on the specific style required for your research output.

There are two ways to cite a reference in the text. If the author's name naturally forms part of a sentence, just include the date next to it as part of the sentence. For example:

Barney (1991) argues that a firm can create competitive advantages if it possesses resources that are valuable, rare, non-imitable and non-substitutable.

A publication with two authors is dealt with in the same way:

Ang and Wight (2009) suggest that firms need sustained performance to generate reputation.

If the citation does not form a natural part of the sentence, you need to enclose the name and year in parentheses, at an appropriate point in the sentence:

The resource-based view suggests that a firm can create competitive advantages if it possesses resources that are valuable, rare, non-imitable and non-substitutable (Barney, 1991).

Reputation is hard to build and easy to be damaged (Ang and Wight, 2009).

In the Harvard system, for a publication with more than two authors you only provide the name of the first author in the in-text citation, followed by 'et al.':

According to Teece et al. (1997), a firm's position includes its technological assets, complementary assets, financial assets and reputational assets.

You may often see 'et al.' italicized; all books and journals vary in their style for this. It is an abbreviation for the Latin 'et alia', meaning 'and others', and the full stop after 'al' must not be omitted. Whichever style you use, be consistent.

If you cite multiple papers by the same author(s), you can place a list of years in parentheses. If there is more than one cited paper in the same year, use letters in alphabetical order to differentiate the papers:

> Variation-selection theory has been used to explain and predict career trajectories, including the longitudinal location of career landmarks and the differences across the various domains of creative achievement (Simonton, 1991a, 1991b, 1997).

Multiple references can be placed in a single list, using semicolons to separate different authors. For example:

> The ability to keep up with the domain of area of research also requires time commitment (Ericsson et al., 1993; McDowell, 1982).

Note that the order of the names can be either alphabetical (as shown above), or chronological (as shown below):

> The ability to keep up with the domain of area of research also requires time commitment (McDowell, 1982; Ericsson et al., 1993).

Check on the preferred style of the research outlet. If there is no guidance, adopt either one but be consistent.

If you are citing parts of a book, it will be desirable to cite the page number(s) that you are referring to. Page numbers are placed after the date, preceded by 'p.' for 'page' or 'pp.' for 'pages', e.g. (2013, pp. 62–78), or the page numbers may simply be preceded by a colon. For example: (2002: 192–205).

> Firms that face low levels of competitive intensity are more likely to attract potential partners, many of whom are facing higher levels of competitive intensity, and thus will have more opportunities to collaborate and to secure favorable terms in these collaborative opportunities (Burt, 1992: 32–8).

A page number will also be appropriate if you quote a particular sentence from an article.

A single list of references should be given at the end of the research output. The list is ordered by name, then year. For works with more than one author, you should list all the authors' names up to a maximum of six, after which you can use et al.

The following are examples of listings for the main types of publication you are likely to be citing. Note that within the Harvard system variations in capitalization and punctuation are acceptable and you may see reference listings that look a little different from these. The important point for you to remember is that you must use your citation format consistently across your project or research output.

Article

Ahuja, G. 2000. The duality of collaboration: inducements and opportunities in the formation of interfirm linkages. *Strategic Management Journal*, 21: 317–43.

Gajraj, A.M., Faria, A.J. and Dickinson, J.R. 1990. A comparison of the effect of promised and provided lotteries, monetary and gift incentives on mail survey response rate, speed and cost. *Journal of the Market Research Society*, 32(1): 141–62.

Book

Hofstede, G. 2001. *Culture's Consequences: Comparing Values, Behaviors, Institutions, and Organizations across Nations*, 2nd edition. Thousand Oaks, CA: Sage Publishing.

Chapter in edited book

Scott, W.R. and Meyer, J.W. 1983. The organization of societal sectors. In J.W. Meyer and W.R. Scott (eds), *Organizational Environments: Ritual and Rationality.* Beverley Hills, CA: Sage Publishing. pp. 1-16.

Report

OECD (Organisation for Economic Co-operation and Development) 2005. *Trends and Recent Developments in Foreign Direct Investment.* Paris: OECD.

Website

UNCTAD. 2005. New UNCTAD Surveys: Foreign Direct Investment Prospects Promising for 2005–2008, www.un.org/News/Press/docs/2005/tad2029.doc.htm (accessed 28 March 2014).

4.6.2 APA referencing style

The **APA referencing** style is similar to the Harvard style in that it uses the author name and the date for the citation, but differs in the way it presents the details, both in the in-text citations and in the list of references. Some of the differences are as follows.

An ampersand ('&' symbol) is always used to link authors' names in the in-text citation if this does not fall within the sentence:

> Reputation is hard to build and easy to be damaged (Ang & Wight, 2009). Ang & Wight (2009) also suggest that firms need sustained performance to generate reputation.

You also link authors' names with '&' in the list of references.

In the APA system, where you cite a publication with more than two, and up to six authors, the first time you give the names of all the authors in the citation (should there be more than six you can give just the first name, followed by 'et al.') as follows:

> Teece, Pisano, and Shuen (1997) suggest that a firm's dynamic capabilities are determined by its organizational processes, positions and paths.

> It has been suggested that a firm's position includes its technological assets, complementary assets, financial assets and reputational assets (Teece, Pisano, & Shuen, 1997).

If you cite this article for a second time, you can use 'et al.':

> According to Teece et al. (1997), a firm's position includes its technological assets, complementary assets, financial assets and reputational assets.

In the references list, the date of publication is always parenthesized and is followed by a full point:

> Gajraj, A.M., Faria, A.J., & Dickinson, J.R. (1990). A comparison of the effect of promised and provided lotteries, monetary and gift incentives on mail survey response rate, speed and cost. *Journal of the Market Research Society*, 32, 141–162.

An edited work is indicated by '(Ed[s].)' in the References list, and in the APA style the page numbers of the contribution will follow the title of the work in parentheses:

> Scott, W.R., & Meyer, J.W. (1983). The organization of societal sectors. In J.W. Meyer and W.R. Scott (Eds), *Organizational Environments: Ritual and Rationality* (pp. 1–16). Beverley Hills, CA: Sage.

In the APA referencing style, the page number of the cited work in the in-text citation is always preceded by 'p.' or 'pp.', e.g. (Mundy, 2001, p. 30), not by a colon.

The APA referencing style is quite prescriptive with regard to punctuation, but comprehensive guidelines for citing many different types of publication are available online (see Additional Reading at the end of this chapter), or your university library should also be able to offer advice.

4.6.3 Vancouver referencing style

The Vancouver referencing style differs from both Harvard and APA by using a number series to indicate cited references. The reference list is based on numerical order as the citations appear in the text. The main advantage of the Vancouver style is that the main text reads more easily. For example:

> Biotech companies often create sophisticated products that take an extraordinarily long time to develop and hence the need for huge capital to fuel product development cycles.[1, 2, 3]

References are listed in numerical order of citation, as below. Note the different position of the date. Often this is a much more economical style than both Harvard and APA, and excessive punctuation, spacing and formatting are absent.

1. Gompers PA, Lerner J. *The venture capital cycle.* The MIT Press, Cambridge, MA; 2004.
2. Finkle TA. The relationships between boards of directors and initial public offerings in biotechnology. *Entrepreneurship: Theory & Practice* 1998; 22(3): 5–30.
3. Robbins-Roth C. *From alchemy to IPO – the business of biotechnology.* Perseus, Cambridge, MA; 2000.

In Vancouver style listing, journal names are sometimes abbreviated:

1. Rosenthal R, DiMatteo MR. Meta-analysis: recent developments in quantitative methods for literature reviews. *Ann Rev Psychol* 2001; 52: 59-82.
2. Stanley TD. Wheat from chaff: meta-analysis as quantitative literature review. *J Econ Perspect* 2001; 15(3): 131-50.

4.7 SOME DOS AND DON'TS OF REFERENCING

As with many aspects of research, the science of referencing also involves some elements of judgement calls. Harzing (2002) provides a technical overview of referencing challenges and offers 12 guidelines for good academic referencing. This section presents six rules of thumb relating to referencing.

4.7.1 Do not follow top journals and top authors blindly

While published articles are the main credible sources of citation, blindly agreeing to all aspects of a source article is generally not advisable. It is more important to read each article with an open mind. By open mind, we mean trusting, but critical; yet not cynical. There is a need to strike a balance between trusting a credible source and being affirmative that the content is trustable, i.e. a credible source is a good place to start, but not always a guarantee of a good article by any means.

It is understandable that citing top journals and top authors provides some degree of persuasion as to the quality of your own work. But this has to be done with some common sense. Good journals, supported by good editors and reviewers, would have filtered out the majority of unreliable information and can therefore be deemed as the best articles to cite (Donohue and Fox, 2000; Judge et al., 2007). But Starbuck (2005) also finds that prestigious journals do not necessarily publish all the best papers submitted to them.

As a researcher, you are still responsible for ensuring that you are citing good material. First, you need to make sure that you have fully understood the article you have read. Most often, it is difficult to make a judgement on the content and quality of an article without understanding the key elements in the whole text. Second, articles should be critically evaluated regardless of who the author is. While good authors tend to publish credible work and have a greater tendency to get cited (Merton, 1968), the quality of the work is the main reason for citation rather than the reputation of the authors.

4.7.2 Adhere strictly to citation of a study, especially authorship order

Whether you are a new researcher or a research student, as a new person stepping into the world of research some things like the actual citation of the articles may appear trivial to you. However, you will learn that the order of authors' names is probably one of the biggest issues that researchers discuss, from the inception of an idea right through to the acceptance of the paper for publication, and even subsequently when one reflects on the contribution of the authors. In other words, it is an issue that will not go away in a collaborative effort to publish an article. Sometimes, disagreements still exist (with respect to contribution) even after an article has been published. It also explains why some collaborative efforts do not go beyond the first article. The author-ship order is thus of great significance to the authors, and you need to cite their names in the correct order to give them proper credit and respect. Recall that Section 1.5.3 discussed the issue of authorship. It is important for us to properly cite the authors as they appear to give proper credits for their work.

4.7.3 Do not misrepresent the content of the references

In research, we want to build a strong base on which our research is grounded. We rely on the authors of published articles to provide accurate and objective information – not just in terms of what they do in their study but also the literature in which it was grounded. From an author's perspective, we will need to ensure that we do the same.

Simple as it sounds, there are at least two common ways in which the content of references can get misrepresented. The first happens when you try to lump references together. Consider the following statement:

> The study is based on transaction cost economics and resource-based arguments (Penrose, 1959; Williamson, 1975).

This statement suggests that the study is grounded in both transaction cost economics and the resource-based perspectives. Any researcher who knows these theoretical perspectives will know that Penrose (1959) provides the background to what we subsequently call the resource-based view in the 1990s. We also know that Williamson is well known for his seminal work on transaction cost economics. However, the statement as given above can confuse any new researcher. Do both Penrose and Williamson discuss transaction cost economics and the resource-based view concurrently? Are these separate discussions or done within a single piece of work?

To avoid the confusion, the proper way to present this citation would be:

> The study is based on transaction cost economics (Williamson, 1975) and resource-based (Penrose, 1959) arguments.

It is clear from this statement that Williamson (1975) introduces the transaction cost economics while Penrose (1959) discusses the resource-based view.

The second type of misrepresentation that is common is to cite references in support of your arguments even though the content of the reference does not reflect exactly what you cite it for. This is mainly due to two reasons. First, you write with an agenda in mind – you expect to prove or disprove a proposition and you need support for that. Sometimes, you cannot find an article that directly supports your viewpoint. Thus, you manoeuvre the findings of the reference article such that it can be used to fit nicely into your viewpoint. Of course, this is just short of engaging in unethical research behaviour. Second, you interpret the findings of the reference article and infer points the author does not explicitly mention. While it is possible that this inference is correct, it is also subjective as the original intention of the author may be different. Inference like this will lead to misrepresentation of the true content of the referenced article.

4.7.4 Avoid 'second-hand' citation

Partially as a result of misrepresentations like those mentioned in the section above, it is advisable not to use a **'second-hand' citation**. A 'second-hand' citation means citing Williamson (1975) for transaction cost economics when you are not aware that Williamson's book in 1975 actually put forth this perspective. The right thing to do is to go back to the source – in this case Williamson (1975) – to ensure that you are citing the right reference. As an extension to this, 'second-hand' citation means that you copy the reference list of the article that cited Williamson (1975). It is often not uncommon to find errors in a reference list as a result of administrative mistakes made by the author. Thus, for this additional reason, going back to the original source of citation is imperative.

It is important to note that you will come across articles that use 'second-hand' citation but acknowledge it, for example: 'Williamson (1975) [cited in Williamson, 1991]'. While there is nothing wrong with this, going back to the original source will still be more appropriate if you have access to the original source article. Otherwise, acknowledging this 'second-hand' citation is acceptable.

In addition, different articles (probably from different related fields) may cite a source article for different purposes. Many articles tend to have more than one contribution. The focal article may be cited for its theoretical contribution by one study but is cited for its inclusion of an important variable by another study. It is essential to get hold of an original copy of the focal article to verify that what you have read about this citation is applicable. Very often, this 'blind' citation of papers that others cite leads to misinterpretation of what the contributions of the original articles are.

4.7.5 Do not cite out-of-date references other than classics

Out-of-date references should be avoided, except for the classics in your research area. We like to associate 'new' with 'time'. In other words, anything that is more recent is regarded as more up-to-date and hence more relevant – in the sense that what happened 30 years ago is perceived to be less relevant than what happened three years ago. In many ways this is certainly the case. If knowledge accumulates, then the state of the field as we see it today is what we should seek to contribute to. Out-of-date references are a major source of rejection criterion of papers submitted for publication in good journals.

The fundamental difference between research and what we read as we acquire knowledge, for example through a magazine, is that in research we are keener to trace the path of the evolution of the field or specific research area. The creation of new theories is becoming scarce as time passes. It is likely then that you will find theoretical groundings from publications dating back to several decades ago. Seminal works like Schumpeter (1934) (in the entrepreneurship area), Williamson (1975) (transaction cost economics area), and Nelson and Winter (1982) (evolutionary economics area) to name a few are household names and must-reads if you are using these theoretical perspectives. It is important that these classics and the subsequent applications built from these seminal works are recognized to avoid a dilution of the actual meaning and assumptions attached to these theoretical perspectives.

4.7.6 Do not try to shun conflicting evidence

In the act of conducting research, you need to argue for your proposed expectations of the relationships between concepts. This would mean that you may be looking for supporting evidence that makes your proposed expectation a convincing one. This, not surprisingly, has led many researchers to believe that the literature review should include only information that supports their belief. This is not true.

There is often conflicting evidence that can come from studies taking an alternative view. Being convincing is not just about finding prior evidence and arguments that support your arguments; you also need to highlight conflicting evidence and include it in your literature review if you are to have a proper coverage of your research topic. The aim is to include all perspectives, while at the same time justifying your viewpoint by balancing these different perspectives. This requires you, at some point, to rule out alternative and counter arguments for some of the relationships you are proposing.

KEY TERMS

- APA referencing style
- Citation
- Contextualized
- Harvard referencing style
- Literature review
- Meta-analysis

- Referencing
- Research contribution
- Review articles
- Second-hand citation
- Synthesis
- Vancouver referencing style

SUMMARY

- A literature review involves corroboration of the output of studies previously conducted in the area, including trends and observations, concepts, perspectives, prior findings, and measurements and variables.
- Article search engines are the key starting point for a literature review.
- When utilizing a source article, look out for research issues and contributions, research arguments, data and samples, and findings, as these are the main areas for synthesis.
- Make sure that the literature review is a collation of the articles, not a mere summary.
- The literature coverage needs to be balanced against the expectations of the outlet, but adequacy and relevancy are essential.
- There are different referencing styles and normally these are determined by your university or publication venue.

- There are some dos and don'ts of referencing and these should be carefully borne in mind when you start referencing.

QUESTIONS

1. What is to be reported in a literature review?
2. What are the key areas to look out for when one seeks to utilize source articles?
3. What is to be collated in a literature review?
4. Briefly discuss the adequacy and relevancy of literature reviews.
5. Provide a list of three differences between the Vancouver and APA referencing styles.
6. List and discuss any five of the dos and don'ts of referencing.
7. Discuss the pitfalls of 'second-hand' citation.

ADDITIONAL READINGS

Reference styles

APA referencing style: www.apastyle.org

Harvard referencing style: see, for example, https://uk.sagepub.com/sites/default/files/sage_harvard_reference_style_0.pdf

Vancouver referencing style: see, for example, https://uk.sagepub.com/sites/default/files/sage_vancouver_reference_style_1.pdf

Bhattacharyya, S. Sekhar and Verma, S. (2019) 'The intellectual core and structure of international business strategies (IBS): a co-citation analysis', *Review of International Business and Strategy*, 29 (3): 180–206.

Calabretta, G., Durisin, B. and Ogliengo, M. (2011) 'Uncovering the intellectual structure of research in business ethics: A journey through the history, the classics, and the pillars of Journal of Business Ethics', *Journal of Business Ethics*, 104 (4): 499–524.

Combs, J.G., Crook, T.R. and Rauch, A. (2019) 'Meta-analytic research in management: Contemporary approaches, unresolved controversies, and rising standards', *Journal of Management Studies*, 56 (1): 1–18.

Cooper, H. (1998) *Synthesizing Research: A Guide for Literature Reviews*, (3rd edition). Thousand Oaks, CA: Sage Publishing.

Culnan, M.J. (1987) 'Mapping the intellectual structure of MIS, 1980–1985: A co-citation analysis', *MIS Quarterly*, 11 (3): 341–53.

Durisin, B., Calabretta, G. and Parmeggiani, V. (2010) 'The intellectual structure of product innovation research: A bibliometric study of the *Journal of Product Innovation Management*, 1984–2004', *Journal of Product Innovation Management*, 27 (3): 437–51.

Edeling, A. and Himme, A. (2018) 'When does market share matter? New empirical generalizations from a meta-analysis of the market share-performance relationship', *Journal of Marketing*, 82 (3): 1–24.

Eriksson, L.T. and Hauer, A.M. (2004) 'Mind map marketing: A creative approach in developing marketing skills', *Journal of Marketing Education*, 26 (2): 174–87.

Fernandez-Alles, M. and Ramos-Rodríguez, A. (2009) 'Intellectual structure of human resources management research: A bibliometric analysis of the *Journal Human Resource Management*, 1985–2005', *Journal of the American Society for Information Science & Technology*, 60 (1): 161–75.

García-Lillo, F., Claver-Cortés, E., Marco-Lajara, B. and Úbeda-García, M. (2017) 'Mapping the intellectual structure of research on "born global" firms and INVs: A citation/co-citation analysis', *Management International Review*, 57 (4): 631–652.

García-Lillo, F., Claver-Cortés, E., Marco-Lajara, B. and Úbeda-García, M. (2019) 'Identifying the "knowledge base" or "intellectual structure" of research on international business, 2000–2015: A citation/co-citation analysis of JIBS', *International Business Review*, 28 (4): 713–26.

García-Lillo, F., Úbeda-García M. and Marco-Lajara, B. (2017) 'The intellectual structure of human resource management research: Abibliometric study of the *International Journal of Human Resource Management*, 2000–2012', *International Journal of Human Resource Management*, 28 (13): 1786–815.

Gilbert, G.N. (1977) 'Referencing as persuasion', *Social Studies of Science*, 7: 113–22.

Grewal, D., Puccinelli, N. and Monroe, K.B. (2018) 'Meta-analysis: Integrating accumulated knowledge', *Journal of the Academy of Marketing Science*, 46 (1): 9–30.

Hoffman, D.L. and Holbrook, M.B. (1993) 'The intellectual structure of consumer research: A bibliometric study of author cocitations in the first 15 years of the *Journal of Consumer Research*', *Journal of Consumer Research*, 19 (4): 505–17.

Hult, G.T.M. (2015) 'JAMS 2010–2015: Literature themes and intellectual structure', *Journal of the Academy of Marketing Science*, 43 (6): 663–9.

Jackson, K.M. and Trochim, W.M..K. (2002) 'Concept mapping as an alternative approach for the analysis of open-ended survey responses' *Organizational Research Methods*, 5 (4): 307–36.

Ma, Z., Liang, D., Yu, K.-H. and Lee, Y. (2012) 'Most cited business ethics publications: Mapping the intellectual structure of business ethics studies in 2001–2008', *Business Ethics: A European Review*, 21 (3): 286–97.

Machi, L.A. and McEvoy, B.T. (2012) *The Literature Review: Six Steps to Success*, (2nd edition). Thousand Oaks, CA: Corwin Press.

Nerur, S.P., Rasheed, A.A. and Natarajan, V. (2008) 'The intellectual structure of the strategic management field: An author co-citation analysis', *Strategic Management Journal*, 29 (3): 319–36.

Palmatier, R., Houston, M. and Hulland, J. (2018) 'Review articles: Purpose, process, and structure', *Journal of the Academy of Marketing Science*, 46 (1): 1–5.

Pilkington, A. and Meredith, J. (2009) 'The evolution of the intellectual structure of operations management – 1980–2006: A citation/co-citation analysis', *Journal of Operations Management*, 27 (3): 185–202.

Ramos-Rodríguez, A.-R. and Ruíz-Navarro, J. (2004) 'Changes in the intellectual structure of strategic management research: A bibliometric study of the *Strategic Management Journal*, 1980–2000', *Strategic Management Journal*, 25 (10): 981–1004.

Ridley, D. (2012) *The Literature Review: A Step-by-step Guide for Students*, (2nd edition). London: Sage Publishing.

Rodríguez-Ruiz, F., Almodóvar, P. and Nguyen, Q.T. K. (2019) 'Intellectual structure of international new venture research: A bibliometric analysis and suggestions for a future research agenda', *Multinational Business Review*, 27(4): 285–316.

Rosenthal, R. and DiMatteo, M.R. (2001) 'Meta-analysis: Recent developments in quantitative methods for literature reviews', *Annual Review of Psychology*, 52: 59–82.

Snyder, H. (2019) 'Literature review as a research methodology: An overview and guidelines', *Journal of Business Research*, 104: 333–9.

Stanley, T.D. (2001) 'Wheat from chaff: Meta-analysis as quantitative literature review', *Journal of Economic Perspectives*, 15 (3): 131–50.

Torraco, R.J. (2016) 'Writing integrative literature reviews: Using the past and present to explore the future', *Human Resource Development Review*, 15 (4): 404–428.

Webster, J. and Watson, R.T. (2002) 'Analyzing the past to prepare for the future: Writing a literature review', *MIS Quarterly*, 26 (2): xiii–xxiii.

REFERENCES

Badger, D., Nursten, J., Williams, P. and Woodward, M. (2000) 'Should all literature reviews be systematic?', *Evaluation and Research in Education*, 14 (3-4): 220–30.

Donohue, J.M. and Fox, J.B. (2000) 'A multi-method evaluation of journals in the decision and management sciences by US academics'. *Omega*, 28 (1): 17–36.

Geyskens, I., Krishnan, R., Steenkamp, J.-B.E.M. and Cunha, P.V. (2009) 'A review and evaluation of meta-analysis practices in management research', *Journal of Management*, 35 (2): 393–419.

Grant, M.J. and Booth, A. (2009) 'A typology of reviews: An analysis of 14 review types and associated methodologies', *Health Information and Libraries Journal*, 26 (2): 91–108.

Harzing, A.-W. (2002) 'Are our referencing errors undermining our scholarship and credibility? The case of expatriate failure rates', *Journal of Organizational Behavior*, 23 (1): 127–48.

Judge, T.A., Cable, D.M., Colbert, A.E. and Rynes, S.L. (2007) 'What causes a management article to be cited – article, author, or journal?' *Academy of Management Journal*, 50 (3): 491–506.

Merton, R.K. (1968) 'The Matthew effect in science', *Science*, 159: 56–63.

Nelson, R.R. and Winter, S.G. (1982) *An Evolutionary Theory of Economic Change*. Cambridge, MA: Harvard University Press.

Nesbit, J.C. and Adesope, O.O. (2006) 'Learning with concept and knowledge maps: A meta-analysis', *Review of Educational Research*, 76 (3): 413–48.

Novak, J.D. and Gowin, D.B. (1984) *Learning How to Learn*. New York: Cambridge University Press.

O'Donnell, A., Dansereau, D. and Hall, R. (2002) 'Knowledge maps as scaffolds for cognitive processing', *Educational Psychology Review*, 14 (1): 71–86.

Palich, L.E., Cardinal, L.B. and Miller, C.C. (2000) 'Curvilinearity in the diversification–performance linkage: An examination over three decades of research', *Strategic Management Journal*, 21 (2): 155–74.

Penrose, E. (1959) *The Theory of the Growth of the Firm*. New York: Oxford University Press.

Post, C., Sarala, R., Gatrell, C. and Prescott, J.E. (2020) 'Advancing theory with review articles', *Journal of Management Studies* (forthcoming), doi.org/10.1111/JOMS.12549

Renfro, C. (2017) 'The use of visual tools in the academic research process: A literature review', *The Journal of Academic Librarianship*, 43 (2): 95–99.

Schumpeter, J.A. (1934) *The Theory of Economic Growth*. Boston, MA: Harvard College.

Seuring, S. and Gold, S. (2012) 'Conducting content-analysis based literature reviews in supply chain management', *Supply Chain Management: An International Journal*, 17 (5): 544–55.

Starbuck, W.H. (2005) 'How much better are the most-prestigious journals? The statistics of academic publication', *Organization Science*, 16 (2): 180–200.

Tranfield, D., Denyer, D. and Smart, P. (2003) 'Towards a methodology for developing evidence-informed management knowledge by means of systematic review', *British Journal of Management*, 14 (3): 207–222.

Verlegh, P.W.J. and Steenkamp, J.-B.E.M. (1999) 'A review and meta-analysis of country-of-origin research', *Journal of Economic Psychology*, 20 (5): 521–546.

Wheeldon, J. and Faubert, J. (2009) 'Framing experience: Concept maps, mind maps, and data collection in qualitative research', *International Journal of Qualitative Methods*, 8 (3): 68–83.

Williamson, O.E. (1975) *Markets and Hierarchies: Analysis and Antitrust Implications*. New York: The Free Press.

Williamson, O.E. (1991) 'Comparative economic organization: The analysis of discrete structural alternatives', *Administrative Science Quarterly*, 36 (2): 269–96.

5
RESEARCH DESIGN

5.1 INTRODUCTION

Upon identifying the research issue and setting up the research question, **research design** is the next important element of research. Regardless of the nature of the issue or which type of researcher you are, there will be some common issues to be addressed at this stage: Which approaches and research designs are appropriate for answering your research question? Is the research issue **time dependent**? Is it context-specific? What should the **unit of analysis** be? Will we be looking at correlational or causal forms of relationships? Will we need a large quantity of data or just a few cases? These are some of the issues considered to be part of a research design and will be covered in this chapter. They form the bedrock upon which subsequent chapters are based.

5.2 TYPES OF RESEARCH DESIGN

Chapter 1 has briefly highlighted that one form of classification of research types is the segregation into quantitative versus qualitative versus mixed methods. Likewise, we can fundamentally classify research designs as being quantitative, qualitative and mixed methods designs.

Quantitative research design usually involves large datasets. Researchers using this design seek to derive predictions and explanations, which will then be tested using various analytical and statistical methods. Thus, quantitative research design is fundamentally positivist and deductive. However, requiring a large quantity of data does not necessarily mean that quantitative research is data-driven, although data consideration is a large part of the approach.

When is the quantitative research design desirable? Quantitative research allows researchers to draw conclusions based on statistical analysis. The more common methods of conducting quantitative research are surveys, archival data collection and, to a lesser extent, experiment. As data quantity is a *sine qua non* for statistical analysis, this research design only makes sense when decently large amounts of data are available and accessible. **Quantitative research design** is also generally expected in research areas where theories are already well established and a significant amount of empirical work has been done previously, i.e. our understanding is relatively advanced. Related to this, when generalizability is an important outcome of a piece of research, then the quantitative research design is often expected to be deployed.

Qualitative research design is usually more interpretative and inductive. In qualitative research, researchers observe behaviours and seek to find explanations for these observations. As a result of the tendency to focus on social processes or the processes of engagement, qualitative research often requires extensive effort for collecting each sample. Partially as a result of the efforts and details required, the qualitative research design often involves a smaller number of observations for analysis.

When is the qualitative approach desirable? On the flip side of the quantitative research design, the qualitative research design is appropriate when a good quantity of data is not available or is inaccessible. This design is also often used when the research inquiry is more exploratory due to our limited understanding, to date, of the relationships proposed in a study. While quantitative research relies on being parsimonious, when a research study requires a lot of details to be teased out without the possibility of collecting information across many cases, a qualitative research design will be highly valuable. The more common methods of conducting qualitative research are case studies, interviews, focus groups, participant observations and experiments.

Historically, quantitative and qualitative research strategies have been viewed as distinct and competing. However, in recent years, there have been many calls for researchers to be open-minded to the use of both methods, as the strengths of one are often the weaknesses of the other (e.g. Cameron, 2011). Thus, quantitative and qualitative research strategies should be viewed as complementary rather than competing strategies. The use of both methods within a single research project or study is called mixed methods. The mixed methods can adopt several forms. The basic forms are: (1) a study uses both quantitative and qualitative methods equally; (2) a study uses predominantly qualitative methods, supplemented by quantitative methods; and (3) a study uses predominantly quantitative methods, supplemented by qualitative methods.

Associated with mixed methods is the concept of triangulation, which is defined as the use of different methods to test the same theoretical issue (Campbell and Fiske, 1959). Early emphasis on triangulation centers around the use of a second method (e.g. quantitative) to cover for the weaknesses of the first method (e.g. qualitative), hence using mixed methods can improve the rigour of a research study. It should be noted here that mixed methods is different from multimethod. When a second quantitative method (e.g. archival data) is being used to cover for the weaknesses of the first method (e.g. survey), which incidentally is also a quantitative method, then this is a study involving multimethods, not a **mixed methods research design**. A mixed methods research design must involve both qualitative and quantitative methods in the same research.

Nonetheless, it should be noted that introducing a second method will mean introducing new weaknesses associated with this method as well. This can potentially create further weaknesses even from using a mixed methods research design. Essentially, we should not be thinking of using mixed methods to reduce weaknesses alone and the thinking should be to build on the strengths of the different methods adopted in a mixed methods research design (Jick, 1979).

Turner et al. (2017) suggest using mixed methods research designs from the perspective of divergence and commonality. In divergence, we seek to offset the weakness of one method by supplementing it with a second. For example, a very detailed case study of how a firm grows from being a medium-sized firm to a large international firm may suffer from external validity issues. A survey of large international firms who have grown from medium-sized in the last two years should help cover this issue of external validity. The approach centers on providing further knowledge of what one method is capable of with the use of additional methods. The commonality element can be instrumental when there is a risk of having divergence in methods that leads to different outcomes, which in essence means triangulation has failed. Commonality, for example, can come in the form of using the same samples with different methods, such as the use of interviews and surveys with the same study subjects.

Triangulation can be difficult due to budget and time constraints, as well as accessibility issues (Jick, 1979). In addition, the purpose of triangulation has often been presented vaguely and the researcher is only expected to report any deviation obtained from introducing a second methodology. The judgement here is that if there is no deviation in rationale or results coming out from using multiple methods, it makes it unnecessary to conduct triangulation in the first place. However, if there is a deviation, it only raises doubts as to the validity of the findings from the first methodology used. Thus, significant caution and justification are needed when adopting a mixed methods research design as it is not always perceived as better than standalone quantitative or qualitative research design.

Given the challenges of using a mixed methods research design, it is not surprising to see in some fields the adoption is still limited, for example international business (Hurmerinta-Peltomäki and Nummela, 2006), environmental management (Molina-Azorin and López-Gamero, 2016) and entrepreneurship (Molina-Azorin et al., 2012). In his interviews with researchers who conduct mixed methods research, Bryman (2007) finds that these researchers express difficulties concerning how to integrate both qualitative and quantitative methods in the same study. For example, our research training tends to make us stronger in either quantitative or qualitative methods. Therefore, when we seek to do a mixed methods study, it will be clear that one part of the findings tends to be presented better than the other. In addressing this, mixed methods studies often involve more than one author, as multiple authors who possess complementary skillsets in methodology are more likely to be able to provide the coverage needed. Even the order of which method comes first or having the two running in parallel is a major decision to be made. Greene et al. (1989) provide a good in-depth discussion on how to design mixed methods studies. More recently, Molina-Azorin et al. (2017) highlight opportunities and challenges surrounding the use of mixed methods research designs. In Figure 5.1, we present some ways to which various quantitative and qualitative methods can be combined. These are by no means exhaustive.

Research Topic	First Method	Second Method
A study on how top management teams make decisions	(Quantitative) Build an online survey to distribute to a mailing list of executives and collect their responses. This can be used to tease out potential questions for the qualitative component.	(Qualitative) Interview a small group of executives who are part of top management teams in their organization, with focus on the process with which their organization makes decisions, building on some of the findings from the quantitative component.
A study on how organizations make decisions about the selection of alliance partners	(Quantitative) Use archival data sources to track alliances that have been established in the last 1-2 years. Identify any pattern regarding alliance partner attributes of a set of organizations.	(Qualitative) Select representative cases from the archival data list based on particular characteristics of the alliances. Based on the alliances formed, interview some managers who have been involved in the alliance partner selection process.
A study on the barriers to small firms growing	(Qualitative) Use a couple of case studies to tease out the factors that might be considered barriers to small firms seeking to grow.	(Quantitative) Use the list of barriers as part of an online survey sent to a wider group of small firms for generalizability.
A study on the functional appeal of a new mobile phone	(Qualitative) Conduct experiments with a focus group on the functionality of the new mobile phone.	(Quantitative) Survey customers in a shopping mall about the appeal of the identified features.

Figure 5.1   Examples of ways in which quantitative and qualitative methods can be combined

The decision to adopt a quantitative, qualitative or mixed methods design can be influenced by many factors. Buchanan and Bryman (2007) provide an extensive discussion on some of these factors, including organizational, historical, political, ethical, evidential and personal properties. For example, the need for access to organizations over time for a **longitudinal study** may impose a huge challenge in quantitative research design due to attrition in subjects or observations. The choice of design is often restricted by limited time to conduct research, such as expectation from a funding agency or a research project undertaken as part of a degree course.

In terms of the choice of research design, one should be aware of the state of the theoretical development in the area of research before making a decision (Edmondson and McManus, 2007). As a general rule of thumb, if you are researching in a field that is well understood from the theoretical perspectives, then quantitative research is more appropriate. On the other hand, if our understanding of a particular area of research is still nuanced, then qualitative research can be instrumental in providing more insights.

With the ever-increasing need for understanding business and management practices, we often have to explore new areas of inquiry. However, new phenomena are likely to involve a limited literature. For this sort of research, the best approach may be to use a **descriptive study**. Descriptive studies provide a basic understanding of the phenomenon under investigation. Some authors also call this type of study an exploratory study. The nature of such studies is to try to get more understanding of a phenomenon.

Researchers approach descriptive studies with open minds. This is mainly due to the uncertainties surrounding the issue to be investigated, as only a limited amount of literature is known. As a result of this approach, descriptive studies are often useful for helping to identify further issues to be addressed in a particular area of research. They are also very useful for identifying potential relationships between constructs for further examination. The nature of descriptive studies suggests the need to observe some patterns of behaviour. It is therefore unusual to see a descriptive study based on a single case study. Researchers often infer from descriptive studies what has been happening in an area, and then provide some further thoughts and explanations that will shed some light.

Due to its characteristics, it is often very difficult applying either quantitative or qualitative research design to a descriptive study. While the objective to identify rough patterns suggests that descriptive studies lean towards quantitative research, the limited observations involved suggest a more qualitative approach.

5.3 UNITS OF ANALYSIS

Research can be conducted on individuals, groups, companies and orgnizations, clusters of companies within an industry, industries, countries and regions. We call these categories the different units of analysis. The nature of data access and availability suggests that the designs for studies with different units of analysis will differ. For example, if we are interested in a study to collect information on goal orientation and task performance of 100 expatriates we can either (a) randomly send surveys out to a mailing list of expatriates in the hope of getting 100 respondents or (b) access three to four multinational corporations so that we get 100 expatriate respondents between them. While the two designs achieve the same goal, it is evident that the research designs are different. The first design is based on random access while the second is based on strata (sampling methods will be discussed in Chapter 6). Nevertheless, it is possible that a single research objective can be achieved through different research designs. Klein et al. (1994) provide a good discussion of some design complications around different units of analysis.

Deciding on the unit of analysis can pose some challenges. For example, let's say we are interested in group behaviour. Now, we can observe group behaviour through direct participation in group discussions to understand the dynamics of the interactions between the group members. But a lot of group activities are often collaborative, meaning that every group member is in charge of different activities. Thus, while we are interested in a group unit of analysis, we cannot raise questions to a group as an entity. Instead, we need to ask the group members questions in order to arrive at a conclusion about the general view of the group; the unit of observation is at an individual level. The group view would then be roughly the aggregate of the group members' views. In such a research scenario, if the responses from the group members align and triangulate, then it is all good. But if there are misalignments between group member responses, then we will run into aggregation issues and need to decide how to reconcile the diverse responses. This example relates to the complications in research that involve data collection at one unit of observation (individuals within groups) and analysis at another unit (groups). A good example of this is illustrated in Staw et al. (1981), where the authors discuss how individuals, groups and organizations behave (rigidly) when faced with threatening situations such as a crisis. They find that there are overlapping common responses at these levels, suggesting that some of the processes that take place in groups are shaped by individual responses and responses at the organizational level can be shaped by both group and individual responses.

Another challenge with different units of analysis occurs when behaviours are affected by attributes at multiple levels of constructs. For example, a firm's behaviour is likely to be affected by its own resources and constraints as well as environmental conditions. The firm's resources and constraints represent firm-level constructs while environmental conditions represent a higher level of construct at the industry or country level. Take yet another example: we are interested in employee perceptions of organizational culture. It is likely that these perceptions are affected by the individual department's operations and it is thus important to control for the nested effects of the department so that we find an accurate picture of employee perceptions of organizational culture. Studies that seek to contribute to one unit of analysis will almost necessarily need the inclusion of constructs at multiple levels of analysis in order to tease out the actual effects at the unit of analysis that is of interest. See for example Ang, Benischke and Doh (2015) in their study of foreign market entry mode, Ang et al. (2018) in their work on interlocked directorships and market entry mode, and Li et al. (2020) in their research on market reaction to cross-border acquisitions.

Yet another challenge relating to the unit of analysis is the fact that macro and micro domains of business and management research tend to be divided. Mathieu and Chen (2011) provide a good background for this discussion and also for the need for a multilevel paradigm that involves challenges such as unit identification, nesting assumptions, multilevel temporal issues, analysis and cross-disciplinary research. Their article is also part of a special issue on bridging of the macro and micro domains in management research (Aguinis et al., 2011).

Regardless of which situations you might run into as illustrated above, the unit of analysis is something that needs to be explicitly documented in any research study. Some studies have more than one unit of analysis, further attesting to the complexities of business and management research. Figure 5.2 provides some guidelines on which levels of constructs should be included for each unit of analysis.

Unit of analysis	Situation	Examples of constructs to account for at different levels
Individuals	Accessing individuals' perceptions of a new brand of headphone	Individual - Demographics and purchasing power - Perception of the new brand of headphone - Ownership of electronics - Experience with using headphones Individual's assessment of other levels of constructs - Industry that they work for - Knowledge of headphone industry - Knowledge of headphone pricing - Knowledge of headphone brands
Groups	Assessing working groups' views of an organization's structure	Individual - Individual's assessment of organization structure to be aggregated into group level, including background of individuals that will affect this assessment Group - Group structure - Group contribution to organization relative to other groups Organization - Characteristics including age, size, industry and various other organizational attributes that affect structure Industry - Type of industry where organization resides - Industry structure

Unit of analysis	Situation	Examples of constructs to account for at different levels
Companies and organizations	Assessing the strategy of an organization in foreign markets	**Organization** - Characteristics including age, size, industry and various other organizational attributes that affect foreign market participation **Industry (both home and foreign)** - Type of industry where organization resides - Industry structure and other industry characteristics that affect strategy **Foreign markets** - Relative foreign market conditions compared to home including market size, competition and other foreign market characteristics that affect strategy

Figure 5.2   Guidelines on levels of constructs to be considered at each unit of analysis

5.4 CORRELATION AND CAUSALITY

Conversation box

Professor: Class, last week we discussed correlation. This week we should look at regression models, which involve causality.

Lyn [Honours student]: Professor, both correlation and causality deal with the relationships between constructs. So why should we bother to conduct one analysis when we have conducted the other?

Professor: In essence, causality infers direction of relationships while correlation does not. In most circumstances, both analyses are required as they provide different insights.

Let's say we observe that a firm is performing well. We infer that it must have excelled in some areas. At the same time, we also observe that the firm has an efficient supply chain that is seamless. We conclude that the efficient supply chain is linked to the better performance observed. Now, while it is a good possibility that the better performance of the firm is in fact partially a result of the efficient supply chain, we are merely observing two phenomena happening at the same time. This is an observation of the **correlation** between supply chain and performance. While an efficient supply chain can lead to better performance, a firm that is better performing is bound to be more resourceful in making a supply chain more efficient. Thus, an observation of correlation does not always allow us to infer **causality**; that it is the supply chain that led the firm to have better performance. Some researchers have noted that in order to establish causality, correlation must exist (Cook and Campbell, 1979; Mulaik and Brett, 1982). Thus, correlation is a necessary but not sufficient condition for causality to occur.

It is not wrong to observe correlation, though it has different implications as compared to observing causality. In the example above, observing correlation does not really allow us to recommend any plan of action though we have advanced our knowledge that a firm with an efficient supply chain tends to perform better or a firm that performs better tends to have an efficient supply chain. On the other hand, if we are able to establish causality, for example a firm with an efficient supply chain will perform better than another firm with a less efficient supply chain, we can then put forth the recommendation that firms should pay adequate attention to make their supply chain efficient, which in turn will enhance their performance.

As we can see here, causality does provide a more in-depth understanding of a phenomenon under study. Causality also implies a time difference. Thus, in order to address causality, we need to take care of the time dimensions of observations. Many aspects of social science research involve a time element. As knowledge advances, we seek to know more by understanding the cause and effect of phenomena. In essence, we are interested in causality. Causality suggests sequences in event occurrence. The time sequence can be in terms of minutes, hours, days, weeks, months, quarters or years. It is imperative for you to take the appropriate time element into consideration when you design your research.

Many real-life corporate issues have embedded time elements. For example, when a company hires a new chief executive officer, when would we expect to see the effect of this new hire in terms of profit or sales performance – six months or two years? It is likely that the latter provides a more reasonable assessment. This means that when investigating an issue such as the one in this example, you will have to assess the performance of the company two years after the new chief executive officer was hired and take account of this possibility when deciding on your design. Measuring the performance at the time when the new chief executive officer was first hired does not allow you to address the above-mentioned research question, leading to erroneous conclusions. Likewise, six months might be too short to see any impact of the new hire. Introducing the appropriate time lags is essential (Mitchell and James, 2001; Ployhart and Vandenberg, 2010).

The type of study that incorporates observing behaviours over time is called a longitudinal study. Longitudinal studies involve research subjects that are observed over a period of time, therefore allowing inferences on causality and **change** behaviours. Longitudinal studies allow us to test theories and phenomena over time and gauge the stability of the relationships that we are testing. Measuring *change* is the primary variable of interest in any longitudinal study (Ployhart and Vandenberg, 2010), even though many longitudinal studies have not accounted for this appropriately (Edwards, 2008; Ployhart and Vandenberg, 2010).

Collecting longitudinal data is difficult, especially if you are conducting surveys or have a relatively large sample that does not rely on archival data. With increasing pressure to publish for academic researchers and the time pressures faced by organizational researchers, longitudinal studies experienced a drop in the 1990s compared to the 1980s (Mitchell and James, 2001). Realizing that the missing time element can be detrimental for progress within a research field, in recent years there have been many calls for the need to address temporal issues in research. Research by Glick et al. (1990) is one major study that incorporates interviews across multiple time periods into a single study as they examine changes within organizations. Their paper also highlights the challenges of having such a research design.

There are many forms of time-varying causal relationships. Thus, while it is easy to imagine the use of time within a research **context**, complexity arises as to which form of time-varying relationship you should use in your research. The following sub-sections provide illustrations of some of those you may consider when designing your research involving causality.

5.4.1 X causes Y

The most basic form of causality is when a deterministic variable (X) has an impact on a dependent variable (Y). X is the cause of Y and the outcome Y takes place in the next time period. This time period is often determined by logical inference. For example, in the example above we expect a new chief executive officer's performance to be reflected in the company's performance after a period of two years (as opposed to merely six months). Thus, Y in this case will be measured at year *t+2* period. As another example, let's say we are interested in testing if an employee's good performance for the year leads to a better salary the following year. As employers conduct performance reviews every year, we would expect that an employee who performs well in the current year may have an increment in salary in the next year.

5.4.2 X causes Y and the relationship is stable over time

In the above example that an employee's good performance for the year leads to better salary in the following year, the focus is on a time-varying relationship between employee's performance and salary. But since this relationship involves time and that salary itself is time dependent (as this is subjected to economic and business cycles), the relationship may not hold true over an extended period of time.

The second form of causality extends the first form to suggest that the X–Y relationship can be proposed to remain stable over time. For example, an employee's good performance in the current year leads to a better salary in the subsequent year. This relationship is true over the period 2008 to 2017.

This second form of causality has implications for research findings on top of the basic X–Y relationship. As mentioned above, this is very useful when either the independent or dependent variable or both are time dependent. When a variable, such as salary, is subjected to adjustments depending on economic and industry conditions, it is considered time dependent. In such cases, finding support using the second form of causality will broaden the implications of your finding – in that the relationship is more generalizable. Conversely, if you do not find support in this form of causality, there is a good chance that your finding has a more restrictive contribution.

5.4.3 X causes Y and Y changes over time

At the start of this section we pose the question of when we should assess a new chief executive officer's profit or sales performance after the hire – six months or two years. While it is likely that we will observe the performance effects two years after the new introduction rather than six months, it will be more difficult to tell the difference in the effects two years, versus three years, down the road. This is the case where the outcome variable Y actually changes over time. For example, completing a Masters degree provides different career advantages at the one-year, three-year and five-year periods. Due to various external conditions and opportunities, some executives take longer than others to reap the benefits of having a graduate degree.

With this form of causality, it is often difficult for researchers to tease out what the appropriate time lags are. The common treatment is to test the causal relationship using dependent variables measured at different time lags. Essentially, this becomes exploratory when it comes to testing when the effect of the independent variable will set in. It is important to emphasize that this form of causality test is useful when the dependent variable is subjected to cyclical movements.

5.4.4 X causes Y, but over repeated exposure to X, Y changes

In many real-life examples, experience counts towards an alteration of behaviour. For example, if you have a bad experience with the product of a particular brand, you are likely to be more cautious in purchasing other products from the same brand. Likewise, when you are hungry, the first bowl of noodles always tastes better than the second one. Such observations suggest that the relationship between X and Y may not always hold depending on the level of exposure of X. Yet another example would be that completing a Masters degree provides different career advantages; however, a second Masters degree provides fewer benefits as compared to the first one.

As illustrated above, many day-to-day occurrences are influenced by experience effects. The first encounter almost always has the strongest impact. This is proven in many management studies, that when we analyze causality relationships, linearity is not always a given. So be it individual, group or organizational behaviour, taking account of this form of causality is essential for actual reflection of a phenomenon of interest that entails experience effects.

5.4.5 X causes Y and a change in X causes a change in Y

Referring back to the basic form of causality in Section 5.4.1, we have logically linked X to Y to infer some causation between the two. To some extent, we can predict the movement in Y as a result of a movement in X. However, this has to be done across the units that are used for analysis. For example, an employee's experience (X) affects their pay (Y). The expectation is that if their experience increases, their salary will rise. But exactly how much will the rise in salary be given, say, for another six months of experience? This question cannot be addressed using the basic form of causality. If we want to imply what changes in X will cause what changes in Y, we will need to use this different form of causality that incorporates change. In essence, this form of testing allows us to offer advice as to how much salary rise will be commensurated with what amount of increase in experience, and thus provides a more accurate assessment of movements in Y in relation to movements in X.

5.4.6 X causes Y that causes a change in X which causes a change in Y

In some relationships, not only does X cause Y, Y will in turn affect a future value of X. In essence, one can argue that X and Y are correlated, as causality can go both ways. For example, Edwards (2008) suggests that using single observations of X and Y as a way to test relationships in a longitudinal study has limitations. Fundamentally, both current value of X and Y, i.e. X_1 and Y_1 respectively can affect a future value of Y, i.e. Y_2. Any reverse causation can be detected by evaluating the effect of Y_1 on X_2, bearing in mind the effect of X_1 on X_2. If reverse causation is established, then we have a scenario that is often associated with longitudinal studies, that X causes Y, that causes a change in X which in turn causes a change in Y. As an example in real terms, one way in which a company can gain reputation amongst investors is to have strong company financial performance. A good reputation in turn can lead to greater trust among customers generating greater revenue and strengthening the company's financial performance. This boost in financial performance in turns generates further reputation increases amongst investors.

5.4.7 X causes Y through M

In Chapter 3, the importance of theorizing has been emphasized. In any research, it is critical to put forth good arguments linking two constructs (X and Y). These are often labelled as the mechanisms or processes leading X eventually to Y. These arguments are often built upon theoretical perspectives or through observations. When a mechanism is observable and measurable, it can potentially become a third construct that links X to Y. This new construct is a mediator to the X–Y relationship.

Mediation exists when the effect of X on Y is carried through a third variable (M), shown in (a) of Figure 5.3 (Baron and Kenny, 1986; James and Brett, 1984; MacKinnon et al., 2002; Shrout and Bolger, 2002). The procedure to establish mediation is slightly different depending on which approach you follow. For example, Baron and Kenny (1986) and James and Brett (1984) have different overlapping criteria sets. Shrout and Bolger (2002) suggests that Baron and Kenny (1986)'s expectations that X and Y has a direct relationship should not be a requirement for mediation to happen (see (b) of Figure 5.3). Nonetheless, it is easy to imagine that Figure 5.3(b) exists in many relationships. For example, we expect competition to affect both a firm's competitive strategy and its financial performance. We also expect the firm's competitive strategy to have a direct effect on financial performance. Testing the effect of competition on financial performance just through competitive strategy may not fully reflect reality, though if one is to test the viability of the introduction of a competitive strategy this is highly appropriate.

Figure 5.3(c) shows that there is potentially more than one mechanism by which X can lead to Y. In our example above, potentially staying focused, i.e. reducing diversification, could be a response to competition that can lead to better financial performance. Therefore, M1 is competitive strategy and M2 is diversification. Figure 5.3(d) is a more complex mediation relationship as illustrated by Ljubownikow and Ang (2020). Due to the fact that X also affects the relationships M1–Y and M2–Y, this is a moderated mediation model (Hayes, 2015; Preacher et al., 2007). In our example, this means competition also has effects on both the competitive strategy-performance and diversification-performance relationships. We will discuss **moderation** in Section 5.5. Holland et al. (2017) provide a good discussion of ways of combining mediation and moderation in our analytical models.

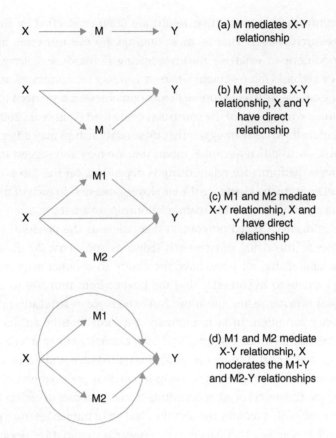

Figure 5.3   Key mediation relationships

As stated earlier, we can treat mediators as the mechanisms linking two constructs. But that does not mean there is no need for arguments linking X to M and also for M to Y. Theorizing the linkages is necessary in all circumstances. Wood et al. (2008) provide a good review of mediation practices in management and make some recommendations of what is needed for good implementation of mediation testing. In the human resource management research area, we are seeing more studies that involve the use of multiple mediators and comparing the effects of these mediators (see for example Ang, et al., 2013; Ang, et al., 2017; Boxall et al., 2011).

5.5 CONTEXT, CONTINGENCIES AND MODERATION

As we deepen our understanding of research, we start to appreciate a lot more that most of the research we do is context contingent (Johns, 2001; Rousseau and Fried, 2001).

By context contingent we mean that results are often moderated by the context in which our research resides. That is, most findings are not universal, and there are boundary conditions to what we are investigating (Edwards and Berry, 2010). This **contingency** becomes more obvious when we conduct cross-industry or cross-border research. For example, when we conduct cross-border research we need to be aware of the cross-cultural equivalence of the constructs being used (Hult et al., 2008). When we test some relationships, we also suggest that these relationships may differ, for example across industries with different capital intensities. We may also suggest that the motivation–employee performance relationship is dependent on the job position of the employee and how much experience the employee possesses. In each of these cases, we are proposing contingencies to the main relationship we are testing.

Testing contingencies based on context does allow us the precision that we need when it comes to theorizing our research (Edwards and Berry, 2010). For example, instead of assuming that all firms have the ability to conduct acquisitions, it may be more appropriate to hypothesize that the linkage from firm size to acquisition is affected by past experience in acquisition. Past experience in acquisition thus becomes the contingency condition. In fact, anormaly can sometimes be attributed to differences in organizational context (Johns, 2001). For example, Ang et al.'s (2013) paper on hospitals, Ang et al.'s (2017) paper on homes for retired men and Boxall et al.'s (2011) paper on compliance in employees working in cinemas are examples of the need to contextualize the constructs of what constitute better outcomes in each context, which affect both measures of outcomes and also the ideal set of human resource practices. On the other hand, it is argued that parsimony in research should drive research to be less context contingent (Rousseau and Fried, 2001). Contextualizing can impose constraints on what we can ultimately provide recommendations for (Johns, 1991).

Conversation box

Isaac [PhD student]:   Would contingencies not make our findings all look tentative? It's as if we are saying 'it depends' all the time.

Professor: Isaac, yes, it seems that way as you phrase it. But we also know that the business and management research areas involve complex interactions between humans and their environments. In other words, it's safe to say that lots of contingencies are to be expected. Moreover, as our understanding of a research area deepens, we will need to learn more by diving into greater details. Testing boundary conditions can become instrumental at this stage.

Recognizing and testing contingencies have become increasingly popular in business and management research. For example, technology is widely recognized as a major contingency factor in determining firm structure and behaviour (e.g. Lawrence and Lorsch, 1967; Perrow, 1967). The contingency approach is recognized as one of the three major approaches in the strategic human resource management area (e.g. Youndt et al., 1996).

In empirical research, we see more and more work done on contingency-type frameworks. We see more testing of interaction and moderating effects of constructs, indicating that a relationship between two constructs depends on a third construct. As indicated in the above conversation box, this is common considering we are trying to go deeper into understanding the research area that we specialize in. Complex relationships need to be as well represented as possible. Gardner et al. (2017) reviews the tests of moderation effects in management and applied psychology studies and concludes that there are mainly three primary moderating effects, namely strengthening, weakening and reversing. They then provide various recommendations about conducting moderation tests. In the business and management area, researchers have also been testing multiple moderation effects simultaneously in recent times (see Ang, 2008; Haans et al., 2016).

5.6 FACTORS TO INFORM RESEARCH DESIGN DECISIONS

5.6.1 Data and sampling

Conversation box

Brianna [Masters student]:   Professor, I would like to conduct my research in the area of cheating in classrooms. The target group involves mainly undergraduate students. Do you think the topic is feasible?

Professor: Sounds like an interesting topic, Brianna. The only challenge for this one will be to have good access to respondents, as this topic is a highly sensitive one.

Access to the entities to be observed is a major influence on the choice of using quantitative or qualitative research design as explained in Section 5.2. In almost all business and management research, the unit of analysis is either individuals, groups of individuals, firms, groups of firms, industries, nations, or regions as discussed in Section 5.3. For our purpose here, it is important to know who or what needs to be accessed in order for you to conduct your research. This decision is related to the decision regarding **research strategy**, as difficulties in accessing these entities will force you to engage in a research strategy manageable within this limitation. This is often one of the major constraints in research.

As the above conversation box shows, access can also be an issue when you have a topic that is challenging to the potential participants. Sensitive topics such as cheating in classrooms will not entice a lot of participants. Potentially the project might not be able to proceed. For the same reason, it is likely that the literature in research areas like this will be thin, as briefly highlighted in Chapter 3.

If you have limited access to your research subjects, whether individuals or organizations, try to talk to people who have greater access. These can be your personal networks, professors or other professional contacts. When you do that, be conscious of data representation which will be discussed in Chapter 6. Researchers also sometimes collaborate in order to reduce the constraints of limited access. Data collection efforts per individual are reduced when more researchers are involved in a research project. In some cases, a collaboration happens as a researcher seeks access to another researcher's privileged knowledge and access to entities. This often happens when observations are needed across country borders. Research that involves data collection across multiple time periods increases the complexity of access. It should be noted that some of the ways to counter constraints, as mentioned here, do not apply to research projects that are tied to the award of study degree, due to the need for such projects to be declared as a researcher's own efforts alone.

5.6.2 Variables and measurements

The use of variables and measurements is yet another deliberation that almost has to be done in conjunction with the decisions about the research strategy and the unit of analysis. Very often in social sciences we run into phenomena that cannot be directly observed. For example, a firm's capabilities are almost not observable and thus we normally use proxies in place to allow us to estimate the firm's capabilities. Researchers have over time started to take up the challenge of finding new ways to measure difficult-to-observe variables. Nevertheless, it is important for a researcher to know all the variables and measurements used in their area of study. This is part and parcel of becoming an expert in the area.

In most areas of research there are established measurements for variables. However, sometimes you may run into situations where existing measurements are inadequate (Chapter 6 provides a more comprehensive discussion on this). In this case, a new measurement is needed, and in introducing a new variable you will need to justify why existing measurements will not cover your requirements well. In other words, what is the value of your newly proposed measurement? Even when using an existing measurement for an existing variable, you will need to explain your choice of this particular measurement as opposed to other existing measurements (most variables in business and management research have more than one existing way of measuring them). Hence, as you can see, deciding on variables and measurements is all about justification and explanation of the research decisions. This is part of the research process.

Conversation box

John, a new research student, is looking at conducting a quantitative study on how compensation systems affect firm performance. After going through a literature search, he has identified variables that are of significance to firm performance. Yet, he is confused as to how he would know which ones are important.

John: Professor, I have found that in order to single out the effects of compensation systems I need to control for other effects on firm performance.

Professor: Yes, you definitely need to include these other potential determinants. Otherwise, you cannot ensure that the impact you observe actually comes from the compensation systems.

John: But there are so many variables – environmental, industry and organizational – that affect firm performance. Which ones should I include? How many do I need?

Professor: John, there is no specific number of variables to be considered. You will have to make sure enough factors are included that represent all levels. For example, industry should matter to compensation and firm performance. So, you need factors at that level. You also need firm level attributes such as firm size, age and public listed or not, to name a few of these factors.

Two issues arise from this conversation. First, how does a researcher decide which variables to include in a study? Other than the key variables, very often we have to include some variables that have an effect on the outcome variable in our analysis in order to control for these effects and single out the effect of the key variables. However, a search of the literature will reveal many such potential other variables that could be included. The response to this is that we will have to include enough variables to allow us to single out the impact of the key variables. In order to do that, we will have to balance the marginal contribution of these potential variables and include only those that have substantive effects on the outcome variable.

Second, research students always like to ask for a number – the number of variables to include for analysis. They need this number to help with their decision as to whether to include certain variables or others. Unfortunately, this is again a judgement call. There is no fixed number of other variables you should include in your study. However, if your sample size is large enough, include as many variables that have an effect. If your sample size is small, for example less than 100, then it is advisable to let your sample size determine the number of variables to include for analysis. This is to allow for degrees of freedom, which will be discussed when we touch on research analytical methods. But for instruments like surveys, it is almost impossible to state a priori what the sample size of your study will be. That is, the response rate is not known beforehand. In such cases, the final number of variables to be included can be determined only after the data are collected. Hence, at the start of your research, you will just have to include all viable variables before narrowing down further depending on the outcomes from the data collection process. Nonetheless, it is always good to bear in mind about the need to be parsimonious yet representative in deciding on the type and number of variables to be included.

5.6.3 Current methodologies

One of the most important elements in conducting any research is a strong grasp of the literature in the research area. The procedures to do that have been laid out in both Chapters 3 and 4. Recall that an extensive literature review also includes the data and empirical aspects of the studies you have encountered. It is this aspect of the literature review that requires special mention in this chapter on research design. That is, in order to zoom into your own research design, you will need to have a good awareness of existing methodologies used in the research area.

To know what best practices of research design exist in your research area, you need to go through the designs of the studies covered in your literature review carefully. You may wish to look at the pros and cons of the research designs used by these prior studies and choose to follow one of the better designs. But you may also want to modify existing designs to bring out the best components of the designs that have been used. On top of this, you may wish to update yourself on other methodological issues relating to your area using articles from research-focused journals presented in Chapter 3.

Conversation box

Jean [Honours student]:	Professor, one of my classmates told me that because we have such good access to data these days, especially via the Internet, quantitative studies are easier to perform. Is this true?
Professor:	This is a misperception, Jean. Yes, data access is becoming easier. But most data that are available are raw and need some work before they can be used for our own research. Another issue to think about is that if data become plentiful, this makes original contributions even harder as information is all out there. This can potentially mean that the expectations of quantitative studies may rise as well.
Jean:	Does that mean qualitative studies could be easier?
Professor:	Probably not. The expectations of the level of richness from qualitative studies are high, making them challenging as well.

In studying the use of research designs adopted in management studies in the top management journals between the periods 1985–7 and 1995–7, Scandura and Williams (2000) find that there was a significant increase in the use of secondary field studies as compared to primary field studies over the two periods. Secondary field studies include mainly archival data, which comes from data previously collected from questionnaires or purely consolidated data from other sources. The increased use of secondary data also reflects the fact that as a field evolves, researchers have accumulated datasets over time allowing increased access to larger datasets. But it is important to note that most publicly available databases do not usually contain the data in the form that we need for our measurement purposes. As such, a lot of data preparation and recoding is often necessary to tailor the data observations to our own needs.

5.6.4 Key directions for future research

It is not surprising to find that sometimes our understanding of a particular field is marred by our application of research design. For example, it is often easier and less time-consuming to collect data at a single point in time. This increases the likelihood that researchers will go for a cross-sectional study rather than spending more time and effort, which comes with risks and demands patience, on performing data collection over multiple periods of time for a longitudinal study.

But clearly, in many areas of research in business and management, we require longitudinal data to validate some predictions. An obvious example is when one needs to observe the outcome of a particular behaviour or policy in place. Let's say Company A implements a pay-for-performance compensation policy for the first time. It would probably be impossible to observe the outcome of this implementation immediately. The best we can do is to observe the outcome, for example employee productivity in the next period of time. This necessitates the need for longitudinal data collected over a period of time. Using data from a single point of time can only allow us to observe the contemporaneous relationship between employee productivity and a pay-for-performance policy. Data collected over a period of time will inform us on how a firm is doing after implementing the new policy, which is probably more insightful. Future research directions will induce the advancement of research designs and methodologies to be used in order to provide more and deeper understanding in those areas. These are important issues to attend to whenever you choose a research design.

5.7 WRITING GOOD HYPOTHESES

Hypotheses are statements derived from an existing body of theory that can be tested using the methods within the field. **Hypothesis** testing establishes the significance of a research finding. The standard research statement of a research objective includes both a null hypothesis and an alternative hypothesis. The null hypothesis almost always predicts that a relationship between the constructs to be tested does not exist. The alternative hypothesis, on the other hand, predicts that a relationship exists between the constructs. This prediction can be positive, negative or bi-directional. It can also adopt other forms, such as curvilinear or staggered. In essence, hypotheses guide the direction of a study.

A good hypothesis must possess three elements. First, it must be adequate for its purpose. The hypothesis must clearly state the constructs (variables) to be tested and their relationships. Second, it must be testable. A testable hypothesis is one that has stated the relationships between the constructs. It is one in which a researcher can reject or accept the null hypothesis with the help of statistical tests. Third, it must require few conditions or assumptions. It is very unusual to have hypotheses that are generic, i.e. that apply to all contexts, for example, across industries and across countries. However, when a hypothesis is based on too many assumptions or conditions, it is not well formulated, leading to questionable results.

Below I provide a few examples of hypothesis statements and suggest some ways in which the forumulation of these statements can be improved.

5.7.1 Hypothesis: good strategy leads to better firm performance

There are two constructs in this hypothesis – good strategy and firm performance. The term 'leads to' suggests a causal link from good strategy to firm performance. This would look like a straightforward and good hypothesis. But let us take a closer look. How does one measure good strategy? Any researcher familiar with firm-level research would know that a good strategy is one that improves a firm's performance! Now, does this hypothesis make any sense if firm performance is the way to tell whether a strategy is good? If a firm's performance is good, then there is a possibility that it has employed good strategy. Thus, the hypothesis statement forms a loop and in effect is not testable. We call this form of hypothesis tautological.

5.7.2 Hypothesis: a pay-for-performance policy leads to (i) more employee motivation and (ii) less employee turnover

There are three constructs in this hypothesis, namely pay-for-performance policy, employee motivation and employee turnover. The term 'leads to' suggests a causal relationship between a pay-for-performance policy and employee motivation, and between a pay-for-performance policy and employee turnover. Now, we see that there are two relationships involved in this hypothesis. First, pay-for-performance policy has a positive impact on employee motivation. Second, it also has a negative effect on employee turnover.

Four outcome scenarios are possible in any empirical test conducted on these relationships: (a) a pay-for-performance policy has a positive effect on both employee motivation and employee turnover; (b) a pay-for-performance policy has a positive effect on employee motivation but a negative effect on employee turnover; (c) a pay-for-performance-policy has a negative effect on both employee motivation and employee turnover; and (d) a pay-for-performance policy has a negative effect on employee motivation but a positive effect on employee turnover.

Note that these scenarios are mutually exclusive. We know that the result in (b) will mean that our hypothesis is supported and that in (d) will mean our hypothesis is not supported. But how do we interpret results in (a) and (c)? In these cases, the hypothesis is partially supported. We neither reject nor accept the hypothesis. We call this complication double-barreled. Double-barreled hypotheses often occur when we try to test two different relationships in one hypothesis. In this example, the single hypothesis should be split into two separate hypotheses to avoid this problem.

5.7.3 Comparing two hypotheses on the effect of a firm's foreign investments on its performance

It is important to note that different ways of formulating a hypothesis imply different methodologies for testing the hypothesis. Let's look at this example of testing the effect of a firm's foreign investments on its performance.

Formulation A: The greater the level of foreign investments, the better the firm performance.

Formulation B: Firms with more foreign investments are likely to perform better.

While the two formulations look similar and have the same objective of testing the effect of a firm's foreign investments on its performance, they are very different in meaning when it comes to testing them. Your choice will depend a lot on what you seek to achieve in your study.

In Formulation A, the phrasing suggests that the measurements are continuous. In testing the hypothesis, we will be able to draw conclusions on whether firms with a greater level of foreign investment perform better or firms with a smaller level of investment perform worse. Notice that level of investment can mean different things: it may mean the dollar amount of foreign investment or it may mean the number of foreign investments.

In Formulation B, the word 'likely' rather than to 'lead' or 'affect' or other similar words is used. The use of the word 'likely' suggests a likelihood component, meaning there are categories we compare against, i.e. less likely or not likely. The specific test to be used for testing this hypothesis would be to divide the firms into groups with varying levels of investment. Then we compare the average performance of each group. This can either be done by using a t-test across groups or by creating dummy variables to represent the groups for regression models. The details of such tests are covered in Chapters 8 and 10.

As shown in the example above, the writing of hypotheses is critical to avoid misleading readers. But there is increasing concern that researchers are slowly ignoring the specificities of phrasing hypotheses. Moreover, you will probably find little coverage in any research textbooks trying to educate researchers on hypothesis writing. Researchers tend to learn from reading hypotheses in good journal articles. Clearly, this is an area that deserves significant attention in research education to ensure that proper research protocols are not lost or neglected.

5.8 RESEARCH DESIGNS: TWO ILLUSTRATIONS

This section will provide a couple of illustrations on crafting research designs. In going through these examples, we will apply some lessons we have learned earlier.

5.8.1 Illustration 1: Top management team and firm performance

Scenario

In trying to review the company's hiring process, your company chief executive officer (CEO) wishes to understand how top management managerial skills affect firm performance and asks you to prepare a research report. Managerial skills are defined as a set of integrated complementary skills possessed by the top management team. Your CEO is expecting an outcome that informs them of how to go about future hiring in the top management team. In order to do that, you will have to find out what managerial skills are essential for good firm performance. Below are some proposed approaches.

Approach 1

Interview top management executives of your company and ask them for a list of desirable managerial skills that contribute to better firm performance. Have a consolidated list of desirable managerial skills. Validate these by asking lower level employees about desirable managerial skills.

Approach 2

Interview top management executives in both your company and a few other companies in the same industry and ask for a list of desirable managerial skills.

(Continued)

Link these with the performance of the companies to ascertain if the list of managerial skills is connected to superior firm performance.

Approach 3

Conduct an extensive literature search and find out what top management managerial skills have been found to be essential for better firm performance.

Approach 4

Conduct an extensive literature search and find out what top management managerial skills have been found to be essential for better firm performance. Using this list, assess the level of top management managerial skills within your company and highlight what is present and what is missing to the CEO.

Approach 5

Conduct an extensive literature search and find out what top management managerial skills have been found to be essential for better firm performance. Using this list, assess the top management managerial skills and performance of companies within your industry to find out if the list of managerial skills is connected to superior firm performance.

The list of approaches above is not exhaustive, but it covers a range of approaches that research students will likely think of when being asked to work on this top management team managerial skills research topic.

Assessment of the approaches

Approach 1

This approach is probably the easiest in that you can access the information needed within a short time and in a convenient way. However, there is potential bias from your company's top management executives' responses. It is very likely that they will give you a list that reflects on who they are, not because they want to portray themselves as good managers, but because that is the easiest point of reference for them. While validating these attributes by asking lower level employees' opinions is a good way to ensure the potential bias in the executives' responses is mitigated, they are likely going to provide responses concerning attributes that they have (good) experiences with. One element missing in this design is that your list of desirable managerial skills is determined to a large extent by the managers' knowledge of what constitute good skills and thus may not reflect the actual list of good practices, of which some are only observable in other organizations. This might be addressed with the help of a literature review to plug the gaps. The other, probably more important element that is missing here is that there is no validation of whether these managerial attributes actually lead to better firm performance. Asking the executives themselves on the assessment of firm performance will create biased responses. Thus, this design does not fully address the research question.

Approach 2

This approach includes more than one company in your study in trying to examine the issue. In this way there is more external validation of desirable managerial skills in this case than in Approach 1. However, again, this approach suffers from the same problem, in the inadequacy of coverage of desirable managerial skills. In addition, comparing the companies might be problematic if the number of companies is too small, since the **level of analysis** is at the firm level. For example, it will be hard to conclude whether a top management team's international experience is instrumental to better firm performance if two of the three firms have top management teams with international experience while the third does not. Thus, the number of companies and representation must be adequate so that differences in managerial skills and firm performance can be observed.

Approach 3

Conducting an extensive literature search and finding out what constitutes top management managerial skills represents a very solid start to identifying good managerial skills. However, this literature review process alone will not be adequate. It is likely that previous findings in this area are derived from different sets of data. If you are working at a New Zealand company, the question is whether previous findings from the United States or Germany are applicable in your context. In addition, these findings are likely to be derived from different study periods. The important question here is whether desirable managerial skills change over time in the corporate world and in some industries as they evolve. These scenarios are likely. Moreover, there is always a good chance that some managerial skills have been found to be beneficial in some studies but not in others, as well as beneficial to some particular industries and companies but not others. Managerial skills can also be country-specific depending on the local cultural and business practices. If this research issue has not been examined in your industry or country previously, questions arise as to how you would be able to figure out which aspects of the literature are applicable to your context. These questions certainly raise validity issues with merely using a background literature search.

Approach 4

This approach is an extension of Approach 3. After generating the list from the extensive literature search, you use this list to assess the top management team of your company. You will then be able to present the attributes that are missing and those that are present to the CEO. However, this approach suffers from not being able to tell if these attributes that you have identified as present are instrumental to your company performance or those that are missing are detrimental to the organization. In essence, this approach allows you a good internal view of what the current set of managerial skills that have been known to be useful out there are. Yet, little can be said about whether these skills would benefit your company.

Approach 5

This approach is an extension of Approaches 3 and 4. Upon generating the list of desirable managerial skills from the extensive literature search, you use this list to assess multiple companies within your industry. As with Approach 2, accessing multiple companies provides greater external validity. The number of companies analyzed needs to be adequate for empirical comparisons. As company performance is relative, it is essential that the companies assessed all come from the same industry. This may then allow you to connect differences in managerial skills with firm performance.

A broader approach

Here it is important to highlight that while the last approach above seems to be the most rigorous of all the five approaches and perhaps the closest to addressing what your CEO seeks, there is a potential bias in that investigation. Recall that the approach is to rely on a literature search to find out what top management managerial skills have been found to be essential for better firm performance. This starting point suggests that the list generated is restricted to skills that have been suggested in previous literature. While there is reason to believe that the literature would likely have enough coverage to produce a comprehensive set of desirable managerial skills, this is still based on the assumption that these skills will be applicable in your context and that there are no omitted essential managerial skills (especially those hard-to-measure ones) and all context-specific skills (i.e. specific to your company) are already incorporated in this set of managerial skills. If this is not the case, then you need to consider incorporating expert opinions to ensure that the generated list from the literature is complete. If the list turns out to be incomplete, then a wider net should be cast as to what should be the final set of managerial skills to be used. This more comprehensive set of managerial skills can then be linked to relative firm performance to address the research question. Further, as the research involves firm performance, it is essential that multiple companies should be investigated to allow comparisons to be made. Otherwise, a longitudinal study of a single company's performance over time may also work.

5.8.2 Illustration 2: Alliances and firm performance

Scenario

Your company CEO wishes to consider cross-border acquisitions as a strategy for the company's continual growth and asks you to conduct a study on the feasibility. The CEO is expecting an outcome that informs him of whether cross-border acquisitions are viable options as vehicles of growth for the company. Below are some proposed approaches.

Approach 1

Interview top management executives of your company and ask their opinions on the possibilities of cross-border acquisitions for growth. Get the top management to rate these cross-border acquisitions in terms of priorities and potential returns.

Approach 2

Consider the cross-border acquisitions that other growing companies in your industry have conducted. Evaluate your company's options based on what you observed.

Approach 3

Conduct an extensive literature search and find out what types of cross-border acquisitions lead to growth. Derive your company's opportunities based on the characteristics of companies and cross-border acquisitions you have found.

Approach 4

Identify companies within your industry that have used cross-border acquisitions. Conduct an analysis of how they have performed (in terms of growth) from the acquisitions. Match your company's strengths and weaknesses with the profiles of the companies you have identified to arrive at your recommendations.

As with the previous example, the list of approaches above is not exhaustive. But it covers a range of approaches that research students will think of when being asked to look into the feasibility of using cross-border acquisitions for firm growth.

Assessment of the approaches

Approach 1

This approach is largely based on your top management's view. An approach like this will normally provide insufficient due diligence. Your top executives' opinions of the possibilities are limited to the time they have to spend on their own scanning processes. Some of them may not have had time to look in detail at such possibilities. Others will have a biased view of how cross-border acquisitions could work for the organization. There is a good possibility that you will get very limited answers from them, restricting your recommendations. Moreover, this outcome may be a wish-list of acquisitions as each executive may wish to use this exercise to draw the attention of the CEO to their ideas.

Approach 2

This approach is based on what you observe of your competitors. This goes beyond Approach 1, which is largely intra-organizational. However, there are some limitations in this approach as well. For example, the position of your organization relative to the competitors you are observing may be different. In that case, what you observe may not be exactly applicable to your company. Let's say your observed competitor has greater financial resources than your company. Your competitor is likely to have more potential acquisition targets and be more able to acquire them than your company. There is also an assumption that what your competitor is doing is right. Thus, using your competitor's acquisitions as a gauge may not provide the basis for recommendations to your CEO.

Approach 3

The literature search should provide a more extensive list of options for you to consider for recommendations than using Approaches 1 and 2. Here, a comparison is made between your company and those that are represented in the literature. Again, this comparison is easier if there are some organizations that are similar to yours. Challenges will occur if none of the organizations in the literature come from the same country or industry. Otherwise, a comparison of similar characteristics and adapting accordingly might do the trick, as long as it is clear that other factors that might affect opportunities are considered, so that we know these similar characteristics are the right attributes to compare.

Approach 4

This approach has the advantage of data being collected from the same context, thereby making it easier for comparison. It is important to make sure that the determinants of the success of cross-border acquisitions are carefully worked out and verified. Otherwise, while we can connect cross-border acquisitions to firm growth, it will remain unclear as to how this is achieved by competitors. This step is also critical to allow us to use these determinants as the comparisons of strengths and weaknesses between company profiles. The other issue with this approach is whether the opportunities that your competitors have exploited are time dependent. If this is so, then the same opportunities may not be available to your company at the current time. Finally, even if these opportunities may still exist, questions should be asked if the same advantages that particular types of cross-border acquisitions have provided for the competitors will be evident in the acquisition opportunities that may present themselves to your company at this point.

KEY TERMS

- Causality
- Change
- Context
- Contingency
- Correlation
- Descriptive study
- Hypothesis
- Level of analysis
- Longitudinal study

- Mediation
- Mixed methods research design
- Moderation
- Qualitative research design
- Quantitative research design
- Research design
- Research strategy
- Time dependent
- Unit of analysis

SUMMARY

- Quantitative, qualitative and mixed methods are the key types of research designs.
- Descriptive studies can be viewed as the middle ground between quantitative and qualitative research.
- The unit of analysis in any study needs to be explicitly documented, and factors at all levels need to be considered in the analysis.
- There are significant differences in what can be implied by correlation analysis as opposed to causality analysis.
- It is important to recognize the time element in research, to model your frameworks based on the relationships and to incorporate time lags.
- Testing context contingencies advances knowledge by setting boundary conditions as to which proposed relationships will hold.
- Business and management research is increasingly adopting mediation and moderation in its hypotheses testing.
- Factors that inform research design decisions include data and sampling, variables and measurements, current methodologies, and key directions for future research.

- A good hypothesis must be adequate for its purposes, must be testable, and must require few conditions or assumptions.

QUESTIONS

1. Under what circumstances would you not use a mixed methods research design and choose instead either a quantitative or qualitative research design?
2. If the unit of analysis of your study is team dynamics, what are the kinds of factors that you will consider in your analysis?
3. What are the differences between correlation and causality?
4. Describe two forms of relationships that may involve a time element in the model and illustrate with examples.
5. What are context contingencies and what value do they provide?
6. Illustrate with examples a research design which uses mediation and moderation simultaneously.
7. Why is it important to consider current methodologies when making research design decisions?

ADDITIONAL READINGS

Abbott, A. (2004) *Methods of Discovery: Heuristics for the Social Sciences*. New York, NY: W.W. Norton & Co.

Bergh, D.D. (1993) 'Watch the time carefully: The use and misuse of time effects in management research'. *Journal of Management*, 19 (3): 683–705.

Blair, J.D. and Hunt, J.G. (1986) 'Getting inside the head of the management researcher one more time: Context-free and context-specific orientations in research', *Journal of Management*, 12 (2): 147–66.

Bliese, P.D., Chan, D. and Ployhart, R.E. (2017) 'Multilevel methods: Future directions in measurement, longitudinal analyses, and nonnormal outcomes', *Organizational Research Methods*, 10 (4): 551–63.

Calder, B.J., Phillips, L.W. and Tybout, A.M. (1981) 'Designing research for application', *Journal of Consumer Research*, 8 (2): 197–207.

Colquitt, J.A. and Zapata-Phelan, C.P. (2007) 'Trends in theory building and theory testing: A five-decade study of the *Academy of Management Journal*', *Academy of Management Journal*, 50 (6): 1281–303.

Creswell, J.W. and Plano Clark, V.L. (2011) *Designing and Conducting Mixed Methods Research*. Thousand Oaks, CA: Sage Publishing.

George, J.M. and Jones, G.R. (2000) 'The role of time in theory and theory building', *Journal of Management*, 26(4): 657–84.

Grunow, D. (1995) 'The research design in organization studies: Problems and prospects', *Organization Science*, 6 (1): 93–103.

Hitt, M.A., Gimeno, J. and Hoskisson, R.E. (1998) 'Current and future research methods in strategic management', *Organizational Research Methods*, 1 (1): 6–44.

James, L.R. (2008) 'On the path to mediation', *Organizational Research Methods*, 11 (2): 359–63.

Johnson, R.B. and Onwuegbuzie, A.J. (2004) 'Mixed methods research: A research paradigm whose time has come', *Educational Researcher*, 33 (7): 14–26.

Kelly, J.R. and McGrath, J.E. (1988) *On Time and Methods*. Thousand Oaks, CA: Sage Publishing.

Klein, K.J., Dansereau, F. and Hall, R.J. (1994) 'Levels issues in theory development, data collection, and analysis', *Academy of Management Review*, 19 (2): 195–229.

Maxwell, S.E. and Cole, D.A. (2007) 'Bias in cross-sectional analyses of longitudinal mediation', *Psychological Methods*, 12(1): 23–44.

Medsker, G.J., Williams, L.J. and Holahan, P.J. (1994) 'A review of current practices for evaluating causal models in organizational behavior and human resources management research', *Journal of Management*, 20(2): 439–64.

Morse, J.M., Niehaus, L., Wolfe, R.R. and Wilkins, S. (2006) 'The role of the theoretical drive in maintaining validity in mixed-method research', *Qualitative Research in Psychology*, 3(4): 279–91.

Mosakowski, E. and Earley, P.C. (2000) 'A selective review of time assumptions in strategy research', *Academy of Management Review*, 25 (4): 796–812.

Short, J.C., Ketchen, D.J. Jr., Combs, J.G. and Ireland, R.D. (2010) 'Research methods in entrepreneurship: Opportunities and challenges', *Organizational Research Methods*, 13 (1): 6–15.

Stone-Romero, E.F. and Rosopa, P.J. (2010) 'Research design options for testing mediation models and their implications for facets of validity', *Journal of Managerial Psychology*, 25 (7): 697–712.

Vancouver, J.B. and Carlson, B.W. (2015) 'All things in moderation, including tests of mediation (at least some of the time)', *Organizational Research Methods*, 18 (1): 70–91.

REFERENCES

Aguinis, H., Boyd, B.K., Pierce, C.A. and Short, J.C. (2011) 'Walking new avenues in management research methods and theories: Bridging micro and macro domains', *Journal of Management*, 37 (2): 395–403.

Ang, S.H. (2008) 'The impact of firm competitive intensity and collaboration on firm growth in different technological environments', *Strategic Management Journal*, 29 (10): 1057–75.

Ang, S.H., Bartram, T., McNeil, N., Leggat, S.G. and Stanton, P. (2013) 'The effects of high-performance work systems on hospital employees' work attitudes and intention to leave: A multi-level and occupational group analysis', *International Journal of Human Resource Management*, 24 (16): 3086–114.

Ang, S.H., Benischke, M.H. and Doh, J.P. (2015) 'The interactions of institutions on foreign market entry mode, *Strategic Management Journal*, 36 (10): 1536–53.

Ang, S.H., Benischke, M.H. and Hooi, A. W.-L. (2018) 'Frequency of international expansion through high control market expansion modes and interlocked directorships', *Journal of World Business*, 53 (4): 493–503.

Ang, S.H., Cavanagh, J., Southcombe, A., Bartram, T., Marjoribanks, T. and McNeil, N. (2017) 'Human resource management, social connectedness and health and well-being of older and retired men: The role of Men's Sheds', *International Journal of Human Resource Management*, 28 (14): 1986–2016.

Baron, R.M. and Kenny, D.A. (1986) 'The moderator-mediator variable distinction in social psychological research: Conceptual, strategic, and statistical considerations', *Journal of Personality and Social Psychology*, 51 (6): 1173–82.

Boxall, P., Ang, S.H. and Bartram, T. (2011) 'Analysing the "black box" of HRM: Uncovering HR goals, mediators and outcomes in a standardized service environment', *Journal of Management Studies*, 48 (7): 1504–32.

Bryman, A. (2007) 'Barriers to integrating quantitative and qualitative research', *Journal of Mixed Methods Research*, 1 (1): 8–22.

Buchanan, D.A. and Bryman, A. (2007) 'Contextualizing methods choice in organizational research', *Organizational Research Methods*, 10 (3): 483–501.

Cameron, R. (2011) 'Mixed methods in business and management: A call to the "first genera-tion"', *Journal of Management and Organization*, 17 (2): 245–67.

Campbell, T. and Fiske, D.W. (1959) 'Convergent and discriminant validation by the multitrait–multimethod matrix', *Psychological Bulletin*, 56 (2): 81–105.

Cook, T.D. and Campbell, D.T. (1979) *Quasi-Experimentation: Design and Analysis Issues for Field Settings*. Boston, MA: Houghton Mifflin.

Edmondson, A.C. and McManus, S.E. (2007) 'Methodological fit in management field research', *Academy of Management Review*, 32 (4): 1155–79.

Edwards, J.R. (2008) 'To prosper, organizational psychology should ... overcome methodo-logical barriers to progress', *Journal of Organizational Behavior*, 29 (4): 469–91.

Edwards, J.R. and Berry, J.W. (2010) 'The presence of something or the absence of noth-ing: Increasing theoretical precision in management research', *Organizational Research Methods*, 13 (4): 668–89.

Gardner, R.G., Harris, T. B., Li, N., Kirkman, B.L. and Mathieu, J.E. (2017) 'Understanding "it depends" in organizational research: A theory-based taxonomy, review, and future research agenda concerning interactive and quadratic relationships', *Organizational Research Methods*, 20 (4): 610–38.

Glick, W.H., Huber, G., P., Miller, C.C., Doty, D.H. and Sutcliffe, K.M. (1990) 'Studying changes in organizational design and effectiveness: Retrospective event histories and periodic assessments', *Organization Science*, 1 (3): 293–312.

Greene, J.C., Caracelli, V.J. and Graham, W.F. (1989) 'Toward a conceptual framework for mixed-method evaluation designs', *Educational Evaluation and Policy Analysis*, 11 (3): 255–74.

Haans, R.F.J., Pieters, C. and He, Z.-L. (2016) 'Thinking about U: Theorizing and testing U- and inverted U-shaped relationships in strategy research', *Strategic Management Journal*, 37 (7): 1177–95.

Hayes, A.F. (2015) 'An index and test of linear moderated mediation', *Multivariate Behavioral Research*, 50 (1), 1–22.

Holland, S.J., Shore, D.B. and Cortina, J.M. (2017) 'Review and recommendations for integrating mediation and moderation', *Organizational Research Methods*, 20 (4): 686–720.

Hult, G.T.M., Ketchen, D.J. Jr, Griffith, D.A., Finnegan, C.A., Gonzalez-Padron, T., Harmancioglu, N. ... and Cavusgil, S.T. (2008) 'Data equivalence in cross-cultural international business research: Assessment and guidelines', *Journal of International Business Studies*, 39 (6): 1027–44.

Hurmerinta-Peltomäki, L. and Nummela, N. (2006) 'Mixed methods in international business research: A value-added perspective', *Management International Review*, 46 (4): 439–59.

James, L.R. and Brett, J.M. (1984) 'Mediators, moderators, and tests for mediation', *Journal of Applied Psychology*, 69 (2): 307–21.

Jick, T.D. (1979) 'Mixing qualitative and quantitative methods: Triangulation in action', *Administrative Science Quarterly*, 24 (4): 602–11.

Johns, G. (1991) 'Substantive and methodological constraints on behaviour and attitudes in organizational research', *Organizational Behavior and Human Decision Processes*, 49 (1): 80–104.

Johns, G. (2001) 'In praise of context', *Journal of Organizational Behavior*, 22 (1): 31–42.

Klein, K.J., Dansereau, F. and Hall, R.J. (1994) 'Levels issues in theory development, data collection, and analysis', *Academy of Management Review*, 19 (2): 195–229.

Lawrence, P.R. and Lorsch, J.W. (1967) *Organization and Environment: Managing Differentiation and Integration*. Boston, MA: Harvard University Press.

Li, C., Arikan, I., Shenkar, O. and Arikan, A. (2020) 'The impact of country-dyadic military conflicts on market reaction to cross-border acquisitions', *Journal of International Business Studies*, 51 (3): 299–325.

Ljubownikow, G. and Ang, S.H. (2020) 'Competition, diversification and performance', *Journal of Business Research*, 112: 81–94.

MacKinnon, D.P., Lockwood, C. M., Hoffman, J.M., West, S.G. and Sheets, V. (2002) 'A comparison of methods to test mediation and other intervening variable effects', *Psychological Methods*, 7 (1): 83–104.

Mathieu, J.E. and Chen, G. (2011) 'The etiology of the multilevel paradigm in management research', *Journal of Management*, 37 (2): 610–41.

Mitchell, T.R. and James, L.R. (2001) 'Building better theory: Time and the specification of when things happen', *Academy of Management Review*, 26 (4): 530–47.

Molina-Azorin, J.F., Bergh, D.D., Corley, K.G. and Ketchen, D.J. Jr. (2017) 'Mixed methods in the organizational sciences: Taking stock and moving forward', *Organizational Research Methods*, 20 (2): 179–92.

Molina-Azorin, J.F. and López-Gamero, M.D. (2016) 'Mixed methods studies in environmental management research: Prevalence, purposes and designs', *Business Strategy and the Environment*, 25 (2): 134–48.

Molina-Azorin, J.F., López-Gamero, M. D., Pereira-Moliner, J. and Pertusa-Ortega, E.M. (2012) 'Mixed methods studies in entrepreneurship research: Applications and contributions', *Entrepreneurship and Regional Development*, 24 (5-6): 425–56.

Mulaik, S.A. and Brett, J.M. (1982) *Causal Analysis: Assumptions, Models and Data*. Beverly Hills, CA: Sage Publishing.

Perrow, C. (1967) 'A framework for the comparative analysis of organizations', *American Sociological Review*, 32 (2): 194–208.

Ployhart, R.E. and Vandenberg, R.J. (2010) 'Longitudinal research: The theory, design, and analysis of change', *Journal of Management*, 36 (1): 94–120.

Preacher, K.J., Rucker, D.D. and Hayes, A.F. (2007) 'Addressing moderated mediation hypotheses: Theory, methods, and prescriptions', *Multivariate Behavioral Research*, 42 (1), 185–227.

Rousseau, D.M. and Fried, Y. (2001) 'Location, location, location: Contextualizing organizational research', *Journal of Organizational Behavior*, 22 (1): 1–13.

Scandura, T.A. and Williams, E.A. (2000) 'Research methodology in management: Current practices, trends, and implications for future research', *Academy of Management Journal*, 43 (6): 1248–64.

Shrout, P.E. and Bolger, N. (2002) 'Mediation in experimental and nonexperimental studies: New procedures and recommendations', *Psychological Methods*, 7 (4): 422–45.

Staw, B.M., Sandelands, L.E. and Dutton, J.E. (1981) 'Threat-rigidity effects in organizational behavior: A multilevel analysis', *Administrative Science Quarterly*, 26 (4): 501–24.

Turner, S.F., Cardinal, L.B. and Burton, R.M. (2017) 'Research design for mixed methods: A triangulation-based framework and roadmap', *Organizational Research Methods*, 20 (2): 243–67.

Wood, R.E., Goodman, J.S., Beckmann, N. and Cook, A. (2008) 'Mediation testing in management research: A review and proposals', *Organizational Research Methods*, 11 (2): 270–95.

Youndt, M.A., Snell, S.A., Dean, J.W. Jr. and Lepak, D.P. (1996) 'Human resource management, manufacturing strategy, and firm performance', *Academy of Management Journal*, 39 (4): 836–66.

6

DATA, MEASUREMENTS
AND SAMPLING

6.1 INTRODUCTION

Data is essential for any research, regardless of whether you are working on a qualitative, quantitative or mixed methods project. Data can come in small or large quantities. Data can range from a single case study of an organization to rich interviews and surveys with managers to a large number of observations from an archival dataset. Data comprises information in its rawest form. Data is meaningless if we do not or cannot attach a meaning to it. Once we attach a meaning to data points, these will be able to help us understand a research issue.

While data exists in our everyday life, unlike physical science where observations can be created within an experiment or laboratory context, research in business and management is often hindered by challenges posed by data observability and availability, with some exceptions. The complex and contemporaneous nature of social and business interactions sometimes make business and management research constructs difficult to quantify. This is especially true considering the number of alternative explanations for any phenomenon under investigation in business and management research. In fact, many interesting ideas in the business and management field cannot be addressed empirically due to the hard-to-codify nature of these ideas.

So, what constitutes data? How do we know what data can be converted to meaningful information? Data are basically known facts. When you observe someone purchasing a mobile phone in a local phone store, you have just registered a data point of a behaviour of mobile phone purchase. When you read in the newspaper that a European company has entered into the Indian market, you are making an observation of a market entry by a company into India. In essence, things that we do or see everyday can become observations that can constitute data. So technically there is an abundance of potential data out there.

Conversation box

Alan [Masters student]: I will leave the worry of data collection till later. I think the research topic is more important. Surely, I will be able to find some data to prove or disprove my theory.

Professor: Alan, the validity of proving or disproving your theory depends on the rigour of the data collection process and quality of data collected. So it is important that these are concurrently thought of when you put forward your theory. While it is likely that data will exist, in reality in many cases the desired data may not be easily accessible.

If you are new to research, you might not have any idea of where all sorts of data generally reside. These days, with the advent of the Internet, you would be conducting a Google or Baidu search the moment you are asked to search for some data sources. You will encounter hundreds if not thousands of hits, making you overwhelmed. Even when you find a potential data source, you will encounter the issue of whether or not this is good data, i.e. whether there is credibility in the observations that you have found. Then there is always some information provided in magazines and news clips. But in some cases, the observations that you would like to work with are not really there. Partially as a result of these complications, many researchers are opting to use **primary data** collection methods. This can include sending out questionnaires to individuals or companies or conducting interviews with executives or consumers. The various methods of data collection will be discussed in Chapter 7.

This chapter will focus on discussing the fundamentals of data. The first section will look at the basic forms of classification of data – primary and **secondary data**. This is followed by a discussion of the different ways of creating measurements and issues with these. Finally, we turn our attention to **sampling** issues, including **sample size**, **sampling errors**, **sampling designs** and some sampling illustrations.

6.2 PRIMARY AND SECONDARY DATA

The basic way to classify data is to label them as primary or secondary data. Primary data refers to data that are collected specifically for your research purpose. There are many ways to collect primary data. These include interviews, focus groups, participant observation, experiments, case studies and surveys. Secondary data, on the other hand, is information collected, usually by someone else for a different purpose and incidentally useful and which can be recoded for your research purpose. Secondary data can come from different sources. Some of these include company reports, news and announcements, surveys, government statistics, studies and reports from transnational organizations, non-governmental organizations, marketing and research institutions, companies' tracking systems of operations and services, and archival data.

Conversation box

Joseph [Masters student]:   Professor, would it not always be true that primary data will have more value than secondary data, given that they are specifically collected for my research purpose?

Professor: One can argue that primary data are more specific and can provide highly relevant value, Joseph. But primary data have their limitations as well. So sometimes secondary data can be complementary, while at other times secondary data may in fact provide a more complete picture of what you seek to investigate.

Primary data can further be classified into two types. One is through direct observations, which can result from you witnessing a behaviour or being a participant of an activity. The other is through interviews and surveys, which is often associated with self-reported data.

A direct observation can be the witnessing of an event happening, such as the purchase of a mobile phone. A direct observation can also happen when you are a participant observer. For example, you may want to observe how company executives make decisions. In order to do that, you attend their meetings as an observer so that you can keep a record of how the process of decision-making comes about.

Both interviews and surveys are designs that rely heavily on self-reported data. For example, you are interested in how the public perceive a new policy set by the government, or how a company perceives its own performance relative to its competitors. These are questions that will rely on the self-reported responses of participants. Self-reported data are useful when more objective data are not available or accessible. They are also useful when a lot of details are needed that are not otherwise available in other formats. Although self-reported data are often needed, the method often invites criticism relating to objectivity. More details on self-reported data will be highlighted when we discuss survey design in Chapter 7.

It is important to note that while self-reported data may have issues with objectivity, more objective forms of data can have shortcomings of their own as well. For example, objective data collected by third parties for other purposes may not be highly appropriate for your variable of interest. In such cases, trying to use these data with a weak proxy can lead to a **measurement** problem for the variable of interest. In addition, there are various attributes and aspects of individual behaviour that simply cannot be assessed well using objective data avenues, because often this means using third party reports from collaterals that are in fact subject to the same types of bias as the subjects in other forms of data collection methods. These will be highlighted in the discussion of archival data collection in Chapter 7.

As mentioned earlier, secondary data are data that are not collected specifically for your research purpose; such data already exist in various forms. There are many databases around, which you can find through a search engine, although the database owners are likely to want to charge you an access fee. Your library will probably have access to some of these databases. It must be noted that in order to find a good database you will initially have to invest a substantial amount of time to go through as many databases as possible, to figure out what information is contained within each of them. It is likely that any study using mainly secondary data will need to access more than one database in order to get adequate information. Nothing is more worthwhile than gaining hands-on experience with some of these databases. This experience will be extremely valuable if you are going down the route of researching using secondary data sources.

It is important to note that secondary data are often useful as supporting materials in research. For example, national-level data can provide the background context within which individuals or companies make decisions. Hence, national-level data can be used for contextualizing the findings and in some cases can be used as control variables in quantitative studies. Some researchers creatively recode and package secondary data to allow them to use large quantities of data points to investigate the phenomena they are interested in.

6.3 MEASUREMENTS

As mentioned earlier in this chapter, we need to attach meaning to data in order to allow the data to be used to address our research questions. Basically, we need to operationalize our constructs in order to test what we propose to investigate in our research. To operationalize is to specify the observable activities or operations that help to quantify the construct. To measure is to assign precise numbers (or a range of numbers) to the attributes of interest. The measurement of any construct can come in various forms. This section will cover the main ones, including **established measurements**, **scales**, **ratios**, difference scores and composite measures.

6.3.1 Established measurements

The general advice is that you should use established measurements if they exist. The use of existing measurements provides legitimacy to your variables, reducing the risks of being challenged on your methodology. Using existing measurements also recognizes the contribution of existing literature and is a good way of building on knowledge accumulated in the research area. It also allows others to locate your work within the literature and can lead to more citations. Nonetheless, there are still a few circumstances where we may have to deviate from using existing measurements. Some of these are presented below.

When existing measurement is inadequate or imprecise

In a lot of well-researched areas you will find many measurements being used for a single construct. For example, many measurements have been used to operationalize firm-level diversification. The same is true for the various human resource practices in the human resource management literature. If you chart the evolution of such literature, you will find that many measurements have been introduced as a result of researchers trying to deepen our understanding of the areas through more refined measurements. Say, for example, a firm that conducts business using a single product is considered focused and not diversified, while another firm that conducts businesses in multiple products is considered to be diversified. This is the most traditional classification of diversification; it is simply a dichotomous classification of the level of firm diversification. As the field evolved, however, researchers have started to look at the difference between related and unrelated diversification. A firm that is diversified can undergo related or unrelated diversification. This dissection clearly helps us to delve deeper into our understanding of diversification behaviours, and this more precise classification has become the preferred means of measurement, unless the key question of a study is about whether to diversify or not. And even so, studies would start using the deeper measurement of whether to diversify (relatedly or unrelatedly) or not at all.

Johnson et al. (1982) notes that altering an existing measurement method has to be done with care, as for example measurements from a Likert scale are not equivalent to measurements using a binary scale. Likewise, Rowe and Morrow (1999) and Tehrani and Noubary (2005) have suggested that the multiple ways to measure firm performance, though correlated, are not exactly the same. In this context, for example, accounting-based firm performance measure is based on financial data, market-based firm performance is based on market data such as stock prices, and perceptual-based firm performance is largely based on assessment by managers or customers. All are valid measures, but depending on the nature of study, one measurement may not be deemed as adequate or precise as another.

When data on existing measurement cannot be accessed

As discussed in earlier chapters, the feasibility of research can sometimes be impeded by factors that lie beyond the research process itself. One of these key factors is data access, as highlighted earlier in this chapter. Data access can hinder a researcher's ability to use a particular measurement, for example, difficulty accessing groups within organizations for a study of inter-groups differences for an assessment of the organization's policies. In yet another example, in my own research on firm competitive intensity, i.e. how a firm is positioned amongst all competitors within its own industry, I find that there is limited data in many countries on industry size, how many players there are in the market and the distribution of companies, e.g. by size within industries. This limits my ability to measure firm competitive intensity in many countries. So as much as we want to achieve rigour and precision in our research, we have to be pragmatic regarding what is achievable given data limitations. When data for the best existing measurement is not accessible, you may have to adopt the second-best option, even to the extent of deriving a new measurement. Otherwise, the possibility of having to give up the variable completely is looming.

When existing measurement needs to be contextualized

Some of the existing measurements may be less generic than we want. This is especially true in cases where the existing measurement was first designed for a particular context, be it the type of organization, industry or country. In Section 5.5, we discussed the contextualization of research. This is quite common in organizational behaviour and human resource management research areas where the research context can just be within one large organization (e.g. Boxall et al., 2011). If this is the case, it becomes necessary for you to adapt the existing measurement accordingly in order to make it fit better with your own research context. For example, as highlighted in Chapter 7, in multiple-country studies involving cross-country comparisons you will need to ensure data equivalence in multi-country studies (Diamantopoulos and Papadopoulos, 2010; Hult et al., 2008; Riordan and Vandenberg, 1994).

When existing measurement is too sophisticated and may impede data collection

Many established measurements in business and management research have been constructed and improved over time. In some research areas, the measurement of key constructs has become sophisticated and will take a lot of effort to collect the necessary data. This happens for example when composite measurements are used (Section 6.3.4). However, with time pressures mounting on most research projects, an expensive data collection process that spans across a long time is highly unrealistic for most research projects. Given this, measurements are often allowed to be parsimonious if they can pass the tests of **reliability** and **validity** (which will be discussed in Section 6.4). To relax on a sophisticated measurement, you will need to back it up with good reasoning and prior literature. This prior literature should support your use of measurement, which will not be the case when the field is relatively new and thereby measurements used are also less advanced. If you are to adapt an existing measurement or coming up with your own, you will have to logically ground that in the literature and test your own proposed measurement for reliability and validity.

6.3.2 Metric scales

A metric scale measures quantitative characteristics or variables. Metric scales are common in surveys. In metric scales, we ask respondents to provide an assessment of an item or question using a range of options or values. The most basic form of metric scale is the *nominal* scale, which provides a classification of attributes into categories. These categories are equal in rank. In other words, no one category is superior to another category. The second form is the *ordinal* scale, where the categories are ranked according to their magnitude in an ordered relationship. The third form of scale is the *interval* scale, where the categories are in order and at the same time the intervals are equal in distance. A fourth form of scale is the *ratio* scale, which on top of the interval scale, has an additional characteristic of the presence of the absolute zero value. Figure 6.1 shows some examples of the use of these different scales.

Type of scale	Examples
Nominal	*Question* Where do you usually travel on business? *Choices* • (1) Asia; (2) Americas; (3) Europe; (4) Africa *Comment* • The order of choices is unrelated to their values. *Question* • What is your favorite breakfast? *Choices* • (1) Bread; (2) Cereal; (3) Congee; (4) Rice; (5) Others *Comment* • The order of choices is unrelated to their values.

(Continued)

Figure 6.1   (Continued)

Type of scale	Examples
Ordinal	*Question* • What is the number of part-time employees in your company? *Choices* • (1) 1–20; (2) 21–50; (3) 51–100; (4) 101 and above *Comment* • Each category is larger than the previous; they do not need to contain the same number of observations. *Question* • Your supervisor is well liked by your peers. *Choices* • (1) Strongly disagree; (2) Disagree; (3) Neutral; (4) Agree; (5) Strongly Agree *Comment* • In this case, the response choices are ranked in order of the degree of agreement with the statement. For example, the fifth category is larger, i.e. more agreement than the fourth category.
Interval	*Question* • How often do you work from home in a year? *Choices* • (1) 1–2 months; (2) 3–4 months; (3) 5–6 months; (4) 7–8 months; (5) 9–10 months; (6) 11–12 months *Comment* • Each category represents two months, i.e. they are equal.
Ratio	*Question* • What is the market share that your company commands in the market? *Choices* • (1) Less than 20%; (2) 20%-40%; (3) 40%-60%; (4) 60%-80%; (5) More than 80% *Comment* • As with interval, the categories are equal. The additional characteristic is the inclusion of the absolute zero value.

Figure 6.1   Examples of the use of different metric scales

Likert items

When you are conducting a survey, very often you will ask questions pertaining to perception. In this kind of question, you will ask the respondents to rate their perception of some items on a scale. The Likert scale, devised by American educator and organizational psychologist Rensis Likert, is grounded in psychometrics, the field of study concerned with the theory and technique of educational and psychological measurement, which includes the measurement of knowledge, abilities, attitudes and personality traits.

Likert items can be used for all sorts of questions. For example, you can ask respondents about their perception (agreement or disagreement) of a certain statement. You can also ask respondents about their behavioural tendency such as whether they are more or less likely to engage in some activity. Likert items come in various ranges: they can be mainly classified as odd-point (i.e. 1–5, 1–7, 1–9) and even-point items (i.e. 1–6,

1–8, 1–10). For a 5-point Likert item, the range of responses can include 'strongly disagree', 'disagree', 'neutral', 'agree' and 'strongly agree' for perception-type questions. For behavioural-type questions, responses can include 'very unlikely', 'unlikely', 'neutral', 'likely' and 'very likely'. The 6-point Likert item equivalent for perception-type questions would be 'strongly disagree', 'moderately disagree', 'disagree', 'agree', 'moderately agree' and 'strongly agree', while that for behavioural-type questions would be 'very unlikely', 'quite unlikely', 'unlikely', 'likely', 'quite likely' and 'very likely'. As you can see, there are only subtle differences between a 5-point Likert item and a 6-point Likert item. So if you are working on your first survey and not utilizing an existing measurement, you may be pondering which of these scales might be more suitable for your construct.

What are the advantages and disadvantages of an odd-point scale versus an even-point scale? The advantage of using odd-point scales is that they do not force respondents to choose either direction, for example to agree or disagree when they are really ambivalent. They can then choose the mid-point neutral. On the flip side, having a middle point can create potential extremity bias, as some respondents may choose to remain neutral for too many questions, leading to loss of information for a research project.

Conversation box

Dean [PhD student]: Professor, when I construct my survey questionnaire using existing items, I find that they use different scale designs. Some provide five categories, others six, and the majority actually use seven. Should I ignore these differences or can I change them to make sure they are consistent, which also makes the survey look better organized?

Professor: Good question, Dean. There is the advantage of being comparable to previous literature if you leave them as they are, even though the temptation is to align them to look more organized and comparable.

One might observe that authors sometimes use items from an established 1–5 scale and modify them into 1–7 option items. Normally this is done to allow a more uniform set of Likert items across the variables for analysis within a single study. It also allows the responses to be spread out and may yield fine-grained results. There is empirical evidence to show that as the number of item response alternatives increases from 2 to 3 to 4 to 5 to 7 (becoming asymptotic around 7), there is a corresponding increase in scale reliability (Lissitz and Green, 1975; Oaster, 1989). The disadvantage of changing scale points is that you cannot compare your results to the original scale, which can sometimes be helpful for you to position your research work within the literature.

In Likert scales, you can also offer an option for 'Not Applicable' or 'Don't Know'. This choice allows a respondent to make a choice of not responding to a particular question. This choice would be eventually coded as missing data as a response, unless your study is using that particular item to help identify differences across groups of respondents. However, some researchers interpret the neutral mid-point as 'Not Applicable'. Nevertheless, if someone is asked to respond on a scale ranging from 1-extremely happy to 5-extremely sad, the mid-point represents how that person feels on this particular dimension of emotions, which is different from saying there is no emotion involved. The additional item of 'Not Applicable' (on top of a Likert item that already includes a neutral mid-point) gives the respondents the option to not rate on an item when it does not apply to them. Without this additional item, it is hard to tell whether a respondent truly has a neutral feeling or whether this is not a question that is applicable to them. That is, being neutral is not exactly the same as not having a feeling or response about a particular item or question.

It is also important to note that the 'Not Applicable' or 'Don't Know' option gives respondents who are a bit tentative or uncommitted in their attitude a way to avoid answering. A less desirable outcome is that this encourages respondents who are cognitive misers to avoid thinking twice before responding – as the option allows an easy way out. If you will have to code this as missing data, it reduces your sample size for statistical analysis. It can be detrimental if the item represents a key construct of your study.

For less typical questions that require a degree of knowledge beyond a respondent's own opinion, a 'Don't Know' option is probably not a bad idea. For example, a measure like 'my organization would support me if I had to report my boss for sexual harassment' is probably difficult for many employees to answer, in which case a 'Don't Know' option would be a legitimate choice, and would probably annoy respondents if it is not available as an option. While this sort of question can and should be avoided if possible as it hovers on the borders of ethics and privacy and may not elicit many responses despite anonymity promises, it is sometimes unavoidable, given the nature of the research. The other concern with treating the mid-point as 'Not Applicable' or 'Don't Know' is that when it comes to analysis, tools often treat Likert-scale data as if it were continuous. Hence, the 'Not Applicable' is interpreted as a score between 'Agree' and 'Disagree', which is not exactly what it is supposed to mean – not applicable. Krosnik et al. (2002) provides some good discussion and advice on this topic.

> **Conversation box**
>
> *Morris [PhD student]:*   Professor, does it matter if I were to use scales ranging from –3 to +3 as opposed to 1 to 7?
>
> *Professor:*   Technically, you should expect no difference between adopting the 1 to 7 scale and the –3 to +3 scale. But according to some studies, there are in fact minor differences. For example, a format that ranges from negative to positive numbers conveys a bipolar dimension, where the two poles refer to the presence of opposite attributes. In contrast, a format that uses only positive numbers conveys a unipolar dimension, referring to different degrees of the same attribute. Thus, it may be wise not to ignore scale anchors when designing the scales for your items.

As Likert scales are common in survey questionnaires, Dillman's (1978) work on survey design also provides a good discussion of using Likert scales. Hinkin (1995, 1998) highlight various issues in the development of measurements in surveys.

6.3.3 Ratios and difference scores

Very often we are interested in the ratios or proportions or the probabilities or likelihood of a certain behaviour being observed. We are thus tempted to ask questions like 'What proportion of your time in the office is spent on answering emails?' or 'What is the ratio of your weekly expenditure on food to your salary?'

But imagine you are the respondent. Do you have a quick idea what these proportions are in your case? While you want to help with the research as a respondent, you will probably be put on the spot as to how to work these ratios out. You may even need a calculator, as you are aware that you spend on average $185 on food on a weekly income of $890. That should give an answer at 20.8%. So now, you are put in the position of working out numbers like these if you are trying hard to help. A few questions of this sort and you start to lose patience with a survey that begins to feel like a maths exam.

If you do not want to be caught in such a position as a respondent yourself, the advice is that you should avoid structuring questions that require your respondents to do the same. In the example above, it is good enough to ask two questions. The first question being 'What is your average weekly expenditure on food?' and the second question will be 'What is your rough weekly salary?' You will then work out the pro-portions upon getting these figures to avoid putting extra stress on your respondents. This will avoid your respondents giving you estimates based on mental calculations or even convenient and arbitrary estimates!

Ratios are useful when you are trying to compare the relative size or importance of two variables. A ratio allows you to have a value that reflects this relativity. For example, you want to test whether people who perceive career advancement as more important than job satisfaction are more likely to be attracted by higher salary packages. A sim-ple way to investigate is to test the ratio of perception of career advancement and job satisfaction. The higher the ratio, the more importance is attached to career advance-ment. An alternative to this is to test the effects of perception of career advancement and perception of job satisfaction on salary packages separately and interpret their relative signs and significance. But somehow, this does not have the same meaning as using the ratio, as it reflects the absolute size difference between the two variables rather than their relative sizes. Firebaugh and Gibbs (1985) provide a good discussion of the use of ratios as measurements. Kronmal (1993) further highlights the challenge of using ratios in quantitative regression analysis.

An alternative to the ratio measurement is the difference scores measurement – taking the difference between two values of the same variable at two different time periods or of two different variables in the same time period. Cronbach and Furby (1970) raise questions about whether the use of difference scores makes sense. Hoffman et al. (1992), in studying the interaction between structure and technology on firm performance, suggest that despite the appeal of using difference scores, the score is likely to have lower reliability than the average of the two values from which the **difference score** is derived from. They further argue that if the difference score variable does not differ-entiate much from the two variables from which it is derived, weak discriminant validity will occur.

Some studies have compared the ratios (relative) and difference scores (absolute). Marino and Lange (1983) discuss various measurements of organizational slack, which tend to be measured either in relative or absolute terms. They conclude that these are not interchangeable and that their use should be observed with care, and are dependent on the research questions among other factors. Hoffman et al. (1992) compare the use of multiplicative model and difference score model for testing interactions and suggest that the multiplicative model is preferred, due to the vari-ous issues with using difference scores as identified in Johns (1981). A major issue with using difference score is the difficulty with identifying the basis against which they are benchmarked (Drazin and Van de Ven, 1985). For an extensive discussion of the use of ratios and difference scores also refer to Fuguitt and Lieberson (1973–4). Johns (1981) provides a comprehensive discussion of the usage and challenges of using difference scores.

6.3.4 Composite measures

Conversation box

Henry [Masters student]:   Professor, one of my key constructs is organizational knowledge. I wonder if I can ask the senior managers directly about
the level of knowledge embedded within their organization?

Professor: Henry, addressing this kind of question will need multiple indicators or questions. As an example, you can ask questions
like 'What is the average number of product innovations generated annually in the last five years?' and 'What is the average
number of process improvements generated annually in the last
five years?' If we believe that product innovations and process
improvements are good indicators of organizational knowledge,
we can then create a composite measure that gives us a proxy
for organizational knowledge from these two questions. In this
way, we can have a better picture of the level of organizational
knowledge embedded within an organization.

A **composite measure** combines the value of its constituent components to provide
a single value for the construct of interest. In combining various components, it is
important to ensure that the values of its components are comparable. For example,
in the above example, if a manager's response to the first question is five (for product
innovation) and the response to the second question is also five (for process improvement), does that mean we can add five to five to make a score of ten? That is, are the
two values of five equivalent such that we can just add them up? One reason for asking
such an equivalent value comparison is the fact that product innovation might take
longer and is probably way more difficult than process improvement. In that case, we
should not expect one process improvement to take the same time, incur the same cost
and expend the same effort as one product innovation.

In order to account for the differences in components and the value of these to the
composite measure, researchers have sought to evaluate ways to combine component
values. Fralicx and Raju (1982) compare five methods to which components can be
combined into a single composite measure. These are unit weight (simply adding the
value of the components), equal weight (multiply component value by its standard
deviation and add all these new values), factor weight (using factor analysis to get
a factor loading), management weight (managers are asked to provide weighting for

each component) and canonical weight (using linear combination of the component values). Likewise, Aamodt and Kimbrough (1985) compare four methods – unit weight, rank order weight (identifical to management weight but just rank order the components), critical incident weight (equivalent to equal weight) and regression weight (using regression analysis to derive the weighting score of each component). Both studies conclude that unit weight and equal weight, though simple, provide good ways to weight component scores for coming up with a composite measure. Subsequent studies have also provided support for the use of unit weight, for example Bobko et al. (2007).

When component values are based on Likert scales, it will be harder to combine two questions using different scales, such as a nominal one with an ordinal one, or using different types of Likert items. Clearly, you also need to make sure that they belong to the same construct – the construct can be explained by a combination of the measures. Keller and Dansereau (2001) found that when additional items are added to an original measurement involving components, the results of the analyses will differ. In other words, one would have to be careful in including new components in the conceptualization of a construct. As discussed in Section 6.3.1, any deviation from an established measurement has to be well grounded.

Some research has looked into how the various ways to measure firm performance are positioned against each other, namely accounting-based, market-based and perceptual-based assessments of firm performance (e.g. Rowe and Morrow, 1999). The general consensus is that these three forms are all valid and distinct measurements of firm performance but their combination to become one dimension needs to be used with care (Rowe and Morrow, 1999). Further, it is unlikely that these measurements are assessed using the same scale or value range, which makes it difficult to combine them. In trying to move a step closer to that, Tehrani and Noubary (2005) have in fact proposed a way to convert objective or archival financial data into scales that can be used for combining with perceptual measures of firm performance.

This section has discussed the various measurement possibilities and challenges. There may be other complex forms of measurements that are not covered here, but those are likely to be a combination or variation of those discussed here. Figure 6.2 presents a summary of the use of different forms of measurements.

Established Measures	• Use as far as possible when they exist, as long as the measure has strong reliability and validity. • Adapt as and when needed, depending on the weakness of the measure. In many cases, there will be a need to prove reliability and validity of the new adapted measure. • Contextualize as needed, such as catering to a particular organization or groups of organizations, or for cross-cultural studies.

Metric Scales	• Choice of categories for scales need to be made with analysis in mind. • Different scales used across variables can lead to difficulty in analysis. The choice of 5-item, 6-item, or 7-item scales should be considered carefully. • Ensure the use of 'neutral', 'don't know' and 'not applicable' categories is appropriate for your research context.
Ratios and Difference Scores	• Ratios are useful when measurement needs to be relative. • Difference scores allow for absolute comparisons. • Whenever possible, these forms of measurements can be replaced by simply including the component scores involved separately. This reduces the possibility of reduced reliability.
Composite Measures	• Be mindful of whether the units of components are comparable that allow simple combination of adding the value of the component values to arrive at the composite measure. • Unit and equal weighting of the components have been proven to be as valid as any other weighting methods. • When scales are used, as far as possible use factor analysis to arrive at the value of the composite measure in these circumstances.

Figure 6.2   Different forms of measurements and their use

6.4 RELIABILITY AND VALIDITY

The recording of the research process and procedures needs to be objectively done with a good level of detail. This is to allow verification and replication of the current research. To explicitly state the procedures is important because it ensures the transparency of reliability and validity. More importantly, it allows you not to forget what decisions and judgement calls have been made in the research process.

6.4.1 Reliability

Reliability is the degree to which measures are free from measurement error and therefore yield consistent results. Reliability reflects the amount of inconsistency or unsystematic fluctuation of individual responses on a measure. That is, does a question elicit similar responses over time and across situations? The test is whether the same question can be repeated with similar outcomes. However, sometimes reliability tests can be problematic when the question relates to the perception of individuals rather than factual information. It is likely that as time elapses, people's perception will change as a result of maturation effect. Reliability testing is important to help ascertain construct validity – though reliability does not necessarily mean validity. The more random errors there are in the measurements, the lower the reliability will be. The greater the reliability, the more a finding can be generalized.

Conversation box

Derek [Masters student]:   Professor, reliability testing requires me to ensure that we have the same responses to the same question when asked over time. Is that a problem if I want the answers to be different so that I can relate before and after?

Professor: If your study was meant to test behaviour or perception changes over time, then it's not a problem. But you need to make sure that the research design allows the changes to be attributed to certain events so that it is clear that we should expect that a difference in the responses to the same question over time is due to the events rather than a measurement error.

Probably the most important question to ask about reliability is how much reliability is enough. In this context, Nunnally (1978) is often cited as suggesting that the cutoff for acceptable reliability is 0.70 (see Lance et al., 2006). However, as Lance et al. (2006) argue, based on the text in Nunnally (1978), this claimed 0.70 cutoff is a myth rather than a rule. In fact, a more appropriate cutoff is probably at 0.80 (Carmines and Zeller, 1979; Lance et al., 2006), and this cutoff really depends on various other factors (see Nunnally, 1978).

The commonly used test model of reliability is the coefficient alpha, often called **Cronbach's alpha** (Cronbach, 1951). Other test models include the split-half, Guttman, parallel and strict parallel. Cronbach's alpha is based on the average inter-item correlations. It is important to note that, while commonly used, Cronbach's alpha is also suggested as not being the best test for all situations in that it is extremely useful to confirm the unidimensionality of the items rather than an exploration of whether these are unidimensional (Cortina, 1993). Traub and Rowley (1991) present an alternative reliability index. The authors suggest that the typically reported reliability is in many cases internal consistency, which is an overestimate of true reliability. Alpha coefficients cannot detect transient error. The degree of reliability is thus better evaluated by referring to its square root value (reliability index), because it is the correlation between observed and true scores that you are interested in, not the squared correlation between observed and true scores (reliability itself).

As empirical test is needed for reliability assessment, it is probably easier to visualize reliability in the context of quantitative research than in qualitative research. Based on this challenge, Riege (2003) provides a good discussion on reliability measures in case studies and more broadly qualitative research. Subsequently, Gibbert et al. (2008) find that case study research in management tends to report reliability and internal validity, but do not do well to discuss external validity.

6.4.2 Validity

Validity is a test of whether a 'measure' measures what it is supposed to measure. There are several forms of validity. As Cortina (1993) indicates, there are two well-known forms of comparison of validity. One is the content–criterion–construct distinction (Messick, 1980). The other is the internal–external–construct–statistical conclusion distinction (Cook and Campbell, 1979). According to Cortina (1993), there has been confusion about what each form of validity covers. For example, while both forms contain construct validity, it has a different meaning in each form. Cortina (1993) clarifies the key differences between these classifications: the former are validation strategies while the latter refer to inferences. In general, when we discuss the extent of validity, we are actually referring to internal–external–construct–statistical conclusion validities (e.g. Calder et al., 1982; MacKenzie, 2003). We will focus on these here.

Internal validity refers to the relationships between the constructs, in particular with causal effects. This should be illustrated in both theoretical development and data analysis. The linkage should be identified through a literature review and further argued as such. The data collection process needs to demonstrate that the cause variable precedes the effect variable and any alternative explanations are eliminated (Sackett and Larson, 1990). The causality will be tested using statistical analysis which will then lead to the question of statistical conclusion validity, which refers to the ability to draw conclusions based on findings (Austin et al., 1998).

External validity refers to generalizability across contexts and across time. If a relationship has external validity, it should also be true in other contexts and stable over time. McGrath and Brinberg (1983) explicitly situate external validity as the next stage after internal validity. They summarize that external validity should cover: the ability to replicate the earlier study; analysis that includes robustness tests; and an identification of boundary conditions under which the findings of the earlier study do not hold. The push towards explaining external validity may sometimes be emphasized in case study research to the extent that internal validity and construct validity are slightly underminded (Gibbert and Ruigrok, 2010; Gibbert et al., 2008). In that line, Calder et al. (1982) and Mook (1983) have contended that some research does not seek to have greater external validity or was not designed as such, so there should be no need to believe that all research should possess strong external validity.

Construct validity refers to how a measurement fits with a theory to the extent that it is consistent with other measurements that are used for the same construct. There are various components of construct validity, most notably content validity, convergent validity, discriminant validity and nomological validity.

Content validity is the most straightforward of these. It means experts in the field will have to agree that the measurement is one that is recognized as a valid measurement for the construct of interest. In essence, this can be done through a literature review process, which should inform us of whether a measure has been used in the past or recognized as a legitimate measure of the construct. In some cases, it may need the assessment of experts through consultation.

Nomological validity is the extent to which theoretical predictions are confirmed and so it is normally done at the analytical level. McGrath (1981) provides a good illustration of how nomological validity fits into the design of research methods.

Convergent validity refers to the relationships between measurements of the same construct (Carlson and Herdman, 2012). For a measurement to have a high convergent validity, it has to be highly correlated to other measurements that have been used to measure the construct. This is normally hard to detect if a study involves only one measurement for each variable. Hence, it has been proposed that in some cases, where the measurement of a key variable of interest can affect the findings of the research, researchers should try to use multiple measurements for this variable (e.g. Boyd et al., 2005; Carlson and Herdman, 2012). This can be done as part of the main analysis or as part of the robustness tests.

Discriminant validity is the extent to which the construct is different from other constructs. Many variables have proxies as measurements. For example, firm performance can be measured in a lot of ways, ranging from financial data such as sales and returns to customer service quality to innovativeness. For this reason, sometimes a proxy used may actually be also a proxy for another construct. Take innovativeness for example: one can argue that innovativeness can be a determinant for sales and returns data which are actual representations of firm performance. Yet, innovativeness is in fact a way to assess the performance of an organization from the technological perspective. So there is a risk of discriminant validity here. Nevertheless, if a study focuses on innovativeness and argues that some firms are performing better in innovativeness than others, then strictly speaking there is nothing wrong to use innovativeness in this case as firm performance. A note of caution is that external validity in this case needs to be assessed accordingly. Hamann et al. (2013) provide a good application of testing reliability, convergent validity, discriminant validity and nomological validity in exploring dimensions of organizational performance. Figure 6.3 provides some guidelines on when the different types of construct validity should be addressed.

Riege (2003) provides a good discussion on validity in case studies and more broadly qualitative research. Scandura and Williams (2000) discuss the various research strategies in management research, including the extent of validities across management studies that were conducted in the 1980s and 1990s. Two good examples of tests of reliability and validity that are needed when a new measure is proposed are Kaptein (2008) and Grégoire et al. (2010). Kaptein (2008) develops a multidimensional measure of unethical behaviour in the workplace through eight steps that would include various construct validity tests in the last stage. Grégoire et al. (2010) provide extensive tests of reliability and validity in their development of a measure for opportunity recognition.

Content validity	• Experts will have to agree that a measurement reflects a specific content domain • Can be done through a literature review (extensive use in the literature)
Convergent validity	• Different ways to measure a construct is in agreement • Can be observed through correlation analysis (high correlation), confirmatory factor analysis (components load onto single factor) and regression analysis (results similar despite using different measurements)
Discriminant validity	• The construct as measured differs from other constructs • Can be observed through correlation analysis (low correlation)
Nomological validity	• The extent to which predictions from a theoretical framework are confirmed • Can be observed through correlation analysis and regression analysis (good explanatory power)

Figure 6.3   Guidelines on addressing the different types of construct validity

A key reason for the complexity of validity tests required is due to the fact that research involves three inter-related but analytically distinct domains, i.e. the conceptual, the methodological and the substantive components (McGrath and Brinberg, 1983). As this book has illustrated to date, these components can also be cyclical and thus some forms of validity can show up in more than one stage of a research. Further, the various forms of validity are also interrelated (Gibbert et al., 2008; MacKenzie, 2003), making the test of multiple validities necessary when introducing a new or adapted measurement. Figure 6.4 shows some examples of how the various forms of validity can affect each other.

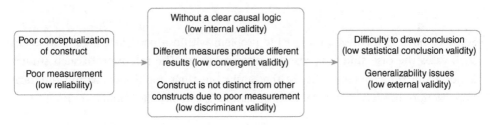

Figure 6.4   How different forms of validity can affect each other

6.5 SAMPLING

In any empirical study, one of the key aspects of the data collection process is sampling. A sample is a sub-group of the population which you want to draw a conclusion on – the target population. The selected sample must be representative of the target population to allow your findings to be generalized to the wider group. The sampling frame consists of a list of all the units in the population to be sampled and sampling units are defined as the non-overlapping collection of elements of the population.

Sampling is important and the process of sampling is critical to the validity of the findings. For example, Short et al. (2002) in their study on the linkage between strategic management and organizational performance suggest that the different sampling techniques utilized can lead to different results, even though the samples are drawn from the same sampling frame. What this means is that we have to be crystal clear in documenting the sampling technique that we use in our research work and justify a priori the sampling criteria used. According to Short et al. (2002), this is badly done in many of the studies that they observed.

Before we look at the various facets of sampling, let us first visit circumstances when we will *not* need to sample in the next sub-section. If these circumstances do not apply to you, then it is likely that you will need to implement a sampling procedure in your research design.

6.5.1 When sampling is not needed

Illustrative case studies

Illustrative case studies are always adopted when there is a lack of a potential medium or large sample to be drawn upon for testing your ideas. This could be due to the emerging nature of the phenomenon under investigation or the fact that the case study is an interesting example from which lessons can be learnt.

Interest in a particular case

Some research is focused on a specific problem within a particular organization. In such cases the case study approach is often adopted. The intention of such studies is not about the generalizability of the results but their application within the focal organization. In such circumstances, the sample is actually the population itself.

Population can be accessed

Instead of sampling, in some situations a researcher may be able to access the entire population for study. For example, you are interested in finding out business postgraduate students' perceptions of having company internships in their programmes. While it is easier to sample by asking for the register of business postgraduate students and sending out a one-page questionnaire, accessing the population is not impossible. Coordinating with course lecturers and distributing the questionnaire in compulsory courses actually gives you a faster and more complete data collection process, though this may mean more work on the outset.

When target subjects, such as individuals or organizations, are hard to access

Some researchers may work on topics that involve target subjects that are hard to access. For example, if you research in the work ethics area, your target units of study can be employees who are involved in either highly ethical or unethical behaviours. Now, employees in the latter group will likely avoid participation as they may find it sensitive. You will then face significant challenges in trying to access a representative number of participants for such research. In this regard, Sudman and Blair (1999) provide some good advice on accessing such elusive populations.

Likewise, there are also hard-to-access organizations that provide challenges for organizational researchers. For example, research on smaller, newer or lesser-known organizations on which limited information can be found even on the Internet. Nonetheless, due to the rising importance of such organizations, researchers have sought ways to get around this hard-to-access problem. Aldrich et al. (1989), Kalleberg et al. (1990) and Katz and Gartner (1988) provide some advice on how to deal with such data situations. Johns (1991) further suggests that there are always contraints enacting on the ability to sample appropriately. In such cases, it is advisable to acknowledge this limitation with good explanations.

6.5.2 Sample size

Conversation box

Winnie [Honours student]: Professor, is there a standard guide to sample size expectation for quantitative studies? I see different sample sizes being used in various studies in my research area.

Professor: It is common to expect hundreds of observations for quantitative studies. There is hardly any upper limit to sample size. However, there may be challenges relating to data access, and time and budget constraints.

What determines sample size? There are different expectations for quantitative vs. qualitative studies. For quantitative studies, a larger sample (up to a point) will always have a better explanatory power. The literature has suggested various answers as to what sample size is considered adequate. For example, Nunnally (1978) recommends a sample size of at least 100 if the number of predictor variables in your study is less than or equal to 3. The sample size can go up to 400 if there are about 10 predictor variables. Combs (2010) further suggests that any quantitative study should at least include 100 observations, taking account of effect size. Nevertheless, the general understanding is that the sample size needed is contingent on the number of predictor variables, and the predictive power and precision required within the study (see Bonett and Wright, 2011; Cohen, 1992; Green, 1991; Kraemer and Thiemann, 1987).

These general rules will have to be contextualized in light of budget and time constraints. Research comes at a cost. It can be the cost of travelling to conduct interviews or the cost of accessing a proprietary database. It can also be the cost of printing and mailing surveys. In all, regardless of your research design, there will always be some costs attached to research. However, not everyone has access to research grants and other financial support, especially if they are a student. Imagine trying to conduct a city household survey of consumption preferences. We know that it would be excellent to access as many respondents as possible (but see below for further discussion); however, for a decent-sized city you will need to access perhaps 200,000 households. Given this scale, you would need a budget that might reach a few hundred thousand dollars. Unless there is financial backing for this study, it is more reasonable to sample say 2,000 representative households and seek to get as large a return as possible from these. Thus, budget constraints can, to an extent, determine the sample size of a study.

Most research work comes with a deadline. An Honours dissertation or a Masters project has to be completed within the stipulated time period in order for the student to obtain their degree. A doctoral degree normally has a maximum date, after which the candidature will expire if the research work is not submitted in time. Some research is done for the purpose of publication in a special issue of a journal. These submissions have deadlines imposed by the individual journals. Most journals set deadlines for articles that require revisions. These are just some deadlines you will see in research projects. In summary, most research projects come with implicit or explicit deadlines. An example of an implicit deadline is when you are writing an article relating a particular event – for example the Asian financial crisis of 1997. Submitting an article in a timely manner, for example not too long after the aftermath of the crisis, will probably generate more value and readership.

Time constraints mean that we cannot hope to achieve much more than we have time for. For example, if you are working on an Honours dissertation for six months, trying to gather survey data from 150 organizations about their expansion plans would be near impossible, as the data collection itself can take six months or more, unless you have privileged access to these organizations. Thus, one can say that a decision to sample is constrained by time limits, and to a larger extent the actual size of the sample is also constrained by time limits.

Conversation box

Lucas [Masters student]: Professor, you have highlighted in your feedback on my proj-ect that I should avoid using time constraints as one of my limitations. But the truth is that time constraints did affect my ability to do a more extensive study.

Professor: You are not wrong, Lucas, but the context of the research contributions expected for your project is shaped by the time constraint itself. In other words, anyone who reads your proj-ect will know that you have done a good job despite the fact that this could be more extensive. But having a more exten-sive study is neither fair nor expected within the boundaries of what can be achieved within the period of the time available for the project. So scope issues are implicitly covered. Beyond that, time constraints are hardly good justification.

Expectation of sample size in qualitative studies tends to be less onerous. This can go as low as one case study. In fact, it has been questioned if the word 'sampling' even applies to qualitative studies (Nakkeeran, 2016). The fact is that qualitative studies are largely driven by particular observations or cases of interest. This necessarily means that the initial sample almost selects itself. Sampling is only possible when a larger pool of potential observations is available for selection to allow for similar data to be collected. Collecting similar data raises a further question on the feasibility of sampling as qualitative studies tend to be contructed as they go along and the collection of data tends to evolve rather than determined a priori. Nonetheless, even with minimal cases, reliability and validity as discussed earlier in Section 6.4 are still critical for qualitative studies for the observations to be relevant (March et al., 1991).

This leads to a further question on the ability to infer from small sample sizes. Guest et al. (2006) investigate how many interviews are considered adequate for infer-ences. With purposive sampling, they examine how far saturation will occur to allow a picture to be formed from interviews. Their findings, while arguably not necessarily generalizable, do suggest that for many research works, though larger samples are gen-erally deemed to be better, there is always a saturation point where the results will start to converge. Tipton et al. (2017) further adds that it is always a challenge to infer from a small set of experiments for a large population. Hence, in sampling, especially for qualitative studies, researchers will need to be mindful of what the broad implications of the work are and use these to inform the selection of the samples.

Overall, increasing sample size can help reduce random sampling errors. There are mainly two types of sampling errors, namely random and systematic. Random sampling errors relate to errors that arise due to chance variation. This component of research error is mostly out of the control of the researcher. But as the sample becomes more representative of the population, of which increasing sample size randomly is one way, random sampling errors can be reduced. Systematic errors relate to errors that arise because of the research study design and the level of rigour in the execution of the design, for example, potential sampling bias. Systematic errors are errors that must be minimized in any research. Systematic errors are signs that extra steps or precaution towards a more rigorous research protocol were not taken. Some examples of sampling errors are illustrated in the sampling situations in Section 6.5.5.

6.5.3 Probability sampling

Conversation box

Ying [Masters student]:   Professor, the textbook provides several options for probability sampling, how do I choose the appropriate one?

Professor: They are quite different, depending on what you seek to achieve in your study. For example, the stratified sampling design is useful if your sampling frame can be divided into sub-groups. If you use the simple random sampling design in this case, then you lose the added information relating to the sub-group classification.

Ying: So there has to be one design that will fit best for my research purpose?

Professor: Sometimes, these designs can be combined to good effect in a single research project as well.

Probability sampling refers to sampling that is based on selection methods involving a known probability for the selection of an element within the sampling frame. Every element has a known, non-zero probability of being selected. The choice of using probability sampling is made on the presumption that there is a population or a segment of population available for selection. In this section we will cover four types of probability sampling, namely **simple random sampling**, **systematic sampling**, **stratified sampling** and **cluster sampling**.

Simple random sampling

The most common probability sampling method is the simple random sampling design. In this design, each element of the population has an equal chance of being included in the sample. Although it sounds straightforward, achieving randomness is not always that easy as the selection process needs to be properly balanced. The most common way to do this is what we often see in a lottery. In a typical lottery, numbers are represented by balls of the same weight, all of which are placed within a glass bowl and spun for each draw. This ensures randomness. We assign a number to each of the elements of the population in this process.

We can also use random number tables to generate our sample. For this, again we first assign a number to each of the elements of the population. If the population consists of a thousand elements, we assign the first element as 000, the second element as 001, etc. The next step is then to use a random number table to pick the sample. Tables of random numbers have the desired properties no matter how the numbers are chosen from the table: by row, by column, diagonally, or irregularly. Ironically, any published (or otherwise accessible) random data table is unsuitable for cryptographic purposes since the accessibility of the numbers makes them effectively predictable. Nowadays, these tables are replaced by computational random number generators.

It is important to note here that in quantitative studies that involve a large population and where sampling is required, it is a common expectation that the sample will be random. The whole notion is to have as representative as a sample as possible. In the case of longitudinal study, for example, Goodman and Blum (1996) assessed the effect of subject attrition in the process of conducting longitudinal studies. They emphasize that there is potential for subjects of particular attributes to drop out in the process, i.e. a systematic reason for a particular group to drop out. Therefore, throughout a longitudinal study, there is a need to manage the design to keep the remaining sample random. In essence, subjects may be deemed to self-select themselves in or out of the sample, leading to sample selection bias (Heckman, 1979). In most recent good empirical studies we also observe the use of analytical models that account for this select-selection **endogeneity** within their analytical models (e.g. Ang et al., 2018; Iyengar and Zampelli, 2009; Shaver, 1998).

Systematic sampling

In the systematic sampling design, the first element is selected through a random process. Subsequently every *n*th element is selected. The sampling interval *n* is calculated by using the population size divided by the sample size. Like the random sampling design, each element in the population in the systematic sampling design has a known and equal probability of being selected. Though systematic sampling is fundamentally similar to simple random sampling, it is much less expensive to carry out as the random process is only executed once.

Just to illustrate, suppose you want to sample 8 houses from a street of 120 houses. We have 120/8 = 15, so every 15th house is chosen after a random starting point between 1 and 15. If the random starting point is 11, then the houses selected are those assigned the numbers 11, 26, 41, 56, 71, 86, 101 and 116.

Conversation box

Wayne [Masters student]:   So, what happens if the population is not evenly divisible? For example, I want to sample 8 houses out of 125 (where 125/8 = 15.625), should I take every 15th or every 16th house?

Professor: Good question. In fact, your situation happens more frequently. If you take every 16th house, then we have 8*16 = 128, so there is a risk that the last house to be chosen does not exist. On the other hand, if you take every 15th house, 8*15 = 120, so the last five houses will never be selected. In such cases, the random starting point should instead be selected as a non-integer number between 0 and 15.625, inclusive on one endpoint only, to ensure that every house has an equal chance of being selected. The interval should now be non-integer (15.625) and each non-integer selected should be rounded up to the next integer. So, for example if the random starting point is 3.3, then the houses selected are the ones with assigned numbers 4, 19, 35, 51, 66, 82, 98, and 113.

In order for the systematic sampling design to be properly executed, we need to ensure that the chosen sampling interval does not elicit a pattern. Any pattern would threaten randomness. For example, suppose you own a restaurant and want to profile the buying habits of your customers. While you can choose to profile the first ten customers in each day for a period of a few weeks to have a decently large sample for analysis, the design may embed a time-related problem as some customers may likely come at the same time slot each day, e.g. for breakfast. This issue can be avoided with the use of sampling across time intervals.

Stratified sampling

In stratified random sampling designs, you first divide the elements into strata. Then you randomly select elements from each stratum. The stratified sampling design is extremely useful when you need each selected category in your population to be represented in the sample. For example, you are conducting a study on the perception of a brand of mobile phone. Customers and potential customers can easily range from a 16-year-old high school student to a retired person. A good study of perception should naturally involve users from all age groups, as each generation will likely look for different functionalities when it comes to the use of mobile phones. Thus, age groups can become the strata in this case. We can then divide a list of potential respondents to your survey into various categories based on age groups. For the purpose of illustration, let's say this turns out to be six groups. We can then use random sampling techniques to choose 50 potential respondents from each of the six groups, resulting in a sample of 300 potential respondents. In this way, we make sure that each group category has equal representation in your study, and respondents within each group are also randomly selected.

Cluster sampling

In cluster sampling designs, you divide the elements into clusters, which need to contain heterogeneous elements within each, yet the means across the clusters should be similar. You then randomly select elements from the randomly selected clusters. The cluster sampling process basically involves two random sampling processes. Instead of grouping the elements into categories through a pre-determined criterion as in the case of stratified random sampling, cluster sampling relies on random sampling to do the segregation. The second procedure is the same as in stratified random sampling – the grouped elements are further selected based on a random sampling process.

6.5.4 Non-probability sampling

Non-probability sampling refers to sampling that is based on selection methods that do not involve a known probability for the selection of elements. Non-probability sampling designs are commonly used when we do not have the luxury of having a good set of elements to start with. In this case, we almost have to rely on an impromptu kind of approach to find the samples we need. It is important to note that this is not the same as saying that an awareness of the boundaries of the target population is not needed. You will still need to define the population that you want to draw your implications on and use this information to guide the non-probability sampling process.

Convenience sampling

Convenience sampling occurs when a researcher obtains sampling units that are most conveniently available. This method is used when the object of study is generic and thus does not require the researcher to aim specifically for certain attributes of the sample units, other than having the population boundary in mind. For example, we want to conduct research about consumer perception of mobile phones with a touch-screen graphical user interface. This requires that a respondent have access to one of these mobile phones to be able to assess its touch-screen functionality. Mobile companies usually do not provide names of clients due to privacy acts. Utilizing the usual sampling methods is likely to result in sampled persons not being eligible for the study, for the reason that they do not have access to a touch-screen mobile phone. In this case, a good approach may be to target some retail stores and, with the permission of both the store and their customers, survey customers who purchase this type of mobile phone at the point of sale. This method allows quick and convenient access to respondents. In this example, care should still be taken so that there is no systematic bias in the sampling process, for example sampling from only one retail store.

Quota sampling

The **quota sampling** design is based on set criteria for certain attributes in selecting elements for the sample. Quota sampling is useful when a particular group or characteristic is relatively rare in the population. An example might be women who are holding leadership roles in large organizations. The proportion of males in these roles is almost always larger than that of females and in order for any study in this area not to be biased by gender, it may be wise to use quota sampling. That is, if there are 250 female leaders in a population of 1,000 leaders, and you wish to have a sample of 200 respondents then your sample should include 50 (= 250/1,000*200) females. Note that quota sampling is not the same as stratified sampling, as the sampling from each group (e.g. male and female) is dependent on the proportion of the groups within the sampling frame.

Snowball sampling

The **snowball sampling** design is sampling that starts with a credible subject and uses this subject, be it a person or an organization, as a gateway for access to subsequent subjects. Initial subjects are selected through a process, but subsequent subjects are selected based on information provided by the initial subjects. This design is useful for locating members of rare populations, for example individuals or organizations that belong to the same professional body. Access to others is easier through members from the same group.

Conversation box

Kelly [PhD student]:   Professor, is it possible to combine probability and non-probability sampling designs in a single study?

Professor: There is no reason why that cannot be done. For example, in our example of quota sampling of female leaders, if access is good, then you can embed random sampling once you have decided on the quota needed. Using mainly a quota sampling design may also need the help of convenience sampling if access to female leaders is an issue.

Systematic matching sampling

The **systematic matching design** is used when you need to control for all other attributes of the subjects except for the key attribute under investigation. This method is good for comparing groups. For example, you would like to find out why some organizations fail while others survived. As it is difficult to access organizations that have failed, sample size is likely to be limited. In order to improve generalizability and since the objective is to see the differences between firms that fail and those that survive, you rely on the attributes of the failure cases to find the equivalent samples among the surviving group. In this way, you can achieve a comparison that allows you to investigate the differences between firms that fail and those that survive.

6.5.5 Sampling situations

Here we present some instances of sampling situations and evaluate whether the proposed method of sample selection is appropriate for obtaining information and drawing implications about the population of interest.

Situation 1

A questionnaire was mailed to a simple random sample of 500 household addresses in a city. Ten were returned as bad addresses, 74 were returned completed, and the rest were not returned. The researcher analyzed the 74 cases and reported that they represented a 'random sample of city households'.

The following issues arise from this situation:

1. *Bad addresses*. Bad addresses in a selected sample should be avoided. It is important that when you mail out surveys, you need to ensure that addresses are valid and checked for accuracy.

2. *Random sampling*. While the originally selected 500 households are randomly selected, it is not clear if the 74 respondents represent a random sample. You will have to conduct a simple comparison of attributes of the respondents and non-respondents to ensure that the respondents do not represent a particular type of household, for example those who live further from a post office may be less likely to return the mail surveys. This is related to the **self-selection bias** explained in Section 6.5.3 and will be discussed further in Chapter 7.

3. *Are 74 respondents adequate?* This is an important question to ask. Seventy-four respondents correspond to 14.8% of the sample of 500. The answer really depends on the population under study. If the sample of 500 is only 10% of the number of households, then our 74 responses constitute only 1.48% of all households in the city. The issue then rests on how representative this 1.48% is of the entire population. It is likely that this is too small a number to be representative. In such cases, it is essential to increase the sample size in order to increase the responses and the representation. Again, it will be essential to check if there is any potential selection bias with this pool of 74 respondents.

Situation 2

In a study of entrepreneurial experience on firm survival, a researcher, with the help of the small and medium enterprises association, sent out a questionnaire to a randomly selected sample of small and medium enterprises from the directory to investigate the research question.

The issue here is one related to the use of the directory. The directory consists of firms that have actually survived. If this is the case, it would not allow the researcher to test their research objective, as the whole sample fits the survival criterion, and no failures were surveyed. In essence, to answer the research question the researcher will also need to access firms that have not survived. In this case, the use of a sample from the directory can at best help the researcher address research questions that relate to why some small and medium enterprises are performing better than others.

Situation 3

In a study of the effect of alliance decision-making processes on firm performance, a questionnaire was mailed to a directory list of alliances established in the last five years.

The following issues arise from this situation:

1. *Directory list of alliances.* It is essential to check on the criteria of listing in this directory of alliances. Successful alliances or alliances by successful firms are more likely to be listed. If this is true, then understanding alliance decision-making processes from this directory list may actually lead to a positive biased view towards these processes. Decision-making processes in alliances not doing well will not be represented.

2. *Respondents to the questionnaire.* Who is the contact person listed in the directory? If an alliance has been in place for a while, the contact person may not be someone who was involved in the alliance formation decision-making process. In order to answer the research question, it is important to have access to the individuals who were involved in the formation of the alliance. Sometimes this becomes tricky when those individuals who were involved in setting up an alliance are no longer working at the company.

3. *Decision-making process.* Information about decision-making processes may be difficult to collect using questionnaires. Open-ended questions are necessary, and these can make the design of the questionnaire complex. Analysis of a predominantly open-ended questionnaire can also be complicated. As such, it is often better to have more than one respondent to these sorts of questions in order to get a fair view of what actually went on in the decision-making process. Thus, some form of triangulation will be needed. The use of surveys and interviews will be discussed in Chapter 7.

Situation 4

In a study of the effect of firm diversification on performance, a researcher chooses the whole population in the global automobile industry for analysis.

The issue in this case centres on the choice of industry for investigating the relationship between firm diversification and performance. While the focus on one industry makes it possible to avoid sampling and hence provide a full picture of the phenomenon using population data, most automobile manufacturers are not diversified, i.e. we are unlikely to observe a lot of diversification behaviours in this industry. This will make the analysis quite difficult, especially regarding the implications of extensive diversification which will be under-represented in the sample.

Situation 5

In order to assess if trade is good for economic development, a researcher conducts a longitudinal study using a sample involving the original 15 European Union (EU) countries over a period of 20 years.

The following issues arise from this situation:

1. *Membership of economic integration region.* Over the period of the 20-year scope of the study, some other countries will have become part of the economic integration region while some member countries may have entered into more free-trade agreements. These would affect the relationship between trade and economic development in the EU region. Accounting for the effects of these movements is important to investigate the real effects of trade taking out the spurious effect of being an EU member country.

2. *The correlation of economic development and EU membership.* By virtue of being an EU member, countries are certified to be developed or have attributes to become a developed country. As such, this may actually become a biased set of countries to test the relationship between trade and economic development. The implications from this study are likely to be significantly reduced in value, as it would be deemed less applicable to developing countries.

KEY TERMS

- Cluster sampling
- Composite measure
- Construct validity
- Content validity
- Convenience sampling
- Convergent validity
- Cronbach's alpha
- Data
- Difference score
- Discriminant validity
- Endogeneity
- Established measurement
- External validity
- Internal validity
- Measurement
- Nomological validity
- Non-probability sampling
- Primary data
- Probability sampling
- Quota sampling
- Ratios
- Reliability
- Sample size
- Sampling
- Sampling design
- Sampling error
- Scales
- Secondary data
- Self-selection bias
- Simple random sampling
- Snowball sampling
- Stratified sampling
- Systematic matching sampling
- Systematic sampling
- Validity

SUMMARY

- Data is information in its rawest form.
- Primary and secondary data are the basic forms of data. Primary data are data collected for a specific research purpose while secondary data are data collected by third parties for another purpose and not tailored to your research.

- Scales, ratios, difference scores and composite measures are key types of measurements.
- Modification of existing measurements is needed when the existing measurement is inadequate or not as precise as desired, when data cannot be accessed, when contextualization is needed and when data collection can be impeded due to the sophisticated nature of the measurement.
- Measurement scales can be nominal, ordinal, interval or ratio.
- Any measurement will need to pass the tests of reliability and validity.
- Key forms of validity include internal validity, statistical conclusion validity, external validity and construct validity.
- A sample is a sub-group of the population upon which a researcher wants to draw a conclusion.
- Sampling is not needed when a researcher works on an illustrative case study, has an interest in a particular case, when a population can be accessed, or when target units are hard to access.
- In general, sample size needed in any empirical study is dependent on the number of predictor variables, predictive power and precision required. This is further limited by budget and time constraints.
- Random and systematic sampling errors are the two common sampling errors.
- In probability sampling, every element has a known, non-zero probability of being selected.
- Simple random sampling, systematic sampling, stratified sampling and cluster sampling are the main types of probability sampling.
- Convenience sampling, quota sampling, snowball sampling and systematic matching are the main types of non-probability sampling.

QUESTIONS

1. When is it necessary to deviate from using established measurements?
2. Discuss the pros and cons of using 5-point, 6-point, and 7-point scales in Likert items.
3. Describe the circumstances to which ratios and difference scores are used. What are some of the challenges when using these?
4. Using an example, describe the process of how to assess reliability and construct validity.
5. In what circumstances is sampling not necessary?
6. Under what conditions is sampling needed?
7. Provide an example of combining both probability and non-probability sampling within a study.

ADDITIONAL READINGS

Arthur, W. Jr., Bell, S.T., Edwards, B.D., Day, E.A., Tubre, T.C. and Tubre, A.H. (2005) 'Convergence of self-report and archival crash involvement data: A two-year longitudinal follow-up', *Human Factors*, 47 (2): 303–13.

Brown, K.A. and Ki, E.-J. (2013) 'Developing a valid and reliable measure of organizational crisis responsibility', *Journalism & Mass Communication Quarterly*, 90 (2): 363–84.

Doty, D.H. and Glick, W.H. (1998) 'Common methods bias: Does common methods variance really bias results?', *Organizational Research Methods*, 1(4): 374–406.

Edwards, J.R. (1994) 'The study of congruence in organizational behavior research: Critique and a proposed alternative', *Organizational Behavior and Human Decision Processes*, 58 (1): 51–100.

Edwards, J.R. (2001) 'Ten difference score myths'. *Organizational Research Methods*, 4 (3): 265–87.

Freeman, J. (1986) 'Data quality and the development of organizational social science: An editorial essay', *Administrative Science Quarterly*, 31 (2): 298–303.

Goffin, R.D. and Gellatly, I.R. (2001) 'A multi-rater assessment of organizational commitment: Are self-report measures biased?', *Journal of Organizational Behavior*, 22 (4): 437–51.

Hamilton, B.H. and Nickerson, J.A. (2003) 'Correcting for endogeneity in strategic management research', *Strategic Organization*, 1 (1): 51–78.

Kuncel, N.R., Credé, M. and Thomas, L.L. (2005) 'The validity of self-reported grade point averages, class ranks, and test scores: A meta-analysis and review of the literature', *Review of Educational Research*, 75 (1): 63–82.

Lee, R.M. (1993) *Doing Research on Sensitive Topics*. London: Sage Publishing.

Martínez, J.F., Schweig, J. and Goldschmidt, P. (2016) 'Approaches for combining multiple measures of teacher performance: Reliability, validity, and implications for evaluation policy', *Educational Evaluation and Policy Analysis*, 38 (4): 738–56.

Revilla, M. and Ochoa, C. (2018) 'Alternative methods for selecting web survey samples', *International Journal of Market Research*, 60 (4): 352–65.

Schuessler, K. (1974) 'Analysis of ratio variables: Opportunities and pitfalls', *American Journal of Sociology*, 80 (2): 379–96.

Shahzad, A.M. and Sharfman, M.P. (2015) 'Corporate social performance and financial performance: Sample-selection issues', *Business & Society*, 56 (6): 889–918.

Towler, A.J. and Dipboye, R.L. (2003) 'Development of a learning style orientation measure' *Organizational Research Methods*, 6 (2): 216–35.

Tversky, A. and Kahneman, D. (1971) 'Belief in the law of small numbers', *Psychological Bulletin*, 76 (2): 105–10.

Venkatraman, N. and Grant, J.H. (1986) 'Construct measurement in organizational strategy research: A critique and proposal', *Academy of Management Review*, 11 (1): 71–87.

REFERENCES

Aamodt, M.G. and Kimbrough, W.W. (1985) 'Comparison of four methods for weighting multiple predictors', *Educational and Psychological Measurement*, 45 (3): 477–82.

Aldrich, H.E., Kalleberg, A.L., Marsden, P.V. and Cassell, J.W. (1989) 'In pursuit of evidence: Sampling procedures for locating new businesses', *Journal of Business Venturing*, 4 (6): 367–86.

Ang, S.H., Benischke, M.H. and Hooi, A.W.-L. (2018) 'Frequency of international expansion through high control market expansion modes and interlocked directorships', *Journal of World Business*, 53 (4): 493–503.

Austin, J.T., Boyle, K.A. and Lualhati, J.C. (1998) 'Statistical conclusion validity for organizational science researchers: A review', *Organizational Research Methods*, 1 (2): 164–208.

Bobko, P., Roth, P.L. and Buster, M.A. (2007) 'The usefulness of unit weights in creating composite scores', *Organizational Research Methods*, 10 (4): 689–709.

Bonett, D.G. and Wright, T.A. (2011) 'Sample size requirements for multiple regression interval estimation', *Journal of Organizational Behavior*, 32 (6): 822–30.

Boxall, P., Ang, S.H. and Bartram, T. (2011) 'Analysing the "black box": of HRM: Uncovering HR goals, mediators and outcomes in a standardized service environment', *Journal of Management Studies*, 48 (7): 1504–32.

Boyd, B.K., Gove, S. and Hitt, M.A. (2005) 'Construct measurement in strategic management research: Illusion or reality?', *Strategic Management Journal*, 26 (3): 239–57.

Calder, B. J., Phillips, L.W. and Tybout, A.M. (1982) 'The concept of external validity', *Journal of Consumer Research*, 9 (3): 240–44.

Carlson, K.D. and Herdman, A.O. (2012) 'Understanding the impact of convergent validity on research results', *Organizational Research Methods*, 15 (1): 17–32.

Carmines, E.G. and Zeller, R.A. (1979) *Reliability and Validity Assessment*. Newbury Park, CA: Sage Publishing.

Cohen, J. (1992) 'A power primer', *Psychological Bulletin*, 112 (1): 155–9.

Combs, J.G. (2010) 'Big samples and small effects: Let's not trade relevance and rigor for power', *Academy of Management Journal*, 53 (1): 9–13.

Cook, T.D. and Campbell, D.T. (1979) *Quasi-experimentation: Design and Analysis for Field Settings*. Chicago, IL: Rand McNally.

Cortina, J.M. (1993) 'What is coefficient alpha? An examination of theory and applications', *Journal of Applied Psychology*, 78 (1): 98–104.

Cronbach, L.J. (1951) 'Coefficient alpha and the internal structure of tests', *Psychometrika*, 16 (3): 297–334.

Cronbach, L.J. and Furby, L. (1970) 'How we should measure "change" – or should we?' *Psychological Bulletin*, 74 (1): 68–80.

Diamantopoulos, A. and Papadopoulos, N. (2010) 'Assessing the cross-national invariance of formative measures: Guidelines for international business researchers, *Journal of International Business Studies*, 41 (2): 360–70.

Dillman, D.A. (1978) *Mail and Telephone Surveys: The Total Design Method*. New York, NY: John Wiley & Sons.

Drazin, R. and Van de Ven, A.H. (1985) 'Alternative forms of fit in contingency theory', *Administrative Science Quarterly*, 30 (4): 514–39.

Firebaugh, G. and Gibbs, J.P. (1985) 'User's guide to ratio variables', *American Sociological Review*, 50 (5): 713–22.

Fralicx, R.D. and Raju, N.S. (1982) 'A comparison of five methods for combining multiple criteria into a single composite', *Educational and Psychological Measurement*, 42 (3): 823–27.

Fuguitt, G.V. and Lieberson, S. (1973–4) 'Correlation of ratios or difference scores having common terms', *Sociological Methodology*, 5: 128–44.

Gibbert, M. and Ruigrok, W. (2010) 'The "what" and "how" of case study rigor: Three strate-gies based on published work', *Organizational Research Methods*, 13 (4): 710–37.

Gibbert, M., Ruigrok, W. and Wicki, B. (2008) 'What passes as a rigorous case study?' *Strategic Management Journal*, 29 (13): 1465–74.

Goodman, J.S. and Blum, T.C. (1996) 'Assessing the non-random sampling effects of subject attrition in longitudinal research', *Journal of Management*, 22 (4): 627–52.

Green, S.B. (1991) 'How many subjects does it take to do a regression analysis?', *Multivariate Behavioral Research*, 26 (3): 499–510.

Grégoire, D.A., Shepherd, D.A. and Lambert, L.S. (2010) 'Measuring opportunity-recognition beliefs: Illustrating and validating an experimental approach', *Organizational Research Methods*, 13 (1): 114–45.

Guest, G., Bunce, A. and Johnson, L. (2006) 'How many interviews are enough? An experi-ment with data saturation and variability', *Field Methods*, 18 (1): 59–82.

Hamann, P.M., Schiemann, F., Bellora, L. and Guenther, T.W. (2013) 'Exploring the dimen-sions of organizational performance: A construct validity study', *Organizational Research Methods*, 16 (1): 67–87.

Heckman, J.J. (1979) 'Sample selection bias as a specification error', *Econometrica*, 47 (1): 153–61.

Hinkin, T.R. (1995) 'A review of scale development practices in the study of organizations', *Journal of Management*, 21 (5): 967–88.

Hinkin, T.R. (1998) 'A brief tutorial on the development of measures for use in survey questionnaires.',*Organizational Research Methods*, 1 (1): 104–21.

Hoffman, J.J., Cullen, J.B., Carter, N.M. and Hofacker, C.F. (1992) 'Alternative methods for meas-uring organization fit: Technology, structure, and performance', *Journal of Management*, 18 (1): 45–57.

Hult, G.T.M., Ketchen, D.J. Jr, Griffith, D.A., Finnegan, C.A., Gonzalez-Padron, T., Harmancioglu, N. ... and Cavusgil, S.T. (2008) 'Data equivalence in cross-cultural international business research: assessment and guidelines', *Journal of International Business Studies*, 39 (6): 1027–44.

Iyengar, R.J. and Zampelli, E.M. (2009) 'Self-selection, endogeneity, and the relationship between CEO duality and firm performance', *Strategic Management Journal*, 30 (10): 1092–112.

Johns, G. (1981) 'Difference score measures of organizational behavior variables: a critique', *Organizational Behavior and Human Performance*, 27 (3): 443–63.

Johns, G. (1991) 'Substantive and methodological constraints on behaviour and attitudes in organizational research', *Organizational Behavior and Human Decision Processes*, 49 (1): 80–104.

Johnson, S.M., Smith, P.C. and Tucker, S.M. (1982) 'Response format of the Job Descriptive Index: Assessment of reliability and validity by the multi-trait, multi-method matrix', *Journal of Applied Psychology*, 67 (4): 500–5.

Kalleberg, A.L., Marsden, P.V., Aldrich, H.E. and Cassell, J.W. (1990) 'Comparing organizational sampling frames', *Administrative Science Quarterly*, 35 (3): 658–88.

Kaptein, M. (2008) 'Developing a measure of unethical behavior in the workplace: A stake-holder perspective', *Journal of Management*, 34 (5): 978–1008.

Katz, J. and Gartner, W.B. (1988) 'Properties of emerging organizations', *Academy of Management Review*, 13 (3): 429–41.

Keller, T. and Dansereau, F. (2001) 'The effect of adding items to scales: An illustrative case of LMX', *Organizational Research Methods*, 4 (2): 131–43.

Kraemer, H.C. and Thiemann, S. (1987) *How Many Subjects? Statistical Power Analysis in Research*. Newbury Park, CA: Sage Publishing.

Kronmal, R.A. (1993) 'Spurious correlation and the fallacy of the ratio standard revisited', *Journal of the Royal Statistical Society: Series A (Statistics in Society)*, 156: 379–92.

Krosnick, J.A., Holbrook, A.L., Berent, M.K., Carson, R.T., Hanemann, W.M., Kopp, R.J. ... and Conway, M. (2002) 'The impact of "no opinion" response options on data quality: Non-attitude reduction or an invitation to satisfice?' *Public Opinion Quarterly*, 66 (3): 371–403.

Lance, C.E., Butts, M.M. and Michels, L.C. (2006) 'The sources of four commonly reported cutoff criteria: what did they really say?' *Organizational Research Methods*, 9 (2): 202–20.

Lissitz, R.W. and Green, S.B. (1975) 'Effect of the number of scale points on reliability: a Monte Carlo approach', *Journal of Applied Psychology*, 60 (1): 10–13.

MacKenzie, S.B. (2003) 'The dangers of poor construct conceptualization', *Journal of the Academy of Marketing Science*, 31 (3): 323–26.

March, J.G., Sproull, L.S. and Tamuz, M. (1991) 'Learning from samples of one or fewer', *Organization Science*, 2 (1): 1–13.

Marino, K.E. and Lange, D.R. (1983) 'Measuring organizational slack: A note on the convergence and divergence of alternative operational definitions', *Journal of Management*, 9 (1): 81–92.

McGrath, J.E. (1981) 'Dilemmatics: The study of research choices and dilemmas', *American Behavioral Scientist*, 25 (2): 179–210.

McGrath, J.E. and Brinberg, D. (1983) 'External validity and the research process: A comment on the Calder/Lynch dialogue', *Journal of Consumer Research*, 10 (1): 115–24.

Messick, S. (1980) 'Test validity and the ethics of assessment', *American Psychologist*, 35 (11): 1012–27.

Mook, D.G. (1983) 'In defense of external invalidity', *American Psychologist*, 38 (4): 379–87.

Nakkeeran, N. (2016) 'Is sampling a misnomer in qualitative research?', *Sociological Bulletin*, 65 (1): 40–9.

Nunnally, J.C. (1978) *Psychometric Theory*, (2nd edition). New York: McGraw-Hill.

Oaster, T.R.F. (1989) 'Number of alternatives per choice point and stability of Likert-type scales', *Perceptual and Motor Skills*, 68 (2): 549–50.

Riege, A.M. (2003) 'Validity and reliability tests in case study research: A literature review with "hands-on" applications for each research phase', *Qualitative Market Research*, 6 (2): 75–86.

Riordan, C.M. and Vandenberg, R.J. (1994) 'A central question in cross-cultural research: Do employees of different cultures interpret work-related measures in an equivalent manner?', *Journal of Management*, 20 (3): 643–71.

Rowe, W.G. and Morrow, J.L. Jr. (1999) 'A note on the dimensionality of the firm financial performance construct using accounting, market, and subjective measures', *Canadian Journal of Administrative Sciences*, 16 (1): 58–70.

Sackett, P.R. and Larson, J.R. Jr. (1990) 'Research strategies and tactics in industrial and organizational psychology', in M.D. Dunnette and L.M. Hough (eds), *Handbook of Industrial and Organizational Psychology*, volume 1, (2nd edition.). Palo Alto, CA: Consulting Psychologists Press. pp. 419–89.

Scandura, T.A. and Williams, E.A. (2000) 'Research methodology in management: Current practices, trends, and implications for future research', *Academy of Management Journal*, 43 (6): 1248–64.

Shaver, J.M. (1998) 'Accounting for endogeneity when assessing strategy performance: Does entry mode choice affect FDI survival?', *Management Science*, 44 (4): 571–85.

Short, J.C., Ketchen, D.J. Jr. and Palmer, T.B. (2002) 'The role of sampling in strategic management research on performance: A two-study analysis', *Journal of Management*, 28 (3): 363–85.

Sudman, S. and Blair, E. (1999) 'Sampling in the twenty-first century', *Journal of the Academy of Marketing Science*, 27 (2): 269–77.

Tehrani, M. and Noubary, R. (2005) 'A statistical conversion technique: objective and perceptive financial measures of the performance construct', *Organizational Research Methods*, 8 (2): 202–21.

Tipton, E., Hallberg, K., Hedges, L.V. and Chan, W. (2017) 'Implications of small samples for generalization: Adjustments and rules of thumb', *Evaluation Review*, 41 (5): 472–505.

Traub, R.E. and Rowley, G.L. (1991) 'An NCME instructional module on understanding reliability', *Educational Measurement: Issues and Practice*, 10 (1): 37–45.

7
DATA COLLECTION METHODS

7.1 INTRODUCTION

In the previous chapter we discussed the essence of data in research and the various issues that are attached to data itself. While data is important, the actual data used in research is the outcome of the data collection process. This makes data collection methods and processes an integral part of research outcomes. Rigorous data collection methods and processes result in quality data. This chapter will look at the various methods that researchers can use to collect data for their research. In particular, we will focus on five key types of data collection methods, namely **interviews**, **focus groups**, **participant observation**, **experiments** and surveys. The chapter also highlights the use of **archival data** and data that spans across industries and countries.

> ## Conversation box
>
> *Amanda [Masters student]:* Professor, I understand there are many ways to go about collecting data. But isn't it about finding the fastest and easiest way to access the data that we need?
>
> *Professor:* Amanda, 'fast' is needed when there is a timeline to completing your research. I am not sure what you mean by easiest. One can argue that there is no 'easiest' way to collect data. Each of the various data collection methods involves hard work. Moreover, depending on the data needed, one method might be deemed to be more appropriate and effective than another method of data collection.
>
> *(Continued)*

Amanda:	Thanks, professor. How then can I decide on which method is the best?
Professor:	To a large extent, you will have to go back to your research question and the literature to help you with that.

7.2 INTERVIEWS

Interviews are usually used in research designs that involve research questions seeking to understand the underlying motivations of attitudes, preferences or behaviours. There are various forms of interviews, the key ones being face-to-face and **telephone interviews**. In any interview, the person being interviewed – the interviewee – is normally regarded as an expert. Through the use of questions asked in a neutral manner, the interviewer seeks to understand the attitudes, preferences or behaviours of the interviewee relating to the research topic at hand.

Interviews are an effective qualitative tool for getting people to talk about their personal feelings, opinions and experiences. They are also an opportunity for researchers to gain insights into how people interpret their surroundings. This is accomplished by the interviewer being attentive to the causal explanations the interviewee provides for what they have experienced, and by actively probing them about the connections and relationships they see between particular events, phenomena and beliefs. Interviews are also especially appropriate for addressing sensitive topics, such as attitudes towards unethical behaviours.

Interview data consist of tape recordings, typed transcripts of tape recordings and the interviewer's notes. Notes may document **observations** about the interview content, the participant and the context. Given the sensitivity of the interview data, sometimes it might not be easy to recruit interviewees when they know you will be recording the interview proceedings. In research that involves people, we have to promise anonymity in almost all cases. This means that whatever was discussed does not get passed around beyond a small, pre-defined set of people. The participant will need to agree on this pre-defined set of people before the interview starts. Keeping a record is necessary for its subsequent use and also for research verification purposes when necessary. Thus, not recording is hardly an option. These rules also apply to other forms of data collection involving people, such as surveys. Interviewees need to fully consent to their involvement, otherwise you cannot include them in your research.

Conversation box

Jane [Masters student]:   Professor, for my Masters project, how many interviews should I conduct to collect my data?

Professor: Jane, it really depends on your research objective. Your research objective will determine what kinds of interviewees you will need. You will then rely on these attributes to identify a pool of potential interviewees. Using a sampling method, you select the representative ones. As to the exact number of interviews that you need, that will depend on the constraints you have and how many it would take for you to arrive at some conclusion.

The actual number of interviews required for each research will be determined by several factors. These include the expectations of the outcomes including whether it is for a journal publication, PhD dissertation or a Masters project, the time and other resource contraints, the breadth and depth of the research topic, the access to potential interviewees and the research conclusions needed such as the general level of consensus of the interviewees needed for this research. It is clear that the number of interviews required is research-specific, so there is no standard answer to this question. Nonetheless, studies have been conducted to determine the number of interviews that need to take place before saturation happens, i.e. general consensus is reached. Guest et al. (2006) show that, in their case, the number of interviews to reach saturation was twelve. They also note that their result might not be as generalizable and provide various discussions on this. As mentioned above, the number of interviews before saturation occurs will be specific to a particular research.

7.2.1 Face-to-face interviews

Face-to-face interviews can be conducted in a structured, semi-structured or unstructured way. Structured face-to-face interviews have carefully worded interview schedules that often allow the interviewee to be brief in their responses. Unstructured interviews involve the interviewer having prompt questions and expecting the interviewee to talk freely. There is often an impromptu element, with the content of the interview depending on the responses made by the interviewee. Semi-structured interviews are a mid-way choice between structured and unstructured interviews. They involve asking a pre-determined set of questions yet allowing the interviewee the freedom to elaborate on their responses.

The face-to-face interview method has several advantages. First, the interviewer has substantial control over the process of data collection. Thus, when detecting any research anomaly in the process, the researcher will be able to adjust accordingly in order to ensure that good quality data is collected. Second, the process allows for full completion of responses required. That is, there is a minimal chance of having missing data and low **response rates**. Third, the method also allows the investigation of motives and feelings, which are difficult to capture using other data collection methods. Tone of voice and facial expression of an interviewee may be detected in face-to-face interviews and can provide additional information to verbal responses. Another useful aspect of face-to-face interviews is that they are often used as piloting for other methods. In other words, researchers often use face-to-face interviews to have some initial understanding of an issue before utilizing other methodologies to collect further data.

Face-to-face interviews are time consuming, however, and even before you start conducting them it is necessary to secure good access to potential interviewees. The search for good interviewees itself will take time. If we are talking about accessing busy executives, that can be an additional hindrance as it is often hard to get these busy people to talk about issues for an hour or so in order for you to understand your research better. While it is advantageous to capture characteristics such as tone of voice and facial expression, as discussed above, interpreting these can sometimes lead to bias. The interviewee may also be someone who is keen to please or impress or portray a good image and thus may provide responses that the interviewer wants to hear. 'Good' responses may also be provided so that the interviewee can end the interview process quicker in order to save time or rush to the next appointment. Extra care needs to be taken during the process of transcribing and analysis as any subjective interpretation can be detrimental to the research outcome. As the nature of the research process relies on the impromptu behaviour of the interviewer, training is also required when multiple interviewers are involved in a research project to ensure the consistent execution of the interviews.

Conversation box

Sven [Masters student]: Professor, given the disadvantages that face-to-face interviews have, would we not assume that this data collection method should be avoided whenever possible?

Professor: Sven, the main problem with avoiding face-to-face interviews is that in many studies that deal with understanding of processes, they provide the best possible way to get something out of the respondents, with the help of open-ended questions using semi-structured or unstructured interviews.

7.2.2 Telephone interviews

Telephone interviews are the other commonly used interview technique. While offering the typical advantages that interviews confer, telephone interviews also enjoy some advantages over face-to-face interviews. It is a relatively cheaper and easier method to operate; for example, you do not have to travel to meet with the interviewee. This also means that telephone interviews can cover a wider geographical area in reaching interviewees. As a result of needing less effort to set up, telephone interviews are always quicker to conduct than face-to-face interviews. Due to these additional advantages, telephone interviews are the preferred technique when a reasonably large number of respondents are desired in your research.

Conversation box

Jan [Masters student]: Professor, telephone interviews seem to be a cheaper option than face-to-face interviews. We should then avoid the use of face-to-face interviews as a larger sample provides more explanatory power, right?

Professor: Jan, of course telephone interviews have some advantages over face-to-face interviews when it comes to getting a large sample size. But face-to-face interviews do have advantages over telephone interviews that make them better vehicles for collecting more in-depth data. Ultimately it is a research decision between getting more data versus getting richer data.

However, telephone interviews have some disadvantages that are not associated with face-to-face interviews. First, a more structured set of questions is often required. Sometimes, it is very hard to improvise on the telephone as you cannot observe the behaviour of the interviewee. Thus, following a script is necessary. Second, as the encounter lacks the 'personal' touch, the interaction in telephone interviews tend to be more formal and the interviewee may be less comfortable with the interviewer as there is a smaller degree of intimacy. This can also lead to irritation, since the interviewer has less awareness of the comfort level of the interviewee. Third, the researcher needs to exercise a lot of patience and tact, as it is never easy to contact someone by phone let alone geting them to talk to you for quite some time for the interview.

It is important to note that telephone interviews are (obviously!) limited to respondents who have phone access. Therefore, it may not be appropriate for studies involving those living in rural areas or people who cannot afford a telephone line in their home or a mobile phone. Sometimes, telephone interviews may lower the authority level of the interviewer as telephone interviews are often associated with marketers selling their products. Thus, if conveying the importance of the respondent's participation is crucial, telephone interviews should be avoided as far as possible.

7.3 FOCUS GROUPS

A focus group is an interview conducted by a trained moderator in a non-structured and natural manner with a small group of participants at the same time. The moderator leads the discussion, and prompts responses from the group. Focus group size usually varies from four to ten participants. Questions are asked in an interactive group setting where participants are free to talk with other group members. The main purpose of focus groups is to gain insights by listening to a group of people with appropriate background talking about a specific research issue. In the area of marketing for example, focus groups are seen as an important tool for acquiring feedback regarding new products and services.

Broadly, focus group interviews can be used for both trying to understand what the issues are and understanding more of an issue at hand. For example, your company wishes to introduce a new health drink for the elderly; however, it is a high-risk venture so knowing the the target group's receptivity towards your health drink is essential for the success of its introduction. Focus group interviews can provide a tool through which you can try to understand the attitude of older people towards health drinks in general and more specifically to your company's health drink.

Conversation box

Zoe [student]:   Why would anyone use focus group interviews when personal interviews can serve the same purposes?

Professor: Focus group interviews have the value of allowing the interaction of participants, and by having discussions among participants, the issue at hand can potentially be better understood than when personal interviews are being used. Discussions among participants can elicit information that may otherwise not be available when there is only interviewee–interviewer interaction. Further, additional interesting points may surface as a result of conversations within focus groups that are otherwise not possible through a one-on-one interview.

As focus groups involve the collection of data in a more natural setting, they provide richer data than one-to-one interviews. Listening to others' verbalized experiences stimulates a participant's own memories, ideas and experiences. This is also known as the group effect (Lindlof and Taylor, 2011). Focus groups also provide an opportunity for disclosure among others in a setting where participants are validated. For example, in the context of workplace bullying, targeted employees often find themselves in situations where they experience lack of voice and feelings of isolation. Focus groups to study workplace bullying therefore serve as both an efficacious and ethical venue for collecting data (Tracy et al., 2006). In essence, focus groups are especially effective for capturing information about social norms and the variety of opinions or views within a target population. Focus groups are also low in cost and produce results relatively quickly (Marshall and Rossman, 2006).

Below are some forms of focus groups:

- Two-way focus group – one focus group watches another focus group and discusses the observed interactions and conclusion.
- Dual moderator focus group – one moderator ensures the session progresses smoothly, while another ensures that all the topics are covered.
- Duelling moderator focus group – two moderators deliberately take opposite sides on the issue under discussion.
- Teleconference focus groups – a telephone network is used.
- Online focus groups – computers or devices (connected via the Internet) are used.

As with all other data collection methods, focus groups also have disadvantages. The researcher has less control over a focus group than in a one-on-one interview, and thus time can be lost on issues irrelevant to the research topic in focus group discussions. Moderators need to be well trained in order to keep the conversations in check and in order so that the discussions remain relevant. Data can also be tough to analyze as very often remarks are made in reaction to the comments of other group members, as opposed to responding directly to the researcher's question.

Very often researchers themselves are not detached observers of the process but are in fact participants in the focus group sessions. Tjaco (2003) advises that researchers must take this into account when conducting their analysis. Rushkoff (2005) further argues that focus groups, smaller ones in particular, are often useless, and frequently cause more problems in research than they help solve, with focus group members often aiming to please rather than offering their own opinions or evaluations, and with data often cherry picked to support a foregone conclusion. For these reasons, researchers will certainly need to ensure the objectivity of research continues to be observed when conducting focus group sessions.

Given the setting, it is hard to ensure anonymity in focus groups, as other participants are also involved. The best one can do is to make the participants sign an agreement to ensure that what gets discussed does not leave the room.

Focus group data consist of tape recordings, transcripts of those recordings, the moderator's and note-taker's notes from the discussion, and notes from the debriefing session held after the focus group session.

7.4 PARTICIPANT OBSERVATION

Participant observation involves recording the behavioural patterns of people, objects and events in a systematic manner. Observational methods may be (1) structured or unstructured; (2) disguised or undisguised; (3) natural or contrived; (4) personal or mechanical; (5) non-participant or participant, with the participant researcher taking a number of different roles.

In structured observation the researcher specifies in detail what is to be observed and how the measurements are to be recorded. This is appropriate when the needed information could be explicitly specified. In unstructured observation the researcher monitors all aspects of the proceedings that are deemed relevant to the issue being investigated. This is appropriate when the research problem is not or could not be explicitly specified a priori, and flexibility is needed in the participant observation process to help identify key components of the problem.

In disguised observation, respondents are unaware that they are being observed. In undisguised observation there are potential Hawthorne effects, i.e. adjustments in behaviour as the result of knowing that one is being observed. Natural observation involves observing behaviour as it takes place in the environment, such as managers in a discussion to arrive at a decision in their corporate boardroom. Contrived observation occurs in an artificial setting, such as getting executive students to participate in a decision-making session to observe how a decision is arrived at.

Personal observation occurs when a researcher observes actual behaviours as they unfold. Mechanical observation is done through the use of devices that record observations. In non-participant techniques, the researcher does not normally question or communicate with the subjects being observed, while in participant observation the researcher actually becomes part of the group being observed. The participant can assume various roles. For a detailed discussion of these roles, see Vinten (1994) and Johnson et al. (2006). Peshkin (1984) highlights the limitations of the human participant observer role.

Observational methods require the researcher to be objective in their observation and in taking notes. As with interviews, there is always a risk of being selective in observation or in taking notes. There will be a tendency for a researcher to include only those observations that align well with their a priori expectations. Again, such tendencies should be avoided.

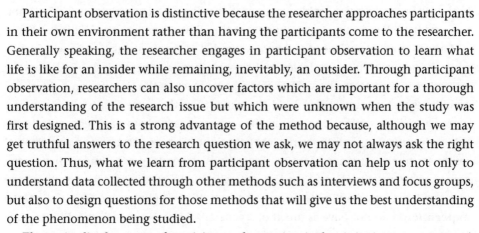

Conversation box

Marcus [student]:   Given that an observer in a focus group is also sometimes perceived as a participant, what is the difference between a focus group and participant observation?

Professor: In focus group sessions, the researcher's main task is to observe. The advice is always for them to distance themselves from accidentally becoming an active participant. The role of the observer is really a moderator rather than a participant. In participant observation, the researcher actively engages in the discussion. Of course, this means they have to stop thinking of themselves as the researcher or moderator to maximize their value as another participant.

Participant observation is distinctive because the researcher approaches participants in their own environment rather than having the participants come to the researcher. Generally speaking, the researcher engages in participant observation to learn what life is like for an insider while remaining, inevitably, an outsider. Through participant observation, researchers can also uncover factors which are important for a thorough understanding of the research issue but which were unknown when the study was first designed. This is a strong advantage of the method because, although we may get truthful answers to the research question we ask, we may not always ask the right question. Thus, what we learn from participant observation can help us not only to understand data collected through other methods such as interviews and focus groups, but also to design questions for those methods that will give us the best understanding of the phenomenon being studied.

The main disadvantage of participant observation is that it is time-consuming. A second disadvantage of participant observation is the difficulty of documenting the data – it is hard to write down everything that is important while you are in the act of participating and observing. As the researcher, you must therefore rely on your memory and on your own personal discipline to write down and expand your obser-vations as soon and as completely as possible. It is easy to tell yourself that you will do this task later, but, because memory fades quickly, postponing the expansion of notes can lead to loss or inaccurate recording of data. The quality of the data there-fore depends on the diligence of the researcher, rather than on technology such as tape recorders.

Participant observation data consist of the detailed field notes that the researcher records in a field notebook. Although typically textual, such data may also include maps and diagrams. Occasionally, participant observation may involve quantification of something and, as a result, produce numerical data. For example, the researcher could count the number of people who enter a particular space and engage in a particular activity during a specified segment of time. Textual notes are entered into computer files, and data of all forms are analyzed and referenced on a regular basis.

7.5 EXPERIMENTS

Recall that in Section 5.4.3 we discussed the difference between correlation and causality in research. In essence, effect should be observed with a time lag after cause. Due to the importance of establishing causality, experiments have been deemed to be an excellent research tool to collect data. Experiments allow a researcher to establish causality with the strong ability to control the conditions and other effects on the outcome variables. This has led to their relatively greater use in organizational research in the 1980s. Nonetheless, evidence suggests that the use of experiments (both laboratory and field) has declined subsequently in the 1990s (Scandura and Williams, 2000).

Laboratory experiments allow a researcher to create a situation in which they control and manipulate variables and expose these to the subjects. Basically, the researcher is keen to see how these participants react to the situation in light of the conditions and manipulations. Field experiments, as the name suggests, happen in a more naturalistic setting. Due to this, the researcher is likely to have less control over the environment and all the variables that might have an effect on the participants' responses to the situation. Due to the settings, laboratory experiments have been argued to be articificial and thus less generalizable to other contexts, i.e. they have issues with external validity (Griffin and Kacmar, 1991; Highhouse, 2009). While **field experiments** do not have as much of a generalizability issue, their inability to have strong control over extraneous effects on outcomes make them subject to scepticism around causality. Further, field experiments in naturalistic settings can mean potential privacy and ethical issues in handling the participants, making field experiments difficult to execute and less convincing to potential participants.

Despite these general challenges, researchers have jumped to the defense of the use of experiments. Dipboye and Flanagan (1979) show that laboratory experiments are no worse than field experiments when it comes to external validity. They suggest that the examination of external validity should be based on the actors, settings and behaviours a researcher wishes to generalize towards. In essence, it is important for us to judge external validity based on the population to which we wish to infer from our research. If your research pertains to the tertiary education fees, then the population should be confined to tertiary actors, rather than any population such as a city or a country. Listing your boundary as tertiary actors will invite little criticism about the generalizability of your outcomes.

Other authors have also provided some compelling reasons for the use of laboratory experiments (e.g. Berkowitz and Donnerstein, 1982; Dobbins et al., 1988; Griffin and Kacmar, 1991). Griffin and Kacmar (1991) further suggest some circumstances where laboratory experiments will be instrumental, for example for exploratory research, when multiple studies or samples are needed (we see a lot of these in the marketing discipline these days), and interdisciplinary research. As student samples are used often for laboratory experiments, questions have been raised about the ability to generalize from a student pool of participants (e.g. Dobbins et al., 1988; Gordon et al., 1986). To that end, again it might be the case that it really depends on the population that you are inferring on. There are also possibilities to combine laboratory and field experiments in a research to provide a more holistic investigation of a phenomenon at hand (Dipboye and Flanagan, 1979; Greenberg and Tomlinson, 2004; Griffin and Kacmar, 1991).

Beyond external validity concerns, experiments are in fact still a strong tool for testing causality. But when it comes to manipulations, it will be good to make sure that construct validity, i.e. convergent validity and discriminant validity, is taken care of (Highhouse, 2009; Perdue and Summers, 1986).

7.6 SURVEY DESIGNS

Conversation box

Heather [Honours student]:	Can interviews be conducted in a survey format?
Professor:	Of course. However, it can become complex to design a survey when there are too many open-ended questions.
Heather:	So, surveys are useful when we do not need to go into great detail?
Professor:	Probably because of the nature of the instruments, surveys are better off used for targeting a larger sample. For greater detail, interviews might be more appropriate, though you are bound to compromise on sample size.

The increase in the availability of archival data has certainly made research easier. However, not all archival data are collected for the purpose of your research. When this happens, you realize that you have to undergo a similar tedious process to collect your data. Worse still, if the data are hard to operationalize and difficult to measure using the basic information often provided by companies, you may start thinking of looking to use case studies. Then you realize you do not have access to good informants and respondents. Even if you manage to hurdle this obstacle, you wonder if the respondent is objective and you feel you really need more opinions. However, a decently large sample is difficult to achieve using the case study approach.

Is there a solution to the kinds of problems encountered above when confronted with data? Facing these challenges, many researchers would end up choosing to conduct their own surveys. Surveys can help researchers find out respondents' (or the larger entity to which they represent) attitudes, beliefs, behaviours and attributes. Respondents' attitudes mainly reflect what people say they want: for example, should the European Union enlarge its membership? Is smoking good or bad? Respondents' beliefs deal with issues that you want the respondents to assess – whether something is correct or incorrect, accurate or inaccurate, or what happened versus what did not happen. We also use surveys to ask the respondents about whether they are engaging or have engaged in certain activities. Finally, we often ask for the attributes of the respondents in order to understand the background of the respondents, which might influence their responses in the survey.

We can classify surveys into structured versus unstructured surveys. Structured surveys are those that contain questions that are closed-ended, where you limit the number of options that the respondents can choose from in each question. Unstructured surveys are those that are open-ended and allow the participants to describe their own responses. The advantage of structured surveys is that it helps to narrow down the options in order to allow easier analysis as the range of responses is restricted. This, in particular, permits quantitative analysis to be conducted. However, this also works on the presumption that you are able to come up with the different options that the respondents might think of. This is by no means easy and it also forces your respondents to make a choice between the prescribed options, hence not providing information that might otherwise prove useful. In a strict research sense, this restriction is unwarranted and should be prevented. Unstructured surveys are used more often in cases where we are less certain about what responses the **survey questions** might generate. So, we prompt the respondents to write down their responses without pre-empting them. Unstructured surveys are also useful for extracting information that is hard to quantify.

Figure 7.1 compares **mail surveys** with face-to-face and telephone interviews across key attributes.

Criterion		Mail surveys	Face-to-face interviews	Telephone interviews
1	Access to a large number of people or organizations	High	Limited	Medium
2	Wide geographic coverage	High	Limited	High
3	Allowable complexity	Low	High	Medium
4	Response rate	Low	High	Medium
5	Time delay whilst waiting for responses	High	None	Limited
6	Success with open-ended questions	Low	High	Medium
7	Success with tedious questions	Low	High	Medium
8	Likelihood that social desirability bias can be avoided	Highly likely	Unlikely	Medium
9	Possible anonymity of respondents	High	Low	Medium
10	Respondents allowed to consider responses	High	Limited	Medium
11	Likelihood that interviewer distortion and subversion can be avoided	Most likely	Unlikely	Medium
12	Potential speed of implementation	High	Low	Medium
13	Costs	Medium	High	Medium
14	Success in avoiding item non-response	Medium	High	High
15	Investigation of motives and feelings	Low	High	Medium
16	Insensitivity to questionnaire construction procedures	Low	High	Medium

Figure 7.1   Comparison of mail surveys with face-to-face and telephone interviews

7.6.1 Designing the survey

Conversation box

Greg [Masters student]: Professor, I have grouped the items together for the survey. Shall I just format them and prepare to send them out?

Professor: Have you checked all aspects of the survey design and format to ensure that they are optimized for response?

Greg: Not sure what you mean by that.

(Continued)

Professor:	Respondents' reaction to your survey can sometimes be affected by the sight of the questionnaire that appears before them. It is important that you tailor the appearance of your questionnaire to the liking of your potential respondents.
Greg:	Seems like an art in itself as you describe it.
Professor:	More like a combination of both art and science.

Beyond the design of survey questions, which we will touch on in the next sub-section, there are a few generic design aspects that apply to any **survey design** and we will cover some key generic aspects here.

Cover letter

Any survey **questionnaire** always has to be accompanied by a cover letter. The cover letter greets the potential respondents to your survey questionnaire. Even if you have contacted the respondents before sending out the survey questionnaire, the cover letter is still necessary.

The cover letter should: (1) state who you are; (2) say what research issue and research question you are addressing; (3) explain what data are required and why; (4) give an assurance of confidentiality and/or anonymity of responses; (5) say 'thank you' in advance to the respondents for responding; and (6) give contact details in case of any queries. In addition to these items, you also need to be explicit with the estimated completion time needed for the survey so that the respondents are not frustrated if the completion time is longer than they were expecting or because they did not know what they have signed up for. In addition, the return date needs to be made obvious so that either the respondent will meet the deadline or knows they are unlikely to respond. Either way, it makes it easier for you to collate your survey responses.

Instructions for completion

You will need to provide clear and unambiguous instructions for completion of the questionnaire. An important aspect to ensure a greater response rate and fewer issues with incomplete questionnaire returns is to facilitate the ease with which the participants can respond to your questionnaire. There may be both general and question-specific instructions, the latter usually spread throughout the questionnaire where specific instructions are needed. When different types of responses are needed across the different questions in the questionnaire, you need to be clear with regard to the response methods needed, such as 'circle', 'tick' or 'tick all that apply'.

Appearance and length

Appearance of a questionnaire is important. Questionnaires with cluttered questions are likely to put off respondents. Inadequate spacing can lead to confusion for respondents as well. So liberal spacing throughout the questionnaire is needed. Using consistent formatting across the questionnaire will take out the need for respondents to second-guess what is required of them. Font style selection is also crucial for legibility.

Length of the questionnaire is a major factor influencing response rate. It is essential to ensure that the questionnaire does not over-tax the respondents on both time and energy needed to respond to your questions. Extremely complex questions should also be avoided as these can be interpreted differently by different respondents or could be too tedious for respondents to answer. When a long questionnaire cannot be avoided, then it may be advisable to leave the page numbers out so that it does not put the respondents off on the strenuous journey ahead of them. The same good practice of not having a long questionnaire will apply to web-based surveys.

Pilot survey

Designing a questionnaire is by no means an easy task. As such, we often have to go through iterations before a questionnaire is finalized. To refine the questionnaire, a **pilot survey** may also be needed. A pilot survey is a trial version of the questionnaire. A pilot survey is needed when you design your own questionnaire or adapt from an existing survey. It allows for feedback on the questions designed; adjustments from such feedback will be incorporated into the next version of the questionnaire. The next version of the questionnaire may need to be re-tested for further refinements. This process is repeated until the questionnaire is finalized and ready to be sent to the actual respondents.

Conversation box

Professor:	It is increasingly common for surveys to be conducted online. A key advantage is that **online surveys** have better reach than traditional mail surveys.
Florence [Honours student]:	Professor, is it easy to set up an online survey?
Professor:	There are many tools these days that provide online survey services. Some of these include SurveyMonkey, Zoomerang, Websurveyor, Qualtrics, and QuestionPro. It is easy to google these and work out your preferences. Most platforms are easy to use. All you need is to have your survey instruments ready. Of course, some may require subscription if you opt for specific types of design.
Florence:	Will there not be privacy issues?
Professor:	Definitely, Florence. You should check out Buchanan and Hvizdak (2009), Cho and Larose (1999), Roberts and Allen (2015), and Stanton and Rogelberg (2001) for extensive discussions on privacy issues and their suggestions on how to tackle those in online surveys.

Incentives

Getting participants to respond to your survey questionnaire can be a major challenge. To you, your research means everything, or it is important enough for you to spend time on it. The reality is that to many of your participants your research may mean little. The context of your work may be too distanced from the participants, so that sometimes it makes sense to provide incentives beyond trying to convince them of the importance of your research.

The kind of incentives depends a lot on the type of people you are going to survey. A small monetary reward tends to work if it is paid before (or at the time of) data collection. This form of incentive does not work as well if a promise is made to provide money after the responses are received (Gajraj et al. 1990; Warriner et al., 1996). Nonetheless, the findings on the outcomes of using money as incentives are mixed. Partly as a result, vouchers are increasingly being used as incentives by survey designers.

Unlike cash, vouchers do not create as much of an impression of 'paying off' respondents for their services.

The two books by Dillman (1978, 2007) provide extensive discussions on other value-added as perceived by participants, beyond providing money and vouchers as incentives.

7.6.2 Survey questions

In interviews and questionnaires with a large number of questions, a researcher should always minimize asking ad hoc questions. In other words, all the questions should be organized according to themes and should not be random. Beyond the need to be cautious about the order of the questions in the questionnaire, there are some rules of thumb that one needs to observe when designing questions for a survey.

1. Make sure the questions are direct and straight to the point. Avoid lengthy questions as they may create ambiguity and subjective interpretations.
2. Avoid using jargon or words that may lead different respondents to have different interpretations. For example, words such as 'generally' and 'normally', which are subject to the individual's interpretation, should be avoided.
3. Do not make incorrect assumptions about the respondents' knowledge of the subject matter of the question. For example, if your questionnaire touches on the issue of capabilities, try to explain what is meant by capabilities first before you go on to ask more specific questions about capabilities.
4. Care must be taken to ask only questions that are related to measuring variables and not to confuse respondents with ad hoc questions, though it may seem tempting to ask more questions out of curiosity. Adequate preparation should be made as to what is expected of the respondent from each question. This is an important element of the process because you must be able to gauge if the respondent is adequately eligible to respond for the purpose of the research, especially for open-ended questions. Ask only the background questions that are necessary for the framework of the research. Do not ask for excessive background information that you do not need for the analysis.
5. As far as possible, ask questions that the respondent can easily answer without having to do memory work or calculations. In the context of asking retrospective questions of survey respondents, the works of Golden (1992, 1997) provide some good discussions on what might work and what might not.
6. Avoid leading questions that force respondents to lean towards a particular response.
7. Avoid the double-barrel problem. Make sure that you are looking for a single response to a single question instead of lumping two or more questions into one. For example, the question 'Does your company hire consultants and ex-employees?' should be split into two separate questions to allow specific responses relating to hiring consultants and hiring ex-employees.

8. Design response choices that are as specific as possible. For example, for a question about how many times one takes a bus ride to the office each week, instead of offering choices like 'a lot', you should use 'five times a week', 'three times a week', etc. as response choices. However, for potentially sensitive questions, such as salary of executives, use bracketed choices rather than asking for an exact figure.

9. In choosing ranges for responses, do take note that the choice of range might affect the perception of respondents, for example a range of 1-10 may be perceived differently to -5 to 5 (Schwarz et al., 1988; 1991). Therefore, the choice options need to be created carefully to allow proper baseline interpretations.

Besides the more generic aspects of designing the survey as discussed above, the wording of survey questions is another critical aspect of getting the maximum value out of the respondents. Dillman (1978) provides extensive discussion of how to design surveys both generically and how to frame the questions. Figure 7.2 highlights some of the risks associated with the phrasing of questions in a survey.

Question	Assessment	Potential solution
More people have used Apple computer products in the last decade than perhaps any other brand. Do you own an Apple product or do you intend to? 1. Yes 2. No	**Bias from establishing a behavioural expectation** You will notice that this question is phrased in a way that is biased. The statement first suggests that the majority of people have used Apple products in the last decade. The actual question is whether the respondent has owned one or intends to own one. This statement actually creates a behavioural expectation – that if the respondent had not owned one, he would be someone who is deemed to behave somewhat unusually in comparison to many others. This puts pressure on the respondents to respond 'yes' to the survey question, potentially biasing the response outcomes from this survey question.	Question 1: Do you own any Apple products? Question 2: If you don't already own an Apple product, do you intend to have one?
Currently our country exports about 350 billion dollars' worth of goods to China. Do you feel this amount should be: 1. Decreased 2. Stay the same 3. Increased a little 4. Increased somewhat 5. Increased a great deal	**Bias from unbalanced categories** You will notice that the 'stay the same' choice – our neutral category – is rated as the second option of the five possibilities. There is only one option relating to a response for a decrease in exports while the three other options are all leaning towards an increase in exports. This creates an unbalanced choice set, which may have reflected the researcher's expectation that the respondents will advocate an increase in exports. This choice set is undesirable. The neutral category needs to be designed to be the mid-point of the range of choices.	Currently our country exports about 350 billion dollars' worth of goods to China. Do you feel this amount should be: 1. Decreased significantly 2. Decreased slightly 3. Stay the same 4. Increased slightly 5. Increased significantly

Question	Assessment	Potential solution
How much was your salary in 2019? _____	**Objectionable question** While this question at first sight does not appear to have an issue, respondents can sometimes be sensitive to questions relating to their salary or age, or any other questions that they feel may have intruded into their privacy. In such cases, a researcher should spare the respondent the hesitancy to provide an honest answer by allowing some choices instead.	Which category best describes your salary in 2019? 1. Less than $20,000 2. $20,000 to $30,000 3. $30,000 to $40,000 4. $40,000 to $50,000 5. $50,000 to $60,000 6. More than $60,000
What percentage of your leisure hours is spent on sports?	**Demanding question** This is a seemingly simple question for the respondent. But if you think of it, it actually requires your respondent to do some mental calculations. Where this might seem easy if the numbers are, for example, 16 leisure hours and 4 hours on sports, which equates to 25 per cent, for most of the time, the calculation is more complicated than this and cannot be done mentally. You could avoid taxing your respondents by asking two questions instead and working out your own calculations.	Question 1: How many leisure hours do you have in an average week? Question 2: How many hours do you spend on sports in an average week?

Figure 7.2   Some examples of the risks associated with the phrasing of questions in a survey

7.6.3 Self-report issues

Surveys are associated with issues of **self-reports** – where respondents self-assess their behaviours or beliefs. Self-reports are used for: (1) obtaining demographic and factual information; (2) gathering personality data; (3) obtaining perceptions or attitudes of a matter; (4) assessing the psychological state of a respondent; and (5) obtaining information about past behaviours. This list is not exhaustive. As many of such data are not observable, in most circumstances the only way to get to them is to use self-reports, in particular through a survey.

Despite their usefulness, self-reports have a few inherent issues. A critical one pertains to **common method variance**. Common method variance occurs when a respondent answers a set of questions concurrently while the responses are tested for causal relationships. There is a chance that when they answer positively to one question, they will also do the same for another. For example, when asked the question 'are you good at picking projects for your unit?' the answer is highly positive. Then when the question 'how well does your unit perform?' is being asked, the response to the earlier question is likely to be on the mind of the respondent, leading to a likely response of positive for the performance question too. Then there are also social desirability questions where respondents answer favourably to provide a good impression.

As pointed out in Section 7.6.2, the phrasing of the questions can be an important element to lower the risk of self-reports. Schwarz (1999) provides a good discussion of how questions will shape answers and how we can minimize the pitfalls of using self-reports. Edwards (2008) and Podsakoff and Organ (1986) further provide ways to consider in order to reduce self-report issues. Gupta and Beehr (1982) compares the results of self-reports with company records and job observations and find that there is only low to moderate agreement between self-reports and these other two sources of data. The authors further suggest that multiple data collection techniques should be considered whenever possible. Nonetheless, surveys continue to provide researchers with a means to collect some data that do not pre-exist and will be hard to access using other data collection methods.

7.6.4 Respondent errors

Respondent errors can occur when you are dealing with human subjects who either represent themselves as an individual or as representatives of their organization. The subject could be taking part in an interview for an individual-level study of perception of social support for the unemployed or responding to a questionnaire on the relationship between organizational support and turnover rates on behalf of their organization. Whatever the situation, whether in the questionnaire case where the respondent is merely facing a piece of paper or in the interview case where there are interactions, there are potential respondent errors lurking. Some of these respondent errors are subtle and unintentional while others are based on the inexperience of the researchers who designed the questionnaire or conducted the interview.

There are several types of response errors that can become problematic for the researcher. In particular, response bias occurs when answers are misrepresented either intentionally or inadvertently. This type of bias can come in various forms. For example, **acquiescent response bias** happens when there is a tendency for respondents to agree with most questions. Some respondents might feel that being agreeable in surveys can help to facilitate an investigation. Others might be thinking that being agreeable means time will be saved. Either way, when responses consistently fall at one end of the scale, it makes it difficult to identify the reason behind this. In this case, the subject will have to be excluded from analysis. **Extremity response bias** occurs when some individuals tend to choose extreme responses, while others tend to respond neutrally. It is hard to eradicate the possibility in surveys that subjects will choose the extremes. But to avoid the tendency to choose the neutral position, it may be wise to choose an even number of choices to avoid choices down the middle, especially for perception questions. These are just two potential respondent errors that can happen as the data is collected. In most circumstances, these can be minimized with carefully designed data collection processes.

7.6.5 Survey response rates and non-response bias

Is there an acceptable survey response rate? This is a question that will arise while a researcher is waiting for survey responses. However, it is likely that 'acceptable' may differ across fields and depends on the size of your initial targeted respondents.

The term 'acceptable' will cover the fact that response bias has been minimized. In order to know that, additional information on both respondents and non-respondents will be required to rule out response bias, unless the response rate is very high. Nevertheless, the issue of response bias is at least if not more critical than response rate because even a response rate as high as 80 per cent is a necessary but not sufficient condition for having no response bias.

In terms of an acceptable response rate for business and management type surveys, Roth and BeVier (1998) reports that studies published from 1990 to 1994 had median response rates of 51 per cent for mailed surveys and 73 per cent for non-mailed surveys. Baruch (1999) examines response rates for studies published in 1975, 1985 and 1995 and also finds evidence of a decline in response rate over time but reported an average response rate of 55.6 per cent. A meta-analysis by Cycyota and Harrison (2006) examining studies published from 1992 to 2003 finds a mean response rate of 32 per cent and evidence that response rates are declining over time. Repsonse rates may also differ depending on the sub-fields. For example, the mean response rates for human resource management and general management areas would be 50 per cent while in international business and marketing the average would be about 35 per cent (Mellahi and Harris, 2016). Further, response rates will also depend on the nature of the survey and the type of respondents. For example, surveys to senior executives are likely to generate lower response rates than those to middle managers, professionals and general population (Baruch, 1999). Surveys designed for individuals can generate around 50 per cent response rate while those seeking organizational responses will bring in a lower return rate of 35 to 40 per cent (Baruch and Holtom, 2008). Anyone who has recently done a survey would find it hard to imagine that such high response rates would be possible. There is no doubt that survey response rates are declining, and many would imagine that a range of 30–40 per cent response rates these days are considered acceptable.

Many reviewers have hang-ups about response rates, based on the assumption that non-response must be indicative of response bias. Goldberg (2003) finds that while non-response affects the means of certain variables, it does not impact the relationships among variables. The widespread practice of comparing mean levels of variables for respondents and non-respondents is largely irrelevant to whether relationships among variables differ for respondents and non-respondents, and it is these relationships, not variable means, that usually constitute the focus of our research. In a similar vein, Schalm and Kelloway (2001) investigate the relationship between response rate and effect size in self-report survey research. The correlation between response rate and effect size was calculated for four variable combinations and found to be non-significant for any of the individual samples. These results suggest further that response rate of a survey has little to do with the relationships between variables.

Ray and Still (1987) introduce a second mailing to try to improve the response rate of their study. This mailing is targeted at non-respondents to the first mailing. While the response rate has in fact improved as a result of the second mailing, analysis shows that there are severe effects of acquiescent response bias, which renders doing a second mailing meaningless. The advice is that additional mailings are not necessarily good and may sometimes increase the likelihood of producing biased outcomes.

Non-response bias relates to the situation where there are some tendencies for potential respondents with particular characteristics to not respond to your research. While this can happen when requesting respondents for interviews, it is more often an issue when one conducts survey research. An example would be a typical poll: when an opinion is sought, it is often the people with a strong view who are responding. Another example can be a questionnaire that necessarily truncates part of the sample, say a questionnaire on malpractices in organizations. This sort of questionnaire will not elicit responses from firms that are very sensitive towards their own deficiencies and can thus result in responses that only include minimum malpractices. This is often labelled as **self-selection**. In essence, respondents have self-selected themselves to be a participant of your survey research. Sometimes, non-response errors can pose a problem as it biases your research towards or away from your expectations.

Trinkoff and Storr (1997) provide a good illustration of checking on non-response bias. In their study, the researchers use a mail survey where the original mailing is followed by four additional mailings. The response rate increased from 43 per cent after the initial mailing to 78 per cent after the final mailing. Their results reveal insignificant differences in drug use across the five waves of mailings. Based on this, one might argue that the initial 43 per cent response rate would be acceptable. Nevertheless, a higher response rate is always welcomed when possible.

Rogelberg and Stanton (2007) presented a feature issue on non-response to organizational surveys. Several of the articles in this feature issue address the topic of e-surveys (i.e. internet-based, emailed, etc.). Tomaskovic-Devey et al. (1994) provide some good advice on how best to design a survey to avoid non-responses.

7.7 ARCHIVAL DATA COLLECTION

We have highlighted various sources of information in Section 3.4. In essence, using archival data as a source of data for research means to track down variables of interest using existing data. Unlike the earlier methods discussed, archival data collection does not usually involve human interactions in the process.

The use of archival data provides several advantages. First, it provides potential for large scale datasets that lend themselves to geater statistical power. This is consistent with the rise of Big Data (e.g. Wenzel and Van Quaquebeke, 2018) and the potential insights that large datasets can provide. Second, it allows the potential to enhance external validity if archival data contains more than one element by which to split the dataset. Third, it allows potential for replication, as when documentation is possible with existing data, there may be other sources of information, such as from other industries or countries that can be used to test similar propositions. This also relates to the above point about enhanced external validity. Fourth, archival data allows the potential to analyze multiple levels of analysis within a single research, as data collection across levels using other data collection methods can be challenging. Fifth, archival data can offer opportunities for longitudinal studies when multiple periods of data are available. Barnes et al. (2018) and Payne et al. (2003) also point out additional benefits of using archival data specific to some areas of research.

Despite the long list of advantages that archival data possess, they do come with a few disadvantages. First, the data is not collected for the purpose of your research and thus may not be as tailor-made. Adjusting your research to fit the data runs the risk of losing sight of research rigour and contributions. Second, related to the first point, as the data is not collected for your specific research purpose, there will be challenges around construct validity when proxies are used (Barnes et al., 2018). Various construct validity issues that we discuss in Chapter 6 would apply. Third, there may also be missing data in the archival sources, leading to potential issues around bias, which will be touched upon in Chapter 8.

Despite some of these disadvantages, increasingly we start to see more archival data being used in research studies. Some of the archival data sources for organizational research would include company records, academic records, previous project data repurposed, government research archives, sports data and media communications. Barnes et al. (2018) compare the strengths and weaknesses of these sources in their study. In fact, archival data can potentially be used to verify or can be done in combination with perceptual data as highlighted in Shortell and Zajac (1990). Payne et al. (2003) also demonstrate how archival data can be converted to make them comparable to data collected through other methods for behavioural type constructs.

It is clear that the use of archival data from documents needs to be done with caution and well documented. The work by Reeves et al. (2005) on the use of archival data is worth noting. Elder et al. (1999) provides good guidelines on how to fit the right dataset to a particular research problem and work from archival data. Lucko and Mitchell (2010) discuss what data preparation would be required when utilizing archival data for analysis. In Figure 7.3, I show some examples of research publications that rely on multiple sources of archival data. As you can see from the figure, several archival data sources are often used for collecting data at different levels, such as the firm, industry and country levels for a single study. Each level of information will require the sources of archival data to be legitimate and possess internal validity. In totality, then it is possible to map these archival data sources together to create variables that can be measured across time and aligned for causality before analysis can occur.

Topic	Variables (measurements)	Data source (data levels used)
The impact of firm competitive intensity and collaboration on firm growth in different technological environments (Ang, 2008)	Firm growth (difference of logarithm of sales growth at time t+1 and t)	Key Business Directory of Singapore (firm level data)
	Collaboration (number count of collaboration)	Business newspaper articles in the only two English language newspapers in Singapore (collaboration level and firm level data)
	Competitive intensity (market share of firm relative to competitors)	Report of the Census of Industrial Production (Singapore) and Key Business Directory of Singapore (firm level and industry level data)
	Industry technology intensity (OECD classification of industries)	OECD (industry level data)
The interactions of institutions on foreign market entry mode (Ang, Benischke and Doh, 2015)	Governance mode of market entry (cross-border acquisitions = 1, cross-border alliances = 0)	SDC Platinum database (collaboration, acquisition and firm level data)
	Mimicking foreign firms (number count of acquisitions conducted by other foreign firms from t-1 to t-3)	SDC Platinum database (collaboration, acquisition and firm level data)
	Mimicking local firms (number count of acquisitions conducted by other local firms from t-1 to t-3)	SDC Platinum database (collaboration, acquisition and firm level data)
	Regulatory distance (six dimensions of governance listed at World Bank)	World Bank Governance Indicators (country level data)
	Normative distance (five indicators selected from World Competitiveness Yearbook through an exploratory factor analysis)	World Competitiveness Yearbook (country level data)

Topic	Variables (measurements)	Data source (data levels used)
Frequency of international expansion through high control market expansion modes and interlocked directorships (Ang, Benischke and Hooi, 2015)	Frequency of international expansion (number count of cross-border greenfield investments and foreign acquisitions)	fDi Markets database for greenfield investments, SDC Platinum for acquisitions and Compustat and Mergent Online databases for firms (greenfield investment, acquisition and firm level data)
	Depth of high control entry mode (HCEM) interlocks (sum of the proportion of interlocks by each director that involves HCEM experience to his total directorships)	Risk Metrics for director, fDi Markets database for greenfield investments, SDC Platinum for acquisitions, and Compustat and Mergent Online databases for firms (greenfield investment, acquisition, firm and director level data)
	Breadth of HCEM interlocks (depth (above) weighted by the total number of interlocked HCEM experience for each director)	Risk Metrics for director, fDi Markets database for greenfield investments, SDC Platinum for acquisitions, and Compustat and Mergent Online databases for firms (greenfield investment, acquisition, firm and director level data)
	Relatedness (in the same SIC-2 industry)	fDi Markets database for greenfield investments and SDC Platinum for acquisitions (greenfield investment, acquisition and firm level data)
Competition, diversification and performance (Ljubownikow and Ang, 2020)	Firm performance (returns on assets at t+2)	Compustat Global (firm level data)
	Related diversification (entropy index within SIC-2 at t+1)	Annual Business Inquiry (industry level data)
	Related diversification (entropy index beyond SIC-2 at t+1)	Annual Business Inquiry (industry level data)
	Competitive intensity (market share of firm relative to competitors)	Compustat Global and Annual Business Inquiry (firm level and industry level data)

Figure 7.3   Examples of using archival data involving multiple data sources

7.8 MULTI-INDUSTRY AND MULTI-COUNTRY DATA

Many of us engage in research that involves **multiple industries**. You may be working on five interviews in five industries, or 100 surveys across five industries, or an archival data collection of 1,000 firms across 30 industries. We all know that industry context plays a part in most of the research that we do. For example, we would expect employee compensation to be different in different industries. Likewise, we would expect policies and practices to differ across industries. We have also discussed contextualization and issues relating to it in Section 5.5.

Examining broad industry contexts is generally not an issue. We know what the software industry constitutes. We know about the large retail stores that compete against one another. But as a researcher, we are expected to have a systematic process in everything that we do – in these cases we have to spell out what the software industry is and what we mean by retail stores. While it may seem straightforward in these examples, there are ambiguities in defining some other industries, such as what constitutes the high-tech and electronics industry.

Let's say we want to define the biotechnology industry and take a large sample of bio-technology firms to investigate their funding sources. In order to access a large number of firms, we need to have a systematic classification of the boundaries of an industry. We turn to the standard industry classification for help. Our research will bring us to the conclusion that the biotechnology industry does not have its own Standard Industry Classification (SIC) or North American Industry Classification System (NAICS) codes, both of which are common classification codes used for defining industries. In the SIC classification, biotech-nology firms would be classified together with chemical companies. A further investigation would bring us to another classification, the Global Industry Classification Standard (GICS), which can also be found in Compustat. This classification by Morgan Stanley actually has a specific code for biotechnology firms – 352010. The complexity of trying to define what constitutes the biotechnology industry suggests that different classifications from different sources are likely to have different criteria. Thus, care must be taken in order to choose an appropriate classification of industries. You will notice that Ljubownikow and Ang (2020) in their study of diversification and competition had to do a similar mapping to allow classifications of industries to be comparable between US and UK data.

Conversation box

Candy [PhD student]:   Professor, what do I have to look out for when conducting a multi-country study?

Professor: It is important to recognize there are country differences. The types of differences vary depending on your topic. For example, business transactions will be dependent on both the regulatory and cultural environment. Yet another example is that surveying consumers across borders will have to take into account country standards and expectations and perhaps language and phrasing used. Clearly, collecting data across countries will introduce a lot of other issues but minimizing those to ensure that the research outcomes from the different sites are comparable is essential.

The increasingly globalized world makes it necessary for us to understand country differences. As we strive for greater generalizability from our research findings it becomes apparent that a lot of what we do is not just about generalizability across organizations or industries, rather it is the generalizability across borders that will provide the ultimate challenge. **Multi-country** studies can range from country comparisons to practices of organizations across borders to how individuals in different countries respond to a particular work incentive.

Collecting data in more than one country poses a huge operational challenge. In the ideal case, you will have three researchers residing in the three countries in which you seek to collect data for your study. This arrangement has resulted in the significant research collaborations across borders that we often see today. Collaboration work might not always work out as well. Then, there are possibilities where a data collection method might not be as effective. For example, mail surveys might not bring as much return in China as compared to the US. In such cases, a multi-country study might in fact need different data collection methods in different countries (Parry et al., 2020).

A bigger challenge in multi-country studies may be cross-country **data equivalence**. This refers to the degree to which the elements of a research design have the same meaning across different cultural contexts. According to Hult et al. (2008), researchers in international business have not done enough to address data equivalence issues.

There are mainly three types of equivalence: construct, measurement and data collection. Construct equivalence relates to whether a concept or behaviour has the same meaning in different contexts and cultures. For example, perception of trust and loyalty may be different as perceived by managers in Japanese corporations compared to managers in US corporations. Measurement equivalence refers to whether the operationalizations of the constructs are comparable across contexts and cultures. For example, the categorization of whether a firm is large, medium or small is different in the US to smaller countries such as New Zealand or Singapore. Singh (1995), in particular, provides a good discussion of four measurement equivalence issues. Finally, data collection equivalence refers to whether the data collection procedure and sample are comparable. For example, Chinese participants may not be as open to face-to-face interviews as US participants. This may result in differing inputs from participants from these countries.

As the above examples illustrate, there are many situations where data equivalence can become an issue in multi-country research. As you read this section, you might have thought of other examples already. Nonetheless, these data equivalence issues can be addressed: take a look at Singh (1995), Hult et al. (2008), Diamantopoulos and Papadopoulos (2010) and Parry et al. (2020) to get more ideas on how to do that. Behling and Law (1999) further provide comprehensive coverage of aspects that need to be treated carefully when translating questionnaires across contexts.

KEY TERMS

- Acquiescent response bias
- Archival data
- Common method variance
- Data equivalence
- Experiment
- Extremity response bias
- Face-to-face interview
- Field experiment
- Focus group
- Interview
- Laboratory experiment
- Mail survey
- Multi-country data
- Multi-industry data

- Non-response bias
- Observation
- Online survey
- Participant observation
- Pilot survey
- Questionnaire
- Respondent error
- Response rate
- Self-report
- Self-selection
- Survey design
- Survey question
- Telephone interview

SUMMARY

- There are three key forms of interactive data collection methods, namely face-to-face interviews, telephone interviews and focus groups.
- Observational methods may be: (1) structured or unstructured; (2) disguised or undisguised; (3) natural or contrived; (4) personal or mechanical; (5) non-participant or participant.
- Laboratory experiments, when appropriate, provide strong cases of observed causality. Field experiments, however, have been argued to have greater external validity.
- Survey questionnaires are useful to reach out to a large sample of potential respondents.
- Some generic aspects of survey questionnaire that need careful attention are the cover letter, instructions for completion, appearance and length of the survey, pilot survey, and online survey tools if the survey is conducted online.
- Writing survey questions is an important aspect of the design of surveys. Avoiding bias from behavioural expectation, unbalanced categories of choice, and objectionable and demanding questions are all crucial.
- An acceptable response rate for surveys varies, but a rule of thumb for business and management research will be 30–40 per cent.
- Self-reports are often associated with issues with common method variance.
- It is often necessary to provide information about the potential response and non-response bias from survey returns.
- Archival data sources allow a researcher to tap into the use of large samples for analysis. They also tend to have better potential for longitudinal studies.
- Multi-industry and multi-country data require the researcher to assess the data equivalence in light of differences in practices and rules across industries and countries.

QUESTIONS

1. What are the advantages of focus groups compared to face-to-face and telephone interviews?
2. Compare and contrast participant observation with laboratory and field experiments.
3. Discuss some important generic aspects of designing a survey.
4. What are some of the risks of bias in writing survey questions?
5. Compare and contrast face-to-face interviews, telephone interviews and mail surveys.
6. Discuss some of the advantages and disadvantags of using archival data for research.
7. Highlight some challenging issues when collecting multi-country and multi-industry data.

ADDITIONAL READINGS

Online survey companies

Qualtrics: www.qualtrics.com
QuestionPro: www.questionpro.com
SurveyMonkey: www.surveymonkey.co.uk
Websurveyor: www.websurveyor.com
Zoomerang: www.zoomerang.com

Chidlow, A., Ghauri, P.N., Yeniyurt, S. and Cavusgil, S.T. (2015) 'Establishing rigor in mail-survey procedures in international business research', *Journal of World Business*, 50 (1): 26–35.

Cotteleer, M.J. and Wan, X. (2016) 'Does the starting point matter? The literature-driven and the phenomenon-driven approaches of using corporate archival data in academic research', *Journal of Business Logistics*, 37 (1): 26–33.

Currall, S.C., Hammer, T.H., Baggett, L.S. and Doniger, G.M. (1999) 'Combining qualitative and quantitative methodologies to study group processes: An illustrative study of a corporate board of directors', *Organizational Research Methods*, 2 (1): 5–36.

DeVellis, R.F. (2003) *Scale Development: Theory and Applications*, (2nd edition). Thousand Oaks, CA: Sage Publishing.

Feldman, J.M. and Lynch, J.G. Jr. (1988) Self-generated validity and other effects of measurement on belief, attitude, intention and behavior', *Journal of Applied Psychology*, 73 (3): 421–35.

Foddy, W. (1993) *Constructing Questions for Interviews and Questionnaires: Theory and Practice in Social Research*. Cambridge: Cambridge University Press.

Fowler, F.J. Jr. (2002) *Survey Research Methods*, (3rd edition). Thousand Oaks, CA: Sage Publishing.

Fox, R.J., Crask, M.R. and Kim, J. (1989) 'Mail survey response rate: A meta-analysis of selected techniques for inducing response', *Public Opinion Quarterly*, 52 (4): 467–91.

Groves, R.M., Fowler, F.J. Jr, Couper, M.P., Lepkowski, J.M., Singer, E. and Tourangeau, R. (2004) *Survey Methodology*. New York: John Wiley.

Harrison, D.A. and McLaughlin, M.E. (1993) 'Cognitive processes in self-report responses: Tests of item context effects in work attitude measures', *Journal of Applied Psychology*, 78 (1): 129–40.

Harzing, A.-W. (2006) 'Response styles in cross-national survey research: A 26-country study', *International Journal of Cross Cultural Management*, 6 (2): 243–66.

Rivers, D.C., Meade, A.W. and Fuller, W..L. (2009) 'Examining question and context effects in organization survey data using item response theory', *Organizational Research Methods*, 12 (3): 529–53.

Schaefer, D.R. and Dillman, D.A. (1998) 'Development of a standard e-mail methodology: Results of an experiment', *Public Opinion Quarterly*, 62 (3): 378–97.

Schafer, J. L. and Graham, J.W. (2002) 'Missing data: Our view of the state of the art', *Psychological Methods*, 7 (2): 147–77.

Schaffer, B.S. and Riordan, C.M. (2003) 'A review of cross-cultural methodologies for organizational research: A best-practices approach', *Organizational Research Methods*, 6 (2): 169–215.

Sheehan K., Bartel and Hoy, M.G. (1999) 'Flaming, complaining, abstaining: How online users respond to privacy concerns', *Journal of Advertising*, 28 (3): 37–51.

Simsek, Z. and Veiga, J.F. (2000) 'The electronic survey technique: An integration and assessment. *Organizational Research Methods*, 3 (1): 93–115.

Stone, A.A., Turkkan, J.S., Bachrach, C.A., Jobe, J.B., Kurtzman, H.S. and Cain, V.S. (eds) (2000) *The Science of Self-report: Implications for Research and Practice*. Mahwah, NJ: Lawrence Erlbaum Associates.

Tipton, E. (2014a) 'Stratified sampling using cluster analysis: A sample selection strategy for improved generalizations from experiments', *Evaluation Review*, 37 (2): 109–39.

Tipton, E. (2014b) 'How generalizable Is your experiment? An index for comparing experimental samples and populations', *Journal of Educational and Behavioral Statistics*, 39 (6): 478–501.

Tourangeau, R., Couper, M.P. and Conrad, F. (2004) 'Spacing, position, and order: interpretive heuristics for visual features of survey questions', *Public Opinion Quarterly*, 68 (3): 368–93.

Tourangeau, R., Rips, L.J. and Rasinski, K. (2000) *The Psychology of Survey Response*. New York: Cambridge University Press.

Van de Vijver, F. and Leung, K. (1997) *Methods and Data Analysis for Cross-cultural Research*. Thousand Oaks, CA: Sage Publishing.

Yammarino, F.J., Skinner, S.J. and Childers, T.L. (1991) 'Understanding mail survey response behavior: a meta-analysis', *Public Opinion Quarterly*, 55 (4): 613–39.

Yang, Z., Wang, X. and Su, C. (2006) 'A review of research methodologies in international business', *International Business Review*, 15 (6): 601–17.

REFERENCES

Ang, S.H. (2008) 'The impact of firm competitive intensity and collaboration on firm growth in different technological environments', *Strategic Management Journal*, 29 (10): 1057–75.

Ang, S.H., Benischke, M.H. and Doh, J.P. (2015) 'The interactions of institutions on foreign market entry mode', *Strategic Management Journal*, 36 (10): 1536–53.

Ang, S.H., Benischke, M.H. and Hooi, A.W.-L. (2018) 'Frequency of international expansion through high control market expansion modes and interlocked directorships', *Journal of World Business*, 53 (4): 493–503.

Barnes, C.M., Dang, C.T., Leavitt, K., Guarana, C.L. and Uhlmann, E.L. (2018) 'Archival data in micro-organizational research: A toolkit for moving to a broader set of topics', *Journal of Management*, 44 (4): 1453–78.

Baruch, Y. (1999) 'Response rate in academic studies – a comparative analysis', *Human Relations*, 52 (4): 421–38.

Baruch, Y. and Holtom, B.C. (2008) 'Survey response rate levels and trends in organizational research', *Human Relations*, 61 (8): 1139–60.

Behling, O. and Law, K.S. (1999) *Translating Questionnaires: Problems and Solutions*. Newbury Park, CA: Sage Publishing.

Berkowitz, L. and Donnerstein, E. (1982) 'External validity is more than skin deep: Some answers to criticisms of laboratory experiments', *American Psychologist*, 37 (3): 245–57.

Buchanan, E.A. and Hvizdak, E.E. (2009) 'Online survey tools: Ethical and methodological concerns of human research ethics committees', *Journal of Empirical Research on Human Research Ethics: An International Journal*, 4 (2): 37–48.

Cho, H. and Larose, R. (1999) 'Privacy issues in internet surveys', *Social Science Computer Review*, 17 (4): 421–34.

Cycyota, C.S. and Harrison, D.A. (2006) 'What (not) to expect when surveying executives: A meta-analysis of top manager response rates and techniques over time', *Organizational Research Methods*, 9 (2): 133–60.

Diamantopoulos, A. and Papadopoulos, N. (2010) 'Assessing the cross-national invariance of formative measures: Guidelines for international business researchers', *Journal of International Business Studies*, 41 (2): 360–70.

Dillman, D.A. (1978) *Mail and Telephone Surveys: The Total Design Method*. New York, NY: John Wiley & Sons.

Dillman, D.A. (2007) *Mail and Internet Surveys: The Tailored Design*, (2nd edition – 2007 update). New York, NY: John Wiley & Sons.

Dipboye, R.L. and Flanagan, M.F. (1979) 'Research settings in industrial and organizational psychology: Are findings in the field more generalizable than in the laboratory?' *American Psychologist*, 34 (2): 141–50.

Dobbins, G.H., Lane, I.M. and Steiner, D.D. (1988) 'A note on the role of laboratory methodologies in applied behavioural research: don't throw out the baby with the bath water', *Journal of Organizational Behavior*, 9 (3): 281–6.

Edwards, J.R. (2008) 'To prosper, organizational psychology should ... overcome methodological barriers to progress', *Journal of Organizational Behavior*, 29 (4): 469–91.

Elder, G.H., Pavalko, E.K. and Clipp, E.C. (1999) *Working with Archival Data*. Thousand Oaks, CA: Sage Publishing.

Gajraj, A.M., Faria, A.J. and Dickinson, J.R. (1990) 'A comparison of the effect of promised and provided lotteries, monetary and gift incentives on mail survey response rate, speed and cost', *Journal of the Market Research Society*, 32 (1): 141–62.

Goldberg, C.B. (2003) 'Who responds to surveys? Assessing the effects of nonresponse in cross-sectional dyadic research', *Assessment*, 10 (1): 41–8.

Golden, B.R. (1992) 'The past is the past – or is it? The use of retrospective accounts as indicators of past strategy' *Academy of Management Journal*, 35 (4): 848–60.

Golden, B.R. (1997) 'Further remarks on retrospective accounts in organizational and strategic management research', *Academy of Management Journal*, 40 (5): 1243–52.

Gordon, M.E., Slade, L.A. and Schmitt, N. (1986) 'The "science of the sophomore" revisited: From conjecture to empiricism', *Academy of Management Review*, 11 (1): 191–207.

Greenberg, J. and Tomlinson, E.C. (2004) 'Situated experiments in organizations: Transplanting the lab to the field', *Journal of Management*, 30 (5): 703–24.

Griffin, R. and Kacmar, K.M. (1991) 'Laboratory research in management: Misconceptions and missed opportunities', *Journal of Organizational Behavior*, 12 (4): 301–11.

Guest, G., Bunce, A. and Johnson, L. (2006) 'How many interviews are enough? An experiment with data saturation and variability', *Field Methods*, 18 (1): 59–82.

Gupta, N. and Beehr, T.A. (1982) 'A test of the correspondence between self-reports and alternative data sources about work organizations', *Journal of Vocational Behavior*, 20 (1): 1–13.

Highhouse, S. (2009) 'Designing experiments that generalize,' *Organizational Research Methods*, 12 (3): 554–66.

Hult, G.T.M., Ketchen, D.J. Jr, Griffith, D.A., Finnegan, C.A., Gonzalez-Padron, T., Harmancioglu, N. ... and Cavusgil, S.T (2008) 'Data equivalence in cross-cultural international business research: Assessment and guidelines', *Journal of International Business Studies*, 39 (6): 1027–44.

Johnson, J.C., Avenarius, C. and Weatherford, J. (2006) 'The active participant-observer: Applying social role analysis to participant observation', *Field Methods*, 18 (2): 111–34.

Lindlof, T.R. and Taylor, B.C. (2011) *Qualitative Communication Research Methods*, (3rd edition). Thousand Oaks, CA: Sage Publishing.

Ljubownikow, G. and Ang, S.H. (2020) 'Competition, diversification and performance', *Journal of Business Research*, 112: 81–94.

Lucko, G. and Mitchell, Z.W. Jr. (2010) 'Quantitative research: Preparation of incongruous economic data sets for archival data analysis', *Journal of Construction Engineering and Management*, 136 (1): 49–57.

Marshall, C. and Rossman, G.B. (2006) *Designing Qualitative Research*, (4th edition). Thousand Oaks, CA: Sage Publishing.

Mellahi, K. and Harris, L. C. (2016) 'Response rates in business and management research: An overview of current practice and suggestions for future direction', *British Journal of Management*, 27 (2): 426–37.

Parry, E., Farndale, E., Brewster, C. and Morley, M.J. (2020) 'Balancing rigour and relevance: The case for methodological pragmatism in conducting large-scale, multi-country and comparative management studies', *British Journal of Management*. https://doi.org/10.1111/1467-8551.12405

Payne, S.C., Finch, J.F. and Tremble, T.R. Jr. (2003) 'Validating surrogate measures of psychological constructs: The application of construct equivalence to archival data', *Organizational Research Methods*, 6 (3): 363–82.

Perdue, B.C. and Summers, J.O. (1986) 'Checking the success of manipulations in marketing experiments', *Journal of Marketing Research*, 23 (4): 317–26.

Peshkin, A. (1984) 'Odd man out: The participant observer in an absolutist setting', *Sociology of Education*, 57 (4): 254–64.

Podsakoff, P.M. and Organ, D.W. (1986) 'Self-reports in organizational research: Problems and prospects', *Journal of Management*, 12 (4): 531–44.

Ray, J. J. and Still, L.V. (1987) 'Maximizing the response rate in surveys may be a mistake', *Personality & Individual Differences*, 8 (4): 571–3.

Reeves, T.C., Ford, E.W., Duncan, W.J. and Ginter, P.M. (2005) 'Communication clarity in strategic management data sources', *Strategic Organization*, 3 (3): 243–78.

Roberts, L.D. and Allen, P.J. (2015) 'Exploring ethical issues associated with using online surveys in educational research', *Educational Research and Evaluation*, 21 (2): 95–108.

Rogelberg, S.G. and Stanton, J.M. (2007) 'Introduction: Understanding and dealing with organizational survey nonresponse', *Organisational Research Methods*, 10 (2): 195–209.

Roth, P.L. and BeVier, C.A. (1998) 'Response rates in HRM/OB survey research: Norms and correlates, 1990–1994', *Journal of Management*, 24 (1): 97–117.

Rushkoff, D. (2005) *Get Back in the Box: Innovation from the Inside Out*. New York, NY: HarperCollins.

Scandura, T.A. and Williams, E. A. (2000) 'Research methodology in management: Current practices, trends, and implications for future research', *Academy of Management Journal*, 43 (6): 1248–64.

Schalm, R.L. and Kelloway, E.K. (2001) 'The relationship between response rate and effect size in occupational health psychology research', *Journal of Occupational Health Psychology*, 6 (2): 160–3.

Schwarz, N. (1999) 'Self-reports: How the questions shape the answers', *American Psychologist*, 54 (2): 93–105.

Schwarz, N., Knäuper, B., Hippler, H.-J., Noelle-Neumann, E. and Clark, L. (1991) 'Rating scales: Numeric values may change the meaning of scale labels', *Public Opinion Quarterly*, 55 (4): 570–82.

Schwarz, N., Strack, F., Müller, G. and Chassein, B. (1988) The range of response alternatives may determine the meaning of the question: Further evidence on informative functions of response alternatives', *Social Cognition*, 6 (2): 107–17.

Shortell, S.M. and Zajac, E.J. (1990) 'Perceptual and archival measures of Miles and Snow's strategic types: A comprehensive assessment of reliability and validity', *Academy of Management Journal*, 33 (4): 817–32.

Singh, J. (1995) 'Measurement issues in cross-national research', *Journal of International Business Studies*, 26 (3): 597–619.

Stanton, J.M. and Rogelberg, S.G. (2001) 'Using internet/intranet web pages to collect organizational research data', *Organizational Research Methods*, 4 (3): 200–17.

Tjaco, W. (2003) 'Avoiding advertising research disaster: Advertising and the uncertainty principle', *Journal of Brand Management*, 10 (6): 403–9.

Tomaskovic-Devey, D., Leiter, J. and Thompson, S. (1994) 'Organizational survey nonresponse', *Administrative Science Quarterly*, 39(3): 439–57.

Tracy, S.J., Lutgen-Sandvik, P. and Alberts, J.K. (2006) 'Nightmares, demons and slaves: Exploring the painful metaphors of workplace bullying', *Management Communication Quarterly*, 20 (2): 148–85.

Trinkoff, A.M. and Storr, C.L. (1997) 'Collecting substance use data with an anonymous mailed survey', *Drug and Alcohol Dependence*, 48 (1): 1–8.

Vinten, G. (1994) 'Participant observation: A model for organizational investigation?', *Journal of Managerial Psychology*, 9 (2): 30–8.

Warriner, K., Goyder, J., Gjertsen, H., Hohner, P. and McSpurren, K. (1996) 'Charities, no; lotteries, no; case, no: Main effects and interactions in a Canadian incentives experiment', *Public Opinion Quarterly*, 60 (4): 542–62.

Wenzel, R. and Van Quaquebeke, N. (2018) 'The double-edged sword of big data in organizational and management research: A review of opportunities and risks', *Organizational Research Methods*, 21 (3): 548–91.

8
DESCRIPTIVE AND EXPLORATORY ANALYSIS

8.1 INTRODUCTION

> ### Conversation box
>
> *Jeremy [Honours student]:* Professor, I've now completed my data collection. What should I do next?
>
> *Professor:* I would assume you've taken the research design course and that should have covered what you should do after you have compiled the data.
>
> *Jeremy:* But there are so many tests possible. I wonder if you can help me get started by pointing me to a place to start with.
>
> *Professor:* OK, first you will need to ensure your data is clean for analysis. You will then need to try to understand your data. This can be done through a data preparation process and some assessments using descriptive and exploratory analysis.

In Chapter 7, we discussed the various **data** collection methods. Good data collection procedures will ensure that you have the data you desire at the end of the collection process. With the data collected, the first thing to do is to document and code the data, so that they are ready for analysis. However, no research process is guaranteed to go according to plan. For example, in the process of preparing the data for analysis, you may encounter quite a few surprises: What happens when there are **missing data**? How do you know whether there are **reliability** and **validity** issues with the data? How do you group and make sense of patterns in the data? If you use a survey design, how do you combine the items into constructs? What are the data descriptives you need to check and present? These are just some of the basic elements of data preparation processes that a researcher should consider when the data arrive. This chapter will touch on these elements.

Let us take another step back now. What if your data is not clean, for example data entry error, error in transcribing or error in the process of merging datasets? Human errors in the data collection process can lead to what we call in general **dirty data** (e.g. De Veaux and Hand, 2005; Kim et al., 2003). Further, data may also be potentially contaminated. For example, if the publication you collect data from changes the criteria of reporting. It would mean that the data that you have collected across different years are based on different baselines. If only aggregate data are provided, then it will not be possible for you to work out comparable statistics across the different years. As another example, companies may change name and if you have not taken steps to ensure that such potential changes are tracked down through the relevant reporting agencies, you will encounter missing data even though the company continues to exist in another name. These are just two examples on how data can be contaminated without human errors. It is possible that dirty data can be dealt with as long as the process of data collection is rigorous. Likewise, a careful data collection process will ensure that human errors will be minimal to non-existent. Kim et al. (2003) provides a good overview of potential sources of dirty data and the interventions required to minimize these. Hand et al. (2000) and Rajagopalan and Isken (2001) illustrate some data preparation processes.

This chapter also covers **descriptive**, univariate and **bivariate** analyses. These are the most fundamental analyses that a researcher should carry out in order to better understand their collected data. Such analyses are also useful for the reader to make sense of the scope and nature of data collected in any study. Finally, we discuss the relevance of **significance testing** and what this represents for reporting findings.

8.2 SOURCES OF DATA ERROR

Various **data errors** can result from the research process. The list of potential errors is endless. It is the researcher's duty to ensure that data errors are minimized. This section will discuss some of the potential sources of data error.

Administrative errors can occur in the course of conducting research. We tend to slip into some sort of boredom when we are dealing with massive data entries or hours after hours of transcribing from interviews. When fatigue sets in, we start to lose focus and concentration level deteriorates. When this happens, we commonly run into data processing errors, which are errors relating to data entry, and data coding and editing. Such mistakes can be as simple as typing a 6 instead of a 9 on the number pad of the keyboard. So, a figure of '6,000' can erroneously become '9,000' with an error in entry. It can also be a simple typo, such as missing the '6' from the figure '557,689' which resulted in '55,789'; a huge difference to the intended value. Nonetheless, in research, you are expected to double check your data entries. The expectation is that no mistake should be made in this process as this is all within the control of the researcher.

Interviews and face-to-face survey research are designed for research that requires some degree of deepened understanding. Normally, responses from the participants are recorded by the researcher. Unless the responses are taped or written down word-for-word, there will be a risk of errors relating to recording of responses. This is a result of selective perception, which occurs when the researcher makes a decision on the spot as to what information is considered relevant and what is not, and chooses only to jot down the information they perceive as relevant. Information has been truncated in this case. While this is not a problem when carefully done, very often a subtle message from the respondents which may not seem to be important at the time of conducting the interview may turn out to be important in hindsight. A more extreme scenario is when a researcher chooses not to jot down information provided by the respondents that goes against their expectations. This is in fact a case of not just administrative error in research, but also has ethical implications in research, as discussed in Chapter 1.

Conversation box

Professor:	Simon, the data and methodology chapter of your thesis is too short. You need to elaborate on your data and also the methodologies used.
Simon [Masters student]:	I have listed whatever I could.
Professor:	Did you include a section on how you arrived at your final sample of the study?
Simon:	But the process is complicated as I made quite a few decisions from the time of downloading the data and coding it and then deleting the cases, and so on.
Professor:	You need to document all these decisions in your chapter. It's part of the research to document these processes. It demonstrates the extent of rigour in your research.

It may seem strange to state that one reason for careful documentation of the research process and procedures is our tendency to forget what we have actually done in the research process. After all, as researchers we are supposed to be meticulous in our work, so why would we expect ourselves to be forgetful? Part of this 'forgetful' reasoning is mainly due to the complication of the research process. Take, for example, the coding of the raw data collected. Let us assume we have 600 data points on a project in international strategy of multinational firms to start with. The next step after the collection of data will be to run some data checks to ensure the data are representative. In order to do that, we will have to do some descriptive statistics and exploratory tests (a few of which can be found in this chapter). We may find out that there are 25 data points with incomplete data. We may also discover that while our sample comes from all regions in the world, there is only one case the multinational firm originates from, Africa, and five originating from Latin America. Considering the importance of controlling for the geographical regions, as the research context is international strategy, these two regions are under-represented and thus should probably be discarded for analysis (this will likely have implications for the scope of the study). We then find that while most firms come from the manufacturing and services sectors, there are 21 cases that come from the agriculture sector. Under-representation would also mean that we have to reconsider and probably discard these cases (this might also mean adjustments to the scope of the study). These three procedures of 'cleaning' reduce the dataset from 600 to 548 data points for analysis. It is not good enough to jump into reporting 548 observations for analysis at the outset. The three procedures that resulted in discarding 52 firms from the analysis have to be documented and well explained. This is also essential as subsequent analysis may suggest, for example, that the agriculture sector data points need to be re-introduced for analysis.

What seems like a straightforward decision, the derivation of data points, as the above research scenario shows, entails a number of judgement calls, for example the decision to discard cases from the agriculture sector. Being transparent in this process will help ensure the replicability and validity of your study.

Smith et al. (1986) provide a list of checks for the detection of errors in the processing of data. It is clear that some of this detection has to be manually done – which again brings us back to the point that researchers need to exercise extra caution when coding and preparing their data for analysis. Kim et al. (2003) provide a list of sources of data error avenues in their paper and suggest some intervention mechanisms to minimize these.

8.3 MISSING DATA

Conversation box

Professor:	Sandra, you have sent me a spreadsheet file with lots of blanks in there. How do I interpret these?
Sandra [Masters student]:	They are missing data, Professor. Is it not possible to run the analysis with missing data?
Professor:	It's possible, Sandra. The only problem with running the analysis with the missing data is that the set of missing data may elicit some patterns, which means that the data that you have collected may be biased. Therefore, it's important for you to check and explain why the data are missing in the first place and rule out potential bias.

Missing data occurs more often when your data collection process involves large quantities of data and when the data collection method is more hands-off. For example, if you are using interviews, the process can be designed to be fluid, in a sense that you can ask the interviewee follow-up questions. On the other hand, if you conduct an online survey and find that the returned responses have missing data, follow up is almost impossible as the respondents may not wish to be contacted and may wish to remain anonymous. Your survey returns may show that some respondents did not respond to all of the questions in the survey. This can be owing to negligence or confusion as to how to respond, or the person just does not want to respond to particular questions. It is of course unethical to fill in those missing responses for the respondent. Yet another example would be that you use secondary data sources and the data for your variable of interest may not be complete for the study period. Overall, to have missing data is unavoidable in many data collection methods. So, how should these missing data be treated?

For data involving large samples, addressing missing data can be less of an issue. It is easy enough just to delete those cases where there are missing data for the key variables of interest. Analysis will then be conducted only with those cases for which all the variables have complete information. This is called **listwise deletion**. When there are a small number of variables involved and only exploratory analysis such as bivariate tests are involved, **pairwise deletion** can be used as only the missing data of the relevant variables are deleted. However, it is important to note that if there are a fair number of missing observations for a particular variable, you should inquire further. In the case of question-naires, this relates to response and non-respondent errors, which were highlighted in Chapter 7. In the case of using archival data, it will be good to go back to the original data sources to check the reasons for those missing observations in your variable of interest. In summary, data must be missing at random. If the data that you are using are not missing at random, then we have undesirable bias issues arising from the data collection process.

Missing data can be painful in research situations when the data collected do not contain a large number of cases. Every one of these cases counts. In such circumstances it may be more appropriate to try to replace the missing values instead of deleting the cases. The most common option is to replace the missing values with the mean score of the rest of the observations for that variable. Gilley and Leone (1991), however, caution that the randomness assumption made in this procedure is often not the usual case. The other option can be to replace a missing value with a value from another observation that has other similar attributes. This is called similar response pattern imputation. With longitudinal, panel or cross-sectional time-series data, if the missing value is between years that you have data for, then you can intrapolate to get an in-between score. If the missing value is adjacent to a few years for which you have data for the same variable, then you can extrapolate from the adjacent data points.

Enders and Bandalos (2001) conducted a Monte Carlo simulation to examine the performance of four missing data methods, namely listwise deletion, pairwise deletion, similar response pattern imputation and full information **maximum likelihood** (FIML). FIML is a means to compute missing data based on data that are available across the sample. Expectation-maximization is also equivalent to FIML. The authors find that FIML is in fact a superior imputation method compared to the other three missing data imputation methods. They further suggest that listwise deletion and simi-lar response pattern should be used with caution. This finding has also been supported in Newman (2003), who examines six missing data techniques in the structural equa-tion modelling context. In fact, the structural equation modelling analytical tool of LISREL uses FIML as the default missing data technique, whenever a researcher speci-fies that there are missing data in his data file. Using such estimation techniques allows the researcher to get the best parameter estimates from his data, rather than discarding the data from partial responses, as listwise deletion does. Schafer and Graham (2002) further provide evidence to support the use of maximum likelihood and Bayesian mul-tiple imputation for addressing missing data.

Despite the fact that the missing data techniques above have advanced to help us address missing data issues, Newman (2003) also finds that all these techniques per-form worse when data are missing non-randomly. Overall, researchers have emphasized that when data is not missing at random or when the missing data mechanisms are unknown it will be difficult to use statistical corrections as demonstrated above (e.g. Goodman and Blum, 1996; Graham and Donaldson, 1993).

It is important to note here that you may sometimes come across studies for which different **sample sizes** are used for analysis depending on the availability of variables. As discussed earlier, if a substantial amount of data is collected, you can avoid replacing missing values as you can afford to delete some cases, as long as the deleted cases do not elicit a pattern. Having a consistent set of observations for analysis allows easier comparisons to be made. However, if deleting observations is not an option due to the need to maintain sample size and representation, then running analysis for different models using slightly different sample sizes would be acceptable. In such cases, care again must be taken to ensure that missing data for each variable occurs at random.

8.4 FACTOR ANALYSIS

In business and management, very often the measurement of a construct will require the combination of a few items from a survey. For example, in Chapter 7 there were a couple of illustrations on the need to ask multiple questions in order to help us operationalize a variable. We have also highlighted one way to combine multiple items: composite meaures in Chapter 7. In the broad context of combining items, especially those from suveys, factor analysis provides a tool for this purpose. Factor analysis is also useful in circumstances where we are not clear as to how items are related and need to explore the possible relationships among the items.

Factor analysis is based on the common factor model. Within the common factor model, items are expressed as a function of common factors, unique factors and errors of measurement. Common factors influence two or more items, while each unique factor influences only one item and does not explain correlations among items. There are two main forms of factor analysis, namely exploratory factor analysis and **confirmatory factor analysis**. Each of these can be used separately and, in many cases, used complementarily as well.

8.4.1 Exploratory factor analysis

Exploratory factor analysis (EFA) helps a researcher identify the underlying relationships between survey items. As the word 'exploratory' suggests, EFA should be used when the researcher has no a priori expectations about factors or patterns of association between items. This is common if the construct in your research does not have any established measurement or it is unclear from the literature what set of items is the best way to measure your construct. In both these cases, subjecting your items to an EFA will help you to see the patterns of relationships among the items and work out a parsimonious set of factors. For example, in Towler and Dipboye (2003), the authors use EFA to tease out how items load onto factors in order to explore the measurement for learning style orientation.

EFA requires the researcher to make a number of important decisions about how to conduct the analysis as there is no single set method. Gerbing and Hamilton (1996) provide a good comparison of the different exploratory factor analysis extraction and rotation methods. An assumption of EFA is that any item may be associated with any factor. This assumption can be strong if there are items that you are not sure are related to your construct at all. Regardless, the items must make sense to be considered as part of the EFA or otherwise using EFA blindly can sometimes lead to absurd items that do not make sense at all being part of a factor.

8.4.2 Confirmatory factor analysis

Confirmatory factor analysis (CFA) allows a researcher to specify the items that should constitute a variable (factor). In other words, CFA takes out the possibility of generating absurd factors, as is possible with EFA, as items are included largely based on a priori theoretical expectations.

When developing a scale, researchers often use EFA first before moving on to CFA. For example, based on EFA, you can develop alternative measurement models that you can test with CFA, such as deleting an item from a factor or moving an item from one factor to another to test the goodness of fit. Van Prooijen and Van der Kloot (2001) provide a good illustration on how this is done. Likewise, Towler and Dipboye (2003) also follow up the EFA with a CFA to confirm the dimensionality and internal consistency reliability of the factors.

An all-encompassing single CFA that includes all constructs in a given theoretical model would always be preferable. The very idea of a factor analysis is to check if the different items load on their respective factors as suggested by theory. Separate CFAs for each factor do not serve that purpose, because convergent validity and discriminant validity cannot be assured. The advantage of an omnibus CFA is to ensure that each of the items load onto the respective factors in the presence of other items or factors. For almost the same reasons, CFA is considered a better method for assessing construct validity than Campbell and Fiske's (1959) approach using multitrait–multimethod matrix (Bagozzi et al., 1991). For an overview of the uses of exploratory and confirmatory factor analyses, refer to the work by Hurley et al. (1997).

8.4.3 Effects of item wording and coding on factor analysis

It is important to note that wording of the items and coding of the responses can affect the outcomes of factor analysis. For example, items that are worded in opposite directions for reason of identifying extremity behaviours of respondents can lead to multiple factors that may overlap (Spector et al., 1997). This suggests that the use of factor analysis will always need to take into account the conceptual background these items are derived from, so that not more than a single factor is created from items that are in fact grounded in the same construct.

Researchers have investigated this phenomenon both from an empirical (e.g. Schmitt and Stults, 1985) and a theoretical (Marsh, 1996) perspective. There is some consensus that in many situations the negatively worded items tend to be linked to one another in a quantitatively, and perhaps qualitatively, different manner than the positively worded items. Schmitt and Stults (1985) investigate the effect of reversing a random number of items in three existing correlation matrices to determine the effects of the reversal procedure on the underlying factor structures. They find that even with a limited number of reverse-scored items, a separate unique factor emerges and accounts for the most **variance** in the multiple factor solutions. They caution researchers to be aware of unique factors that emerged based solely on negatively worded items. Marsh (1996) provides similar evidence. The CFA he conducts also provides support for a two-factor solution rather than the hypothesized unidimensional construct.

Mook et al. (1991) investigate dispositional optimism using negatively and positively worded items. They illustrate using a two-factor solution indicating optimistic and pessimistic attitudes. The optimistic outcomes are associated with positively phrased items whereas the pessimistic outcomes are associated with negatively worded items. In this case the items are designed to measure different constructs that result in the hypothesized outcomes. However, the implications of this result lead to questions concerning factors intended to demonstrate levels of intensity for positive traits but which use negative statements.

All these findings suggest that caution should be exercised about how questions are worded in a survey. The wording and ultimately the coding of the items may have adverse effects on factor analysis outcomes.

8.4.4 Number of items in your scale

Let's say you have designed a set of questions that are not derived directly from a previous study. You face the challenge of having to make sure that these questions have adequate reliability and validity. How do you decide how many items to retain in a scale after conducting an EFA of 50 items and four factors emerge, each having between 10 and 15 item loadings above 0.4 and few cross-loadings? Is there a benefit in having an equal number of items for each construct that is being measured?

The answer depends on internal consistency. However, it is unclear how many items it will take to arrive at a reasonable **Cronbach's alpha** coefficient to demonstrate internal consistency, as it depends on the construct and items (Cortina, 1993). Moreover, we need to be concerned about content validity, and whether the scale represents the entire construct. You can begin with the factors, including items for subscales that have strong loadings on one factor and low loadings on the others. Take a look at the alpha coefficients for the subscales. If alpha coefficients are very high, try to reduce the number of items as a shorter list is more parsimonious. Often you can eliminate quite a few items with little reduction in alpha coefficients. While it may be neat to try to keep the number of items for each factor identical, this is not always possible or necessary. One advantage of keeping identical numbers of items per factor is that if you create subscale scores as sums, the **range** is the same if the number of items is the same. Of course, you can get around that by computing the average response per item.

If you are interested in further reducing the length of the measure after executing EFA and accumulating more validity, you might also consider subjecting your scales to additional, and perhaps more rigorous analysis such as CFA using another independent sample. CFA will help confirm whether your four-factor model is in fact a good measurement model.

If you are using an existing measure, then you can skip EFA and move directly to CFA, testing the measurement model that corresponds to the design of the measure. If some of the items do not perform well, for example low loadings on assigned factors, then you might consider dropping the problematic items. However, it is not advisable for you to modify the measure and test substantive hypotheses with the same sample, because doing so can capitalize on chance sampling variability (Campbell, 1976). As an alternative approach, you can search the literature for previous CFAs of the measure to see whether problems have been detected by other researchers, use these results to construct an alternative measurement model, and use your data to compare this model with the one that corresponds to the original measure. If the re-specified model performs better than the original, then you can use the new model in your research. This approach would avoid using your data for both EFA and CFA.

8.5 BASIC DESCRIPTIVES

Basic descriptives are normally presented to provide an overview of the observations in your data – to provide a feel of the data for you and your readers. These include **distribution** of observations, measures of **central tendency**, measures of variation, and **univariate test**. In fact, even when there are only a few cases in your sample, presenting some basic descriptives is encouraged.

8.5.1 Distribution of observations

Figure 8.1 shows the **frequency distribution** of grades across a class of 100 students in a business studies programme. A frequency distribution is a listing of intervals of possible values for a variable, together with a tabulation of the number of observations in each interval. The intervals must be mutually exclusive. Figure 8.2 presents the **relative frequency** – the **proportion** of the sample observations that fall within that interval. The relative frequency is directly computed from the frequency distribution.

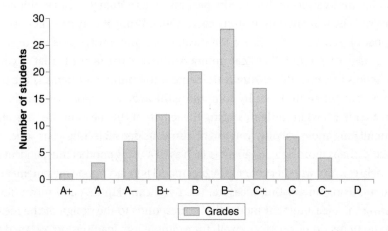

Figure 8.1   Frequency distribution

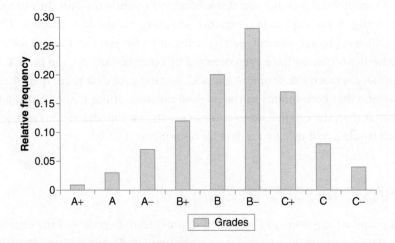

Figure 8.2   Relative frequency distribution

8.5.2 Measures of central tendency

Mean

The **mean** of a sample of n observations $Y_1, Y_2, ..., Y_n$ is calculated as:

$$\bar{Y} = \frac{\sum\limits_{i-1}^{n} Y_i}{n}$$

where $\bar{Y}$, the sample mean, is an estimate of the population mean μ.

Properties of the mean

- The mean is appropriate only when $Y_1, Y_2, ..., Y_n$ are metric (numeric) data, and not appropriate for nominal scales with three or more categories.
- The mean of nominal scales of two categories that are assigned the values of 0s and 1s represent the percentage of the sample that has a value of 1 for the measurement.
- The mean can be highly influenced by outliers.

Median

The **median** is the observation that falls in the middle of an ordered sample. When the sample size is odd, a single observation occurs in the middle. When the sample size is even, the median is the midpoint of the two middle observations in the sample.

Properties of the median

- Appropriate for metric (numeric) data, but not for nominal data.
- For symmetrical distributions, median = mean.
- For skewed distributions, the mean lies toward the direction of skew (the longer tail) relative to the median.
- The median is insensitive to the distances of the observations from the middle.
- The median is unaffected by outliers.

Mode

The **mode** is the value that occurs most frequently among the observations.

Properties of the mode

- Appropriate for all types of data.
- mode = mean = median for normal distribution.

8.5.3 Measures of variation

Range

The range is the difference between the largest and smallest observations. In Figure 8.3, the mean values for the distributions of weekly rental rate for a car park slot for Nations A and B are the same. However, it is clear that the range of the distributions differs. In Nation A, the weekly rental rate for a parking slot ranges from US$28 to US$42. On the other hand, the weekly rental rate for that in Nation B ranges from US$20 to US$50. While the ranges are different, the means for both nations are the same, i.e. US$35.

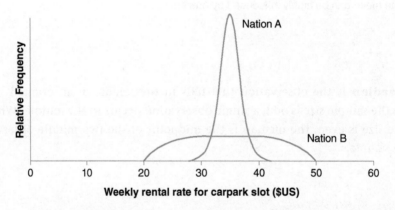

Figure 8.3   Range of distribution

Variance and standard deviation

The variance of a sample of n observations $Y_1, Y_2, ..., Y_n$ is calculated as:

$$s^2 = \frac{\sum_{i-1}^{n} (Y_i - \bar{Y})^2}{n-1}$$

where s^2, the sample variance, is an estimate of the population variance σ^2.

The **standard deviation** s is defined as the positive square root of variance:

$$S = \sqrt{\frac{\sum_{i-1}^{n}(Y_i - \bar{Y})^2}{n-1}}$$

Properties of the standard deviation

- $s \geq 0$, equality occurs only when the distribution is uniform.
- Changes if data is rescaled or transformed.

In Figure 8.4, we can see that the ranges of yearly income in Nations A, B and C are the same. However, if you observe the concentration of the area below each graph, which helps us observe variance, it is evident that these areas differ in their construction. For example, in the case of Nation B, the distribution is relatively extreme, with many observations at the lower and upper ends of the yearly income distribution. Nation A, on the other hand, has observations concentrating around the mean yearly income value of US$25,000. In Nation C, the distribution is uniform across various income levels.

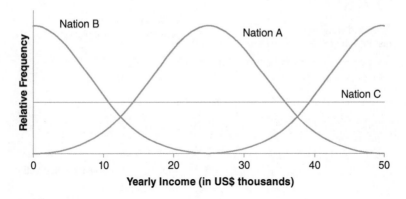

Figure 8.4   Variance of distribution

When the data are approximately bell-shaped (such as in the case of Nation A in the above example):

1. about 68% of the observations will fall between $(\bar{Y} - s)$ and $(\bar{Y} + s)$;
2. about 95% of the observations will fall between $(\bar{Y} - 2s)$ and $(\bar{Y} + 2s)$; and
3. about 99.7% or nearly all the observations will fall between $(\bar{Y} - 3s)$ and $(\bar{Y} + 3s)$.

Outliers

An observation is an **outlier** if it falls more than 1.5 IQR (interquartile range) above the upper quartile or more than 1.5 IQR below the lower quartile. Interquartile range is calculated by the difference between the lower quartile (25 per cent of observations) and the upper quartile (75 per cent of observations).

8.5.4 Univariate tests

When one variable is available for analysis, univariate tests are performed. Univariate tests are the most basic form of analysis. The test used is largely dependent on the distribution of the observations for that variable of interest. Before we move on to highlight the various distributions and tests, it is essential to consider two elements that are key components of parametric tests – point estimator and **confidence interval**.

A point estimator of a parameter is a simple statistic that predicts the value of that parameter. A good point estimator is one with a sampling distribution that (a) is centred around the parameter (unbiased) and (b) has as small a standard error as possible (efficient). In Figure 8.5, we can see that Graph A seems to come closer to the population distribution in terms of its shape. Yet this is based on biased sampling resulting in its mean being different from μ. On the other hand, Graph B has estimated $\overline{Y} = \mu$ Thus, Graph B produces better point estimators in comparison to Graph A.

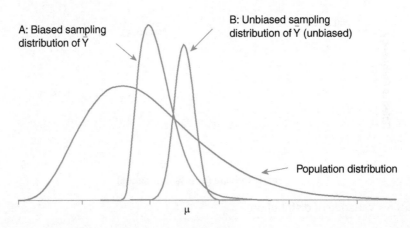

Figure 8.5 Biased and unbiased point estimators

A confidence interval for a parameter is a range of numbers the parameter is believed to fall within. The probability that the confidence interval contains the parameter is called the confidence coefficient. This is a chosen number close to 1, such as 0.95 or 0.99.

Referring to Figure 8.6, Sample A clearly contains the mean μ in the confidence interval of $\overline{Y} \pm 1.96\sigma_{\overline{Y}}$, which is an interval estimate for μ with confidence coefficient 0.95, called a 95% confidence interval. However, in the case of Sample B, μ is found to be outside the range of the confidence interval.

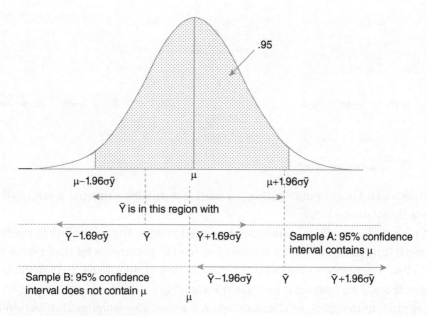

.95

$\mu-1.96\sigma\bar{y}$ μ $\mu+1.96\sigma\bar{y}$

$\bar{Y}$ is in this region with

$\bar{Y}-1.69\sigma\bar{y}$ $\bar{Y}$ $\bar{Y}+1.69\sigma\bar{y}$ Sample A: 95% confidence
                                                                              interval contains μ

Sample B: 95% confidence $\bar{Y}-1.96\sigma\bar{y}$ $\bar{Y}$ $\bar{Y}+1.96\sigma\bar{y}$
interval does not contain μ
                                                      μ

Figure 8.6   Confidence interval

A large sample confidence interval for μ is

$$\bar{Y} \pm z\sigma_{\bar{Y}} = \bar{Y} \pm z\left(\frac{s}{\sqrt{n}}\right)$$

The z-value is such that the probability under a normal curve within z standard errors of the mean equals the confidence coefficient. For 95% and 99% confidence intervals, z equals 1.96 and 2.58. In addition, if we repeatedly select random samples of n and each time construct a 95% confidence interval, then in the long run about 95% of the intervals constructed should contain μ. It is important to note that the width of a confidence interval (1) increases as the confidence coefficient increases, and (2) decreases as the sample size increases.

Normal distribution

The **normal distribution** is a symmetric, bell-shaped curve, characterized by its mean μ and standard deviation σ. For each fixed number z, the probability concentrated within z standard deviations of μ is the same for all normal distributions. In particular, the probability equals 0.68 within z = 1 standard deviation, 0.95 within z = 2 standard deviations, and 0.997 within z = 3 standard deviations, as shown in Figure 8.7.

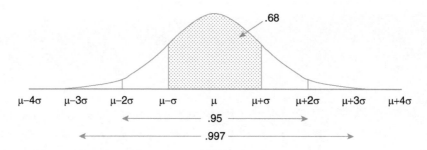

Figure 8.7   Normal distribution

The standard normal distribution is a normal distribution that has mean $\mu = 0$ and standard deviation $\sigma = 1$.

A number Y is $z = (Y-\mu)/\sigma$ standard deviations from μ. The probability in the tail of a normal distribution beyond a number Y is the tail probability for that z-score from the z table. The z table is available in most books on quantitative research methods and accessible from the Internet if you search for 'z table'.

For random sampling, as the sample size n grows, the sampling distribution of $\bar{Y}$ approaches a normal distribution. An illustration is presented in Figure 8.8.

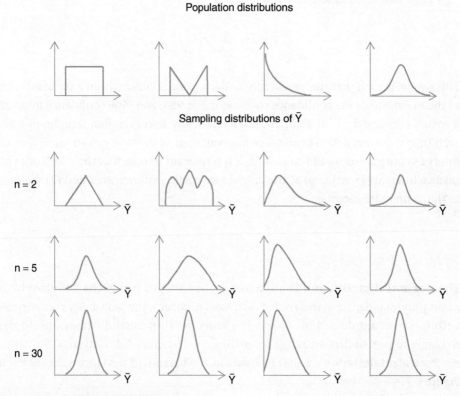

Figure 8.8   Sampling distribution

Significance test for a mean

The significance test for mean value for normal distributions requires a random sample of $n \geq 30$. The variable has to be quantitative. The test refers to the population mean of the variable, μ.

The **null hypothesis** has the form

$$H_0: \mu = \mu_0$$

where μ_0 is some particular number.

The **alternate hypothesis** has the form

$$H_a: \mu \neq \mu_0$$

This alternate hypothesis is two-sided as it includes values falling both below and above the value μ_0 listed in H_0.

Test statistic

$$z = \frac{\bar{Y} - \mu_0}{\hat{\sigma}_{\bar{Y}}} = \frac{\bar{Y} - \mu_0}{s/\sqrt{n}}$$

Rule: The larger the absolute value of z ($|z|$), the stronger the evidence against H_0.

Suppose $z = -1.5$. This is the z-score resulting from a sample mean $\bar{Y}$ that is 1.5 standard errors below μ_0. The *p*-value is the probability that $z \geq 1.5$ or $z \leq -1.5$. From the normal distribution table, (this is also accessible in most quantitative research methods books and from the Internet), the probability in one tail above $z = +1.5$ is 0.0668, so the probability for two tails is 0.1336. For a given size of effect, smaller *p*-values result from larger sample sizes.

In Chapter 6, we discussed sampling issues, the challenges with sample size and what sample sizes would deem to be adequate for a particular research. While the general rule is that for statistical power, the larger the sample the merrier, there are often situations where a large sample size is not easily achievable. In such situations, and when the population and sample is possible to follow a normal distribution, it is possible to work backwards to derive a minimal target for sample size.

Let B denote the desired bound on error. The sample size n ensuring that, with fixed probability, the error of estimation of μ by $\bar{Y}$ is no greater than B, is

$$n = \sigma^2 \left(\frac{z}{B}\right)^2$$

The z-score is the one for a confidence interval with confidence coefficient equal to the fixed probability. Figure 8.9 provides a graphical demonstration of the importance of ensuring that the sample size is adequate. In the first sampling distribution, where sample size is 100, the range covered by (μ–B, μ+B) does not reflect the 95% confidence interval that we seek to achieve. As we move further, to 300 and finally to 500 for sample size, we get closer to achieving the desired confidence interval of 95%.

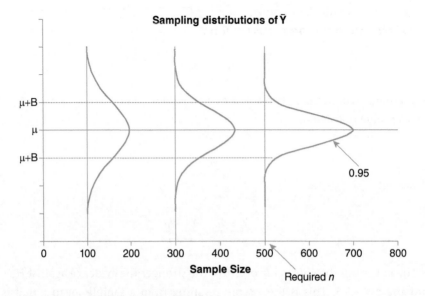

Figure 8.9   Sample size for estimation

There are research situations that may require you to test a mean that has a value equivalent to a proportion or ratio. We have highlighted the use of ratios in Chapter 6 when we discussed measurements. When it comes to testing the significance of a proportion, the following significance test should be applied.

Assumptions: the test requires a random sample of n ≥ 30. The variable is quantitative, with mean μ.

Null and alternate hypotheses

$$H_0: \mu = \mu_0$$
$$H_a: \mu \neq \mu_0 \text{ (or } H_a: \mu > \mu_0 \text{ or } H_a: \mu < \mu_0)$$

Test statistic

$$z = \frac{\hat{\pi} - \pi_0}{\sigma_{\hat{\pi}}} = \frac{\hat{\pi} - \pi_0}{\sqrt{\pi_0(1-\pi_0)/n}}$$

Rule: The larger the value of $|z|$, the stronger the evidence against H_0 (two-sided test).

A large sample confidence interval for a population proportion π, based on a sample proportion $\hat{\pi}$, is

$$\hat{\pi} \pm z\hat{\sigma}_{\hat{\pi}} = \hat{\pi} \pm z\sqrt{\frac{\hat{\pi}(1-\hat{\pi})}{n}}$$

A somewhat larger sample is needed if the proportion is relatively small or large – at least 10 observations in the category and at least 10 not in it.

In the case of sample size required for estimating a proportion π, the sample size n ensuring that, with fixed probability, the error of estimation of π by the sample proportion $\hat{\pi}$ is no greater than B is

$$n = \pi(1-\pi)\left(\frac{z}{B}\right)^2$$

The z-score is the one for a confidence interval with confidence coefficient equal to the fixed probability; for instance, $z = 1.96$ for probability 0.95 and $z = 2.58$ for probability 0.99. Using this formula requires guessing π or taking the safe but conservative approach of setting $\pi(1-\pi) = 0.25$.

It is important to highlight that significance testing contains some standard items. Below are the elements of any significance test.

- Assumptions: type of data, e.g. quantitative/qualitative; population distribution, e.g. normal; method of sampling, e.g. random; minimum sample size.
- Hypotheses: null and alternate hypotheses.
- Test statistic: a statistic calculated from the sample data to test the null hypothesis.
- p-value: the p-value is the probability, when H_0 is true, of a test statistic value at least as contradictory to H_0 as the value actually observed. The smaller the p-value, the more strongly the data contradict H_0. The p-value is denoted by p.
- Conclusion: report p-value and formalize decision.

t-Distribution

The **t-distribution** is bell-shaped and symmetric about 0. The spread of the t-distribution depends on the degrees of freedom (*df*). The standard deviation of the

t-distribution $\sqrt{df / (df - 2)}$ always exceeds 1 but decreases towards 1 as df increases. Though the t-distribution is bell-shaped about 0, the probability falling in the tails is higher than that for the standard normal distribution. Figure 8.10 shows the difference between the t-distribution and the standard normal distribution. The larger the df value, however, the more closely the t-distribution resembles the standard normal distribution. In the limit as df increases indefinitely, the two distributions are identical.

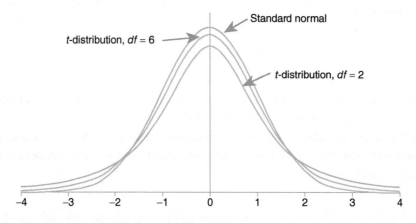

Figure 8.10 The t-distribution

For testing the mean value of the t-distribution, the statistic for t is:

$$t = \frac{\overline{Y} - \mu}{\hat{\sigma}_{\overline{Y}}} = \frac{\overline{Y} - \mu}{s / \sqrt{n}}$$

and is called the t-distribution with $(n-1)$ degrees of freedom.

For a random sample from a normal population distribution, a 95% confidence interval for μ is

$$\overline{Y} \pm t_{0.025}\, \hat{\sigma}_{\overline{Y}} = \overline{Y} \pm t_{0.025}\left(\frac{s}{\sqrt{n}}\right)$$

where $df = n-1$ for the t-value.

Binomial distribution

For observations on a nominal variable with two categories, the **binomial distribution** applies when the following three conditions hold:

1. For a fixed number of observations n, each observation falls into one of the two categories.
2. The probability of falling into each category, π for the first category and $(1-\pi)$ for the second category, is the same for every observation.
3. The outcomes of successive observations are independent; that is, the category that occurs for one observation does not depend on the outcomes of other observations.

Denote the probability of the first category, for each observation, by π. For a sample of n independent observations, the probability that Y of them will fall in that category equals

$$P(Y)=\frac{n!}{Y!(n-Y)!}\pi^Y (1-\pi)^{\pi-Y}, \quad Y = 0, 1, 2, ..., n.$$

The symbol $n!$ is called n *factorial* and represents $n! = 1 \times 2 \times 3 \times .... \times n$.

8.6 BIVARIATE ANALYSIS

8.6.1 Comparing two means

Let $\bar{Y}_1$ and $\bar{Y}_2$ denote the sample means of the population Y_1 and Y_2 with population means μ_1 and μ_2 respectively.
The confidence interval for $\mu_2 - \mu_1$ is

$$\left(\bar{Y}_2 - \bar{Y}_1\right) \pm z\sigma_{\bar{Y}_2 - \bar{Y}_1}$$

When two estimates are formed from independent samples, the sampling distribution of their difference has variance equal to the sum of the variances of the sampling distributions of the separate estimates.
Thus, the large-sample confidence interval for $\mu_2 - \mu_1$ is

$$\left(\bar{Y}_2 - \bar{Y}_1\right) \pm z\sqrt{\frac{s_1^2}{n_1} + \frac{s_2^2}{n_2}}$$

for $n_1 \geq 20$ and $n_2 \geq 20$.

Rule:

1. If the confidence interval contains only positive values, then $\mu_2 > \mu_1$.
2. If the confidence interval contains only negative values, then $\mu_2 < \mu_1$.
3. If the confidence interval contains 0, then there is insufficient evidence to conclude which of μ_1 or μ_2 is larger.

The standard form for a **z-test** statistic is

$$z = \frac{\left(\bar{Y}_2 - \bar{Y}_1\right) - \left(\mu_2 - \mu_1\right)}{\hat{\sigma}_{\bar{Y}_2 - \bar{Y}_1}}$$

For small sample methods that make the assumption that the two groups have the same variability, the common value of σ of σ_1 and σ_2 is estimated by

$$\hat{\sigma} = \sqrt{\frac{\sum\left(Y_{1i} - \bar{Y}_1\right)^2 + \sum\left(Y_{2i} - \bar{Y}_2\right)^2}{n_1 + n_2 - 2}} = \sqrt{\frac{(n_1 - 1) S_1^2 + (n_2 - 1) S_2^2}{n_1 + n_2 - 2}}$$

The confidence interval for $\mu_2 - \mu_1$ has the form

$$\bar{Y}_2 - \bar{Y}_1 \pm t\sigma_{\bar{Y}_2 - \bar{Y}_1}$$

The t-score comes from the t–table with $df = n_1 + n_2 - 2$.

8.6.2 Comparing two proportions

Let $\hat{\pi}_1$ and $\hat{\pi}_2$ denote the sample proportions of the random samples n_1 and n_2 with population proportions π_1 and π_2 respectively.

The large-sample confidence interval for $\pi_1 - \pi_2$ is

$$\hat{\pi}_2 - \hat{\pi}_1 \pm z\hat{\sigma}_{\hat{\pi}_2 - \hat{\pi}_1} = \left(\hat{\pi}_2 - \hat{\pi}_1\right) \pm z\sqrt{\frac{\hat{\pi}_1\left(1 - \hat{\pi}_1\right)}{n_1} + \frac{\hat{\pi}_2\left(1 - \hat{\pi}_2\right)}{n_2}}$$

The sample is considered large if, for each sample, more than five observations fall into the category for which the proportion is estimated, and more than five observations do not fall in this category.

The standard form for a z-test statistic is

$$z = \frac{\left(\hat{\pi}_2 - \hat{\pi}_1\right) - \left(\pi_2 - \pi_1\right)}{\hat{\sigma}_{\hat{\pi}_2 - \hat{\pi}_1}}$$

8.6.3 Chi-squared test of independence

Two nominal variables are *statistically independent* if their conditional distributions within the population are identical. The variables are *statistically dependent* if the conditional distributions are not identical.

Let's take for example a business school that is keen to understand the attributes of postgraduate students who are enrolled in its programmes in order to establish a marketing strategy moving forward.

Figure 8.11 shows the distribution of students and computations of probabilities. The first entry in each cell is the actual number of students in the categories. Numbers in brackets represent the percentages within rows. The two sets of percentages for females and males are the conditional distributions on the programmes. The rows (25.9, 74.1) and (7.7, 92.3) are the genders' estimated conditional probabilities for the programmes.

	Research Masters	**Taught Masters**	**Total**
Female	7 (25.9) 5.4	20 (74.1) 21.6	27 (100)
Male	1 (7.7) 2.6	12 (92.3) 10.4	13 (100)
Total	8	32	40

Figure 8.11   Chi-squared test of independence

In some cases, eye balling the data may suggest that there are some tendencies, for example females tend to enrol in research Master's programmes. But using eye balling for inference is hardly scientific. There are various statistical tests that can be conducted in order to replace this eye balling as support for observing these tendencies. The **chi-squared test** of independence would be the most common one used.

Let f_o denote an observed frequency in a cell of the table.

Let f_e denote an expected frequency; this is the count expected in a cell if the variables were independent.

The expected frequency f_e for a cell equals the product of the row and column totals for that cell, divided by the total sample size (see numbers in italics in the Figure).

The chi-squared (χ^2) test statistic is

$$\chi^2 = \sum \frac{(f_o - f_e)^2}{f_e}$$

Rule: The larger the χ^2 value, the greater the evidence against the null hypothesis of independence.

The chi-squared test should be used only when $f_e \geq 0$. Otherwise, use a small sample exact test. It also does not apply when each row has the same subjects, in which case the McNemar's test is more appropriate. For large sample sizes, the sampling distribution of χ^2 is the chi-squared **probability distribution**. Figure 8.12 shows some examples of chi-squared distributions.

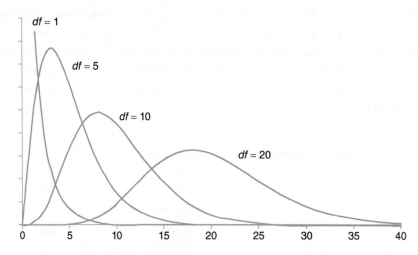

Figure 8.12   Chi-squared distributions

Properties of chi-squared distribution

- It is always positive and skewed to the right. The precise shape of the distribution depends on the *df*. For testing independence in a table with r rows and c columns, the formula for the degrees of freedom is $df = (r – 1) (c – 1)$.
- The mean μ and the standard deviation σ of the chi-squared distribution depend on the *df* value, with $\mu = df$ and $\sigma = \sqrt{2df}$.
- The chi-squared statistic does not reflect the nature of strength of the association.

The chi-squared test of independence is suitable for testing with nominal variables. If your variables of interest are ordinal by nature, then you will have to adopt other tests such as Goodman and Kruskal's gamma, Kendall's tau-b and tau-c, Spearman's rho-b and rho-c and Somers' d. These tests are available with a click of a button in most statistical software.

8.6.4 One-way and two-way ANOVA

The z- and **t-tests** presented in earlier sections are parametric tests. Parametric tests are statistical tests that are based on assumptions of the probability distributions of the sample. The z- and t-tests, as shown above, are useful for testing the differences between two sample groups. However, when the comparison cuts across more than two sample groups, the z- and t-tests will no longer be appropriate tests. In these circumstances, the **one-way ANOVA** and the **two-way ANOVA** are the commonly used tests.

The one-way ANOVA test is used when the multiple sample groups of your study are independent. Take for example, a comparison of the job satisfaction levels across three groups of employees. Although it is easy just to enter the data in your statistical software for them to generate a result from the one-way ANOVA test, it is important for you to understand how these are derived and will help in interpreting from the findings. The illustration below shows the procedures for testing using the one-way ANOVA.

Research objective: To find out whether job satisfaction levels of workers in subsidiary A, B and C differ.

Sample: A sample of 50 workers in each subsidiary is selected and a survey is conducted on their job satisfaction level.

Next, take an average score for each firm: e.g. $\overline{X}_A = 60.3$; $\overline{X}_B = 64.0$; $\overline{X}_C = 78.7$.

$$\text{We have } H_0: \ \mu_A = \mu_B = \mu_C$$

$$H_1: \text{One of the equalities does not hold}$$

Then we take the variance within each group, square it and add their sum together, we have within-group variation:

$$SSE = \sum_{1}^{50}(X_{Ai} - \overline{X}_A) + \sum_{1}^{50}(X_{Bi} - \overline{X}_B) + \sum_{1}^{50}(X_{Ci} - \overline{X}_C) = 1122.2$$

Between-groups variation is:

$$SSG = (60.3 - 64.0)^2 + (60.3 - 78.7)^2 + (64.0 - 78.7)^2 = 1894.47$$

Rule: Reject H_0 if $F \geq F_{0.05, 3, 147} = 2.44$, setting $\sigma = 0.05$

$$\text{The } F\text{-statistic} = (SSG/3) \ / \ (SSE/147) = 82.72$$

Hence, we reject H_0 at the 5% level of significance, as $F \geq F_{0.05, 3, 147}$.

To find out if each pair is different, the Tukey's Test can be used.

$$\text{Test statistic: HSD} = q_{\alpha, k, n-k} \sqrt{\frac{MSE}{n_i}}$$

where k is the number of groups, n is the total number of observations, and n_i is the number of observations in a sample group.

Rule: Any pair of $\left(\overline{X}_i - \overline{X}_j\right) > HSD$ is significantly different.

The two-way ANOVA is used when there is a controlling effect to the above research situation. For example, if subsidiary B is the supplier to both subsidiary A and subsidiary C, then the job satisfaction levels of employees within one subsidiary can be affected by the job satisfaction levels of employees in another subsidiary, i.e. not independent. In such circumstances, the two-way ANOVA is more appropriate.

8.6.5 Non-parametric tests

Non-parametric tests are used in situations where we are not certain of the assumptions underlying the probability distribution. They are also useful in circumstances where response measurements cannot be quantified. For example, in consumer research a question like 'do you prefer product A to product B?' does not allow us to accurately assess the degree of preference for A and B. Non-parametric tests are thus useful for testing data that are in nominal and ordinal scales.

As non-parametric tests often use ranking systems for their calculations of the index, information can be lost as numerical values get ranked. A result of this is that non-parametric tests are normally less efficient than parametric tests. Figure 8.13 depicts the equivalent non-parametric tests for two or more independent and related sample groups.

	Two sample groups		More than two sample groups	
	Independent	Related	Independent	Related
Parametric tests	*t*-test; z-test	*t*-test	1-way ANOVA	2-way ANOVA
Non-parametric tests	Mann–Whitney	Wilcoxon signed rank	Kruskal–Wallis	Friedman

Figure 8.13 Non-parametric tests

Mann–Whitney test

The **Mann–Whitney test** is used to compare the distribution of two populations (independent random samples). It is important to note that when the sample gets large or the underlying populations are normal, then the *t*-test or z-test is used.

Procedure

1. Pool all observations from both samples.
2. Rank them in ascending order (assign rank of 1 to the smallest).
3. If sample 1 and sample 2 are from the same populations (or the distributions of the populations are the same), then we would expect:

   Sum of ranks (sample 1) (M_1) = Sum of ranks (sample 2) (M_2).

4.   Thus, we have:

H_0: $M_1 = M_2$ (no difference)

H_i: $M_1 \neq M_2$ (there is a difference).

Test statistic: $U - S - \dfrac{n_1(n_1+1)}{2}$ where S is the sum of ranks of sample 1.

5.   Rule: Reject H_0 if U is very small or very large, i.e. $U < U_{\alpha/2}$ or $U > U_{1-\alpha/2}$ where $U_{\alpha/2}$ is the critical value of U in the Mann–Whitney table (can be accessed from quantitative research methods books or from the Internet).

Wilcoxon signed-rank test

The **Wilcoxon signed-rank test** is used to compare two related distributions. Let's say we want to test if the difference in the average income of professionals between two cities is less than \$15,000:

Thus, we have

$$H_0 : \mu \geq 15{,}000$$

$$H_1 : \mu < 15{,}000$$

Procedure

1.   Find $d_i = X_i - \mu_0$.
2.   Take the rank of $|d_i|$ (if there is a tie, take the mean). Smallest value will be assigned the value of 1. Also note that cases where $|d_i| = 0$ are eliminated from analysis.
3.   Get signed rank of $|d_i|$, i.e. if $d_i < 0$, then the rank will be negative.
4.   Test statistic: Compute T_+ : sum of positive ranks.

Compute T_- : sum of negative ranks.

5.   Rule: Reject H_0 if T_+ or T_- is very small.

In this case, we hypothesize that the income is less than \$15,000, therefore if T_+ is very small, we will reject H_0.

Kruskal–Wallis test

The **Kruskal–Wallis test** is used to compare more than two independent samples.

H_0: Mean score is the same for the four cities

H_i: Mean score is not the same for the four cities

	City A	City B	City C	City D
	27 (40)	13 (17.5)	11 (7.5)	7 (1)
	17 (29.5)	13 (17.5)	13 (17.5)	13 (17.5)
	21 (35)	14 (24)	19 (33.5)	14 (24)
	26 (39)	11 (7.5)	13 (17.5)	9 (4)
	25 (38)	13 (17.5)	16 (26.5)	12 (10.5)
	18 (32)	13 (17.5)	13 (17.5)	8 (2)
	17 (29.5)	9 (4)	12 (10.5)	12 (10.5)
	23 (36.5)	13 (17.5)	17 (29.5)	12 (10.5)
	17 (29.5)	14 (24)	19 (33.5)	9 (4)
	23 (36.5)	10 (6)	16 (26.5)	13 (17.5)
Total rank	345.5	153	220	101.5

Figure 8.14   Kruskal–Wallis test

Procedure

1. Rank all observations as if they are from the same population. Rank presented in brackets in Figure 8.14.
2. Sum the ranks of all the four samples.

$$Test\,statistic: H = \frac{12}{n(n+1)} \sum_{j=1}^{4} \frac{R_j^2}{n_j} - 3(n+1)$$ where n is the total number of observations = 40

and n_j is the number of observations in City j.

3. Rule: Reject H_0 if $H > \chi_{1-\alpha}^2$ (df = no. of cities − 1).

In this case, $\chi_{0.99}^2$ (df =3) =11.345 (using the χ^2 table that can be accessed from quantitative research methods books or the Internet) and H = 24.43. Thus, we reject H_0 at the 1% significance level.

Friedman test

The **Friedman test** is used to compare more than two related samples.

H_0: Mean score is the same for the three dyes

H_1: Mean score is not the same for the three dyes

	Fabric	Dye A	Dye B	Dye C
	1	74 (1)	81 (2)	95 (3)
	2	78 (1)	86 (2)	99 (3)
	3	76 (1)	90 (2.5)	90 (2.5)
	4	82 (1)	93 (3)	87 (2)
	5	77 (2)	73 (1)	93 (3)
Total rank		6	10.5	13.5

Figure 8.15   Friedman test

Procedure

1. Rank the dyes with respect to individual fabric (the smallest value will be assigned the rank of 1). The ranks are shown in brackets in Figure 8.15.
2. Total the ranks of each dye.

    Test statistic: $\chi^2 = \dfrac{12}{nk(k+1)} \displaystyle\sum_{j-1}^{k} R_j^2 - 3n(k+1)$ where n is the number of blocks (= 5) and

    k is the number of treatments (= 3).
3. *Rule*: Reject H_0 if T is very small or very large, i.e. $T > W_{\alpha/2}$ or $T > W_{1-\alpha/2}$.

    In this case, $\chi^2 = 5.7$ and from the χ^2 table that can be accessed from quantitative research methods books or the Internet we have p-value = 0.0705, thus we cannot reject H_0 at the 5% significance level.

8.7 BIVARIATE CORRELATION

In Section 5.4, we briefly compared correlation and causality. In essence, correlation is a necessary but not sufficient condition for causality to occur. Correlation can cover both positive and negative correlation, i.e. can go in either direction. Correlation tests also do not allow deeper implications to be made when compared to causality tests. It is almost mandatory that the **bivariate correlations** of all the variables used in a study are presented. The bivariate correlation matrix shows all the pairwise relationships between any two variables used in a study. It measures the strength of the association and range between –1 and 1. The stronger the relationship between two variables, the closer the bivariate correlation is to the value of 1 or –1. The value 0 shows that two variables are not related at all.

High bivariate correlations can become a problem relating to multicollinearity for statistical testing, which will be demonstrated in Chapter 10 when we discuss quantitative analysis. But what level of correlation is considered 'high'? As Spencer (1995) finds in his investigation of psychological and medical research, 'high' would mean an absolute value of 0.7 or above, i.e. ≥0.7 or ≤ -0.7. 'Low' would mean an absolute value of about 0.30. These would be roughly the same rules that business and management researchers apply.

8.8 SIGNIFICANCE TESTING

When you read the presentation of the results of a study, you will see '$p < 0.05$' or '$\alpha = 0.05$' or 'significance at 5% level'. These forms of presentation are different ways to reflect that the results that you observe are significant at the 5% level, which means that 95% of the time you should observe the results that you have found. The levels of 1%, 5% and 10% are the commonly used significance cut-off points.

Despite the importance of significance testing, there have been discussions about its misuses (Carver, 1978; Cohen, 1994). Bettis (2012), for example, highlights that researchers often search for the results that they need to support their theories by snooping the data and searching for significance in their analyses. Schmidt (1996) suggests that perhaps the most appropriate way to obtain results might be to use point estimates and confidence intervals as opposed to using significance levels. Others have also suggested similar alternative tests (e.g. Abelson, 1997; Cohen, 1994). Cortina and Dunlap (1997: 170) however add that the idea of replacing Null Hypothesis Significance Testing (NHST) with confidence intervals is nonsensical. The two are based on exactly the same information, and both involve an exclusionary decision of some kind. Chow (1988) finds that an alternative such as effect size is not necessarily better than significance testing as well.

Nonetheless, as Sauley and Bedeian (1989) suggest, there is no right or wrong level of significance and the selection of this significance level should be treated like any other research parameter. This would mean that the selection of significance level is yet another judgement call of practice in research in business and management. As such, we all have to be mindful of over-reliance on significance testing itself (Gelman and Stern, 2006).

KEY TERMS

- Alternate hypothesis
- Binomial distribution
- Bivariate analysis
- Bivariate correlation
- Central tendency
- Chi-squared test
- Confidence interval
- Confirmatory factor analysis
- Cronbach's alpha
- Data
- Data error
- Descriptive analysis
- Dirty data
- Distribution
- Exploratory factor analysis
- Frequency distribution
- Friedman test
- Kruskal–Wallis test
- Mann–Whitney test
- Maximum likelihood

- Mean
- Median
- Missing data
- Mode
- Non-parametric test
- Normal distribution
- Null hypothesis
- One-way ANOVA
- Outlier
- Probability distribution
- Proportion
- Range
- Relative frequency distribution
- Reliability
- Sample size
- Significance testing
- Standard deviation
- t-distribution
- t-test
- Two-way ANOVA

- Univariate test
- Validity
- Variance
- Wilcoxon signed-rank test
- z-test

SUMMARY

- There are many sources of data error; some due to human errors, while others are due to contaminated data.
- Missing data need to be handled with care and there are several ways to handle missing data situations.
- The exploratory factor analysis and confirmatory factor analysis can be used separately and simultaneously.
- The exploratory factor analysis and confirmatory factor analysis can be used to adjust the number of items represented in a scale.
- Wordings within items can affect the outcomes of factor analysis from a survey.
- The common measures of central tendency are the mean, median and mode.
- The measures of variation include range, variance and standard deviation.
- The normal distribution applies to large samples while the t-distribution applies to small samples.
- The z-test and t-test are used for cases where there are two independent or related sample groups in your testing.
- The one-way ANOVA and two-way ANOVA tests are used when there are more than two independent or related sample groups in your testing.
- Non-parametric tests are used in situations where we are not certain of the assumptions underlying the probability distribution. They are also useful in circumstances where response measurements cannot be quantified.
- Bivariate correlation refers to the association between two variables.
- There is no right or wrong level of significance required for testing. The most common ones are 1%, 5% and 10%. The selection of this significance level should be treated like any other research parameter.

QUESTIONS

1. Discuss some ways to handle missing data, including the pros and cons.
2. Compare and contrast exploratory factor analysis and confirmatory factor analysis.
3. Discuss the effects of negatively and positively worded items on factor analysis.
4. What are the differences between the test statistics used for samples following a normal distribution versus those following a t-distribution?
5. Describe the chi-squared test of independence with the help of an example.
6. What are the advantages and disadvantages of non-parametric analysis?
7. Illustrate the procedure for two of the following non-parametric tests: (1) Mann–Whitney, (2) Wilcoxon signed-rank, (3) Kruskal–Wallis and (4) Friedman.

ADDITIONAL READINGS

Agresti, A. and Finlay, B. (2009) *Statistical Methods for the Social Sciences* (4th edition). Upper Saddle River, NJ: Pearson Prentice Hall.

Austin, J.T., Boyle, K.A. and Lualhati, J.C. (1998) 'Statistical conclusion validity for organizational science researchers: A review', *Organizational Research Methods*, 1 (2): 164–208.

Carmines, E.G. and Zeller, R.A. (1979) *Reliability and Validity Assessment*. Newbury Park, CA: Sage Publishing.

Cook, T.D. and Campbell, D.T. (1979) *Quasi-experimentation: Design and Analysis for Field Settings*. Chicago, IL: Rand McNally.

Cronbach, L.J. (1951) 'Coefficient alpha and the internal structure of tests', *Psychometrika*, 16 (3): 297–334.

Kanji, G.K. (2006) *100 Statistical Tests* (3rd edition). Thousand Oaks, CA: Sage Publishing.

Lance, C.E., Butts, M.M. and Michels, L.C. (2006) 'The sources of four commonly reported cutoff criteria: what did they really say?' *Organizational Research Methods*, 9 (2): 202–20.

Levitin, A.V. and Redman, T.C. (1998) 'Data as a resource: Properties, implications, and prescriptions', *Sloan Management Review*, 40 (1): 89–101.

Little, R. J.A. and Schenker, N. (1995) 'Missing data', In G. Arminger, C.C. Clogg and M.E. Sobel (eds), *Handbook of Statistical Modeling for the Social and Behavioral Sciences*. New York, NY: Plenum Press. pp. 39–75.

Mazen, A., Magid, M., Hemmasi, M. and Lewis, M.F. (1987) 'Assessment of statistical power in contemporary strategy research', *Strategic Management Journal*, 8 (4): 403–10.

Messick, S. (1980) 'Test validity and the ethics of assessment', *American Psychologist*, 35 (11): 1012–27.

Nunnally, J.C. (1978) *Psychometric Theory* (2nd edition). New York: McGraw-Hill.

Peterson, R.A. (1994) 'A meta-analysis of Cronbach's Coefficient Alpha', *Journal of Consumer Research*, 21 (2): 381–91.

Redman, T.C. (1998) 'The impact of poor data quality on the typical enterprise', *Communications of the ACM*, 41 (2): 79–82.

Riege, A.M. (2003) 'Validity and reliability tests in case study research: A literature review with "hands-on" applications for each research phase', *Qualitative Market Research*, 6 (2): 75–86.

Rozebloom, W.W. (1960) 'The fallacy of the null-hypothesis significance test', *Psychological Bulletin*, 57 (5): 416–28.

Rubin, D.B. (1976) 'Inference and missing data', *Biometrika*, 63 (3): 581–92.

Sackett, P.R. and Larson, J.R. Jr. (1990) 'Research strategies and tactics in industrial and organizational psychology', in M.D. Dunnette and L.M. Hough (eds), *Handbook of Industrial and Organizational Psychology*, volume 1, (2nd edition.). Palo Alto, CA: Consulting Psychologists Press. pp. 419–89.

Scandura, T.A. and Williams, E.A. (2000) 'Research methodology in management: Current practices, trends, and implications for future research', *Academy of Management Journal*, 43 (6): 1248–64.

Sussmann, M. and Robertson, D.U. (1986) 'The validity of validity: An analysis of validation study designs', *Journal of Applied Psychology*, 71 (3): 461–8.

Traub, R.E. and Rowley, G.L. (1991) 'An NCME instructional module on understanding reliability', *Educational Measurement: Issues and Practice*, 10 (1): 37–45.

REFERENCES

Abelson, R.P. (1997) 'On the surprising longevity of flogged horses: Why there is a case for the significance test', *Psychological Science*, 8 (1): 12–5.

Bagozzi, R.P., Yi, Y. and Philips, L.W. (1991) 'Assessing construct validity in organizational research', *Administrative Science Quarterly*, 36 (3): 421–58.

Bettis, R.A. (2012) The search for asterisks: Compromised statistical tests and flawed theories. *Strategic Management Journal*, 33(1): 108–13.

Campbell, D.T. and Fiske, D.W. (1959) 'Convergent and discriminant validation by the multi-trait–multimethod matrix', *Psychological Bulletin*, 56 (2): 81–105.

Campbell, J.P. (1976) 'Psychometric theory', in M.D. Dunnette (ed.), *Handbook of Industrial and Organizational Psychology*, Volume 1. Chicago, IL: Rand McNally. pp. 185–222.

Carver, R.P. (1978) 'The case against statistical significance testing', *Harvard Educational Review*, 48 (3): 378–99.

Chow, S.L. (1988) 'Significance test or effect size?', *Psychological Bulletin*, 103 (1): 105–10.

Cohen, J. (1994) 'The Earth is round (p <0.05)'. *American Psychologist*, 49 (12): 997–1003.

Cortina, J.M. (1993) 'What is coefficient alpha? An examination of theory and applications', *Journal of Applied Psychology*, 78 (1): 98–104.

Cortina, J.M. and Dunlap, W.P. (1997) 'On the logic and purpose of significance testing', *Psychological Methods*, 2 (2): 161–72.

De Veaux, R.D. and Hand, D.J. (2005) 'How to lie with bad data', *Statistical Science*, 20 (3): 231–8.

Enders, C.K. and Bandalos, D.L. (2001) 'The relative performance of full information maximum likelihood estimation for missing data in structural equation models', *Structural Equation Modeling*, 8 (3): 430–57.

Gelman, A. and Stern, H. (2006) 'The difference between "significant" and "not significant" is not itself statistically significant', *The American Statistician*, 60 (4): 328–31.

Gerbing, D.W. and Hamilton, J.G. (1996) 'Validity of exploratory factor analysis as a precursor to confirmatory factor analysis', *Structural Equation Modeling*, 3 (1): 62–72.

Gilley, O.W. and Leone, R.P. (1991) 'A two-stage imputation procedure for item nonresponse in surveys', *Journal of Business Research*, 22 (4): 281–91.

Goodman, J.S. and Blum, T.C. (1996) 'Assessing the non-random sampling effects of subject attrition in longitudinal research', *Journal of Management*, 22 (4): 627–52.

Graham, J.W. and Donaldson, S.I. (1993) 'Evaluating interventions with differential attrition: The importance of nonresponse mechanisms and use of follow-up data', *Journal of Applied Psychology*, 78 (1): 119–28.

Hand, D. J., Blunt, G., Kelly, M.G. and Adams, N.M. (2000) 'Data mining for fun and profit', *Statistical Science*, 15 (2): 111–26.

Hurley, A.E., Scandura, T.A., Schriesheim, C.A., Brannick, M.T., Seers, A., Vandenberg, R.J. and Williams, L.J. (1997) 'Exploratory and confirmatory factor analysis: Guidelines, issues, and alternatives', *Journal of Organizational Behavior*, 18 (6): 667–83.

Kim, W., Choi, B.-J., Hong, E.-K., Kim, S.-K. and Lee, D. (2003) 'A taxonomy of dirty data', *Data Mining and Knowledge Discovery*, 7 (1): 81–99.

Marsh, H.W. (1996) 'Positive and negative global self-esteem: A substantively meaningful distinction or artefactors?' *Journal of Personality & Social Psychology*, 70 (4): 810–19.

Mook, J., Kleijn, W.C. and van der Ploeg, H.M. (1991) 'Symptom-positively and -negatively worded items in two popular self-report inventories of anxiety and depression', *Psychological Reports*, 69 (2): 551–60.

Newman, D.A. (2003) 'Longitudinal modeling with randomly and systematically missing data: A simulation of ad hoc, maximum likelihood, and multiple imputation techniques', *Organizational Research Methods*, 6 (3): 328–62.

Rajagopalan, B. and Isken, M.W. (2001) 'Exploiting data preparation to enhance mining and knowledge discovery', *IEEE Transactions on Systems, Man, and Cybernatics – Part C: Applications and Reviews*, 31 (4): 460–7.

Sauley, K.S. and Bedeian, A.G. (1989) '.05: a case of the tail wagging the distribution', *Journal of Management*, 15 (2): 335–44.

Schafer, J.L. and Graham, J.W. (2002) 'Missing data: Our view of the state of the art', *Psychological Methods*, 7 (2): 147–77.

Schmidt, F.L. (1996) 'Statistical significance testing and cumulative knowledge in psychology: Implications for training of researchers', *Psychological Methods*, 1 (2): 115–29.

Schmitt, N. and Stults, D.M. (1985) 'Factors defined by negatively keyed items: The result of careless respondents?' *Applied Psychological Measurement*, 9 (4): 367–73.

Smith, P.C., Budseika, K.A., Edwards, N.A., Johnson, S.M. and Bearse, L.N. (1986) 'Guidelines for clean data: Detection of common mistakes', *Journal of Applied Psychology*, 71 (3): 457–60.

Spector, P.E., Van Katwyk, P.T., Brannick, M.T. and Chen, P.Y. (1997) 'When two factors don't reflect two constructs: How item characteristics can produce artefactual factors', *Journal of Management*, 23 (5): 659–77.

Spencer, B. (1995) 'Correlations, sample size, and practical significance: A comparison of selected psychological and medical investigations', *Journal of Psychology*, 129 (4): 469–75.

Towler, A.J. and Dipboye, R.L. (2003) 'Development of a learning style orientation measure' *Organizational Research Methods*, 6 (2): 216–35.

Van Prooijen, J.-W. and Van der Kloot, W.A. (2001) 'Confirmatory analysis of exploratively obtained factor structures', *Educational and Psychological Measurement*, 61 (5): 777–92.

9
QUALITATIVE METHODS AND ANALYSIS

9.1 INTRODUCTION

The first chapter of this book has briefly highlighted the key attributes of **qualitative research** as compared to quantitative research. Qualitative researchers aim to gain an in-depth understanding of human and organizational behaviours, the reasons driving these behaviours, and their differences. In qualitative studies, this is often done through the **contextualization** of the research setting, where findings are explained in light of the research context and environment. Although the reasoning behind qualitative research is largely inductive, both inductive and deductive processes are at work when one conducts qualitative research.

The process of qualitative research is often an emergent one. Many aspects of a research study get adjusted as themes and other discoveries emerge during the research process. This is in contrast to a typical quantitative research where the process follows a pre-defined script. For example, the research questions in a qualitative study may be refined in the process of conducting the research as the researcher learns more about additional questions to ask study participants after the initiation process, or a general pattern of understanding may emerge from some initial data collected, which then develops into broader themes that will mean adjustments to the research framework. In a nutshell, as Morgan and Smircich (1980) put it, in qualitative research the human researcher will not just merely be an observer, they will actively contribute to the creation of the observations. This means that observations within the qualitative sphere may be contextualized by a researcher's interpretation of the situation. It is this contextualization that can lead to richness of data that good qualitative research often brings.

The various forms of data collection methods commonly used in qualitative research have been highlighted in Chapter 7. This chapter will focus on when qualitative methods are considered appropriate, and the different approaches to qualitative research.

It will also discuss data recording and organization, **data analysis** and interpretation, and the **validation process** in qualitative research in detail.

9.2 WHEN ARE QUALITATIVE RESEARCH METHODS APPROPRIATE?

One key advantage of qualitative research methods is the use of open-ended questions that allow the researcher to probe the informants, hence providing more depth to the data collected as opposed to getting them to choose from a pre-defined set of options as would normally be used in quantitative research. Basically, the researcher can go deeper into the topic by constantly asking 'how' and 'why' until they get to the root of the topic. The flexibility to probe is not possible using more structured forms of inquiry. In qualitative research, we also use 'informants' as opposed to 'respondents' in labelling participants (Nakkeeran, 2016).

Because the nature of qualitative research evolves throughout the process, the prescription for when to perform qualitative research tends to be more fluid. For example, within a research area the use of qualitative research may be better suited for one aspect than another. Downey and Ireland (1979) demonstrate this. The authors look at the research area dealing with the assessment of an organization's environment. This area can be broadly classified into two dimensions, one regarding the participants' interpretations of the environment, and the other regarding environmental attributes. Based on an assessment of the extent to which these two dimensions use qualitative versus quantitative data, the authors conclude that qualitative data may be better placed to help with operationalizing environmental attributes, which have predominantly been measured using quantitative metrics that are far from producing satisfactory proxies. Contextualized measurements can mean that a large quantity of data are unavailable or are hard to collect. For the same reason, it is also a common understanding that qualitative research may not entail an a priori sampling strategy. Qualitative research also makes the investigation of sensitive topics possible, owing to the ability to engage directly and build rapport with informants (Dundon and Ryan, 2010).

In settings involving multiple participants – such as focus groups – interactions and the ability to allow the conversations to evolve also opens up an avenue for informants to build on each other's comments and ideas, potentially creating synergies from the discussions and potentially leading to a new line of inquiry. In addition, qualitative research methods provide the opportunity for the researcher to record and interpret non-verbal communications such as body language and expressions. Such additional information allows the contextualization of the responses provided by the informants. Due to the evolving nature of qualitative data collection, it should be noted that data collected from different groups, for example in focus groups, can result in different interpretations of a situation (Rentsch, 1990). In such cases, different interventions will have to be introduced to allow comparisons to be made across groups by aligning the interpretations of the situation.

Figure 9.1 provides a brief comparison of qualitative and quantitative research in terms of strategies of inquiry, analytical objectives and practices.

	Qualitative	Quantitative
Strategies of inquiry	• Ethnographic research • Grounded theory • Case study research	• Surveys • Archival data
Analytical objectives	• To describe variation • To describe and explain relationships • To describe individual experiences or group norms	• To quantify variation • To predict relationships, both causal and non-causal • To describe characteristics of a population
Practices of research	Researcher ... • Positions themselves in the context of the research and brings personal values into the study • Collects participant meanings • Focuses on a single concept or phenomenon • Studies the context or setting of participants, sometimes in collaboration with participants • Validates the accuracy of findings • Makes interpretations of the data	Researcher ... • Tests or verifies theories • Identifies variables to study • Uses standards of validity and reliability • Observes and measures information numerically • Uses unbiased approaches • Employs statistical procedures

Figure 9.1 Comparison of qualitative and quantitative approaches

In summary, what distinguishes qualitative from quantitative research methods is their flexibility. It is important to note, however, that there is a range of flexibility among methods used in both quantitative and qualitative research and that flexibility is not an indication of how scientifically rigorous a method is. Rather, the degree of flexibility reflects the nature of understanding of the problem that is being pursued using the chosen method.

Qualitative research can be used mainly for: (1) developing propositions and hypotheses that are used for further empirical testing, which can also include setting the parameters and boundaries for a quantitative study; (2) understanding the meaning of the data obtained from a quantitative study in order to further contextualize the findings; (3) further understanding the feelings, values and perceptions that underlie and influence behaviours; and (4) exploring future customer needs to generate new product ideas.

In comparing the reasons for choosing qualitative versus quantitative research, Edmondson and McManus (2007) propose a framework based on the dimensions of theoretical and empirical development. They broadly propose that nascent theories are best investigated using qualitative research methods to allow exploratory understanding, while mature theories should usually be tested using quantitative research methods as understanding in these areas is already developed. Thus, the choice of research approach will largely depend on the stage of the development of the theory and the extent of how far a field has evolved empirically.

While deviations from the proposed framework by Edmondson and McManus are possible, the authors also suggest that poor fit between methods used and the theoretical development of the topic in question can lead to potential problems. For example, using qualitative research methods in conducting research in mature research areas can result in discoveries that are really reinventing the wheel. There are limited opportunities in mature research areas for generating insightful findings using the qualitative approach. Even when used in conjunction with quantitative research methods, i.e. mixed methods, qualitative data may add little value to complement quantitative methods in research that involves mature theories. Conversely, using quantitative methods for nascent research areas can be challenging, as constructs are likely to be new, and reliability and validity of measurements are untested. This can pose operationalization issues, resulting in a tendency to mine the data using broad measurements.

Conversation box

This is a conversation between two research students.

Tracy [Masters student]: We have four months before the research project is due for submission. I'm rushing to get the survey responses back in time for analysis.

Paul [Masters student]: I've yet to send out my survey because I adjusted my topic only a couple of weeks ago. In the worst case, I will just conduct several in-depth interviews as time may run out for getting enough responses from the survey for proper quantitative analysis.

Tracy: Can you justify your logic for changing the approach from a quantitative to a qualitative one at this late stage in the project? Will the structure of the project look different if you adjust?

Paul: I think I'll state that there was a time limitation for data collection due to unforeseen circumstances.

While the open-mindedness and high flexibility inherent in the execution of qualitative research methods are strengths that make them pretty usable in any research context, it must be noted that they are not always the best mechanism for investigating all research areas, as pointed out by Edmondson and McManus (2007).

An additional point to note is that qualitative research methods should not be used as substitutes for quantitative research methods for reasons of time and budgetary constraints when quantitative analysis can be more telling. In the conversation box above, Paul has decided that he is likely to move on to use in-depth interviews, using a qualitative research method as a backup plan if he runs out of time to collect enough survey responses for quantitative analysis. In fact, this is a very common behaviour and mentality among research students who are not fully exposed to the fundamental differences between the two types of research methodologies. But this sort of research mindset of using qualitative research methods as a backup plan is hardly ideal. The choice of any methodological approach should be justified logically and should be the best fit for the research topic, rather than being used due to time constraints, especially when this is judged to be feasible in the conception of the research. If time is an issue, then the research topic itself should be looked at again instead of falling back on adjustments only on the methodology used.

Conversation box

A professor is having a conversation with a research fellow.

Professor:	Steven, we can either use in-depth interviews or open-ended questionnaires for this project.
Steven [Research fellow]:	I agree. Do you have a preference, Professor because I'm more comfortable with open-ended questionnaires than doing in-depth interviews, particularly the face-to-face ones?
Professor:	Let's talk about this. We should avoid making a methodological decision based on personal preferences, though I can understand why.

The conversation box above illustrates a discussion about the methodology to be adopted in a study. The research fellow is keen on the open-ended questionnaire method as he is more comfortable with that. That is his personal preference. If you are a new researcher, then you are less entrenched in particular methods. You are then probably more open-minded as to which method should be used, though it must be said that some of us are more number-oriented while others are more qualitatively inclined. Over time, however, as researchers are trained in particular tools, they tend to use the same or similar tools repeatedly – hence the tendency expressed by the research fellow. As noted by the professor, however, making a methodological choice based on personal preference should be avoided. The most appropriate method of investigation for a particular research question should always prevail, even when making comparisons within a suite of qualitative approaches.

Properties	Rationale
Organizational	The methodological choice is dependent on the stability of research site and access. For example, an ethnographic research can involve observations over an extended period of time within an organization. However, if the internal structure and personnel within the hierarchies of the organization that you choose to study change during the study period, it makes observations over time impossible. Likewise, access to an organization undergoing change can be challenging, as a previous contact for access may no longer be working for the organization.
Historical	Past research field conditions are the basis for many future method decisions. It is often advisable to allow past experience and knowledge to influence future choices of research methods. Deviations are possible and will need to be justified to be transparent as to how your research fits within the literature. Even when the research context is an individual organization, there is room for taking into account the knowledge accumulated from other similar research projects or research in other similar contexts.
Political	Researchers are regularly engaged in political actions through negotiated objectives, partisan conclusions and the politics of publishing. For example, very often our research is shaped by journals' preference of what they publish. Yet for example, a research student is keen to make sure that their potential supervisor likes the research area that they choose to work with in order to entice the interests of the potential supervisor to take them on as a research student.
Ethical	As discussed in Chapter 1, ethics is an important component of research. But the pressures to research and publish are huge, and ethical behaviours are becoming a major challenge as the time allowed for researchers to complete their work is reduced. The open-ended nature of qualitative inquiry can sometimes pose an ethical concern as the qualitative researcher may probe further into an area that may embarrass the informant or ethical restraints may even be breached. Relatedly, some research questions are likely to suffer from pushbacks on qualitative designs because of ethical concerns, such as a topic on cheating or a topic on misbehaviours in the workplace.
Evidential	Every piece of research work has an audience. Clearly, this audience has to be identified appropriately at the outset of the research. In some ways the audience helps to define the topic as well. The challenge for the researcher is to ensure that the audience's questions are answered. For example, managers may want to know the details of what recommendations would be appropriate from your study given some new environmental conditions. Given this then, the research and methodologies should be shaped to allow your work to arrive at conclusions from which the audience, in this case the managers, can extract value.
Personal	The choice of topic and research method can also depend on personal interests and preferences of the researchers. For example, with good access to social networks, it might be easier to access respondents using a snowballing effect, provided this is an appropriate sampling method for the research topic. Likewise, interpersonal skills are highly essential for interviews and there will be tendencies for a researcher with good interpersonal skills to lean towards using interviews in their research. But as discussed above, such personal preferences should be adopted with care.

Figure 9.2   Reasons for methodological choice

Buchanan and Bryman (2007) suggest that methodological choice in organizational research needs to be made in light of the contexts of the research. They propose six observable attributes for contextualization. These are organizational, historical, political, ethical, evidential and personal properties as highlighted in Figure 9.2.

Conversation box

Julian [PhD student]: Professor, if a choice of method is shaped by so many properties, as Buchanan and Bryman (2007) suggested, would these properties provide the same constraints for the choice of topic?

Professor: You are right, Julian. It is likely that topic selection is shaped by the same factors, to different degrees for each attribute perhaps. Just to give you an example, personal properties are implicitly shaping what we want to research. That's understandable. However, if personal preference for methods leads to use of a sub-optimal tool to examine a particular topic, that is not acceptable.

Further to the purposes of qualitative research methods and the appropriateness and constraints surrounding their use, Silverman (2006) has highlighted two key criticisms of qualitative research. The first criticism is that qualitative researchers do not always show contextual sensitivity, as they sometimes neglect the role the informants play in the setting. In this sense, a really good qualitative study is by no means easier to conduct than a quantitative study involving a large sample. In addition, qualitative research is regularly miscategorized as a relatively minor methodology and is thus contemplated only at the exploratory stage of a research project. The problem that then arises is how a qualitative researcher goes about categorizing the events or activities described. This is sometimes known as the reliability problem. Shortage of space means that many qualitative studies provide readers with little more than brief data descriptions. The reliability of the interpretation of transcripts may also be weakened by a failure to note trivial yet often crucial body movements or expressions.

The second criticism of qualitative research methods that Silverman (2006) advances relates to the soundness of the explanations provided by qualitative methods. This is sometimes known as the anecdotalism problem, revealed in the way in which research reports sometimes appeal to a few telling examples of some apparent phenomenon, without any attempt to analyze less clear or even contradictory data. This complaint of anecdotalism often raises questions about the **validity of qualitative research**.

9.3 THE KEY APPROACHES TO QUALITATIVE RESEARCH

In the business and management field, the most frequently used qualitative research approaches are **ethnographic research**, **grounded theory** and **case study** research. These are featured in this section.

9.3.1 Ethnographic research

Ethno, in essence, means a way of life. The ethnographer participates in the daily lives of the informant or organization under research for an extended period of time – observing, asking questions and collecting other relevant data. Culture is central to **ethnography**, i.e. ethnographic research is used for investigating a culture by participating in activities relating to the culture and collecting and describing data that are intended to help in the development of a theory. Typical ethnographic research employs three kinds of data collection, namely interviews, observations and documents. These were discussed in Chapter 7. These data collection methods in turn produce three kinds of data, namely quotations, descriptions and excerpts of documents. The ethnographer then observes, conducts interviews and scrutinizes relevant archives to arrive in one product – narrative description. This narrative description often includes charts, diagrams and additional artefacts that help to tell the story (Hammersley, 1990).

Punch (2005) lists six features of ethnographic research. First, ethnographic research has the assumption that shared cultural meanings of the observed population are crucial to the understanding of their behaviours. Second, ethnographic research is sensitive to the fact that behaviours, events and actions are contextualized in the eyes of the participants involved. Third, the ethnographer is part of the natural setting of the research. Fourth, ethnographic research evolves and is not pre-structured. Fifth, data collection in ethnographic research is eclectic and not restrictive. Multiple tools are often utilized simultaneously. The diversity of these tools also allows the ethnographer to triangulate the accuracy of the data collected. And finally, ethnographic research takes time and often requires repetitive data collection processes.

In ethnographic research, an ethnographer has to gather data around informants' conceptualization of the setting. This will involve tracking down operational and presentational data (Van Maanen, 1979). Operational data relates to the conversations and activities that the ethnographer is a part of throughout the process. Presentational data pertains to what informants seek to present to the ethnographer or outsiders. As Van Maanen (1979: 542) puts it, 'data in this category are often ideological, normative, and abstract, dealing far more with a manufactured image of idealized doing than with the routinized practical activities actually engaged in by members of the studied organization.'

He further adds that if this distinction of data is not appropriately observed, presentational data will mask operational data leading to confusion of what is fact and what is fiction.

The presentational data and operational data collected will form part of the informants' conception of the setting. The next step is then for the ethnographer to analyze these data using their own conceptions of the setting, i.e. using theories to explain the observations. These ethnographer's conceptions are based on common knowledge amongst the population of the informants. Van Maanen (1979) summarizes these conceptions as merely the statements that show the relationships between certain properties observed to co-vary in the setting that may occasionally converge with the informants' conceptions.

Despite our common understanding of what ethnographic research constitutes, there is hardly any single methodological approach to it (Van Maanen, 2006). In recent times, however, there have been extensions to what ethnographic research used to involve. For example, multi-site studies, where the same people or groups of people are tracked across different settings, are becoming more common (Marcus, 1998). Van Maanen (2006) discusses some other areas where ethnographic research has evolved over the years.

Conversation box

Kirsty [Masters student]:	Professor, would you say the emphasis of having observations over time and the researcher being part of the research context as a participant observer represent the unique characteristics of ethnographic research?
Professor:	These are two important features of ethnographic research, but they are by no means unique to ethnographic research. For example, grounded theory and case study research approaches also encourage observations over a period of time.

Van Maanen (2006) succinctly describes the process of conducting ethnographic research. His review of the literature suggests that ethnography remains free from technical jargon and abstraction, and discovery remains at the forefront of the approach. In addition, he also notes that this freedom from jargon and abstraction has allowed the approach to continually interest researchers who are not specialized in this field. A focus on empirics and a lack of standard methodology also characterize the current state of ethnographic research. These characteristics together make ethnographic research likely to overlap with other research approaches. As illustrated in the conversation box above, for example, ethnographic research is not mutually exclusive from grounded theory or case study research. These two other approaches will be discussed in the following sections.

The basic issues that need to be covered while writing up your research using the ethnographic approach include:

a)   what you seek to research;
b)   the reason for conducting this research, including the contribution to the understanding of social life;
c)   the arguments that you propose and how convincing these arguments are;
d)   the adequacy of the evidence presented;
e)   your role as the ethnographer in the research and the extent of intrusion if any;
f)   the self-awareness and self-exposure of yourself as the ethnographer to allow the reader to make judgements about the proposed point of view; and
g)   the credibility of the work from a cultural, social, individual or communal sense of reality.

Golden-Biddle and Locke (1993) discuss extensively how to write ethnographic research. The authors suggest that the goal is to convince, and authenticity, plausibility and criticality are the three dimensions central to be convincing. Authenticity relates to the ability of the text to convey the vitality of everyday life encountered by the researcher in the field. Plausibility is the ability to connect observations in the field back to the community of the readers. Criticality is about the ability of the text to probe readers to reconsider their taken-for-granted ideas and beliefs.

As ethnographic research emphasizes contextualization, its focus is deep, rather than broad. The nature of being sensitive to context means that writing up field notes as soon as possible after data is collected is essential. The process of recording every observation can be time consuming, and so being able to jot them down while you are fresh in the data collection process is crucial for providing accurate information. Sanday (1979) reiterates the importance of note taking in the context of participant observation. In ethnographic research, it is not good enough to just be observing. Knowing how to record, categorize and code are essential skills of the ethnographer.

9.3.2 Grounded theory

Grounded theory is an inductive type of research that, as the name suggests, is 'grounded' in the observations or data from which it was developed. The grounded theory approach uses a variety of data sources, including quantitative data, review of records, interviews, observations and surveys. The basic idea of the grounded theory approach is to identify variables and establish their interrelationships through the data collected. The implicit assumption is always that variables interact in complex ways and thus a simple world of additive relationships does not accurately represent reality.

Conversation box

Janet [Masters student]:   Professor, grounded theory in essence is about finding a theory to explain the data. Does that mean whatever evolves has to be new, and given that we do not make a priori predictions, I wonder how would I be able to set the boundaries for my literature review?

Professor: Janet, no doubt you will not be making a priori predictions in this case. However, the ability to attach meaning to the data has to be based on your knowledge of the subject matter, which has to come from the literature. Without that preparatory work, the whole research process becomes a data mining process. We must not treat grounded theory as nothing but data mining.

This conversation rules out that grounded theory is operating in a vacuum. Background understanding of the literature is still essential, though preconceived constructs and hypotheses are not needed for guiding data collection (Shah and Corley, 2006). Yet, there is still substantial confusion as to what the grounded theory approach constitutes (see Suddaby, 2006). While Suddaby (2006) does not explicitly spell out what grounded theory covers, he suggests that grounded theory is not:

1. an excuse to ignore the literature (as theory grounded from new data will have to be new and cannot be built on existing literature);
2. a mere presentation of raw data (as the data themselves will show a phenomenon and hence in themselves potentially represent a theory without any need to go deep into explaining the data);
3. in itself theory testing or content analysis (as analyzing the data and reporting the analysis can naturally become a testing of hypotheses);
4. a routine application of formulaic technique to data (as rigid rules get to be imposed on the process, such as when saturation happens);
5. straightforward (as it is specific, so few flaws can be traced, and with data the analysis should be straightforward); and
6. an excuse for the absence of a methodology (as the data and the coding of the data will themselves constitute a methodology).

Jones and Noble (2007) trace the history of the two main schools represented in grounded theory, namely the Glaserian (Glaser, 2001, 2003, 2005) and the Straussian (Strauss and Corbin, 1990, 1998). The roots of these schools can be traced back to Glaser and Strauss' publication in 1967. Based on a review of the schools of thought and their application in 32 studies, the authors conclude that qualitative researchers have adopted a loose definition of grounded theory to the extent that any inductive analysis grounded from data can be classified as grounded theory. They further propose that researchers adopting the grounded theory approach should adhere closely to the key aspects of grounded theory. Below is the procedure that we should expect from a research study using the grounded theory approach.

The open coding stage and the data collection stage occur simultaneously and continue until the core theme emerges. Open coding is the part of the analysis concerned with identifying, naming, categorizing and describing the phenomena found in the text. Essentially, each line, sentence, paragraph etc. is read in search of the answer to the repeated questions – 'What is this about?' and 'What is being referenced here?' These labels refer to the nouns and verbs of a conceptual world. Part of the analytic process is to identify the more general categories that these things are part of, such as institutions, work activities, relationships and outcomes. We also seek out the adjectives and adverbs that constitute the properties of these categories. It is important to have fairly abstract themes in addition to very concrete ones, as the abstract ones help to generate general theory.

Next, the axial coding is the process of relating themes and properties to each other, via a combination of inductive and deductive thinking. To simplify this process, rather than looking for any and all kinds of relationships, researchers using the grounded theory approach emphasize causal relationships. It should be noted again that a fallacy of some grounded theory work is that it takes the informant's understanding of what influences the truth. That is, they see the informant as an insider expert and the model they create must be equal to reality. There is no doubt that this is frequently the case, but the researcher should always make a judgement as to the degree of accuracy in causal relationships as articulated by the informant and interpret information given accordingly. In both coding processes, it is important to practise the constant comparative method, which emphasizes that the coding of a new data point or theme need to be compared to previous data points or categories to assess alignment and deviation.

Selective coding for the core theme and related themes then follows. Selective coding is the process of choosing one theme to be the core theme and relating all other themes to it. The goal here is to develop a single storyline that everything else is related to. Selective coding is about finding the key driver for the story. Sometimes, further sampling is needed in order to develop the theory and help with saturating the core theme and related themes. Throughout the whole process, theoretical sampling needs to be adopted to support the development of theoretical framework, which is the ultimate goal of the research (Locke, 2001). The various themes and new themes to be created need to face constant scrutiny as to how relevant and distinct they are. Writing notes throughout the entire research process is imperative as it helps with this saturation process. As can be seen, this process involves both analysis and data collection in iterative ways. Saturation occurs when additional data points provide little further value to the existing dataset and do not alter the themes created (Goulding, 2002). When this occurs, the researcher will move to the key task of attaching meaning to the themes and their relationships.

In a brief review of the execution of grounded theory research, O'Reilly et al. (2012) find that only 35 per cent of research that identified itself as using a grounded theory approach has in fact described its process in totality. For the most part, the researchers tend to only describe the data analysis process rather than include the whole process of using grounded theory across data collection, analysis and writing. O'Reilly et al. (2012) further add that using this 'a la carte' approach has several pitfalls. For example, limited use of theoretical sampling will restrict the boundaries set on data collection and the failure to use the constant comparative method will not allow a new data point to access the insights and learning gained from earlier data points.

The above coding processes entail significant care and judgement calls. It is important that you observe these steps if you are not familiar with the grounded theory approach and are preparing to use it in your research. In a research collaboration or group context, it will be wise to have different coders to see how coding aligns across the different coders to allow a test of validity. It is crucial that triangulation can be made. Even if you are working alone, it might pay to hire a second independent coder to help validite the coding. Suddaby (2006), Jones and Noble (2007) and O'Reilly et al. (2012) provide some good practices on the use of this approach and help you avoid falling into the grounded theory trap when it comes to execution.

In terms of writing up, Gioia et al. (2012) provide some guidelines on the necessary components. First and foremost, the reader needs to be able to see how the data are coded and categorized and explanations given for each of the themes and their connectivity. New and emergent key concepts and themes also need to be highlighted. The theorizing part using grounded theory then weave the parts together. It will be worthwhile to take a look at the detailed discussion this paper provides.

Sometimes it is common to see propositions or hypotheses as conclusions in grounded theory research (e.g. Clark et al., 2010; Gioia et al., 2010). This is not formally necessary but encouraged as discussed in Gioia et al. (2012). Clark et al. (2010) is a good example of an execution of the grounded theory approach using data from semi-structured interviews and participant observations. Likewise, Gioia et al. (2010) present this approach using five data sources, namely semi-structured interviews, archival data, archived communications (written and electronic), non-participant observations, and private journals of a key informant.

Overall, the procedures specified in grounded theory research (Glaser and Strauss, 1967) suggest that it is more rigid than the research adopted in ethnographic research. This has led to concerns around how researchers can further adapt to research methods requirements over time (Fendt and Sachs, 2008). In essence, a more pragmatic approach to conduct grounded theory research is encouraged. Nonetheless, as raised earlier, at the very least, a researcher should seek to properly weave the process together to avoid a poor execution of the approach.

9.3.3 Case study research

The term case study usually refers to a fairly intensive examination of a single unit such as a person, a small group of people, or a single company. Case studies enable the researcher to explore, unravel and understand problems, issues and relationships. In many instances, however, case studies do not allow the researcher to generalize from the results, findings or theory developed to other contexts or situations as the focal case may be unique.

> # Conversation box
>
> *Igor [Honours student]:* Given that it's a challenge to generalize from a case study, would it not make sense that we should try to avoid using this data collection avenue?
>
> *Professor:* A case study offers a lot of value and depth into a research issue. While there are certainly challenges associated with generalization, with care and rigour, it is certainly possible to learn from case studies. Take a look at the article by March et al. (1991).

The case study approach involves mainly four steps:

1. Determine the present situation.
2. Gather background information about the past and key variables.
3. Analyze the information for possible hypotheses. In this step, specific evidence about each hypothesis can be gathered. This step aims to eliminate possibilities that conflict with the evidence collected and to gain confidence for the proposed hypotheses. The culmination of this step might be the development of an experimental or quantitative design to test the developed hypotheses.

4. Check that the hypotheses tested actually work out in practice. Some action, correction or improvement is made, and a re-check carried out on the situation to see what effect the changes have brought about.

Probably the most cited book on case study methodology is Yin (2009). He provides extensive coverage on various aspects to look out for when one uses the case study method. Siggelkow also focuses on the value of conducting case studies and provides some key principles for working in this way. He advises that the use of case studies for presenting conceptual contribution be treated with caution. In his view, 'an open mind is good; an empty mind is not' (2007: 21). Clearly, while case studies can help to single out some things that are unique, they are also subjected to the same requirement of being backed up by existing work. Researchers adopting the case study approach should not have a 'let's wait and see' mentality without any a priori expectations of what is needed from the case.

Case studies allow the qualitative researcher to engage with rich data using multiple sources and to apply multiple levels of analysis of the dynamics within a single research setting (Eisenhardt, 1989). Often, case studies are used as a backdrop against which theoretical constructs and propositions are put forward (Eisenhardt, 1989). Some of the common methods of data collection that are used in case studies are documents, archival records, interviews, direct observations, participant observation and artefacts. Case studies are likely to be much more convincing and accurate if they are based on several different sources of information, which allows for triangulation. Rigorous case studies emphasize the presence of internal validity, construct validity, external validity and reliability. Gibbert et al. (2008) add that case study research published in top journals tends to have a good balance of these validities, while articles published in other journals tend to have an over-emphasis on external validity. The balanced approach represents a more rigorous way to conduct case studies.

Conversation box

Priscilla [PhD student]:   Professor, this morning I attended a seminar on research design. The focus of the seminar was on quantitative designs. The presenter mentioned that a key element of research outcomes is to ensure generalizability. Now, does that mean I should also ensure that the eight cases that I will be using for my thesis are chosen to be generalizable?

Professor: Generalizability is not as straightforward in the case of qualitative designs as compared to quantitative designs. The ability to generalize is good but insights from those eight cases may or may not be able to achieve that. That does not mean the outcome is suboptimal when some of these cases are not generalizable.

A case study enables rich information to be gathered from which potentially useful hypotheses can be generated. It can be a time-consuming process. It is also inefficient in researching situations that are already well structured and where the important variables have been identified. As case studies provide lots of detail about individual cases, there is a common perception that these cases are unique; however, very often this uniqueness is exaggerated (Martin et al., 1983). But let's say that this uniqueness holds true; this means that learning from this case cannot be applied elsewhere. This is the irony: the case loses its purpose once we argue that it is totally unique.

Hence, a major challenge of case study research is in fact the selection of case(s). A case may be selected as a key case because of a unique attraction in the case or the circumstances surrounding it. It may also be chosen because of a researcher's in-depth local knowledge, thereby offering strong reasoned lines of explanation based on this rich knowledge of setting and circumstances. Given that generalizations deriving from these case(s) are essential, one would imagine that the case selected should be as representative as possible. However, this would mean we would be selecting cases that are likely to be an average case. An 'average' case will pose the challenge of the degree of interest it might generate within the discipline (Barley, 2006; Bartunek et al., 2006). More often than not, it is useful to select cases that offer an interesting, unusual or particularly revealing set of circumstances. A case selection that is based on representation, however, will seldom be able to produce these kinds of insights, i.e. outlier cases reveal more information than representative cases. This dilemma (and the judgement call needed) of case study research should be seriously considered when a qualitative researcher chooses their case(s).

Piekkari et al. (2009) conduct a review of 157 journal articles published in four international business journals and make several observations. The authors find that the usefulness of a case study is interpreted differently even within the field. Historical use has been to use case studies as a backup in situations when there are not enough observations for quantitative analysis. Then subsequently, multiple thin case studies or case surveys are adopted by convention, while single case studies that are rich in content are used as an alternative practice in the field. There are also concerns about case studies from a more positivist approach which can cause conflicting messages within the case. Further, it is becoming common to have one case study context that involves various analyses within. This is related to the contextualized design that we have discussed in Chapter 5. In the human resource management area for example, various studies have examined various relationships within a single case study (or context) such as hospitals in Ang et al. (2013), retired homes for men in Ang et al. (2017) and cinemas in Boxall et al. (2011).

It is important to note that in case studies, as with any qualitative descriptive research, while a qualitative researcher begins his study with one or several questions that influence what he will be looking out for during the data collection process, he may encounter new lines of inquiry emerging during this process. Even when these do not have much bearing on the researcher's guiding questions, the new variables may become the basis for new questions asked at the end of the report, thus linking to possibilities for further research.

In a case study approach, researchers strive to make sense of their data as the data are collected. Generally, researchers interpret their data in one of two ways – holistically or through coding. Holistic analysis does not attempt to break the evidence into parts, but rather to draw conclusions based on the text as a whole. Coding, on the other hand, allows researchers to dissect the text into various components. One can argue that this approach is equivalent to the grounded theory approach where information is codified into categories. Since coding is inherently subjective, more than one coder is usually employed (e.g. Berkenkotter et al., 1988). Multi-modal case study researchers often corroborate and balance the results of their coding with data from interviews or reflections of their own work. Thus, the outcomes can become highly contextualized.

Once key variables have been identified, they can be analyzed. Reliability becomes a key concern at this stage, and many case study researchers go to great lengths to ensure that their interpretations of the data will be both reliable and valid. Because issues of validity and reliability are an important part of any study in business and management, it is important to identify some ways of dealing with these. As is the case with other research methodologies, issues of external validity, construct validity and reliability need to be carefully considered. Gibbert and Ruigrok (2010) provide some strategies for ensuring rigour when adopting the case study method.

While the case study approach is generally better understood compared to the grounded theory approach, misunderstandings about the approach still exist. Flyvbjerg (2006) identifies five such common misunderstandings: (1) general, theoretical knowledge is more valuable than concrete, practical knowledge; (2) one cannot generalize on the basis of an individual case and, therefore, the case study cannot contribute to scientific development; (3) the case study is most useful for generating hypotheses, whereas other methods are more suitable for hypothesis testing and **theory building**; (4) the case study contains a bias toward verification, i.e. a tendency to confirm the researcher's prior expectations; and (5) it is often difficult to summarize and develop general propositions and theories on the basis of specific case studies. These statements can be said to represent the cautionary view of case studies in the conventional philosophy of science. Flyvbjerg (2006) also adds that these statements are too categorical and argued for the value of phenomenological insights gained by closely examining contextualized expert knowledge.

Conversation box

Anya [Masters student]:   Professor, using multiple case studies can pose a problem as each case may be rich enough on its own and thus the outcomes from these may become extremely onerous to report.

Professor: When multiple case studies are involved, Anya, one should always seek patterns if possible. Take a look at Larsson's (1993) paper on observing patterns across case studies.

The problem with using single case studies and the significant value added by having more than one case study is illustrated in Campbell (1975). Even though Campbell's discussion concerns the study of cultures using ethnographic research, his illustration demonstrates how using single case studies can lead to ambigious results. In essence, observations within a single case study sometimes cannot rule out whether the inference is derived from the effect of the observer or the activity or behaviour being observed.

The support of the use of multiple case studies is also discussed in Eisenhardt and Graebner (2007) and Lee et al. (2007). It is noted that while single case studies can be rich and provide great value, multiple case studies typically provide a stronger base for theory building (Yin, 2009). The choice of multiple case studies should be done for theoretical reasons regarding replication, extension of theory, contrary replication and elimination of alternative explanations. For example, the use of polar examples, i.e. extreme cases using a particular attribute that set boundary conditions within which other observations can be placed.

The next step will then be to be able to compare across case studies. Larsson (1993) provides 12 steps for doing this. These processes involve coding of themes using a coding scheme. The coding scheme can be designed with the help of a closed-ended questionnaire. This is commonly known as **case survey methods** (Larsson, 1993; Yin and Heald, 1975). For better rigour, it is always advisable to use multiple coders for triangulation.

Two variations of the case survey methods are worth noting. Leonard-Barton (1990) combines two forms of case studies, a longitudinal single-site three-year case study and nine retrospective case studies about the same phenomenon. This case study multimethod allows one method to address the weaknesses of the other. Due to the strengths as discussed in the paper, mainly regarding the fact that both cross-sectional and longitudinal perspectives are accounted for, this method is useful for generating hypotheses and for studying processes. Another variation is the **case cluster method** (McClintock et al., 1979). In essence, this is similar to the case survey, but only involves tracking substantial activities within a case study and the ability to document patterns, be it events, choice situations or tasks. These can effectively become three units of analysis to which sampling and quantitative data (coded) are traced within the case study for analysis.

9.4 DATA RECORDING AND ORGANIZATION

The various approaches to qualitative research have been highlighted in Section 9.3. In Chapter 7 we also discussed various data collection methods. This section will focus on what happens after the data have been collected, including recording, organizing and storing the data.

9.4.1 Data recording and coding procedures

In terms of data recording, a qualitative researcher will have to first identify what data needs to be recorded. Data recorded normally include both actual observations, such as a description of the physical setting, accounts of particular activities, and reflective notes, such as the researcher's personal thoughts, feelings and impressions. The notes should also include contextual information about the time, place and setting where the observations take place.

For qualitative interviews, an interview protocol will be needed to help guide the information recording process. This protocol should include a heading, instructions to the interviewer (opening statements), the key research questions, probes to follow key questions, transitional messages for the interviewer, space for recording the interviewer's comments and space in which the researcher records reflective notes. The recording can be in the form of handwritten notes, audiotaping or videotaping. Many informants may not be comfortable with videotaping. In such circumstances, a researcher should not insist on doing so unless the videotaping is absolutely necessary, such as to record facial expressions.

The recording of documents and visual materials can be based on the researcher's structure for taking notes. Typically, notes reflect information about the document or other materials as well as key ideas in the documents. For documents, it is helpful to note whether the information represents primary materials, i.e. information related directly to the people or situation under study, or secondary materials, i.e. second-hand accounts of the people or situation documented by others.

9.4.2 Organizing and storing data

Because they capture the thoughts and experiences of individual people, every set of qualitative data collected is distinct. In addition, individual researchers inevitably have differences in style that affect how data are managed. Different locations also have unique logistics constraints that may impede organizing data in similar ways. There is no one single way to organize and analyze qualitative data (Bansal and Corley, 2011). Thus, systematically comparing and analyzing qualitative data in raw form is challenging. Organizing data in a rigorous, standardized way is essential to their security and to the validity of the results from the analysis. Consistency is important for every study but is especially crucial for large, team-based projects involving extensive amounts of data collected from multiple sites.

Preparing recorded data for analysis requires transcribing all tapes and notes and converting them into computer files. Backup copies of the tapes are necessary and ideally these should be securely stored in a separate location from the original tapes. These days we have the benefit of digital tapes with large capacities, so duplicating them is very easy. In many cases the storage would be simply a USB memory stick.

For focus groups and interviews, after transcribing all relevant recordings, the transcriptionist types up the interviewer's or focus group moderator's corresponding handwritten field notes. These typed notes could either be appended to the transcript within the same file or kept as a separate file. It is advisable that tapes of interviews and focus groups should be processed as soon as they are archived, rather than being allowed to accumulate. Field notes should also be typed as soon as the data collector has expanded them.

To transcribe an audio recording, the transcriptionist listens to the tape and simultaneously writes down or types everything that is recorded on the tape. The transcription is usually performed by the data collector or their assistant. When the transcriptionist is not the person who collected the recorded data, the data collector should review the completed transcripts for accuracy. In some cases, transcripts may also need to be translated into the language(s) of the organization sponsoring the study.

It is becoming more common for researchers to outsource the process of transcribing their taped data as there are many transcriptionists out there. Using professional transcriptionists can ensure that nothing gets left out. It might also be quicker. However, the process of outsourcing also distances you from your data, i.e. you have one less chance to get familiar with your data. In addition, the fact that you were involved in collecting the data means that the transcribing process will mean more than just jotting down what was on the tape; it may also allow you to reflect on the data collection process and procedures and highlight any feelings and impressions involved rather than merely the words being used. As previously mentioned, you will of course have to check the accuracy of the transcribed materials when you are not directly involved in the transcription process.

Conversation box

In a conversation between two Masters research students.

Ellie: Have you finished your data collection?

Mary: No, one last interview to go before the transcribing starts.

Ellie: Are you transcribing by yourself? Did you attend any course on how to do it?

Mary: Not decided yet. In fact, I heard there are professional transcriptionists who can do it.

Ellie: Can we do that? That sounds good to me. I'm just not sure if I will be able to do it myself even if I attend training courses.

When more than one person is involved in the transcription process, as the amount of materials to transcribe may be too much for one person to do it alone, it is highly recommended that everyone involved in a given study uses a common format for transcribing. That is, there should be standard conventions for identifying the researcher and individual participants throughout the transcript. There should also be a uniform way of presenting information on the location, date and type of data collection event. These conventions should be detailed in a project-specific transcription protocol that specifically outlines procedures and formats for transcribing recorded data. The transcription protocol you develop for your own study should similarly reflect any formatting or other requirements of the software that you will use. It is important to determine such requirements before the first transcription occurs. Even if you find that the software you use does not require any specific format, it is nonetheless still important for you to design a systematic and consistent transcription protocol when multiple persons are involved in the transcription process.

Complications can also arise in organizing responses from open-ended questionnaires or interviews. Open-ended questions can elicit rich responses from informants, so much so that they should be considered for inclusion in public opinion polls (Geer, 1991). Their relative lower use can be attributed more about the greater time and cost in coding and analyzing the data as opposed to the issue with the mechanism (Erickson and Kaplan, 2000; Geer, 1991). Nonetheless, using best practices for qualitative analysis such as those illustrated above for ethnographic, grounded theory and case study research, responses from open-ended questions can provide rich information on processes and themes.

9.5 DATA ANALYSIS AND INTERPRETATION

Discussion of the plan for analyzing the data might have several components. The process of data analysis involves preparing the data for analysis, conducting different analyses, moving deeper and deeper into understanding the data, and making an interpretation of the wider meaning of the data.

Researchers need to tailor the data analysis beyond the more generic approaches to specific types of qualitative research strategies. Grounded theory, for example, has systematic steps. These involve generating themes of information (open coding), selecting one of the themes and positioning it as a core theme (axial coding) and then explicating a story from the interconnections of these themes (selective coding). These aspects are discussed in more detail in the earlier section on grounded theory research. This process is different from those highlighted in ethnographic research and case study research.

Despite these analytic differences depending on the type of design used, qualitative research often involves a generic process of data analysis. An ideal situation is to blend the generic steps with the specific research design steps. Broadly, the five generic steps are described in Figure 9.3.

Step 1: General overview of data collected	Go through all the data once to get a general sense of the information and to reflect on the overall meaning of the data. A holistic picture of what data were collected and how they might fit together is an important starting point. This can involve the general ideas that informants have put forth in the data collection process and also the researcher's overall impression of the depth and credibility of the information.
Step 2: Working out a coding scheme	Begin detailed analysis with a coding process. A systematic coding procedure may not be easy to determine before the actual coding process begins. There may be some learning along the way during the process of coding. As the process evolves, the pattern will reach a plateau, which will become an eventual coding system. The coding process is used to generate a description of the setting or people as well as themes for analysis. This analysis is useful in designing detailed descriptions for case studies, ethnographies and narrative research projects. A small number of themes, perhaps four to seven, will also emerge. These themes represent separate headings in the results section of a research study. They should represent multiple perspectives and be supported by diverse quotations and specific evidence.
Step 3: Consolidate themes	Beyond identifying the themes during the coding process, qualitative researchers can also build additional layers of complex analysis. For example, researchers can connect the themes into a storyline (as in narratives) or develop them into a theoretical model (as in grounded theory). Themes are analyzed for each individual case and across different cases (as in case studies). Deep qualitative studies tend to go beyond description and theme identification into complex thematic connections.

Step 4: Identify potential links between themes and how they relate	Use an appropriate way to convey the findings of the analysis. A narrative is commonly used. This might be a discussion that mentions a chronology of events, the detailed discussion of several themes (complete with sub-themes, specific illustrations, multiple perspectives and quotations), or a discussion using interconnecting themes. Many qualitative researchers also use visuals, figures, or tables as supplements to the discussion. These are represented using a process model (as in grounded theory), a drawing of the specific research site (as in ethnographic research), or descriptive information about each participant in a table (as in case studies and ethnographic research).
Step 5: Derive and attach meanings to data and themes	This final step in data analysis involves making an interpretation or deriving meaning from the data, i.e. the lessons learned (Lincoln and Guba, 1985). These lessons could be the researcher's personal interpretation, couched in their understanding from their own cultural background and experiences. It could also be a meaning derived from a comparison of the findings with the extant literature. In this way, the researcher will relate their findings to past findings, whether they are confirmatory or contradictory. New questions may also arise from findings that the researcher had not foreseen earlier in the study. One common way for ethnographers to end a study is in fact to ask further questions (Wolcott, 1994). The questioning approach is also used in advocacy and participatory approaches to qualitative research. Moreover, when qualitative researchers use a theoretical lens, they can form interpretations that call for action agendas for reform and change. Thus, interpretation in qualitative research can take many forms, be adapted for different types of designs and be flexible to convey personal, research-based and action meanings.

Figure 9.3   Typical qualitative data analysis

Some highly structured qualitative data, for example open-ended responses from surveys or tightly defined interview questions, are typically coded without the need for additional segmentation of the content. In such cases, codes are often applied as a layer on top of the data. Quantitative analysis of these codes is typically the capstone analytical step for this type of qualitative data.

A frequent criticism of coding methods is that they seek to transform qualitative data into quantitative data, thereby draining the data of its variety, richness and individual characteristics. Researchers respond to this criticism by clearly explaining their definitions of codes and linking those codes soundly to the underlying data, and in this process bring back some of the richness that might be absent from a mere list of codes.

However, not all qualitative datasets are analyzed with the help of coding. A common method of analysis of qualitative data without coding is **recursive abstraction** (see Polkinghorne and Taylor, 2019), where datasets are summarized several times until saturation occurs. The end result is a more compact summary that would have been difficult to accurately discern without the preceding steps of distillation. However recursive abstraction can lead to the final conclusions containing information that is several times removed from the underlying data. While it is true that poor initial summaries will certainly yield an inaccurate final report, qualitative researchers can minimize the risk of using recursive abstraction by documenting in detail the reasoning behind each summary step, citing examples from the data where statements are included, and where statements are excluded from the intermediate summary.

Visual maps are becoming a common tool for helping qualitative research identify links. These are especially useful for process-type data and identifying causality (Langley, 1999; Langley and Traux, 1994; Lyles and Reger, 1993). In fact, some researchers also suggest the use of such maps to help guide the data collection process (e.g. Meyer, 1991; Wheeldon and Faubert, 2009) and as a way to analyze open-ended responses (e.g. Jackson and Trochim, 2002). The aforementioned articles provide good illustrations and guidelines on how to use visual maps in different situations. My personal experience suggests that visuals also assist with the thinking process relating to designing a research, writing hypotheses and interpreting results.

9.6 THE VALIDATION PROCESS

Validity in qualitative research does not carry the same connotations as it does in quantitative research. In a limited way, qualitative researchers can use reliability to check for consistent patterns of theme development among several researchers on a team. They can also generalize some facets of multiple case analysis to other cases (Yin, 2009). Overall, however, unlike in quantitative research, reliability and generalizability play a relatively minor role in qualitative research.

Validity, on the other hand, is recognized as a strength of qualitative research. There are many different ways of establishing validity in qualitative research (Lincoln and Guba, 1985). These can include member checking, triangulation, thick description, peer reviews and external audits. Researchers engage in one or more of these procedures and report results in their investigations.

With member checking, the validity procedure shifts from the researcher to the informants in the study. It consists of taking the data and interpretations back to the informants in the study so that they can confirm the credibility of the information and narrative account. With the lens focused on informants, the researchers systematically check the data and the narrative account.

Triangulation is a validity procedure where researchers search for convergence among multiple and different sources of information to form themes in a study. Denzin (1978) identifies four types of triangulation: across data sources (i.e. informants), theories, methods (i.e. interview, observations, documents) and among different investigators. As a validity procedure, triangulation is a step taken by researchers employing only the researcher's lens, and it is a systematic process of sorting through the data to find common themes by eliminating overlapping areas. A popular practice is for qualitative researchers to provide corroborating evidence collected through multiple methods, such as observations, interviews and documents to locate core and minor themes. The narrative account is valid because researchers go through this process and rely on multiple forms of evidence rather than a single incident or data point in the research.

A good example of using triangulation to validate qualitative studies is demonstrated by Jonsen and Jehn (2009). Specifically, the authors illustrate how three complementary triangulation methods can be used for validation in qualitative studies. Beyond triangulation, however, there are other forms of checks for validity in qualitative studies. Creswell and Miller (2000) summarize validity procedures using two dimensions, namely paradigm assumptions and lens. Paradigm assumptions consist of postpositivist, constructivist and critical paradigms. Lens can be from the perspective of the researcher, participants or people external to the study, such as reviewers. In their framework, triangulation is a validity procedure using the postpositivist assumption paradigm from the lens of the researcher. As highlighted in a few earlier chapters, validity is essential to research, and in the case of qualitative research, due to the inherent small number of observations, having high validity is even more imperative. Tracy et al. (2006) provide a good illustration of using multiple sources of data for triangulation.

Another procedure for establishing credibility in a study is to describe the setting, the informants and the themes of a qualitative study in rich detail. The purpose of a thick description is that it creates statements that relate to the audience how they feel they have experienced, or could experience, the events being described in a study. Thus, credibility is established through the lens of readers who read a narrative account and are transported into a setting or situation. To use this procedure for establishing credibility, researchers employ a constructivist perspective to contextualize the people or site. The purpose of writing using thick description is to provide as much detail as possible.

A peer review or debriefing is the review of the data and research process by someone who is familiar with the research or the phenomenon being explored. A peer reviewer provides support, plays devil's advocate, challenges the researcher's assumptions, pushes the researcher to the next step methodologically, and asks hard questions about methods and interpretations (Lincoln and Guba, 1985).

The credibility of a study can also be established by turning to individuals who are external to the project, such as auditors. In establishing an audit trail, a researcher provides clear documentation of all research decisions and activities. They may provide evidence of the audit trail throughout the account of the study or in the appendices.

9.7 QUALITATIVE ANALYSIS SOFTWARE

Contemporary qualitative data analyses are commonly supported by computer programs termed broadly as **Computer-Assisted Qualitative Data Analysis Software**

(CAQDAS). These programs do not supplant the interpretative nature of coding but are rather aimed at enhancing the researcher's efficiency at applying the codes to the data. Many programs offer efficiencies in editing and revising coding, which allow for files and work sharing, as well as recursive examination of data.

Mechanical techniques, which rely on counting words, phrases, or coincidences of tokens within the data, are often adopted in CAQDAS. Often referred to as content analysis, the output from these techniques is amenable to many advanced statistical analyses.

Mechanical techniques are particularly well suited for a few scenarios. One such scenario is for datasets that are simply too large for a human to effectively analyze. Another scenario is when the main value of a dataset is the extent to which it contains specific information that you desire from the dataset. A frequent criticism of mechanical techniques, however, is the absence of a human interpreter. While sophisticated software claims to mimic some human decisions, the bulk of the analysis is nonetheless labelled as non-human.

The majority of CAQDAS will require you to have the transcripts to use. The most commonly used CAQDAS software are QSR **NVivo**, **ATLAS.ti** and **MAXQDA**. Lewins and Silver (2007) provides good guidelines on how qualitative researchers can analyze data using such software, with specific focus on examples using the three types of software mentioned.

KEY TERMS

- ATLAS.ti
- Case cluster method
- Case study
- Case survey method
- Computer-Assisted/Aided Qualitative Data Analysis (CAQDAS) Software
- Contextualization
- Data analysis
- Ethnographic research
- Ethnography

- Grounded theory
- Glaserian school
- MAXQDA
- NVivo
- Qualitative research
- Recursive abstraction
- Straussian school
- Theory building
- Validation process
- Validity of qualitative research

SUMMARY

- Qualitative and quantitative research are different in terms of strategies of inquiry, analytical objectives and practices.
- Qualitative research methods should not be used as a substitute for quantitative research methods because of time and budgetary constraints when quantitative evaluation is critical.

- Making a methodological choice based on personal preference should be avoided.
- Methodological choice in organizational research needs to be made in light of the contexts of the research, such as organizational properties, historical properties, political properties, ethical properties, evidential properties and personal properties.
- The three main approaches to qualitative research in business and management studies are ethnographic research, grounded theory research and case study research.
- Ethnographic research is not mutually exclusive with grounded theory or case study research.
- The two main schools represented in grounded theory are the **Glaserian** and the **Straussian schools**. These can be traced back to Glaser and Strauss (1967).
- While single case studies can be rich and provide great value, multiple case studies typically provide a stronger base for theory building.
- The most commonly used Computer Assisted/Aided Qualitative Data Analysis (CAQDAS) software packages are QSR NVivo, ATLAS.ti and MAXQDA.

QUESTIONS

1. What are the broad purposes of qualitative research?
2. What are some of the reasons why the contextualization of methodological choice in organizational research is necessary?
3. Describe the three main approaches to qualitative research.
4. List any four of the features of ethnographic research.
5. Based on Suddaby (2006), discuss what grounded theory is not.
6. What are some of the common misunderstandings about case study research?
7. Beyond triangulation, what are some of the other procedures that a researcher can put in place to ensure the validity of his qualitative research?

ADDITIONAL READINGS

CAQDAS software:

ATLAS.ti: https://atlasti.com
MAXQDA: www.maxqda.com
QSR NVivo: www.qsrinternational.com/nvivo-qualitative-data-analysis-software/home

Alvesson, M. and Kärreman, D. (2007) 'Constructing mystery: Empirical matters in theory development', *Academy of Management Review*, 32 (4): 1265–81.

Clandinin, D.J. and Connelly, F.M. (2000) *Narrative Inquiry: Experience and Story in Qualitative Research*. San Francisco, CA: Jossey–Bass.

Creswell, J.W. (2003) *Research Design: Qualitative, Quantitative, and Mixed Methods Approaches* (2nd edition). Thousand Oaks, CA: Sage Publishing.

Creswell, J.W. (2013) *Qualitative Inquiry and Research Design: Choosing Among Five Traditions* (3rd edition). Thousand Oaks, CA: Sage Publishing.

Creswell, J.W. and Miller, D.L. (2000) 'Determining validity in qualitative inquiry', *Theory Into Practice*, 39 (3): 124–30.

Denzin, N.K. and Lincoln, Y.S. (eds) (2011) *The Sage Handbook of Qualitative Research* (4th edition). Thousand Oaks, CA: Sage Publishing.

Dubois, A. and Gadde, L.-E. (2002) 'Systematic combining: An abductive approach to case research', *Journal of Business Research*, 55 (7): 553–60.

Emigh, R.J. (1997) 'The power of negative thinking: The use of negative case methodology in the development of sociological theory', *Theory and Society*, 26 (5): 649–84.

Fine, G.A., Morrill, C. and Surianarain, S. (2009) 'Ethnography in organizational settings', in D.A. Buchanan and A. Bryman (eds), *The Sage Handbook of Organizational Research Methods*. Thousand Oaks, CA: Sage Publishing. pp. 602–19.

Fitzgerald, L. and Dopson, S. (2009) 'Comparative case study designs: their utility and development in organizational research', in D.A. Buchanan and A. Bryman (eds), *The Sage Handbook of Organizational Research Methods*. Thousand Oaks, CA: Sage Publishing. pp. 465–83.

Goulding, C. (2009) 'Grounded theory perspectives in organizational research', in D.A. Buchanan and A. Bryman (eds), *The Sage Handbook of Organizational Research Methods*. Thousand Oaks, CA: Sage Publishing. pp. 381–94.

Henderson, N. R. (2009) 'Managing moderator stress: Take a deep breath. You can do this!', *Marketing Research*, 21 (1): 28–9.

Isabella, L.A. (1990) 'Evolving interpretations as a change unfolds: How managers construe key organizational events', *Academy of Management Journal*, 33 (1): 7–41.

Klein, H.K. and Myers, M.D. (1999) 'A set of principles for conducting and evaluating interpretive field studies in information systems', *MIS Quarterly*, 23 (1): 67–93.

Krippendorff, K. (2004) *Content Analysis: An Introduction to Its Methodology* (2nd edition). Thousand Oaks, CA: Sage Publishing.

Lindlof, T.R. and Taylor, B.C. (2011) *Qualitative Communication Research Methods* (3rd edition). Thousand Oaks, CA: Sage Publishing.

Loseke, D.R. and Cahill, S.E. (2007) 'Publishing qualitative manuscripts: lessons learned', in C. Seale, G. Gobo, J.F. Gubrium and D. Silverman (eds), *Qualitative Research Practice*. Thousand Oaks, CA: Sage Publishing. pp. 491–506.

Marshall, C. and Rossman, G.B. (2006) *Designing Qualitative Research* (4th edition). Thousand Oaks, CA: Sage Publishing.

Miles, M.B. (1979) 'Qualitative data as an attractive nuisance: The problem of analysis', *Administrative Science Quarterly*, 24 (4): 590–601.

Peterson, M.F. (1998) 'Embedded organizational events: The units of process in organization science', *Organization Science*, 9 (1): 16–33.

Rossman, G.B. and Rallis, S.F. (2012) *Learning in the Field: An Introduction to Qualitative Research* (3rd edition). Thousand Oaks, CA: Sage Publishing.

Seale, C. (1999) 'Quality in qualitative research', *Qualitative Inquiry*, 5(4): 465–78.

Seale, C., Gobo, G., Gubrium, J.F. and Silverman, D. (eds) (2004 [concise edition 2007]) *Qualitative Research Practice*. Thousand Oaks, CA: Sage Publishing.

Stake, R.E. (1995) *The Art of Case Study Research*. Thousand Oaks, CA: Sage Publishing.

Tjaco, W. (2003) 'Avoiding advertising research disaster: Advertising and the uncertainty principle', *Journal of Brand Management*, 10 (6): 403–9.

Toma, J.D. (2000) 'How getting close to your subjects makes qualitative data better', *Theory Into Practice*, 39 (3): 177–84.

Van Maanen, J. (1988) *Tales of the Field: On Writing Ethnography*. Chicago, IL: University of Chicago Press.

REFERENCES

Ang, S.H., Bartram, T., McNeil, N., Leggat, S.G. and Stanton, P. (2013) 'The effects of high-performance work systems on hospital employees' work attitudes and intention to leave: A multi-level and occupational group analysis', *International Journal of Human Resource Management*, 24 (16): 3086–114.

Ang, S.H., Cavanagh, J., Southcombe, A., Bartram, T., Marjoribanks, T. and McNeil, N. (2017) 'Human resource management, social connectedness and health and well-being of older and retired men: The role of Men's Sheds', *International Journal of Human Resource Management*, 28 (14): 1986–2016.

Bansal, P.and Corley, K. (2011) 'The coming of age for qualitative research: Embracing the diversity of qualitative methods', *Academy of Management Journal*, 54 (2): 233–7.

Barley, S.R. (2006) 'When I write my masterpiece: Thoughts on what makes a paper interesting', *Academy of Management Journal*, 49 (1): 16–20.

Bartunek, J.M., Rynes, S.L. and Ireland, R.D. (2006) 'What makes management research interesting, and why does it matter?', *Academy of Management Journal*, 49 (1): 9–15.

Berkenkotter, C., Huckin, T.N. and Ackerman, J. (1988) 'Conventions, conversations, and the writer: Case study of a student in a rhetoric Ph.D. program', *Research in the Teaching of English*, 22 (1): 9–44.

Boxall, P., Ang, S. H. and Bartram, T. (2011) 'Analysing the 'black box' of HRM: Uncovering HR goals, mediators and outcomes in a standardized service environment', *Journal of Management Studies*, 48 (7): 1504–32.

Buchanan, D.A. and Bryman, A. (2007) 'Contextualizing methods choice in organizational research', *Organizational Research Methods*, 10 (3): 483–501.

Campbell, DT. (1975) '"Degrees of freedom" and the case study', *Comparative Political Studies*, 8 (2): 178–93.

Clark, S.M., Gioia, D.A., Ketchen, D.J. Jr. and Thomas, J.B. (2010) 'Transitional identity as a facilitator of organizational identity change during a merger', *Administrative Science Quarterly*, 55 (3): 397–438.

Creswell, J.W. and Miller, D.L. (2000) 'Determining validity in qualitative inquiry', *Theory Into Practice*, 39 (3): 124–30.

Denzin, N.K. (1978) *The Research Act: A Theoretical Orientation to Sociological Methods* (2nd edition). New York, NY: McGraw-Hill.

Downey, H.K. and Ireland, R.D. (1979) 'Quantitative versus qualitative: Environmental assessment in organizational studies', *Administrative Science Quarterly*, 24 (4): 630–37.

Dundon, T. and Ryan, P. (2010) 'Interviewing reluctant respondents: Strikes, henchmen, and Gaelic games', *Organizational Research Methods*, 13 (3): 562–81.

Edmondson, A.C. and McManus, S.E. (2007) 'Methodological fit in management field research', *Academy of Management Review*, 32 (4): 1155–79.

Eisenhardt, K.M. (1989) 'Building theories from case study research', *Academy of Management Review*, 14 (4): 532–50.

Eisenhardt, K.M. and Graebner, M.E. (2007) 'Theory building from cases: Opportunities and challenges', *Academy of Management Journal*, 50 (1): 25–32.

Erickson, P.I. and Kaplan, C.P. (2000) 'Maximizing qualitative responses about smoking in structured interviews', *Qualitative Health Research*, 10 (6): 829–40.

Fendt, J. and Sachs, W. (2008) 'Grounded theory method in management research: Users' perspectives', *Organizational Research Methods*, 11 (3): 430–55.

Flyvbjerg, B. (2006) 'Five misunderstandings about case-study research', *Qualitative Inquiry*, 12 (2): 219–245.

Geer, J.G. (1991) 'Do open-ended questions measure "salient" issues?', *Public Opinion Quarterly*, 55 (3): 360–70.

Gibbert, M. and Ruigrok, W. (2010) 'The "what" and "how" of case study rigor: Three strategies based on published work', *Organizational Research Methods*, 13 (4): 710–37.

Gibbert, M., Ruigrok, W. and Wicki, B. (2008) 'What passes as a rigorous case study?', *Strategic Management Journal*, 29 (13): 1465–74.

Gioia, D.A., Corley, K.G. and Hamilton, A.L. (2012) 'Seeking qualitative rigor in inductive research: Notes on the Gioia methodology', *Organizational Research Methods*, 16 (1): 15–31.

Gioia, D.A., Price, K.N., Hamilton, A.L. and Thomas, J.B. (2010) 'Forging an identity: An insider-outsider study of processes involved in the formation of organizational identity', *Administrative Science Quarterly*, 55 (1): 1–46.

Glaser, B.G. (2001) *The Grounded Theory Perspective: Conceptualization Contrasted with Description*. Mill Valley, CA: Sociology Press.

Glaser, B.G. (2003) *The Grounded Theory Perspective II: Description's Remodelling of Grounded Theory Methodology*. Mill Valley, CA: Sociology Press.

Glaser, B.G. (2005) *The Grounded Theory Perspective III: Theoretical Coding*. Mill Valley, CA: Sociology Press.

Glaser, B.G. and Strauss, A.L. (1967) *The Discovery of Grounded Theory: Strategies for Qualitative Research*. Chicago, IL: Aldine de Gruyter.

Golden-Biddle, K. and Locke, K. (1993) 'Appealing work: An investigation of how ethnographic texts convince', *Organization Science*, 4 (4): 595–616.

Goulding, C. (2002) *Grounded theory. A Practical Guide for Management, Business and Market Researchers*. London: Sage Publishing.

Hammersley, M. (1990) 'What's wrong with ethnography? The myth of theoretical description', *Sociology*, 24 (4): 597–615.

Jackson, K.M. and Trochim, W.M.K. (2002) 'Concept mapping as an alternative approach for the analysis of open-ended survey responses', *Organizational Research Methods*, 5 (4): 307–36.

Jones, R, and Noble, G. (2007) 'Grounded theory and management research: a lack of integrity?', *Qualitative Research in Organizations and Management: An International Journal*, 2 (2): 84–103.

Jonsen, K. and Jehn, K.A. (2009) 'Using triangulation to validate themes in qualitative studies', *Qualitative Research in Organizations and Management: An International Journal*, 4 (2): 123–50.

Langley, A. (1999) 'Strategies for theorizing from process data', *Academy of Management Review*, 24 (4): 691–710.

Langley, A. and Truax, J. (1994) 'A process study of new technology adoption in smaller manufacturing firms', *Journal of Management Studies*, 31 (5): 619–652.

Larsson, R. (1993) 'Case survey methodology: Quantitative analysis of patterns across case studies', *Academy of Management Journal*, 36 (6): 1515–46.

Lee, B., Collier, P.M. and Cullen, J. (2007) 'Reflections on the use of case studies in the accounting, management and organizational disciplines', *Qualitative Research in Organizations and Management: An International Journal*, 2(3): 169–78.

Leonard-Barton, D.A. (1990) 'A dual methodology for case studies: Synergistic use of a longitudinal single site with replicated multiple sites', *Organization Science*, 1 (3): 248–66.

Lewins, A. and Silver, C. (2007) *Using Software in Qualitative Research: A Step-by-step Guide*. London: Sage Publishing.

Lincoln, Y. S. and Guba, E.G. (1985) *Naturalist Inquiry*. Beverly Hills, CA: Sage Publishing.

Locke, K. (2001) *Grounded Theory in Management Research*. London: Sage Publishing.

Lyles M.A. and Reger, R.K. (1993) 'Managing for autonomy in joint ventures: A longitudinal study of upward influence', *Journal of Management Studies*, 30 (3): 383–404.

March, J.G., Sproull, L.S. and Tamuz, M. (1991) 'Learning from samples of one or fewer', *Organization Science*, 2 (1): 1–13.

Marcus, G.E. (1998) *Ethnography through Thick and Thin*. Princeton, NJ: Princeton University Press.

Martin, J., Feldman, M.S., Hatch, M.Jo and Sitkin, S.B. (1983) 'The uniqueness paradox in organizational stories', *Administrative Science Quarterly*, 28 (3): 438–53.

McClintock, C.C., Brannon, D. and Maynard-Moody, S. (1979) 'Applying the logic of sample surveys to qualitative case studies: The case cluster method', *Administrative Science Quarterly*, 24 (4): 612–29.

Meyer, A.D. (1991) 'Visual data in organizational research', *Organization Science*, 2 (2): 218–36.

Morgan, G. and Smircich, L. (1980) 'The case for qualitative research', *Academy of Management Review*, 5 (4): 491–500.

Nakkeeran, N. (2016) 'Is sampling a misnomer in qualitative research?', *Sociological Bulletin*, 65 (1): 40–9.

O'Reilly, K., Paper, D. and Marx, S. (2012) 'Demystifying grounded theory for business research', *Organizational Research Methods*, 15 (2): 247–62.

Piekkari, R., Welch, C. and Paavilainen, E. (2009) 'The case study as disciplinary convention: Evidence from international business journals', *Organizational Research Methods*, 12 (3): 567–89.

Polkinghorne, M. and Taylor, J. (2019) 'Switching on the BBC: Using recursive abstraction to undertake a narrative inquiry-based investigation into the BBC's early strategic business and management issues', *SAGE Research Methods Cases in Business and Management*, DOI: https://dx.doi.org/10.4135/9781526473134.

Punch, K.F. (2005) *Introduction to Social Research: Quantitative and Qualitative Approaches* (2nd edition) London: Sage Publishing.

Rentsch, J.R. (1990) 'Climate and culture: Interaction and qualitative differences in organizational meanings', *Journal of Applied Psychology*, 75 (6): 668–81.

Sanday, P.R. (1979) 'The ethnographic paradigm(s)', *Administrative Science Quarterly*, 24 (4): 527–38.

Shah, S.K. and Corley, K.G. (2006) 'Building better theory by bridging the quantitative–qualitative divide', *Journal of Management Studies*, 43 (8): 1821–35.

Siggelkow, N. (2007) 'Persuasion with case studies', *Academy of Management Journal*, 50 (1): 20–4.

Silverman, D. (2006) *Interpreting Qualitative Data: Methods for Analysing Talk, Text and Interaction* (3rd edition). London: Sage Publishing.

Strauss, A.L. and Corbin, J.M. (1990) *Basics of Qualitative Research: Grounded Theory Procedures and Techniques*. Newbury Park, CA: Sage Publishing.

Strauss, A.L. and Corbin, J.M. (1998) *Basics of Qualitative Research: Techniques and Procedures for Developing Grounded Theory* (2nd edition). Thousand Oaks, CA: Sage Publishing.

Suddaby, R. (2006) 'From the editors: What grounded theory is not', *Academy of Management Journal*, 49 (4): 633–42.

Tracy, S.J., Lutgen-Sandvik, P. and Alberts, J.K. (2006) 'Nightmares, demons, and slaves: Exploring the painful metaphors of workplace bullying', *Management Communication Quarterly*, 20 (2): 148–85.

Van Maanen, J. (1979) 'The fact of fiction in organizational ethnography', *Administrative Science Quarterly*, 24 (4): 539–50.

Van Maanen, J. (2006) 'Ethnography then and now', *Qualitative Research in Organizations and Management: An International Journal*, 1 (1): 13–21.

Wheeldon, J. and Faubert, J. (2009) 'Framing experience: Concept maps, mind maps, and data collection in qualitative research', *International Journal of Qualitative Methods*, 8 (3): 68–83.

Wolcott, H.F. (1994) *Transforming Qualitative Data: Description, Analysis, and Interpretation*. Thousand Oaks, CA: Sage Publishing.

Yin, R.K. (2009) *Case Study Research: Design and Methods* (4th edition). Los Angeles, CA: Sage.

Yin, R.K. and Heald, K.A. (1975) 'Using the case survey method to analyze policy studies', *Administrative Science Quarterly*, 20 (3): 371–81.

10
QUANTITATIVE METHODS AND ANALYSIS

10.1 INTRODUCTION

Quantitative research methods are used when you need to establish relationships between two or more constructs using a large number of observations. Analysis using a larger number of observations provides a researcher with more certainty and potentially greater precision when attempting to relate constructs to one another. While a few observations may have been enough for us to see the linkages between these constructs if there are obvious patterns across case studies (as discussed in Chapter 9), when it comes to relationships that are likely to be dependent on contexts and conditions, greater number of observations will allow for greater degrees of freedom to ascertain certain relationships. More generalizable relationships can potentially be derived from availability of detailed data, when the intention is to have more external validity. In this process, the level of significance of a relationship is quantified. Not only do quantitative research methods help to confirm a relationship, they are also useful for assessing the strength of this relationship.

Quantitative research methods further allow us to relate multiple constructs across observations. That is, if your data are set up for analysis to be done using quantitative methodologies, it allows you to test the relationship of more than two constructs at the same time. This is often done with the help of statistical methods such as multiple analysis of variance (MANOVA) and multiple **regression models**.

The fact that quantitative research methods typically involve a large number of observations suggests that the constructs chosen in your study must be observable across entities. That is, what you observe is interpreted as the same for different entities (reliability and internal validity). If this is not possible, then the use of the quantitative research design is not viable.

In Chapter 5 we discussed the differences between correlation and causality. It is important to highlight here that quantitative methods allow us to conduct both forms of research. Chapter 8 has highlighted tests that are associated with correlation techniques, i.e. those that do not consider directional relationships between constructs. In this chapter, the focus will be on analytical methods that allow us to relate constructs with inference on causality.

10.2 TYPES OF DATASET

Data coding is an essential component of quantitative studies. As mentioned above, for quantitative studies, constructs need to be observable across multiple entities. Once the data are collected, the same rule will apply to the data coding process. Observations across units need to be comparable to allow patterns of behaviour to be tracked. Depending on what kind of inferences you intend to derive from your analysis, the data coding process and the organization of the data can take many different forms. Some of the forms of organizing quantitative data are highlighted in this section. This section also includes some advice of when **data transformation** is needed and how this can be done.

10.2.1 Different coding of data

Conversation box

Charles [Masters student]:   Professor, you asked me to sign up for a couple of statistics courses so that I can start preparing myself for quantitative analysis. I came across a course on data coding and wonder if it's worthwhile to do a course on data coding alone.

Professor: Charles, the natural order of the research process flows from data collection to analysis. But between these two processes, there is a major research step and that is data coding. While it's more often not treated like a major step in the research process, bad data coding can cause lots of problems for all subsequent processes such as analysis and the interpretation of results. I would strongly encourage you to attend this course, so you can understand why the process deserves some attention.

Chapter 6 has listed the various forms that data can take. Data can be presented as scales, which include nominal, ordinal, interval and ratio. Data can also be measured via ratios and difference scores, and in many instances composite measures can be utilized. The simplest form of data are continuous data, where the values reflect the actual measurements of the observations.

Nominal data include categories of equal rank. When it comes to coding nominal data, this is often represented by a variable that takes values of 1, 2, 3, ..., where each of these values represents one category. Therefore, in the example in Figure 6.1, the value of '1' represents Asia, '2' represents 'Americas' etc. For analytical purposes, however, coding these categories using the numerics above will lead to erroneous analysis as most software and analytical methods will read these as ranked order. Instead of having one variable consisting of five categories in this example, the software will require the researcher to split this variable and code the construct into five variables, with each variable representing one category only. Therefore, a new variable such as 'Asia' may be introduced for cases where the responses are 'Asia'. This dummy variable will take the value of '1' for these cases and '0' for all cases not classified as 'Asia', i.e. in any one of the other four categories. Such a variable is created for every category.

It is important to note that statistically, if we are to run the descriptive statistics of the single variable with the five categories, the mean value does not have any meaning attached to it at all. For example, you run the descriptive statistics and find that the mean value is 2.56; this falls between 'Americas' (2) and 'Europe' (3). We cannot interpret this value as 'the mean value falls between Americas and Europe'. Hence, splitting the variable into five different dummy variables has its merit to help prepare the data for analysis. With the dummy variables, the mean of each variable is basically the percentage of observations that falls into that category.

The coding of ordinal data is more straightforward. This can be coded using one variable. The mean value of a variable with ordinal data does represent its actual value, i.e. a mean value of 2.56 suggests that the average falls between the values of 2 and 3. Likewise, interval data can be coded in the same way, though the value of mean has to be interpreted in light of the intervals used in the measurement.

While integers and truncated values are usually not an issue in data coding, they are to be treated differently from the typical interval and ratio scales. This is because if these variables are the outcome variables in your study, it will suggest the use of different types of statistical analysis. For example, while a typical continuous-type **dependent variable** can be analyzed using multiple linear regression models, a count-type dependent variable, such as the number of overseas business trips made in a year, will require the Poisson, Negative Binomial or similar regression models to help with the analysis.

Beyond the coding of the individual variables, data also need to be organized such that every observation (equivalent to every row in a spreadsheet) represents a unit of analysis. For example, in a study of the impact of human resource practices on company performance, if you measure a company's performance using the inputs of survey responses from two of its senior executives, then you will need to try to aggregate the scores provided by these two senior executives so that each company has only one score for performance given the analysis is at the company level. In this example, the company score can just be an average of the scores provided by the two senior executives, or a composite measure using some weighting.

In the above example, scores obtained at a more micro level (executives) are being converted into a score at a more macro level (company). However, it must be noted that it is impossible to do the reverse. You cannot get a sense of the response provided by each individual employee solely through an aggregate score given by an employer. As also mentioned in Chapter 7, some archival data will be hard to access as the source document only provides aggregate data. Before any data is collected, a researcher needs to take into account the challenge of collecting data at one level and analyzing it at another, as mentioned in Chapter 5. There needs to be a good awareness of the unit of observation vs. the unit of analysis before data collection and coding.

A cross-sectional dataset contains data that are collected at the same point in time, for example, an analysis of responses of businesses during the first three months of the Coronavirus Pandemic in 2020. Pooled cross-sectional samples include observations that may start at different points in time but are stacked together to be compared. For example, business responses can be studied during the first three months during a crisis, and this is done across the three crises of the Asian Financial Crisis in 1997, Global Financial Crisis in 2008 and Coronavirus Pandemic in 2020. A longitudinal dataset is a dataset in which data of each individual unit are collected over multiple periods of time that also allows for the analysis of changes with units over time. If all units are observed across similar periods of time, then we call this a panel dataset; for example a set of firms are tracked on their responses in each of the three months since the outbreak of the Coronavirus Pandemic.

10.2.2 Transformation of data

Beyond coding the raw data to the extent that these are packaged well and ready for analysis in statistical software, we may find ourselves needing to do some data transformation in the actual analysis itself. Data transformation is sometimes necessary, as while the coded data are clean, the attributes of the data do not fulfil the assumptions needed to fit into the statistical models for analysis.

For example, from a large enough sample of firms, we hope to get a normal distribution of diversity in terms of, say, the performance of firms. But if the return on assets data (as a measurement of firm performance) shows a range of between 2% and 500%,

Conversation box

Professor:	Robert, I believe some of your variables need logarithm transformation.
Robert [PhD student]:	What do you mean by that, Professor?
Professor:	Take this for example: you use the actual value of total assets of firms in your analysis. This variable takes values ranging from five million to three billion dollars. If you plot this on a diagram, you might find that some of the data points are quite far apart. This is due to the big range represented in your variable. Extreme values can affect your results. Logarithm transformation can narrow the range and reduce the effects of extreme values may have on your analysis.

there is a genuine concern that the range in itself may suggest the presence of outliers. Outliers can have a significant influence on results (Stevens, 1984). A normal distribution of the return on assets data when used as a dependent variable will allow us to use the most fundamental model of multiple linear regression, which will be discussed later in this chapter. At the time of coding, it is unlikely that we can tell if the data follow a normal distribution. When coding is done, we will perform the descriptive and exploratory analyses discussed in Chapter 8. Upon normality tests, it may be discovered that the return on assets distribution does not follow a normal distribution. It is in such research situations that it becomes necessary for us to transform the data (in this case return on assets) to allow us to analyze the dataset using multiple linear regression, if this is the appropriate type of analysis needed in your context. It is important to note that if we do not believe that the outcome variable itself should follow a normal distribution, then transformation of the data may not be required. In such cases, other forms of regression model will be needed for analysis.

The illustration above on the return on assets is clearly a simple scenario that data transformation will have to take place. According to Ryan (1997), transformations are needed to (1) transform a non-linear model to a linear model (if a linear model is necessary for analysis); (2) transform the predictor and/or outcome variables in such a way that the transformed variables have a stronger linear relationship than the original variables (if a linear model is necessary for analysis); (3) obtain a relatively constant error variance; and (4) ensure approximate normality for the distribution of the error terms (1997: 89).

Conversation box

Cindy [Masters student]:   Professor, do we focus on checking on the outcome variable to assess if our data is appropriate for analysis or not?

Professor: The fit of outcome variable for analysis is the first thing to check, Cindy. As you will realize from our lessons about regression models, it is however not the only variable that one should check. For example, sometimes you will have to transform the predictor variables to make them possible for analysis as well.

Nonetheless, the decision of whether to transform the data is not an easy one (Draper and Smith, 1998). Both Ryan (1997) and Weisberg (2005) provide some discussions around the basic transformations. The Box–Cox transformation is a major form of transformation (Box and Cox, 1964). The method basically replaces the original variable by using a function of its geometric mean, getting it closer to a normal distribution to allow for testing using the multiple linear regression models. Manning and Mullahy (2001) extensively discuss the various forms of transformation using logarithm models. For transforming non-positive variables, Weisberg (2005) provides some suggestions while Zhang et al. (2000) propose an inverse hyperbolic sine transformation for this purpose.

Referring back to the outlier example mentioned earlier around return on assets data, sometimes outliers may not appear to be obvious in a dataset. A good illustration is provided in Kahn and Udry (1986). Aguinis et al. (2013) present 14 different definitions of outliers. The authors further provide 39 outlier identification techniques for researchers, such as the single-construct techniques, the multiple-construct techniques, and the influence techniques. Transformation of data as mentioned above is also just one of the 20 outlier handling techniques discussed in this paper. It is worth noting here that an easy way to handle outliers is just to delete them when there are plenty of observations in a dataset. On this, some researchers advise the risk of deleting outliers as one needs to take account for sample representation and bias (see Cortina, 2002 for a brief discussion).

10.3 DIFFERENT TYPES OF REGRESSION MODELS

A regression analysis is concerned with describing and evaluating the relationship between a given variable Y (often called the dependent variable) and one or more other variables X_1, X_2, ..., X_n (often called explanatory, predictor or independent variables). Regression models where there is only one independent variable are called simple regression models. Simple regression models are similar to a typical bivariate test between two variables, except in the simple regression models there is inference on causality. Regression models that contain more than one independent variable are called multiple regression models.

As highlighted earlier, the commonly used regression models assume linearity, i.e. there is a linear relationship between the independent variables and the dependent variable. This linearity can either be positive or negative. Regression analysis seeks to identify the best line that explains this relationship, usually through the use of the least-squares method. The essence of the least-squares method is to find a linear line of relationship between constructs where the sum of the squared values of the distances between data points and the line is at the minimum.

Conversation box

Mia [PhD student]:   Professor, there are so many books on regression models. I wonder if there's one that provides a good overview of all the different types of regression models. That would be a helpful starting point.

Professor: I would suggest starting with basic books, for instance Aiken and West (1991) or Kleinbaum et al. (2013). Most regression models that are designed for specific purposes possess the same fundamental attributes as the basic multiple regression models. You will need to have a strong grasp of the fundamentals to allow you to go deep in search of the specific regression models that you can use to analyze your data.

As this book focuses on how to get a research project set up with discussion on the key components, it is not the intention here to be overly focused on the specifics of each of the different types of regression models. However, it is important to note that the choice of regression model depends largely on the attributes of the outcome variables, and to a much lesser extent on the independent variables. Assumptions about what the dependent variable and the independent variables should look like in any regression model should be observed. It is these assumptions that sometimes make it necessary for us to transform our variables so that we can appropriately use the different analytical methods.

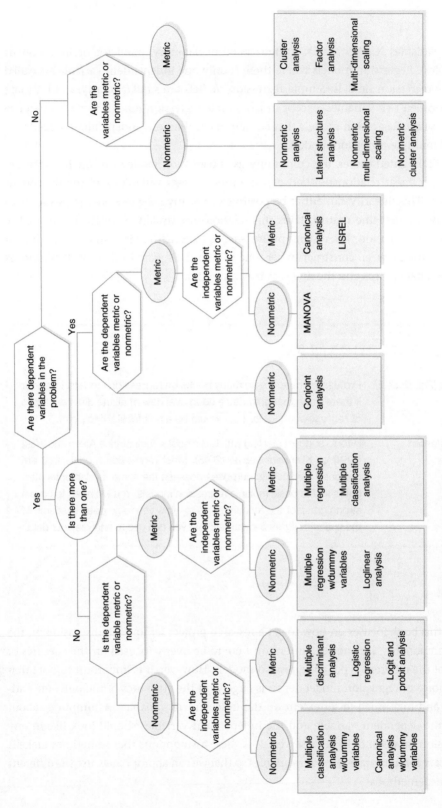

Figure 10.1 Roadmap of the types of regression models to use

Figure 10.1 shows a roadmap of how we may determine the type of regression model that is required in our different research situations. The decisions required when using the roadmap presented in Figure 10.1 depend on whether the variable in question is metric or not. Recall that metric means there is a number associated with the variable in question. Non-metric means that the variable is not represented by numbers but rather by categories.

Just as an illustration, say you are trying to test the relationship between the adoption of different total quality control practices by companies and their performance. You use a survey to ask top executives in your target sample companies to respond to Likert scale-type questions that represent your variables. For the questions on practices, you ask the respondents to rate the extent of their use of the different total quality control practices. For the questions on performance, you ask the respondents to rate their performance relative to their competitors across various dimensions. Referring to Figure 10.1, the first decision point is whether there is a dependent variable in your study. The answer would be 'yes' – performance being the dependent variable. The second decision point is whether there is more than one dependent variable. The answer is 'no' in this case. The third decision point is whether your dependent variable is a metric variable or not. In this case, it would be a 'yes' response. The fourth decision point is whether the independent variable is a metric variable. In this case, the answer would be a 'yes' again. This would lead us to the potential analytical methods of multiple regression analysis or multiple classification analysis.

The essence of a roadmap as illustrated in Figure 10.1 is its ability to guide us to decision points that will necessarily force us into making a major decision when facing dilemmas. Many variations of regression models have been generated due to the implicit assumptions of previous models. As such, there are a lot of complexities concerning the analytical methods we see today. Having a decision tree to guide the process will make the research decision more systematic as opposed to using judgement calls as a way to resolve the dilemma.

Beyond a roadmap like the one in Figure 10.1, it is evident across many books that some classifications can be made by just focusing on the type of dependent variable that your study involves. For example, the following models are common:

- Continuous response models (multiple regression)
- Limited/semicontinuous models (truncated regression, tobit regression, **self-selection/ endogeneity** models)
- Binomial response models (**logistic regression**, logit regression and probit regression)
- Count response models (**Poisson regression** and negative binomial regression, and their truncated and zero-inflated variations)
- Multinomial response models (ordered logistic regression, ordered probit regression, multinomial logistic regression and multinomial probit regression)

10.4 MULTIPLE LINEAR REGRESSION ANALYSIS

In a multiple regression analysis, a continuous-type dependent variable is regressed against a set of **predictor variables**. The analysis seeks to find a linear relationship between two constructs, controlling for the effects of other constructs that are fed into the analysis. As mentioned earlier, all regression models have their assumptions. Section 10.4.1 lists the key assumptions made in **multiple linear regression models**.

10.4.1 Assumptions

Measurement

The dependent variable is continuous, unbounded and measured on an interval or ratio scale. All independent variables are nominal, ordinal, interval or ratio. All variables are measured without error. We have touched on these topics in Chapter 6.

Error term

The expected value of the error, ε, is zero.

Homoscedasticity

The variance of the error term, $\text{Var}(\varepsilon)$, is the same, or constant, for all values of the independent variable.

Normality of error terms

The errors are normally distributed for each set of values of the independent variables.

Autocorrelation

There is no correlation among the error terms produced by different values of the independent variables. Mathematically, $E(\varepsilon_i, \varepsilon_j) = 0$.

Correlation with error terms

There is no correlation between the error terms and the independent variables. Mathematically, $E(\varepsilon_i, X_j) = 0$.

Multicollinearity

None of the independent variables is a perfect linear combination of the other independent variables.

10.4.2 Regression outputs: an illustration

Nowadays there is a decent number of statistical software applications available that allow us to run quantitative analysis with relative ease. But knowing the reasons why you are seeing what are presented as outputs from such statistical software is essential. In this, researchers have warned against the hunger in search of significant results in a study without observing the underlying reasons for seeing what has been found (Bettis, 2012; Goldfarb and King, 2016). Bettis (2012) labels this as researchers doing 'data snooping' while Goldfarb and King (2016) call it scientific apophenia, i.e. the tendency to find connections where none exist. Bettis (2012) reiterates the need to understand how a software package arrives at the results, stating that

> these [software] packages all include many esoteric models and tests for which one only needs to push the 'enter' key. Learning to appropriately use and interpret powerful statistical software, without a rigorous understanding of the theory of statistical testing, is a prescription for disaster and can turn both science and art of rigorous statistical research into a paint-by-numbers exercise fraught with oversights and errors. (2012: 113)

It is in this spirit that this section will kick off with some statistical demonstration of how the multiple regression models operate so that we are not interpreting the statistical results blindly.

Conversation box

Roger [Masters student]: Professor, I'm not sure which software is the best for analyzing my data. It seems different people are using different software.

Professor: There is no 'best' software for analyzing quantitative data. The key ones that I use are STATA and SPSS. In fact, I use different software for different analyses. Regardless of which software you use, it will be good to refer to the statistical software manuals as different software may use slightly different assumptions and mechanisms for some tests.

In order to do that, let's use an example. The dataset used for illustration involves collaboration data of firms residing in Singapore in the period 1994–96. A firm can appear in
one, two or all three years of the data, i.e. this is a cross-sectional dataset. It is important
to note here that this is not a panel dataset as not all firms appear in all three years of the
sample period. The resulting dataset contains 4,805 observations for analysis. The research
question here is to examine the relationship between the competition that a firm faces and
both the collaboration it conducts in response to competition and its sales growth.

Figure 10.2 shows the multiple regression statistical outputs from testing the relationship between competition (*Comp_Int*) and sales growth (*Rel_Sales_Growth*). This
output is obtained from using the STATA software. Figure 10.3 shows the output of the
same analysis using the **SPSS** software.

```
. regress Rel_Sales_Growth Firm_Age No_of_Bus_Lines Sub_Triad Sub_Asia_minus_Sin_Jpn Large
> _Size_Firm Medium_Size_Firm Small_Size_Firm Year95 Year96
note: Small_Size_Firm omitted because of collinearity
```

Source	SS	df	MS			
Model	75091.7918	8	9386.47398			
Residual	11051597.6	4796	2304.33646			
Total	11126689.4	4804	2316.13019			

	Number of obs =	4805
	F(8, 4796) =	4.07
	Prob > F =	0.0001
	R-squared =	0.0067
	Adj R-squared =	0.0051
	Root MSE =	48.004

Rel_Sales_Growth	Coef.	Std. Err.	t	P>|t|	[95% Conf. Interval]	
Firm_Age	-.2678937	.0760636	-3.52	0.000	-.4170133	-.1187741
No_of_Bus_Lines	1.029185	.7755256	1.33	0.185	-.4912012	2.549571
Sub_Triad	.9111096	1.480434	0.62	0.538	-1.991221	3.81344
Sub_Asia_minus_Sin_Jpn	3.899335	3.504319	1.11	0.266	-2.970738	10.76941
Large_Size_Firm	2.381969	2.211547	1.08	0.282	-1.953677	6.717615
Medium_Size_Firm	3.291845	1.520537	2.16	0.030	.3108954	6.272794
Small_Size_Firm	0	(omitted)				
Year95	2.692736	1.812499	1.49	0.137	-.8605924	6.246065
Year96	7.616803	1.802306	4.23	0.000	4.083456	11.15015
_cons	-.9175834	1.897363	-0.48	0.629	-4.637286	2.802119

Figure 10.2 STATA output

© Copyright 1996–2020 StataCorp LLC.

```
REGRESSION
/MISSING LISTWISE
/STATISTICS COEFF OUTS R ANOVA
/CRITERIA=PIN(.05) POUT(.10)
/NOORIGIN
/DEPENDENT Rel_Sales_Growth
/METHOD=ENTER Firm_Age No_of_Bus_Lines Sub_Triad Sub_Asia_minus_Sin_Jpn Large_Size_Firm Medium_Size_Firm Small_
Size_Firm Year95 Year96.
```

Regression

[DataSet1]

Variables Entered/Removed[a]

Model	Variables Entered	Variables Removed	Method
1	Year96, Small_Size_Firm, Sub_Asia_minus_Sin_Jpn, No_of_Bus_Lines, Sub_Triad, Year95, Firm_Age, Large_Size_Firm[b]	.	Enter

a. Dependent Variable: Rel_Sales_Growth
b. Tolerance = .000 limits reached.

Model Summary

Model	R	R Square	Adjusted R Square	Std. Error of the Estimate
1	.082[a]	.007	.005	48.0035046

a. Predictors: (Constant), Year96, Small_Size_Firm, Sub_Asia_minus_Sin_Jpn, No_of_Bus_Lines, Sub_Triad, Year95, Firm_Age, Large_Size_Firm

ANOVA[a]

Model		Sum of Squares	df	Mean Square	F	Sig.
1	Regression	75091.792	8	9386.474	4.073	.000[b]
	Residual	11051597.644	4796	2304.336		
	Total	11126689.436	4804			

a. Dependent Variable: Rel_Sales_Growth
b. Predictors: (Constant), Year96, Small_Size_Firm, Sub_Asia_minus_Sin_Jpn, No_of_Bus_Lines, Sub_Triad, Year95, Firm_Age, Large_Size_Firm

Coefficients[a]

Model		Unstandardized Coefficients		Standardized Coefficients	t	Sig.
		B	Std. Error	Beta		
1	(Constant)	2.374	2.006		1.184	.237
	Firm_Age	−.268	.076	−.053	−3.522	.000
	No_of_Bus_Lines	1.029	.776	.020	1.327	.185
	Sub_Triad	.911	1.480	.009	.615	.538
	Sub_Asia_minus_Sin_Jpn	3.899	3.504	.016	1.113	.266
	Large_Size_Firm	−.910	2.118	−.007	−.430	.667
	Small_Size_Firm	−3.292	1.521	−.033	−2.165	.030
	Year95	2.693	1.812	.022	1.486	.137
	Year96	7.617	1.802	.063	4.226	.000

a. Dependent Variable: Rel_Sales_Growth

Excluded Variables[a]

Model		Beta In	t	Sig.	Partial Correlation	Collinearity Statistics Tolerance
1	Medium_Size_Firm	.[b]	.	.	.	.000

a. Dependent Variable: Rel_Sales_Growth
b. Predictors in the Model: (Constant), Year96, Small_Size_Firm, Sub_Asia_minus_Sin_Jpn, No_of_Bus_Lines, Sub_Triad, Year95, Firm_Age, Large_Size_Firm

Figure 10.3   SPSS output

Other variables included to predict sales growth are: (1) age of the firm (*Firm_Age*); (2) number of business lines that the firm participates in (*No_of_Bus_Lines*); (3) the firm is a subsidiary of a parent originating from the Triad nations, i.e. US, Europe and Japan (*Sub_Triad*); (4) the firm is a subsidiary of a parent originating from Asian countries other than Singapore and Japan (*Sub_Asia_minus_Sin_Jpn*); (5) the firm is a large-sized firm, i.e. more than 500 employees (*Large_Size_Firm*); (6) the firm is a medium-sized firm, i.e. between 100 and 500 employees (*Medium_Size_Firm*); (7) the firm is a small-sized firm, i.e. fewer than 100 employees (*Small_Size_Firm*); (8) the observation is made in Year 1994 (*Year94*); (9) the observation is made in Year 1995 (*Year95*); and (10) the observation is made in Year 1996 (*Year96*).

While there might be some differences in the presentation of results from the same analysis using different software, there are some elements of the outputs that are common. The first such element is the **Analysis of Variance (ANOVA)**. We have touched on the basic bivariate case of ANOVA in Section 8.6.4.

ANOVA in a multiple regression model relates to the goodness of fit of the model, i.e. how much of the dependent variable can be explained by the set of predictor variables that are introduced in the regression model.

Model wise, let's say $Y_i = a + bX_i$

where $i = 1, 2, \ldots n$ is the number of observations.

We obtain the estimates of a and b, i.e. $\hat{a}$ and $\hat{b}$.

Substituting back to the equation allows us to obtain estimate of Y_i, i.e. $\hat{Y}_i$, corresponding to each value of X_i.

We have $\hat{Y}_i = \hat{a} + \hat{b}X_i$

and mean $\overline{Y}$.

Then $\left(Y_i - \overline{Y}\right) = \left(\hat{Y}_i - \overline{Y}\right) + \left(Y_i - \hat{Y}_i\right)$

Squaring both sides and taking the sum gives:

$$\sum\left(Y_i - \overline{Y}\right)^2 = \sum\left(\hat{Y}_i - \overline{Y}\right)^2 + \sum\left(Y_i - \hat{Y}_i\right)^2$$

This equation basically says that the total sum of squares of differences (SST) is equal to the ('explained') sum of squares of differences from the regression (SSR) and the ('unexplained') sum of squares of error (SSE).

The Y values must be independent, i.e. the value of Y observed for a particular value of X, X_i does not depend on the value of Y observed at another value of X, X_j. In addition, for each value of X, there is a subpopulation of Y values. These subpopulations must be normally distributed, with

$$\text{Mean: } E(Y_i)=a+bE(X_i)$$

$$\text{Variance: } Var(Y_1) = Var(Y_2)=.....=Var(Y_k)$$

Using the SPSS output as illustration, we have

$$Y_i =a+ b_1X_{1i}+ b_2X_{2i}+ .....+b_kX_{ki}$$

Hypothesis will be:

$H_0: b_1, b_2, ... , b_k =0$ (no linear relationship)

H_i: Some $b_i \neq 0$ (linear relationship)

Rule: Reject H_0 if $F \geq F_{\alpha,k,n-(k+1)}$

Looking at the degrees of freedom of the rejection rule,

(a) the degrees of freedom of SSR is the number of X_i s, (in this case is $k = 8$). Mean sum of regression (MSR) = 9,386 (SSR/no. of degrees of freedom)
(b) the degrees of freedom of SSE is the number of observations ($n = 4,805$) – number of parameters to be estimated [$n-(k+1) = 9$]. Mean sum of error (MSE) = 2,304 (SSE/no. of degrees of freedom)

F is calculated by MSR/MSE = 4.073, which is highly significant at $p<0.001$ in this case.

The *test statistic* for the significance of individual variables is $t = \dfrac{b}{S_b}$

where $S_b^2 = MSE / \Sigma(X_i - \bar{X})^2$

Rule: Reject H_0 if $|t| \geq t_{1-\alpha/2,n-(k+1)}$

For example, in the case of firm age, we have $t = -3.52$, which is highly significant at $p<0.001$.

The confidence interval for b is computed by $b \pm t_{1-\alpha/2} S_b$. Based on this example, we are 95% confident that the true value of b for firm age will lie within the interval of (–0.42, –0.12) as shown in the STATA output (SPSS can be programmed to include confidence intervals in the output as well). An alternative interpretation is that if we are to perform the analysis using different samples, each analysis will give us one interval and 95% of these intervals will contain the true value of b.

R^2 measures the proportion of total variation in Y that can be explained by the predictor variables Xs.

$$R^2 = (SST–SSE)/SST = SSR/SST$$

In our example, only 7% of the variation in sales growth can be explained by the predictor variables used for the analysis.

It can be shown that adding any additional independent variables will increase the value of R^2, regardless of whether these variables are good predictors of Y or not. To remedy the problem, we must take into consideration the number of variables used. This goes back to the fundamentals of being parsimonious in our modelling.

We can recalculate:

$$\text{Adjusted } R^2 = 1 - \left[\frac{\frac{SSE}{n-k-1}}{\frac{SST}{n-1}} \right] = 1 - (n-1)\left(\frac{S_e^2}{SST} \right)$$

In this calculation, (1) if additional variables are good predictors of Y, then S_e^2 decreases, and therefore R_{adj}^2 increases; (2) R_{adj}^2 may increase or decrease as more independent variables are added; (3) if R^2 and R_{adj}^2 are very different, we would suspect at least one of the X_i variables contributes very little to the prediction of Y. In our example, R_{adj}^2 as opposed to $R^2 = 0.007$.

The assessment of the fit of any regression model is largely reliant on both the t-values of the predictor values and the R^2 of the model. Figure 10.4 shows the action required depending on the outcomes for the two criteria.

t-Value	R Squared	Action
Pass	Low	Try to find more variables which can explain the pattern of Y
Pass	High	Good Model
Fail	Low	Do all over again
Fail	High	Reevaluate: The form of some of the variables is not correct

Figure 10.4   Criteria for assessing fit of regression model

Residual analysis

Figure 10.4 has highlighted that when t-values are insignificant and yet R^2 remains high, there may be a case that the form of the regression model is mis-specified. In other words, there may be a potential non-linear relationship between the dependent variable and the predictor variables. In such cases, running residual analyses may reveal some patterns in the relationship.

The **residual analysis** would show if the current regression line is the best possible line of relationship between these variables.

$$\text{Given the equation } Y_i = a + bX_i$$

$$\text{We have } \hat{Y}_i = \hat{a} + \hat{b}X_i$$

We define residual as $\left(Y_i - \hat{Y}_i \right)$. These residuals are often provided in statistical outputs.

The concept of residual analysis is to plot the residuals with their corresponding X values. If the residual plot shows a certain pattern, then it suggests another form of the model may be more appropriate. If there is a curvilinear relationship for example, then the following models may be appropriate:

$$\hat{Y}_i = \hat{a} + \hat{b}X_i + \hat{c}X_i^2$$
$$\hat{Y}_i = \hat{a} + \hat{b}X_i + \hat{c}X_i^3$$
$$\hat{Y}_i = \hat{a} + \hat{b}X_i + \hat{c}\frac{1}{X}$$
$$\hat{Y}_i = \hat{a} + \hat{b}X_i + \hat{c}e^{-x}$$

The aim of residual analysis is to ensure that the model can explain the data well. As we always propose first-order linear models, i.e. positive or negative linear, there is a likelihood that we will miss out on the possibility that the data conforms to second-order models shown above. The models will only explain the data well when the residuals are scattered without a pattern in the residual plot.

Autocorrelation

Autocorrelation occurs when there is a distinct tendency for the residuals to have long positive or negative runs, i.e. e_t is related to e_{t-1}.

The Durbin-Watson d test is the best test for the presence of autocorrelation.

$$d = \frac{\sum\limits_{t=2}^{n}(\hat{e}_t - \hat{e}_{t-1})^2}{\sum\limits_{t=1}^{n}\hat{e}_t^2}$$

$$d \approx 2\left(1 - \frac{\sum\limits_{t=2}^{n}\hat{e}_t\,\hat{e}_{t-1}}{\sum\limits_{t=1}^{n}\hat{e}_t^2}\right)$$

The rule is:

> If the residuals are not correlated, then $d \approx 2$; if the residuals are highly positively correlated, then $d \approx 0$; and if the residuals are highly negatively correlated, then $d \approx 4$.

For a given sample size and a given number of independent variables, find the critical value of the upper bound (d_U) and the lower bound (d_L). Then follow the decision rule depicted in Figure 10.5. The Durbin-Watson table for the critical values can be accessed in many quantitative research methods books and from the Internet.

The straightforward remedial measure when autocorrelation is detected is to transform the data, such as taking the first-order difference equation, i.e.

$$Y_t - Y_{t-1} = \beta(X_t - X_{t-1}) + (e_t - e_{t-1})$$
$$= \beta(X_t - X_{t-1}) + u_t$$

Null Hypothesis	Decision	If
No positive autocorrelation	Reject	0 < d < dL
No positive autocorrelation	No decision	dL ≤ d ≤ dU
No negative autocorrelation	Reject	4-dL < d < 4
No negative autocorrelation	No decision	4-dU ≤ d ≤ 4-dL
No autocorrelation, +ve or −ve	Do not reject	dU < d < 4-dU

Figure 10.5 Decision criteria for the Durbin-Watson d test

Multicollinearity

High R^2 but few statistically significant t-ratios can also mean a potential **multicollinearity** issue. High pair-wise correlations among independent variables can cause multicollinearity issues. Generally, high bivariate correlations of more than 0.7 or 0.75 would become suspect cases for multicollinearity. There are statistical tests for the presence of multicollinearity, rather than relying on judgements. The most comon one would be the variance inflation factor (VIF), computed using $(1 - R_k^2)^{-1}$, where R_k^2 is derived from regressing each predictor X_k on the other predictor variables. A low R_k^2 will lead to a small VIF value closer to 1 (lowest possible value) and a high R_k^2 will lead to a large VIF value. The typical cut-off point for VIF for multicollinearity is 10 (Marquardt, 1970; Kutner et al., 2004).

When highly correlated predictor variables are included in a regression model, there is a chance that their interactions will lead to one of the variables having an opposite effect on the dependent variable from what it is supposed to have without this collinearity issue. Just as an example, both X_1 and X_2 have separate positive significant effects on Y.

Conversation box

Will [Masters student]:   Professor, to avoid multicollinearity issues, isn't the safest way just to delete the variable deemed to have collinear relationships with other variables?

Professor: Not when the variable is a key variable in your study. You can potentially justify deletion of a control variable without much loss to the quality of the research. But for a key variable, deletion is hardly an option. So other remedial measures need to be considered.

The correlation between X_1 and X_2 is 0.88. As we include them in a single regression model, X_1 continues to have a positive significant effect on Y but X_2 now has a negative significant effect on Y. This observation is quite common, and Kalnins (2018) clearly illustrates why that is the case. This is one of the ways in which collinearity gets picked up as a potential issue, though running a VIF test would have identified the problem earlier as well.

There are some ways to handle multicollinearity issues (Mason and Perreault, 1991). While most of the time dropping a variable when faced with potential multicollinearity issues can work, sometimes this is not practical, as pointed out in the conversation box above. For example, dropping a variable can cause a model to be mis-specified or make it difficult to compare the importance of predictor variables (Mason and Perreault, 1991). Some other possible remedial measures for potential multicollinearity issues include changing the form of the model and even increasing the sample size if practically possible. Together, these remedial measures can simultaneously be used if the situation of multicollinearity is deemed to be serious. Mason and Perreault (1991) also provide discussions about other means of dealing with such situations.

Control variables

A fundamental component to evaluating whether X could cause Y is the study of whether their association remains when we remove the effects of other variables on this association. Control variables are those other variables that have effects on the dependent variable, but which are not the focus of the study. Thus, the control variables to be used are dependent on what the dependent variable is. In our illustration, the control variables are firm age, firm origin, firm size and year of observation.

Conversation box

Karen [Masters student]: Professor, given the risks of multicollinearity, is there any guideline as to how many control variables I can use in my research?

Professor: There's no such guideline, Karen. Ideally, we should always include control variables that allow us to control the effects of these variables. In an ideal situation, that means as many as possible. We also want to include representative variables such that the control variables are not representing the similar constructs to the extent that their controlling effects are duplicating or significantly overlapping. Distinct control variables should ensure that multicollinearity issues are avoided.

Control variables are an essential element of a multiple regression model. Such a model adds more rigour to the analysis linking the dependent variable to the independent variables. Yet researchers have found that the use of control variables is frequently not well justified (Atinc et al., 2012; Becker, 2005; Spector and Brannick, 2011). Other notable issues include unclear descriptions of measurements (Becker, 2005), incomplete reporting of results of control variables (Becker, 2005), and little discussion of the linkage between the control variables and the dependent variable (Atinc et al., 2012).

The inclusion of control variables can potentially cause issues due to the assumptions needed to perform multiple regression models. There are conditions not just for the individual control variables but also the relationship between a **control variable** with all other variables. Given these, control variables should not be added to a regression model blindly, bearing in mind the need to be parsimonious.

It is easy to imagine researchers neglect the practice for treating control variables seriously as they are not the focus of a study. Yet, in the grand scheme of things, a control variable of one study can be a key variable in another study for the same dependent variable, making it imperative for researchers to treat them with care as well for use by subsequent research (Becker, 2005). Thus, good practices on why control variables are included, their measurements, how they are contributing to the study and their linkages with other variables especially with the dependent variable, and the results and reporting of their effects should become a core element in any quantitative study. Atinc et al. (2012), Becker (2005) and Carlson and Wu (2012) provide overviews of the practices needed in regard to control variables.

Group-type variables

Let D_{1i} = 1 if firm i has a parent company from the US, Europe and Japan

D_{1i} = 0 if firm i has a parent company not from the US, Europe and Japan

D_{2i} = 1 if firm i has a parent company from Asia except Japan and Singapore

D_{2i} = 0 if firm i has a parent company not from Asia except Japan and Singapore

D_{3i} = 1 if firm i has a parent company from Singapore

D_{3i} = 0 if firm i has a parent company not from Singapore

There are three indicator variables above. However, in a regression model, only (3–1 = 2) of the indicator variables are included for analysis. The one group omitted serves as the baseline group.

$$E(Y) = \alpha + \beta_1 D_{1i} + \beta_2 D_{2i}$$

In the case when D_{1i} = 0 and D_{2i} = 0, the firm has a parent company from Singapore. In this case, α is the effect of the baseline group on the dependent variable.

Referring back to Figures 10.2 and 10.3, for the firm origin dummy variables, the third category of subsidiary of a Singaporean firm has been intentionally omitted from the model. Likewise, for the year of observation, *Year94* is intentionally omitted for the same reason.

The figures also show that all categories of the firm size variable are included in the analysis. In Figure 10.2 using the STATA software, the output clearly states that the *Small_Size_Firm* variable has been omitted from the table. As stated above, both the statistics relating to *Large_Size_Firm* and *Medium_Size_Firm* are relative to the *Small_Size_Firm* variable. For example, medium-sized firms experience greater sales growth than small-sized firms (b = 3.29, $p<0.05$). The baseline group in this case contains small-sized firms.

You will see a slightly different output presented in Figure 10.3 using the SPSS software. In this case, the missing category is *Medium_Size_Firm*, which is now the baseline group. The output here also confirms that medium-sized firms experience greater sales growth than small-sized firms (b = –3.29, $p<0.05$). It also allows comparison between large-sized firms and medium-sized firms, but not between large-sized firms and small-sized firms. The output in Figure 10.2 on the other hand allows this latter comparison.

It is evident from this comparison between the outputs of the two software that each software runs its own algorithm and they can differ. This actually can be avoided if we just include two of the categories for this firm size variable, as with the firm origin and year of observation variables. Therefore, understanding how software packages treat variables and generate analysis is essential when using them.

10.4.3 Incremental contribution of added variable

Figure 10.6 shows the outputs of a multiple regression model involving an additional variable relating to competition (*Comp_Int*). In Figure 10.4, *Comp_Int* is found to be negative and significant ($b = -0.315$, $p<0.05$). In other words, competition has a negative significant effect on sales growth, i.e. firms facing greater competition are experiencing smaller growth.

REGRESSION
/MISSING LISTWISE
/STATISTICS COEFF OUTS R ANOVA
/CRITERIA=PIN(.05) POUT(.10)
/NOORIGIN
/DEPENDENT Rel_Sales_Growth
/METHOD=ENTER Firm_Age No_of_Bus_Lines Sub_Triad Sub_Asia_minus_Sin_Jpn Large_Size_
Firm Medium_Size_Firm Small_Size_Firm Year95 Year96 Comp_Int.

Regression
[DataSet1]

Variables Entered/Removed[a]

Model	Variables Entered	Variables Removed	Method
1	Comp_Int, Year96, Sub_Asia_ minus_Sin_Jpn, Medium_ Size_Firm, Sub_Triad, No_of_ Bus_Lines, Year95, Firm_Age, Large_Size_Firm[b]	.	Enter

a. Dependent Variable: Rel_Sales_Growth
b. Tolerance = .000 limits reached.

Model Summary

Model	R	R Square	Adjusted R Square	Std. Error of the Estimate
1	.087[a]	.008	.006	47.9888640

a. Predictors: (Constant), Comp_Int, Year96, Sub_Asia_minus_Sin_Jpn, Medium_Size_Firm, Sub_ Triad, No_of_Bus_Lines, Year95, Firm_Age, Large_Size_Firm

ANOVA[a]

Model		Sum of Squares	df	Mean Square	F	Sig.
1	Regression	84134.986	9	9348.332	4.059	.000[b]
	Residual	11042554.450	4795	2302.931		
	Total	11126689.436	4804			

a. Dependent Variable: Rel_Sales_Growth
b. Predictors: (Constant), Comp_Int, Year96, Sub_Asia_minus_Sin_Jpn, Medium_Size_Firm, Sub_ Triad, No_of_Bus_Lines, Year95, Firm_Age, Large_Size_Firm

Coefficients[a]

Model		Unstandardized Coefficients		Standardized Coefficients	t	Sig.
		B	Std. Error	Beta		
1	(Constant)	−1.298	1.906		−.681	.496
	Firm_Age	−.207	.082	−.041	−2.526	.012
	No_of_Bus_Lines	1.177	.779	.023	1.512	.131
	Sub_Triad	1.004	1.481	.010	.678	.498
	Sub_Asia_minus_Sin_Jpn	3.580	3.507	.015	1.021	.307
	Large_Size_Firm	3.951	2.348	.029	1.682	.093
	Medium_Size_Firm	3.297	1.520	.034	2.169	.030
	Year95	2.561	1.813	.021	1.412	.158
	Year96	7.432	1.804	.062	4.119	.000
	Comp_Int	−.315	.159	−.034	-1.982	.048

a. Dependent Variable: Rel_Sales_Growth

Excluded Variables[a]

Model		Beta In	t	Sig.	Partial Correlation	Collinearity Statistics
						Tolerance
1	Small_Size_Firm	.[b]	.	.	.	.000

a. Dependent Variable: Rel_Sales_Growth
b. Predictors in the Model: (Constant), Comp_Int, Year96, Sub_Asia_minus_Sin_Jpn, Medium_Size_Firm, Sub_Triad, No_of_Bus_Lines, Year95, Firm_Age, Large_Size_Firm

Figure 10.6   Multiple linear regression outputs

As with Figure 10.3, clearly the model is significant in explaining sales growth ($F = 4.059$, $p<0.001$). However, this does not single out the contribution that *Comp_Int* makes. In order to work out this incremental contribution, it is necessary to compare the explanatory power of both models.

Since the main difference between the models is the addition of the competition variable, it can be inferred that the comparison of the two models will help work out the added contribution of the competition variable.

This difference can be calculated by: $F = \dfrac{(R_{new}^2 - R_{old}^2)/(df_{new} - df_{old})}{(1 - R_{new}^2)/(n - df_{new} - 1)}$

which follows a *F*-distribution.

In our example, $F = 52.22$ ($df_1 = 1$, $df_2 = 4{,}804$). This is significant at $p<0.001$, suggesting that the competition variable significantly adds to the contribution of the regression model in explaining sales growth.

The literature has also touched on the relative importance of predictors in multiple regression models. Johnson and LeBreton (2004) review the various methods and conclude that dominance analysis (Budescu, 1993) is a preferred option for such comparisons. Dominance analysis takes into account all possible relationships between independent variables and a dependent variable. Meng et al. (1992) also provide a formula to compare correlation coefficients. One may argue that it is never easy to compare the coefficients if the variables are not measured using the same dimensions and metric. Nonetheless, comparison methods often use standardized coefficient to reduce the effect of such incompatibility. Johnson (2000) also proposes a heuristic model to test the relative strength of predictor variables.

10.4.4 Endogeneity models

In Chapter 6, we have highlighted the self-selection bias (Heckman, 1979) that may occur when non-respondents to a survey are self-selected, i.e. possess certain common attributes or the choice of a data source rules out a particular set of firms for a sample. This self-selection bias can cause problems in any analysis around validity. Sample selection bias can be fixed through various mechanisms as also discussed in Chapter 6.

A related self-selection issue can occur in regression models when a predictor variable is linked to an outcome variable based on certain conditions that are influencing the predictor variable. For example, the effect of a firm's alliances on its performance is dependent on the firm's ability to ally in the first place, and this in turn may depend on firm performance itself. In technical terms, the predictor variable is correlated with the error terms of the model, leading to this endogeneity issue (Echambadi et al., 2006). As the authors clearly explain, the sources of self-selection and endogeneity differ – self-selection occurs when the dependent variable is observed only for a restricted, non-random sample while endogeneity surfaces around the exogeneity of a predictor variable.

In reality, many decisions are nested, therefore endogeneity models are expected to proliferate. Researchers have started to incorporate endogeneity factors into their regression models (e.g. Ang et al., 2018; Ruiz-Moreno et al., 2007; Shaver, 1998; Wolfolds and Siegel, 2019). Shaver's (1998) study of linking entry mode to performance suggests that the results from incorporating self-selection of entry mode choice are different from those without accounting for this. Likewise, Ruiz-Moreno et al. (2007) also find evidence of a two-stage process in the linkage between foreign direct investment ownership structure and diversification mode.

The Heckman two-step procedure is the most common method used to deal with endogeneity issues. But researchers are generally of the view that not a single method is the best for all circumstances (Stolzenberg and Relles, 1997), and some have expressed concerns about Heckman's two-step procedures being sensitive to violations of its assumptions about the way selection occurs (Winship and Mare, 1992; Wolfolds and Siegel, 2019). There is also added complexity regarding different factors which may affect the two stages within an endogeneity model (Ruiz-Moreno et al., 2007). Nevertheless, Heckman's methods continue to be the main procedures used, but researchers do provide other options (Stolzenberg and Relles, 1997; Winship and Mare, 1992; Wolfolds and Siegel, 2019). In essence, it is essential to use instrumental variables for any regression models involving endogeneity (Ang et al., 2018; Bascle, 2008).

10.4.5 Mediation effects in multiple linear regression

Mediation is the other commonly used technique for testing the relationships among more than two variables. This is more often seen in the more micro studies, such as those in organizational behaviour and human resource management. We have highlighted how mediation works and the various mediation relationships in Section 5.4.7 (depicted in Figure 5.3).

According to MacKinnon et al. (2002), there are 14 methods to test the **mediation effects**. The authors provide a good comparison of these methods. The most common test of full mediation are the procedures demonstrated in Baron and Kenny (1986). Let's say it is proposed that X_2 mediates the relationship between Y and X_1. For full mediation, four conditions need to be satisfied. First X_1 must have a relationship with X_2 in the predicted direction. Second, X_1 must have an effect on Y. Third, X_2 also needs to have a relationship with Y. Finally, when both X_1 and X_2 are concurrently tested in their relationships with Y, the effect of X_1 on Y is reduced as a result of the inclusion of X_2.

The Sobel test is commonly used to test the effect of the fourth condition listed above (e.g. Ang et al., 2013; Ang et al., 2017; Boxall et al., 2011; Wood et al., 2008). Seemingly unrelated regression can further be used to test the individual and collective mediation effects of multiple mediators (Ang et al., 2013; Ang et al., 2017). Subsequent research has also used the bootstrapping approach which does not make assumptions such as the normality of the change using the Sobel test (MacKinnon et al., 2002; Shrout and Bolger, 2002).

As researchers seek to unveil the unknowns embedded in the processes of business and management, there has also been additional interest in mediation effects (Shaver, 2005; Wood et al., 2008). Taylor et al. (2008) provide a good illustration of a three-path mediated model, which was also used in Ang et al. (2013), Ang et al. (2017) and Boxall et al. (2011), all in the human resource management context.

10.4.6 Interaction effects in multiple linear regression

Statistical interaction (also called moderation) occurs when the relationships between two variables change according to the value of a third variable (Aguinis, 2002; Aiken and West, 1991). We have highlighted moderation in Section 5.5 when we also cover context (Johns, 2001; Rousseau and Fried, 2001) and contingencies (Delery and Doty, 1996; Schoonhoven, 1981).

For example, suppose the relationship between X_1 and the mean of Y is $E(Y) = 2+5X_1$ when $X_2 = 0$, it is $E(Y) = 4+15X_1$ when $X_2 = 50$, and it is $E(Y) = 6+25X_1$ when $X_2 = 100$. The slope for the partial effect of X_1 changes markedly as the fixed value for X_2 changes. Then, there is an interaction between X_1 and X_2 in their effects on Y.

The most common approach in the **interaction effects** is the cross-product terms.

$$E(Y) = \alpha + \beta_1 X_1 + \beta_2 X_2 + \beta_3 X_1 X_2$$

We can rewrite the equation to:

$$E(Y) = (\alpha + \beta_2 X_2) + (\beta_1 + \beta_3 X_2) X_1 = \beta' + \beta' X_1$$

So, for fixed X_2, the mean of Y changes linearly as a function of X_1. Both the intercept and the slope depend on X_2.

Figure 10.7 shows the multiple regression analysis results when an interaction term is introduced. In this case, it is hypothesized that the effect of competition on sales growth is affected by the number of business lines that a firm participates in. In the above equation, Y = sales growth, X_1 = competition and X_2 = number of business lines.

```
REGRESSION
/MISSING LISTWISE
/STATISTICS COEFF OUTS R ANOVA
/CRITERIA=PIN(.05) POUT(.10)
/NOORIGIN
/DEPENDENT Rel_Sales_Growth
/METHOD=ENTER Firm_Age No_of_Bus_Lines Sub_Triad Sub_Asia_minus_Sin_Jpn Year95 Year96 Comp_Int ZComp_IntxBus_Lines.
```

Regression
[DataSet1]

Variables Entered/Removed[a]

Model	Variables Entered	Variables Removed	Method
1	ZComp_IntxBus_Lines, Year95, Sub_Asia_minus_Sin_Jpn, Sub_Triad, No_of_Bus_Lines, Year96, Firm_Age, Comp_Int[b]	.	Enter

a. Dependent Variable: Rel_Sales_Growth
b. All requested variables entered.

Model Summary

Model	R	R Square	Adjusted R Square	Std. Error of the Estimate
1	.086[a]	.007	.006	47.9874945

a. Predictors: (Constant), ZComp_IntxBus_Lines, Year95, Sub_Asia_minus_Sin_Jpn, Sub_Triad, No_of_Bus_Lines, Year96, Firm_Age, Comp_Int

ANOVA[a]

Model		Sum of Squares	df	Mean Square	F	Sig.
1	Regression	82462.437	8	10307.805	4.476	.000[b]
	Residual	11044226.999	4796	2302.800		
	Total	11126689.436	4804			

a. Dependent Variable: Rel_Sales_Growth
b. Predictors: (Constant), ZComp_IntxBus_Lines, Year95, Sub_Asia_minus_Sin_Jpn, Sub_Triad, No_of_Bus_Lines, Year96, Firm_Age, Comp_Int

Coefficients[a]

Model		Unstandardized Coefficients		Standardized Coefficients	t	Sig.
		B	Std. Error	Beta		
1	(Constant)	1.975	1.992		.991	.322
	Firm_Age	−.178	.082	−.035	−2.181	.029
	No_of_Bus_Lines	1.033	.787	.020	1.312	.190
	Sub_Triad	1.638	1.469	.016	1.115	.265
	Sub_Asia_minus_Sin_Jpn	3.480	3.506	.014	.993	.321
	Year95	2.513	1.813	.021	1.386	.166
	Year96	7.312	1.804	.061	4.053	.000
	Comp_Int	−.902	.327	−.097	−2.759	.006
	ZComp_IntxBus_Lines	1.300	.591	.076	2.199	.028

a. Dependent Variable: Rel_Sales_Growth

Figure 10.7   Interaction effects in multiple linear regression

IBM® SPSS®. Reprint Courtesy of International Business Machines Corporation, © International Business Machines Corporation.

IBM, the IBM logo, ibm.com, and SPSS are trademarks or registered trademarks of **International Business Machines Corporation**, registered in many jurisdictions worldwide. Other product and service names might be trademarks of IBM or other companies. A current list of IBM trademarks is available on the Web at IBM Copyright and trademark information at www.ibm.com/legal/copytrade.shtml.

In order to test the interaction effect, we calculate the cross-product term, i.e. X_1X_2. This interaction term is represented by the variable *ZComp_IntxBus_Lines* in Figure 10.7. In Figure 10.7, the term *ZComp_IntxBus_Lines* is shown to have a positive significant effect on sales growth ($b = 1.300$, $p<0.05$). In addition, it is also observed that the coefficient of *Comp_Int* continues to have a negative direct impact on sales growth with the addition of *ZComp_IntxBus_Lines*, though it is less significant in comparison to Figure 10.6. The interpretation is that the negative effect of competition on sales growth increases as the number of business lines increases. In other words, the competition–sales growth relationship is more negative for firms involved in more business lines.

This illustration has used a metric type variable as the interaction term. When it comes to using a dummy variable as an interaction term, extra caution is needed.

Yip and Tsang (2007) provide a good guideline on the use of dummy variables as interaction terms. As noted in Cohen (1983) and Maxwell and Delaney (1993), dichotomizing variables can lead to false significance and the loss of statistical power. Therefore, as far as possible, when an interaction variable is metric, always try to use the interaction term created from the product of the original variables rather than splitting the sample.

Given the complexity of business and management research, it is not surprising to see more and more studies testing interaction effects among variables. Other than interaction effects, one can also use piecewise or spline regressions when there is belief that the regression line might differ across segments within the sample. With piecewise regression, you code a dummy variable that segregates cases into segments, and the product of this dummy variable with the independent variable captures the difference in slopes (this is also covered in Yip and Tsang, 2007). Spline regression (Marsh and Cormier, 2001) is useful when it is not clear where the cut-off of the segments might be. Spline regression uses non-linear estimation methods to locate the points on the X-axis where the slope changes.

The measuring of **moderation effects** has also reached a high level of complexity. It is now widely recognized that the interaction effects can be tested in multiple stages (Ang, 2008; Haans et al., 2016). The theorizing of moderation can be complex alone given the extent to which we also observe a lot more 'too-much-of-a-good-thing' effect of behaviours and activities in the sense that even the benefits of desirable behaviours and activities can reach a plateau or even turn negative (Pierce and Aguinis, 2013). Likewise, when supply and demand becomes imbalanced, a desirable option may no longer be available (e.g. Ang, 2008). Thus, the observation of complex multi-way inter-action effects start to become more common (Ang, 2008; Dawson, 2014; Haans et al., 2016). While multi-way interactions come closer to reality, their theorizing is diffi-cult and normally not well done (Gardner et al., 2017; Haans e al., 2016). A lot more precision will be necessary to ensure that moderating effects are theorized and tested effectively, such as with the use of inflection points (Ang, 2008; Haans et al., 2016).

In Section 7.7 when we discussed archival data collection, Figure 7.3 was presented showing data collected from multiple sources. You will also notice that these data col-lected are on different levels, e.g. country, industry and firm level, all within a single study. The fact that decisions made by firms will likely be influenced by country and industry factors causes the decisions to be nested in all likelihood. We have briefly touched on this in the endogeneity models section. But analytically, what it also means is the need to recognize this nested effect on decisions, hence the advent of the **multilevel analysis**. Some good examples of the use of multilevel analysis that will assist you in either making an assessment to conduct multilevel analysis or not, or what to do should you need to do one, can be found in Ang et al. (2015), Bliese et al. (2007), Li et al. (2020) and Staw et al. (1981).

10.5 REGRESSION MODELS WITH NOMINAL DEPENDENT VARIABLE

There are several common regression analyses that are used when the research involves **nominal dependent variables** (Lloyd, 1999). These include the logistic, the logit and the probit regression analysis. The basic mechanisms for these methods are the same. As such, this section will cover only one of these commonly used methods – the logistic regression (Hosmer and Lemeshow, 2000).

The logistic regression is the statistical technique used when the dependent variable in a multiple regression model is dichotomous (e.g. head or tail). In logistic regression, the probability of an event (dependent variable) occurring is estimated. The relationship between this probability and the independent variables is non-linear and takes the form:

$$\text{Logit}(Y) = \alpha + \beta_1 X_1 + \beta_2 X_2 + \ldots + \beta_k X_k$$

The 'log odds' of each probability is tested for linear associations with a vector of covariates X_i. The parameter vector β_i of the model is estimated using the maximum-likelihood method (unlike the linear regression model that uses the least-squares method), i.e. the coefficients that make the observed results 'most likely' are selected. Since the logistic regression is non-linear, an iterative algorithm is necessary for parameter estimation.

Figures 10.8 and 10.9 show logistic regression outputs. Figure 10.8 presents the baseline model that includes only the control variables while Figure 10.9 shows the full model with an additional variable competition. The analysis here uses the same dataset used in our earlier illustration of the multiple linear regression model. However, this time around the dependent variable here is whether a firm is engaged in a collaboration ($Y = 1$) or not ($Y = 0$).

LOGISTIC REGRESSION VARIABLES Coll_Yes_or_No
/METHOD=ENTER Firm_Age No_of_Bus_Lines Sub_Triad Sub_Asia_minus_Sin_Jpn Large_Size_Firm Medium_Size_Firm Small_Size_Firm Year95 Year96/
CRITERIA=PIN(.05) POUT(.10) ITERATE(20) CUT(.5).

Logistic Regression
[DataSet1]

Case Processing Summary

Unweighted Cases[a]		N	Percent
Selected Cases	Included in Analysis	4805	100.0
	Missing Cases	0	.0
	Total	4805	100.0
Unselected Cases		0	.0
Total		4805	100.0

a. If weight is in effect, see classification table for the total number of cases.

(Continued)

Figure 10.8   (Continued)

Dependent Variable Encoding	
Original Value	Internal Value
0	0
1	1

Block 0: Beginning Block

Classification Table[a],[b]

Observed			Predicted		
			Coll_Yes_or_No		Percentage Correct
			0	1	
Step 0	Coll_Yes_or_No	0	4501	0	100.0
		1	304	0	.0
	Overall Percentage				93.7

a. Constant is included in the model.
b. The cut value is .500

Variables in the Equation

		B	S.E.	Wald	df	Sig.	Exp(B)
Step 0	Constant	−2.695	.059	2068.309	1	.000	.068

Variables not in the Equation[a]

			Score	df	Sig.
Step 0	Variables	Firm_Age	28.125	1	.000
		No_of_Bus_Lines	163.774	1	.000
		Sub_Triad	46.036	1	.000
		Sub_Asia_minus_Sin_Jpn	.647	1	.421
		Large_Size_Firm	271.949	1	.000
		Medium_Size_Firm	1.059	1	.303
		Small_Size_Firm	116.679	1	.000
		Year95	.353	1	.552
		Year96	11.031	1	.001

a. Residual Chi-Squares are not computed because of redundancies.

Block 1: Method = Enter

Omnibus Tests of Model Coefficients

		Chi-square	df	Sig.
Step 1	Step	455.021	8	.000
	Block	455.021	8	.000
	Model	455.021	8	.000

Model Summary

Step	-2 Log likelihood	Cox & Snell R Square	Nagelkerke R Square
1	1811.640[a]	.090	.240

a. Estimation terminated at iteration number 7 because parameter estimates changed by less than .001.

Classification Table[a]

	Observed		Predicted		
			Coll_Yes_or_No		Percentage Correct
			0	1	
Step 1	Coll_Yes_or_No	0	4482	19	99.6
		1	280	24	7.9
	Overall Percentage				93.8

a. The cut value is .500

Variables in the Equation

		B	S.E.	Wald	df	Sig.	Exp(B)
Step 1[a]	Firm_Age	.004	.006	.380	1	.538	1.004
	No_of_Bus_Lines	.471	.056	70.365	1	.000	1.601
	Sub_Triad	-1.459	.164	78.981	1	.000	.232
	Sub_Asia_minus_Sin_Jpn	-.623	.356	3.059	1	.080	.536
	Large_Size_Firm	2.968	.220	182.131	1	.000	19.458
	Medium_Size_Firm	1.343	.210	40.781	1	.000	3.830
	Year95	-.275	.169	2.666	1	.103	.759
	Year96	-.739	.193	14.660	1	.000	.477
	Constant	-4.515	.224	406.929	1	.000	.011

a. Variable(s) entered on step 1: Firm_Age, No_of_Bus_Lines, Sub_Triad, Sub_Asia_minus_Sin_Jpn, Large_Size_Firm, Medium_Size_Firm, Year95, Year96.

Figure 10.8   Logistic regression outputs – baseline model

IBM® SPSS®. Reprint Courtesy of International Business Machines Corporation, © International Business Machines Corporation.

IBM, the IBM logo, ibm.com, and SPSS are trademarks or registered trademarks of **International Business Machines Corporation**, registered in many jurisdictions worldwide. Other product and service names might be trademarks of IBM or other companies. A current list of IBM trademarks is available on the Web at IBM Copyright and trademark information at www.ibm.com/legal/copytrade.shtml.

LOGISTIC REGRESSION VARIABLES Coll_Yes_or_No
/METHOD=ENTER Firm_Age No_of_Bus_Lines Sub_Triad Sub_Asia_minus_Sin_Jpn Large_Size_Firm Medium_Size_Firm Small_Size_Firm Year95 Year96 Comp_Int
/CRITERIA=PIN(.05) POUT(.10) ITERATE(20) CUT(.5).

Logistic Regression
[DataSet1]

Case Processing Summary

Unweighted Cases[a]		N	Percent
Selected Cases	Included in Analysis	4805	100.0
	Missing Cases	0	.0
	Total	4805	100.0
Unselected Cases		0	.0
Total		4805	100.0

a. If weight is in effect, see classification table for the total number of cases.

Dependent Variable Encoding

Original Value	Internal Value
0	0
1	1

Block 0: Beginning Block

Classification Table[a,b]

	Observed			Predicted		
				Coll_Yes_or_No		Percentage Correct
				0	1	
Step 0	Coll_Yes_or_No		0	4501	0	100.0
			1	304	0	.0
	Overall Percentage					93.7

a. Constant is included in the model.
b. The cut value is .500

Variables in the Equation

		B	S.E.	Wald	df	Sig.	Exp(B)
Step 0	Constant	−2.695	.059	2068.309	1	.000	.068

Variables not in the Equation[a]

			Score	df	Sig.
Step 0	Variables	Firm_Age	28.125	1	.000
		No_of_Bus_Lines	163.774	1	.000
		Sub_Triad	46.036	1	.000

			Score	df	Sig.
		Sub_Asia_minus_Sin_Jpn	.647	1	.421
		Large_Size_Firm	271.949	1	.000
		Medium_Size_Firm	1.059	1	.303
		Small_Size_Firm	116.679	1	.000
		Year95	.353	1	.552
		Year96	11.031	1	.001
		Comp_Int	257.826	1	.000

a. Residual Chi-Squares are not computed because of redundancies.

Block 1: Method = Enter

Omnibus Tests of Model Coefficients

		Chi-square	df	Sig.
Step 1	Step	485.713	9	.000
	Block	485.713	9	.000
	Model	485.713	9	.000

Model Summary

Step	-2 Log likelihood	Cox & Snell R Square	Nagelkerke R Square
1	1780.949[a]	.096	.256

a. Estimation terminated at iteration number 7 because parameter estimates changed by less than .001.

Classification Table[a]

	Observed		Predicted		
			Coll_Yes_or_No		Percentage Correct
			0	1	
Step 1	Coll_Yes_or_No	0	4479	22	99.5
		1	273	31	10.2
	Overall Percentage				93.9

a. The cut value is .500

Variables in the Equation

		B	S.E.	Wald	df	Sig.	Exp(B)
Step 1[a]	Firm_Age	−.012	.007	3.004	1	.083	.988
	No_of_Bus_Lines	.441	.058	57.739	1	.000	1.554
	Sub_Triad	−1.587	.173	84.307	1	.000	.205
	Sub_Asia_minus_Sin_Jpn	−.522	.355	2.160	1	.142	.593
	Large_Size_Firm	2.757	.225	150.017	1	.000	15.750
	Medium_Size_Firm	1.375	.210	42.767	1	.000	3.957

(Continued)

Figure 10.9   (Continued)

	B	S.E.	Wald	df	Sig.	Exp(B)
Year95	−.257	.171	2.253	1	.133	.773
Year96	−.718	.196	13.390	1	.000	.488
Comp_Int	.049	.009	31.164	1	.000	1.051
Constant	−4.359	.226	370.589	1	.000	.013

a. Variable(s) entered on step 1: Firm_Age, No_of_Bus_Lines, Sub_Triad, Sub_Asia_minus_Sin_Jpn, Large_Size_Firm, Medium_Size_Firm, Year95, Year96, Comp_Int.

Figure 10.9   Logistic regression outputs – full model

IBM® SPSS®. Reprint Courtesy of International Business Machines Corporation, © International Business Machines Corporation.

IBM, the IBM logo, ibm.com, and SPSS are trademarks or registered trademarks of **International Business Machines Corporation**, registered in many jurisdictions worldwide. Other product and service names might be trademarks of IBM or other companies. A current list of IBM trademarks is available on the Web at IBM Copyright and trademark information at www.ibm.com/legal/copytrade.shtml.

To assess the goodness of fit in a logistic regression model, one can examine how likely the sample is observed, given the parameter estimates. The probability of the observed results given the parameter estimates is known as the likelihood. It is customary to use −2 times the log of the likelihood (−2 Log Likelihood) as a measure of how well the estimated model fits the data. This is presented under model summary in the figures. A good model is one that results in a high likelihood of the observed results. This translates to a small value for −2 Log Likelihood.

Under the null hypothesis that the model fits perfectly, −2 Log Likelihood has a chi-square distribution with $N - k$ degrees of freedom, where N is the number of cases and k is the number of parameters estimated. The significance of the model can be found under the heading of omnibus tests of model coefficients. In essence, the significance presented here is also a reflection of the significance of the value of −2 Log Likelihood.

To test the significance of a second model over the first, in this case the contribution of the added variable *Comp_Int*, the difference of the −2 Log Likelihood value of the models is taken. This difference has degrees of freedom equal to the difference of the two models' degrees of freedom and follows the chi-square distribution. In our example, the difference in the −2 Log Likelihood values is (1811.640 − 1780.949) = 30.691 with $df = 1$. Referring to any chi-square table, we have $p<0.001$. In addition, the coefficient of *Comp_Int* is shown to be highly significant ($e^{0.049}$, $p<0.001$). Thus, the added contribution of *Comp_Int* is highly significant. It is noted here that unlike the case of multiple linear regression, the coefficient value reflected in the table is not the actual effect of the predictor variable on the dependent variable. The actual effect takes the value of $e^{coefficient}$.

Kleinbaum et al. (2002) provide a good step-by-step guide to logistic regression, while Peng et al. (2002) provide a good set of guidelines on what is expected of researchers who use the logistic regression when it comes to the analysis and reporting.

10.6 REGRESSION MODELS WITH COUNT DEPENDENT VARIABLE

Count variables (e.g. number of children) do not really follow the normal distribution that a dependent variable for multiple linear regression assumes. As such, using the multiple linear regression model to analyze relationships involving **count-dependent variables** can lead to inefficient, inconsistent and biased estimates (Cameron and Trivedi, 1998; Coxe et al., 2009).

The Poisson regression model is the most basic model as far as analyzing count variables is concerned. The other key count model is the negative binomial regression model, which caters to situations where there are a large number of zeros in the count observations (Gardner et al., 1995). Long (1997) provides a good comparison of four regression models for count-dependent variables, namely the Poisson, the negative binomial, the zero-inflated Poisson and the zero-inflated negative binomial.

We illustrate here using the Poisson regression model. The probability of an occurrence using a Poisson regression model is determined by a Poisson distribution, where the mean of the distribution is a function of the independent variables. A critical assumption of a Poisson process is that events are independent. This means that the chance that an event occurs is not dependent on previous events that occurred.

Figures 10.10 and 10.11 show the outputs from the Poisson regression analysis. Figure 10.10 presents the baseline model while Figure 10.11 shows the full model. The dependent variable in these cases is the number of collaborations that a firm engages in. The Poisson regression model also uses the Log Likelihood algorithm. As you can see from Figure 10.10, the statistical output reports the Log Likelihood (−1763.105) and the LR chi-square (1202.37) values and the significance of the model 'Prob > chi 2'.

In Figure 10.11, it is found that *Comp_Int* has a positive significant effect on the number of collaborations at $p<0.001$. For the significance of the added contribution, again we refer back to the difference in the models' explanatory power. The difference is $(1249.28 - 1202.37) = 46.91$ with $df = 1$. Using the chi-square table, this is highly significant.

```
. poisson No_of_Coll Firm_Age No_of_Bus_Lines Sub_Triad Sub_Asia_minus_Sin_Jpn Large_Size_
> Firm Medium_Size_Firm Small_Size_Firm Year95 Year96
note: Small_Size_Firm omitted because of collinearity


Iteration 0:   log likelihood = -1971.5511
Iteration 1:   log likelihood = -1765.7986
Iteration 2:   log likelihood = -1763.1122
Iteration 3:   log likelihood =  -1763.105
Iteration 4:   log likelihood =  -1763.105
```

Poisson regression		Number of obs	=	4805
		LR chi2(8)	=	1202.37
		Prob > chi2	=	0.0000
Log likelihood = -1763.105		Pseudo R2	=	0.2543

No_of_Coll	Coef.	Std. Err.	z	P>|z|	[95% Conf. Interval]	
Firm_Age	.0066662	.0030633	2.18	0.030	.0006623	.01267
No_of_Bus_Lines	.426748	.0304364	14.02	0.000	.3670938	.4864022
Sub_Triad	-1.753509	.1249816	-14.03	0.000	-1.998469	-1.50855
Sub_Asia_minus_Sin_Jpn	-1.077605	.2811447	-3.83	0.000	-1.628638	-.5265714
Large_Size_Firm	2.96203	.1659432	17.85	0.000	2.636787	3.287273
Medium_Size_Firm	1.623736	.164344	9.88	0.000	1.301628	1.945845
Small_Size_Firm	0	(omitted)				
Year95	-.2119317	.1048371	-2.02	0.043	-.4174087	-.0064547
Year96	-.4436065	.1141803	-3.89	0.000	-.6673958	-.2198172
_cons	-4.115569	.1673583	-24.59	0.000	-4.443585	-3.787553

Figure 10.10   Poisson regression outputs – baseline model

© Copyright 1996–2020 StataCorp LLC.

```
. poisson No_of_Coll Firm_Age No_of_Bus_Lines Sub_Triad Sub_Asia_minus_Sin_Jpn Large_Size_
> Firm Medium_Size_Firm Small_Size_Firm Year95 Year96 Comp_Int
note: Small_Size_Firm omitted because of collinearity


Iteration 0:   log likelihood = -4771.6472
Iteration 1:   log likelihood = -3126.1583
Iteration 2:   log likelihood = -2580.8566
Iteration 3:   log likelihood = -1794.9131
Iteration 4:   log likelihood = -1743.1214
Iteration 5:   log likelihood = -1739.6594
Iteration 6:   log likelihood = -1739.6488
Iteration 7:   log likelihood = -1739.6488
```

Poisson regression		Number of obs	=	4805
		LR chi2(9)	=	1249.28
		Prob > chi2	=	0.0000
Log likelihood = -1739.6488		Pseudo R2	=	0.2642

No_of_Coll	Coef.	Std. Err.	z	P>|z|	[95% Conf. Interval]	
Firm_Age	-.0070838	.0034603	-2.05	0.041	-.0138658	-.0003018
No_of_Bus_Lines	.3751569	.0312499	12.01	0.000	.3139082	.4364056
Sub_Triad	-1.805679	.1261769	-14.31	0.000	-2.052981	-1.558377
Sub_Asia_minus_Sin_Jpn	-.9774349	.2815582	-3.47	0.001	-1.529279	-.4255908
Large_Size_Firm	2.802828	.1690645	16.58	0.000	2.471468	3.134188
Medium_Size_Firm	1.671273	.1642663	10.17	0.000	1.349317	1.993229
Small_Size_Firm	0	(omitted)				
Year95	-.2038655	.1049785	-1.94	0.052	-.4096196	.0018886
Year96	-.4038249	.1142716	-3.53	0.000	-.6277932	-.1798567
Comp_Int	.0305841	.0042315	7.23	0.000	.0222904	.0388777
_cons	-3.909989	.1694464	-23.08	0.000	-4.242098	-3.57788

Figure 10.11   Poisson regression outputs – full model

© Copyright 1996–2020 StataCorp LLC.

10.7 QUANTITATIVE ANALYSIS SOFTWARE

There is no shortage of software for the analysis of quantitative data. Back in the 1990s, quantitative analysis software often required the researcher to learn some type of programming language in order to get the software to execute the required command. These days, most of the software are preprogrammed to do that, and only require the researcher to use some simple syntax if they choose to vary from the standard analysis.

The SPSS Statistics package is becoming the most commonly used quantitative analysis software in the marketing and psychology areas. Because of its origin in the social sciences, it is widely used for analysis of survey data. **SAS** and **STATA** are two other quantitative analysis software packages commonly used in business and management. Like SPSS, both are user-friendly. These packages also tend to cover a wider range of analytical tools, modelling in particular. Partly as a result, both provide extensive documentation to allow researchers to vary their conditions when analyzing their data.

As mentioned earlier in the coding process, it is important for you to decide which software you want to use before finalizing all the coding. As these softwares try to preprogram as much as they can to make analysis easier for the user, this does influence what kind of data they read and in what form. For example, coding a categorial variable with three options into a single column may work in one software but not another. Likewise, it may work in one type of analysis within a software package but yet does not fit the data expectation of another type of analysis (in which case the tool might be looking for three dummy variables represented by three columns) in the same software. Therefore, make sure you understand what each of these programs expects before you decide what to use and before you code your data.

Acock (2005) provides a good comparison of SAS, STATA and SPSS. The UCLA Institute for Digital Research & Education Statistical Consulting (n.d.) also provides a good source for using these softwares to conduct different statistical tests. If you search the Web for statistical software, you will also find a huge list of packages that cater to different types of **data analysis**. It is worthwhile to remind again that even when a researcher is familiar with a software tool, they should not let the analytical methods be guided by the comfort of use and hence decide how the analysis be conducted based on what this particular tool provides. I recall I had to learn three software packages to conduct an analysis related to the paper Ang et al. (2015) in order to iron out the nitty-gritty of the multilevel analysis that we use in that paper. In this analysis, the three softwares also provided slightly different results for the same statistical analysis, leading me back to the assumptions made in each one. Further, as also mentioned earlier, it is essential to know the background of the methods before using the software tools, as otherwise interpretations of findings can be a mechanical exercise rather than one that is driven by rigorous theory with statistical support.

KEY TERMS

- Analysis of variance (ANOVA)
- Autocorrelation
- Control variable
- Count dependent variable
- Data analysis
- Data transformation
- Dependent variable
- Endogeneity
- Interaction effect
- Logistic regression
- Mediation effect
- Moderation effect

- Multicollinearity
- Multilevel analysis
- Multiple linear regression analysis
- Nominal dependent variable
- Poisson regression
- Predictor variable
- Regression models
- Residual analysis
- SAS
- Self-selection
- SPSS
- STATA

SUMMARY

- Quantitative analysis is useful for establishing a general relationship between two constructs with the help of a large number of observations.
- Data are coded differently for analysis, at times depending on the statistical software used.
- Transformation of data is often needed to reduce the effect of extreme values.
- Regression models are often classified based on the type of dependent variable used.
- The outputs from different software can be different although the fundamentals of analysis are the same.
- Residual analysis is used to detect if the relationship between constructs is not linear.
- Autocorrelation occurs when the residuals are correlated across time.
- Dropping a variable, changing the form of the model and increasing sample size are some remedial measures for dealing with multicollinearity issues.
- Mediation occurs when the relationship between two variables necessarily has to go through a pathway involving a third variable.
- Interaction or moderation occurs when the relationship between two variables changes depending on the value of a third variable.
- Multilevel analysis is needed when decisions are nested within multiple levels of data.
- The most commonly used quantitative statistical software packages are SAS, SPSS and STATA.

QUESTIONS

1. Highlight a few ways in which data can be transformed.
2. Draw a typical roadmap that allows a researcher to decide on the type of analytical methods to use.

3. How does a researcher assess the effect of an independent variable on a dependent variable? Discuss with the help of an example.
4. How can a researcher check for multicollinearity? How can multicollinearity be avoided if there are concerns?
5. How does a researcher test the incremental contribution of an added variable in multiple linear regression? How is that different in logistic regression?
6. Compare and contrast the use of interaction and mediation effects in studies.
7. Compare and contrast regression models with nominal dependent variables and regression models with count dependent variables.

ADDITIONAL READINGS

Statistical software

SAS: www.statisticssolutions.com/statistical-analysis-software-sas/
STATA: www.stata.com
SPSS: www.ibm.com/uk-en/analytics/spss-statistics-software
General listing: https://en.wikipedia.org/wiki/List_of_statistical_software

Abelson, R.P. (1985) 'A variance explanation paradox: When a little is a lot', *Psychological Bulletin*, 97 (1): 129–33.

Abelson, R.P. (1997) 'On the surprising longevity of flogged horses: Why there is a case for the significance test', *Psychological Science*, 8 (1): 12–5.

Aguinis, H. and Beaty, J.C. (2005) 'Effect size and power in assessing moderating effects of categorical variables using multiple regression: A 30-year review', *Journal of Applied Psychology*, 90 (1): 94–107.

Aguinis, H., Edwards, J.R. and Bradley, K.J. (2013) 'Improving our understanding of moderation and mediation in strategic management research', *Organizational Research Methods*, 20 (4): 665–85.

Aguinis, H. and Stone-Romero, E.F. (1997) 'Methodological artefacts in moderated multiple regression and their effects on statistical power', *Journal of Applied Psychology*, 82 (1): 192–206.

Alcácer, J., Chung, W., Hawk, A. and Pacheco-de-Almeida, G. (2018) 'Applying random coefficient models to strategy research: identifying and exploring firm heterogeneous effects', *Strategy Science*, 3 (3): 533–53.

Amore, M.D. and Murtinu, S. (2019) 'Tobit models in strategy research: Critical issues and applications', *Global Strategy Journal*, in press. doi.org/10.1002/gsj.1363

Antonakis, J., Bendahan, S., Jacquart, P. and Lalive, R. (2010) 'On making causal claims: A review and recommendations', *The Leadership Quarterly*, 21 (6): 1086–120.

Becker, C. and Gather, U. (1999) 'The masking breakdown point of multivariate outlier identification rules', *Journal of the American Statistical Association*, 94 (447): 947–55.

Bliese, P.D. and Ployhart, R.E. (2002) 'Growth modeling using random coefficient models: Model building, testing, and illustrations', *Organizational Research Methods*, 5 (4): 362–87.

Chin, H.C. and Quddus, M.A.I (2003) 'Modeling count data with excess zeroes: an empirical application to traffic accidents', *Sociological Methods and Research*, 32 (1): 90–116.

Chow, S.L. (1988) 'Significance test or effect size?', *Psychological Bulletin*, 103 (1): 105–10.

Dalal, D.K. and Zickar, M.J. (2012) 'Some common myths about centering predictor variables in moderated multiple regression and polynomial regression', *Organizational Research Methods*, 15 (3): 339–62.

Denton, F.T. (1985) 'Data mining as an industry', *Review of Economics and Statistics*, 67 (1): 124–7.

Dielman, T.E. (1989) *Pooled Cross-sectional and Time Series Data Analysis*. New York, NY: Marcel Dekker.

Echambadi, R. and Hess, J.D. (2007) 'Mean-centering does not alleviate collinearity problems in moderated multiple regression models', *Marketing Science*, 26 (3): 438–45.

Edwards, J.R. and Lambert, L.S. (2007) 'Methods for integrating moderation and mediation: a general analytical framework using moderated path analysis', *Psychological Methods*, 12 (1): 1–22.

Fern, E.F. and Monroe, K.B. (1996) 'Effect-size estimates: Issues and problems in interpretation', *Journal of Consumer Research*, 23 (2): 89–105.

Glick, W.H. (1985) 'Conceptualizing and measuring organizational and psychological climate: pitfalls in multilevel research', *Academy of Management Review*, 10 (3): 601–16.

Green, B.F. and Hall, J.A. (1984) 'Quantitative methods for literature reviews', *Annual Review of Psychology*, 35: 37–53.

Grubbs, F.E. (1969) 'Procedures for detecting outlying observations in samples', *Technometrics*, 11 (1): 1–21.

Hayes, A.F. (2015) 'An index and test of linear moderated mediation', *Multivariate Behavioral Research*, 50 (1), 1–22.

Holland, S.J., Shore, D.B. and Cortina, J.M. (2017) 'Review and recommendations for integrating mediation and moderation', *Organizational Research Methods*, 20 (4): 686–720.

Iversen, G.R. and Norpoth, H. (1976) *Analysis of Variance*. Beverly Hills, CA: Sage Publishing.

Iyengar, R.J. and Zampelli, E.M. (2009) 'Self-selection, endogeneity, and the relationship between CEO duality and firm performance', *Strategic Management Journal*, 30 (10): 1092–112.

Jaccard, J.J. and Turrisi, R. (2003) *Interaction Effects in Multiple Regression*, (2nd edition). Thousand Oaks, CA: Sage Publishing.

James, L.R. and Brett, J.M. (1984) 'Mediators, moderators, and tests for mediation', *Journal of Applied Psychology*, 69 (2): 307–21.

Kaplan, D. (ed.) (2004) *The Sage Handbook of Quantitative Methodology for the Social Sciences*. Thousand Oaks, CA: Sage Publishing.

Kenny, D.A. (1996) 'Models of non-independence in dyadic research', *Journal of Social and Personal Relationships*, 13 (2): 279–94.

Kenny, D.A. and Judd, C.M. (1986) 'Consequences of violating the independence assumption in analysis of variance', *Psychological Bulletin*, 99 (3): 422–31.

Langford, I.H. and Lewis, T. (1998) 'Outliers in multilevel data', *Journal of the Royal Statistical Society. Series A*, 161 (2): 121–60.

Lindner, T., Puck, J. and Verbeke, A. (2020) 'Misconceptions about multicollinearity in international business research: Identification, consequences, and remedies. *Journal of International Business Studies*, 51 (3): 283–98.

MacCullum, R.C. and Mar, C.M. (1995) 'Distinguishing between moderator and quadratic effects in multiple regression', *Psychological Bulletin*, 118 (3): 405–21.

MacKinnon, D.P., Fairchild, A.J. and Fritz, M.S. (2007) 'Mediation analysis', *Annual Review of Psychology*, 58: 593–614.

Meyer, A.D., Tsui, A.S. and Hinings, C.R. (1993) 'Configurational approaches to organizational analysis', *Academy of Management Journal*, 36 (6): 1175–95.

Murphy, K.R. and Russell, C.J. (2017) 'Mend it or end it: Redirecting the search for interactions in the organizational sciences', *Organizational Research Methods*, 20 (4): 549–73.

Nielsen, B.B. and Raswant, A. (2018) 'The selection, use, and reporting of control variables in international business research: A review and recommendations', *Journal of World Business*, 53 (6): 958–68.

Ployhart, R.E. and Vandenberg, R.J. (2010) 'Longitudinal research: The theory, design, and analysis of change', *Journal of Management*, 36(1): 94–120.

Preacher, K.J., Rucker, D.D. and Hayes, A.F. (2007) 'Addressing moderated mediation hypotheses: Theory, methods, and prescriptions', *Multivariate Behavioral Research*, 42 (1), 185–227.

Prentice, D.A. and Miller, D.T. (1992) 'When small effects are impressive', *Psychological Bulletin*, 112 (1): 160–4.

Press, S.J. and Wilson, S. (1978) 'Choosing between logistic regression and discriminant analysis', *Journal of the American Statistical Association*, 73 (364): 699–705.

Rosenthal, R. and DiMatteo, M.R. (2001) 'Meta-analysis: Recent developments in quantitative methods for literature reviews', *Annual Review of Psychology*, 52: 59–82.

Sawyer, A.G. and Ball, A.D. (1981) 'Statistical power and effect size in marketing research', *Journal of Marketing Research*, 18 (3): 275–90.

Simmons, J.P., Nelson, L.D. and Simonsohn, U. (2011) 'False-positive psychology: undisclosed flexibility in data collection and analysis allows presenting anything as significant', *Psychological Science*, 22 (11): 1359–66.

Simonsohn, U., Nelson, L.D. and Simmons, J.P. (2014) 'P-curve: a key to the file-drawer', *Journal of Experimental Psychology*, 143 (2): 534–47.

Sorescu, A., Warren, N.L. and Ertekin, L. (2017) 'Event study methodology in the marketing literature: an overview', *Journal of the Academy of Marketing Science*, 45 (2): 186–207.

Stanley, T.D. (2001) 'Wheat from chaff: Meta-analysis as quantitative literature review', *Journal of Economic Perspectives*, 15 (3): 131–50.

Venkatraman, N. and Prescott, J.E. (1990) 'Environment-strategy coalignment: An empirical test of its performance implications', *Strategic Management Journal*, 11 (1): 1–23.

Yeaton, W.H. and Sechrest, L. (1981) 'Meaningful measures of effect', *Journal of Consulting and Clinical Psychology*, 49 (5): 766–7.

Yuan, K.-H. and Zhong, X. (2008) 'Outliers, leverage observations, and influential cases in factor analysis: Using robust procedures to minimize their effect', *Sociological Methodology*, 38: 329–68.

REFERENCES

Acock, A.C. (2005) 'SAS, Stata, SPSS: A comparison', *Journal of Marriage and Family*, 67 (4): 1093–5.

Aguinis, H. (2002) 'Estimation of interaction effects in organization studies', *Organizational Research Methods*, 5 (3): 207–11.

Aguinis, H., Gottfredson, R.K. and Joo, H. (2013) 'Best-practice recommendations for defin-ing, identifying, and handling outliers', *Organizational Research Methods*, 16 (2): 270–301.

Aiken, L.S. and West, S.G. (1991) *Multiple Regression: Testing and Interpreting Interactions*. Newbury Park, CA: Sage Publishing.

Ang, S.H. (2008) 'The impact of firm competitive intensity and collaboration on firm growth in different technological environments', *Strategic Management Journal*, 29 (10): 1057–75.

Ang, S.H., Bartram, T., McNeil, N., Leggat, S.G. and Stanton, P. (2013) 'The effects of high-performance work systems on hospital employees' work attitudes and intention to leave: A multi-level and occupational group analysis', *International Journal of Human Resource Management*, 24 (16): 3086–114.

Ang, S.H., Benischke, M.H. and Doh, J.P. (2015) 'The interactions of institutions on foreign market entry mode', *Strategic Management Journal*, 36 (10): 1536–53.

Ang, S.H., Benischke, M.H. and Hooi, A.W.-L. (2018) 'Frequency of international expansion through high control market expansion modes and interlocked directorships', *Journal of World Business*, 53 (4): 493–503.

Ang, S.H., Cavanagh, J., Southcombe, A., Bartram, T., Marjoribanks, T. and McNeil, N. (2017) 'Human resource management, social connectedness and health and well-being of older and retired men: the role of Men's Sheds', *International Journal of Human Resource Management*, 28 (14): 1986–2016.

Atinc, G., Simmering, M.J. and Kroll, M.J. (2012) 'Control variable use and reporting in macro and micro management research', *Organizational Research Methods*, 15 (1): 57–74.

Baron, R.M. and Kenny, D.A. (1986) 'The moderator–mediator variable distinction in social psychological research: Conceptual, strategic, and statistical considerations', *Journal of Personality and Social Psychology*, 51 (6): 1173–82.

Bascle, G. (2008) 'Controlling for endogeneity with instrumental variables in strategic man-agement research', *Strategic Organization*, 6 (3): 285–327.

Becker, T.E. (2005) 'Potential problems in the statistical control of variables in organizational research: A qualitative analysis with recommendations', *Organizational Research Methods*, 8 (3): 274–89.

Bettis, R.A. (2012) 'The search for asterisks: Compromised statistical tests and flawed theo-ries', *Strategic Management Journal*, 33 (1): 108–13.

Bliese, P.D., Chan, D. and Ployhart, R.E. (2017) 'Multilevel methods: Future directions in measurement, longitudinal analyses, and nonnormal outcomes', *Organizational Research Methods*, 10 (4): 551–63.

Box, G.E.P. and Cox, D.R. (1964) 'An analysis of transformations', *Journal of the Royal Statistical Society: Series B (Methodological)*, 26 (2): 211–46.

Boxall, P., Ang, S.H. and Bartram, T. (2011) 'Analysing the "black box" of HRM: Uncovering HR goals, mediators and outcomes in a standardized service environment', *Journal of Management Studies*, 48 (7): 1504–32.

Budescu, D.V. (1993) 'Dominance analysis: a new approach to the problem of relative impor-tance of predictors in multiple regression', *Psychological Bulletin*, 114(3): 542–51.

Cameron, A.C. and Trivedi, P.K. (1998) *Regression Analysis of Count Data*. New York, NY: Cambridge University Press.

Carlson, K.D. and Wu, J. (2012) 'The illusion of statistical control: Control variable practice in management research', *Organizational Research Methods*, 15 (3): 413–35.

Cohen, J. (1983) 'The cost of dichotomization', *Applied Psychological Measurement*, 7 (3): 249–53.

Cortina, J.M. (2002) 'Big things have small beginnings: An assortment of "minor" methodological misunderstandings', *Journal of Management*, 28 (3): 339–62.

Coxe, S., West, S.G. and Aiken, L.S. (2009) 'The analysis of count data: A gentle introduction to Poisson regression and its alternatives', *Journal of Personality Assessment*, 91 (2): 121–36.

Dawson, J.F. (2014) 'Moderation in management research: What, why, when, and how', *Journal of Business and Psychology*, 29 (1): 1–19.

Delery, J.E. and Doty, D.H. (1996) 'Modes of theorizing in strategic human resource management: Tests of universalistic contingency, and configurational performance predictions', *Academy of Management Journal*, 39 (4): 802–35.

Draper, N.R. and Smith, H. (1998) *Applied Regression Analysis* (3rd edition). Hoboken, NJ: John Wiley & Sons.

Echambadi, R., Campbell, B. and Agarwal, R. (2006) 'Encouraging best practice in quantitative management research: An incomplete list of opportunities', *Journal of Management Studies*, 43 (8): 1801–20.

Gardner, R.G., Harris, T.B., Li, N., Kirkman, B.L. and Mathieu, J.E. (2017) 'Understanding "it depends" in organizational research: A theory-based taxonomy, review, and future research agenda concerning interactive and quadratic relationships', *Organizational Research Methods*, 20 (4): 610–38.

Gardner, W., Mulvey, E.P. and Shaw, E.C. (1995) 'Regression analyses of counts and rates: Poisson, overdispersed Poisson, and negative binomial models', *Psychological Bulletin*, 118 (3): 392–404.

Goldfarb, B. and King, A.A. (2016) 'Scientific apophenia in strategic management research: Significance tests and mistaken inference', *Strategic Management Journal*, 37 (1): 167–76.

Haans, R.F.J., Pieters, C. and He, Z.-L. (2016) 'Thinking about U: Theorizing and testing U- and inverted U-shaped relationships in strategy research', *Strategic Management Journal*, 37 (7): 1177–95.

Heckman, J.J. (1979) 'Sample selection bias as a specification error', *Econometrica*, 47 (1): 153–61.

Hosmer, D.W. Jr and Lemeshow, S. (2000) *Applied Logistic Regression* (2nd edition). New York: John Wiley & Sons.

Johns, G. (2001) 'In praise of context', *Journal of Organizational Behavior*, 22 (1): 31–42.

Johnson, J.W. (2000) 'A heuristic method for estimating the relative weight of predictor variables in multiple regression', *Multivariate Behavioral Research*, 35 (1): 1–19.

Johnson, J.W. and LeBreton, J.M. (2004) 'History and use of relative importance indices in organizational research', *Organizational Research Methods*, 7 (3): 238–57.

Kahn, J.R. and Udry, J.R. (1986) 'Marital coital frequency: Unnoticed outliers and unspecified interactions lead to erroneous conclusions', *American Sociological Review*, 51 (5): 734–7.

Kalnins, A. (2018) 'Multicollinearity: How common factors cause Type 1 errors in multivariate regression', *Strategic Management Journal*, 39 (8): 2362–85.

Kleinbaum, D.G., Klein, M. and Pryor, E.R. (2002) *Logistic Regression: A Self-Learning Text* (2nd edition). New York: Springer.

Kleinbaum, D.G., Kupper, L.L., Nizam, A. and Rosenberg, E.S. (2013) *Applied Regression Analysis and Other Multivariable Methods* (5th edition). Boston, MA: Cengage Learning.

Kutner, M.H., Nachtsheim, C.J., Neter, J. and Li, W. (2004) *Applied Linear Statistical Models* (5th edition). Chicago, IL: McGraw-Hill/Irwin.

Li, C., Arikan, I., Shenkar, O. and Arikan, A. (2020) 'The impact of country-dyadic military conflicts on market reaction to cross-border acquisitions', *Journal of International Business Studies*, 51 (3): 299–325.

Lloyd, C.J. (1999) *Statistical Analysis of Categorical Data*. New York, NY: John Wiley & Sons.

Long, J.S. (1997) *Regression Models for Categorical and Limited Dependent Variables*. Thousand Oaks, CA: Sage Publishing.

MacKinnon, D.P., Lockwood, C.M., Hoffman, J.M., West, S.G. and Sheets, V. (2002) 'A comparison of methods to test mediation and other intervening variable effects', *Psychological Methods*, 7 (1): 83–104.

Manning, W.G. and Mullahy, J. (2001) 'Estimating log models: To transform or not to transform?' *Journal of Health Economics*, 20 (4): 461–94.

Marquardt, D.W. (1970) 'Generalized inverses, ridge regression, biased linear estimation, and nonlinear estimation', *Technometrics*, 12 (3): 591–612.

Marsh, L.C. and Cormier, D.R. (2001) *Spline Regression Models*. Thousand Oaks, CA: Sage Publishing.

Mason, C.H. and Perreault, W.D. Jr. (1991) 'Collinearity, power, and interpretation of multiple regression analysis', *Journal of Marketing Research*, 28 (3): 268–80.

Maxwell, S.E. and Delaney, H.D. (1993) 'Bivariate median splits and spurious statistical significance', *Psychological Bulletin*, 113 (1): 181–90.

Meng, X.-L., Rosenthal, R. and Rubin, D.B. (1992) 'Comparing correlated correlation coefficients', *Psychological Bulletin*, 111 (1): 172–5.

Peng, C.-Y. J., Lee, K.L. and Ingersoll, G.M. (2002) 'An introduction to logistic regression analysis and reporting', *Journal of Educational Research*, 96 (1): 3–14.

Pierce, J.R. and Aguinis, H. (2013) 'The too-much-of-a-good-thing effect in management', *Journal of Management*, 39 (2): 313–38.

Rousseau, D.M. and Fried, Y. (2001) 'Location, location, location: Contextualizing organizational research', *Journal of Organizational Behavior*, 22 (1): 1–13.

Ruiz-Moreno, F., Mas-Ruiz, F.J. and Nicolau-Gonzálbez, J.L. (2007) 'Two-stage choice process of FDI: Ownership structure and diversification mode', *Journal of Business Research*, 60 (7): 795–805.

Ryan, T.P. (1997) *Modern Regression Methods*. New York, NY: John Wiley & Sons.

Schoonhoven, C.B. (1981) 'Problems with contingency theory: Testing assumptions hidden within the language of contingency "theory"', *Administrative Science Quarterly*, 26 (3): 349–77.

Shaver, J.M. (1998) 'Accounting for endogeneity when assessing strategy performance: Does entry mode choice affect FDI survival?', *Management Science*, 44 (4): 571–85.

Shaver, J.M. (2005) 'Testing for mediating variables in management research: Concerns, implications, and alternative strategies', *Journal of Management*, 31 (3): 330–53.

Shrout, P.E. and Bolger, N. (2002) 'Mediation in experimental and nonexperimental studies: New procedures and recommendations', *Psychological Methods*, 7 (4): 422–45.

Spector, P.E. and Brannick, M.T. (2011) 'Methodological urban legends: The misuse of statistical control variables', *Organizational Research Methods*, 14 (2): 287–305.

Staw, B.M., Sandelands, L.E. and Dutton, J.E. (1981) 'Threat-rigidity effects in organizational behavior: A multilevel analysis', *Administrative Science Quarterly*, 26 (4): 501–24.

Stevens, J.P. (1984) 'Outliers and influential data points in regression analysis', *Psychological Bulletin*, 95 (2): 334–44.

Stolzenberg, R.M. and Relles, D.A. (1997) 'Tools for intuition about sample selection bias and its correction', *American Sociological Review*, 62 (3): 494–507.

Taylor, A.B., MacKinnon, D.P. and Tein, J.-Y. (2008) 'Tests of the three-path mediated effect', *Organizational Research Methods*, 11 (2): 241–69.

UCLA Institute for Digital Research & Education Statistical Consulting (n.d.) 'Choosing the correct statistical test in SAS, STATA, SPSS and R', https://stats.idre.ucla.edu/other/mult-pkg/whatstat/.

Weisberg, S. (2005) *Applied Linear Regression* (3rd edition). Hoboken, NJ: John Wiley & Sons.

Winship, C. and Mare, R.D. (1992) 'Models for sample selection bias', *Annual Review of Sociology*, 18: 327–50.

Wolfolds, S.E. and Siegel, J. (2019) 'Misaccounting for endogeneity: The peril of relying on the Heckman two-step method without a valid instrument', *Strategic Management Journal*, 40 (3): 432–62.

Wood, R.E., Goodman, J.S., Beckmann, N. and Cook, A. (2008) 'Mediation testing in management research: a review and proposals', *Organizational Research Methods*, 11 (2): 270–95.

Yip, P.S.L. and Tsang, E.W.K. (2007) 'Interpreting dummy variables and their interaction effects in strategy research', *Strategic Organization*, 5(1): 13–30.

Zhang, M., Fortney, J.C., Tilford, J.M. and Rost, K.M. (2000) 'An application of the inverse hyperbolic sine transformation – a note', *Health Services and Outcomes Research Methodology*, 1 (2): 165–71.

11
WRITING UP

11.1 INTRODUCTION

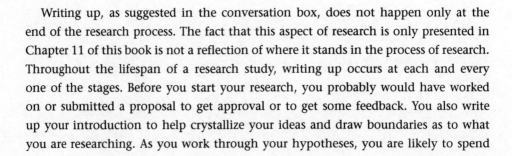

Conversation box

Professor:	Sheryl, you should get some writing done while waiting for your survey responses.
Sheryl [Masters student]:	I will try, Professor, but I will have to start incorporating new materials into the literature review and introduction chapters.
Professor:	This is precisely why you need to be constantly writing even though you are engaged in the process of collecting data, as previous written work can be outdated and it can take a while for you to catch up and to update with new materials.

Writing up, as suggested in the conversation box, does not happen only at the end of the research process. The fact that this aspect of research is only presented in Chapter 11 of this book is not a reflection of where it stands in the process of research. Throughout the lifespan of a research study, writing up occurs at each and every one of the stages. Before you start your research, you probably would have worked on or submitted a proposal to get approval or to get some feedback. You also write up your introduction to help crystallize your ideas and draw boundaries as to what you are researching. As you work through your hypotheses, you are likely to spend substantial time on crafting the linkages between constructs in your work. You write up the methodology to ensure the entire data collection process is well documented and transparent to the reader. You describe your data and weave some of the results together, especially when mixed methods or multimethods are used. You then write up the results so that the contributions of the study can be presented. While each part of this writing can differ in the nature of what is covered and what is not, there are some good practices that we can apply while writing up our research.

The writing up process is by no means straightforward. In fact, the writing up process entails lots of rewriting for greater clarity. Few of us are expert writers who get it right in our first draft. Further, as we are immersed in the process of writing, we also tend to make assumptions in our writing about what the readers know. But writing for the customer is essential (Aguinis et al., 2010). If you speak to seasoned researchers, they can also tell you it is common to need a dozen rewrites if not more before a research paper is ready for submission to a journal, and often with external feedback between rewrites. Therefore, it is good practice to ensure that writing is done constantly as opposed to waiting for the 'right moment' to write. This chapter covers materials that are useful for guiding your writing and rewriting of your research.

As with different expectations of quality of work for different degress of study and for publication outlets of different status as discussed in Chapter 1, writing expectations can also differ. Further, there may be differences in institutional practices in terms of structure of content and writing styles, and in that I have highlighted the practices regarding plagiarism policies that a researcher needs to check when enrolling as a foreign student in an institution. This was also covered in Chapter 1. Studies have also found that international students do need to make adjustments in order to adapt their writing styles to a foreign environment (e.g. Angelova and Riazantseva, 1999). Therefore, it is more important if you are an international student that you recognize that the writing advice in this chapter will form a base from which you start adjusting your writing to your institution's requirements.

11.2 TYPICAL SECTIONS OF A RESEARCH PROJECT

While there is no prescribed format in the order of organizing the presentation of your research project, and this tends to be dependent on the degree programme, there is a rough guideline that is commonly adopted. You might also find a resemblance of this guideline in the way the chapters are organized in this book.

Whether your study is a quantitative or qualitative one, your research project layout is likely to comprise of the following sections: (1) summary or abstract; (2) introduction; (3) background and literature review; (4) industry or location context (if research topic is highly industry- or location-specific); (5) development of theory and propositions or hypotheses development; (6) data and methodology; (7) results; (8) discussion;

(9) conclusions; (10) references; and (11) tables, figures and appendices. Some projects and papers also include acknowledgements as a separate section.

The order of the appearance of the sections might differ depending on the type of study, e.g. qualitative or quantitative. Note that this is only a guideline – some researchers may think having this many sections is too cumbersome. Then for example, it will be good to combine discussion and conclusions into one section. Others might feel a need to have even more sections. Further, there will be some expectations imposed by your institution such as restrictions to the length of the work, formatting such as double-line spacing, which is commonly adopted, and referencing format. Regardless, you should use the structure that best allows the message of your research to be presented as clearly as possible to the audience.

This section will highlight the main expectations in each of the sections listed above in terms of reporting and writing.

11.2.1 The summary or abstract

The **summary** or **abstract** is a brief synopsis of the entire research work. It contains a quick summary of the motivation of the study, the objectives of the study, the data, the key findings and conclusions of the study, and most importantly the main contributions of the research. This section allows the audience to develop a preliminary appreciation of the content of the study. It also provides the audience with a quick overview of the relevance of the study to their own work. As the coverage of the summary or abstract includes most components of a research study, the content of this section will evolve throughout the duration of your research. An alternative way to handle this is to start preparing this when writing up the full draft of the research itself. It is only when the findings are revealed and discussed that the author gets a clear and concise picture of the whole study, providing all materials needed for this section.

11.2.2 The introduction

The **introduction** section plays a significant role in research outreach and perception of the work, as it sets the scene for how the study fits in the overall picture, both in terms of the research literature and practice. Not that the other sections are not important, it's just that this is the section that creates the reader's first impressions of your work. You must take this first opportunity to state the importance and value of your work and to contextualize it for the reader. Given a choice of not continuing to read a project beyond this section, it is this section that sways the reader in one way or another. As a researcher, you might also find that the introduction section of a paper allows you to assess if the paper is of use to your own work. The introduction of a research project serves the same purpose for the project. When your introduction section is badly structured and boringly written, your audience will get turned off from the start and cannot appreciate why your study is important and deserves their attention. This is what you don't want to happen. It is important to relate to the reader to entice them to keep on reading your work. This is by no means an easy task, as what is important to you may not be a priority for your reader. Further, given the length of research projects, it is a major commitment for a reader to read from cover to cover. What they need to know is what knowledge and insights they will gain by reading your work. That is, what is the missing link in the literature that motivated you to conduct this research? The introduction section should also highlight the research questions, research objectives and contributions, and provide some background to your work.

A well-written introduction section provides a clear indication of the depth and breadth of the research, as well as the content and the structural presentation of the work. Since the purpose of the introduction section is to provide a rationale for your research, it must successfully establish the position of your research within the larger knowledge base of the discipline. This requires clearly constructed logics and explicit arguments that clarify how this work will contribute to the knowledge of the field.

The introduction section often starts with some context information or a problem statement. These can sometimes come in a form of a business issue or a company-specific challenge, depending on the nature of the research project. To establish the need for the research, the author must adequately justify the limitations of previous research, the gaps identified within previous projects, such as conflicting findings, and new developments that are required for knowledge accumulation in the field. A more applied research project will have some coverage of the above with added materials around why the problem deserves attention and is worthwhile of a research project to address it. These aspects were discussed in Chapter 3 in regard to generating research questions.

The problem statement is often followed by a statement of the aims of the research. It is crucial for every research study to have clear and concise research aims at the outset. Research aims state what the author hopes to achieve by the end of the research, giving the reader a pathway to the rest of the work. In addition, the introduction section also needs to include an outline of the approach the author has adopted, and briefly list the key decision choices made regarding conceptual or theoretical lenses, data and methodology.

Overall, the introduction section generally moves from general information providing background and contextual information of the research field to more specific information about the research itself, culminating in an outline of the subsequent sections. By making this section interesting and informative it helps to generate audience interest to read further, and in the process sets the scene for subsequent sections.

Due to its critical role, it is advisable to write up the introduction section in the early stages of the research as it can provide a good way to help crystallize your own thinking and the boundaries for your study. Nonetheless, this is also a section that should be revisited throughout the entire research process, as more information about the field, decisions around your research, and findings emerge.

11.2.3 Background and literature review

Chapter 2 has discussed extensively the conduct of the **literature review**. As highlighted in that chapter, what needs to be included in a typical literature review section are a discussion of the trends and observations of the phenomenon and context of interest in your study, the relevant theoretical perspectives being used to test aspects of the phenomenon in your research, prior findings related to the issues you are investigating in your research, and the variables and measurements used in these other relevant previous studies.

A literature review is an attempt by the author of the research to summarize and evaluate existing studies in the field, and this section serves to complement the introduction section. By conducting a literature review, the author can learn from the findings and thought processes of others and expand their view of the field, as well as becoming familiar with any existing theories and parallel developments. The end-product is a demonstration of the author's efforts in exploring and recognizing the existing literature to provide the background and justification for their own research. A good literature review needs to be more than a simple description of what others have published in the form of a set of summaries. It should take the form of a critical discussion, showing insights and an awareness of differing arguments, theories and approaches used in the literature. It should be a synthesis and analysis of the relevant published works that are linked to your research-specific purpose and rationale. Sometimes, it can be extremely useful to use review articles or articles that applied bibliometric analysis to spot intellectual structure gaps (e.g. Zha et al., 2020; Zupic and Cater, 2015). It is worth noting that for qualitative exploratory work, a good literature review will still be needed to set the scene so that results can be linked back to the literature (Rynes and Gephart, 2004; Siggelkow, 2007).

Information relevant to the topic needs to be synthesized into something that is more logical and comprehensible for the reader. There are several ways to construct a literature review. For example, it may be suitable for the articles to be integrated into a chronological perspective to help the reader understand how ideas have evolved over time. Another useful way is to organize the review based on key constructs; each section would represent a construct. With each section, the content of the literature can be further organized chronologically or by using sub-headings. This also allows you to use existing limitations from previous research to build a convincing rationale for your own methodology. There is no yardstick as to which is the better approach to present a literature review. Usually the decision depends on how your constructs relate to each other and the organization of the literature review should ensure that theorizing flows smoothly from this section.

11.2.4 Industry or location context

> ## Conversation box
>
> *Jack [student]:*   Professor, as you're aware, my research relates directly to the biotech-nology industry. Do I need to have a separate chapter on the industry in my thesis?
>
> *Professor:*   Your thesis seeks to examine the relationship between venture capital funding and venture success. Your research context is the biotechnol-ogy industry but in your case the choice of industry is an empirical decision. Your focus is still around the general understanding of the relationship between venture capital funding and venture success. As such, you will just need to include a brief discussion section of the bio-technology industry in your data chapter instead of devoting an entire chapter to this.

If a research is industry- or location-specific, and this context shapes the findings significantly and may not be highly applicable to other industries, you should consider having a separate section on the specific industry or location of study. Examples of this would be a study of information technology use in the steel industry and a study of the customs regulations of the Netherlands. In this form, we should expect to see justifica-tions as to how the choice of industry or location shape the research question. When the research question is generic and applicable more broadly, then its construction does not require a separate contextualized discussion of the industry or location. Considering the research published out there, we tend to see more generic research questions than contextualized ones. For studies with generic research questions, the industry or location choice is just another research context, as highlighted in the conversation box above. It is also worth noting here that the decision can sometimes be a judgement call – hence it is essential to make sure the decision is discussed and consulted, especially with respect to the content of a thesis or project. In such cases, as the Professor advises, covering industry or location information in the data section will suffice.

11.2.5 Development of theory, propositions and hypotheses development

For quantitative studies, this section usually comes after the background and literature review section. For qualitative studies, it appears normally after the findings section. This section mainly involves the propositions or hypotheses to be tested in or derived from your study and the arguments supporting these propositions or hypotheses. The arguments presented consist of your inferences that link the constructs involved, grounded with the help of both the literature and logic. For quantitative studies, these serve as the basis of formulating the propositions and hypotheses to be tested empirically. For qualitative studies, these are the outcomes of interpreting the findings from your research. It is worth noting here, as discussed in Chapter 9, propositions and hypotheses are not a necessary outcome of qualitative research (Gioia et al., 2012).

Writing propositions and **hypotheses development** is by no means easy. Ask any researcher who has submitted articles to the top journals for consideration for publication and you will hear that many articles are rejected due to inadequate theoretical development. There is a tendency to make assumptions when we write hypotheses development. Implicitly we assume that for the most part the audience knows what we are thinking. As such, sometimes our explanations can be brief – too brief, to the extent that the ideas are jumping around, and the logic and thoughts are not linked together. It is not fair to expect the reader to piece the puzzles together. For a reviewer for your paper submission, this may mean expecting them to help you theorize – and this often results in a paper getting rejected from a top journal.

It is essential when you write this section that every process of linking one variable to another is explicitly explained. Only then can the theorizing be clear to the audience. A mapping diagram involving asking all the 'why' questions is always a good starting point to help with this. That is, for every explanation that you have written down, you seek to go further with another 'why?' Keep doing this and you will be a step closer to better theory development. In addition, try to avoid the tendency to merely find citations to link the arguments together. The logic behind the linkages should always come first, followed by the citations. There is also a tendency to present post hoc hypotheses as a priori (Kerr, 1998; Leung, 2011), i.e. writing arguments that support the results and adjusting the hypotheses accordingly. To what extent this act is unethical is debatable. But potentially, doing it this way around might even mean that the theoretical and conceptual framework needs to be adjusted and a new framework needs to be introduced, affecting all other components of the research as well. For the most part, using the results to inform the theory will be an interpretivistic approach to research but doing this for a positivist approach may not gel well.

11.2.6 Data and methodology

The data and **methodology** section includes a description of the data that you are using in your study, the variables and measurements of the constructs, as well as the analytical methods used. The description of the data includes the data collection process as well. As often mentioned throughout this book, the documentation of the research process is equally, if not more important than the research findings themselves.

The data and methodology section answers two critical questions: (1) 'How did you go about conducting your research?' and (2) 'Why did you do it that way?' It is often the most vigorously scrutinized part of the research, as flaws in methodology can lead to results being deemed as weak or unreliable. It is probably also true that this is a section that is easy pickings for errors. Since there is often more than one possible method to go about investigating a relationship between two or more constructs, an author needs to give a good summary of available methods and theoretical approaches for the research topic and then justify their own choices. This will be followed by a description of the way that particular method was applied and the reasons behind this. The author will need to indicate how the sample was selected and why. It is critical that some efforts are made to justify the actions and decisions made in each aspect of this section.

Conversation box

Kim [Masters student]:   Professor, how much detail do I need to include in my data reporting about the interviews, given that there were open-ended questions?

Professor: Kim, you must give as much detail as you can. Of course, this will have to be balanced against the space available for reporting and also against the relative weight given to other parts of the research.

Kim: Can you elaborate?

Professor: We usually have constraints in research. Any paper submission to journals is restricted to a certain length. The same guidelines can apply to theses and projects as well. In addition, given these constraints, you do not want to focus too much on data and sacrifice space available for other parts of the research.

No method is perfect and there is often a gap between the ideal and what can realistically be implemented. Every study will be influenced by factors that are both under and out of the researcher's control. Therefore, a well-presented methodology section often includes a discussion of the necessary compromises and judgement calls made and discusses the impacts of such decisions, including risk minimization regarding validity and reliability. Overall, this section must provide the right kind of data, facts, examples and details such that there is sufficient evidence to be persuasive and the audience can trust the findings you obtained.

11.2.7 Results and discussion

The **results** section reports all the findings from the analysis. It is important to mention here that while some research has found that there is a bias against studies that show non-results (e.g. Cortina and Folger, 1998; Stanley, 2005), this is hardly good practice so the advice here is that it is acceptable to *not* find support for some of your propositions or hypotheses. After all, your research linkages may have alternative explanations. An author needs to present the results as they emerge from the analysis and highlight those that are interesting. If there is any result that is contradictory, or a lack of support for a prediction, this must also be reported. Explanations for such counterintuitive observations need to be provided. Sometimes, non-results may prove to be as, if not more interesting than the confirmation of predictions.

One caveat about non-results is that I would advise against any study where all the propositions or hypotheses show no results. If a research is well conceived and executed, with reliability and validity for the measurements used for testing with the appropriate methodology, we should not expect non-results for all propositions or hypotheses proposed. In other words, non-results for some propositions or hypotheses are acceptable, but a study with all non-results is not.

It is common for data to be presented in the form of tables or graphs as they help illustrate trends to the audience. Avoid over-crowding the text with tables. Only those tables central to interpreting the results that support predictions should appear in the results section; any remaining tables in the context of a thesis or project should be placed in appendices. All tables and graphs should be used diligently. In quantitative studies, results are organized by hypotheses. Results and observations beyond this are usually represented in a separate sub-section. In qualitative studies, the results are generally organized by themes.

As the **discussion** and the results sections are mutually dependent, the structure of the discussion is often similar to that of the results section. More often, they are combined into one section, similar to how this section is organized.

There are several key elements that make up a discussion section. The first is the 'so what' question. In the introduction section, the author will have already made a case for the importance of his research. It is important that in the discussion section, they follow this up with a discussion on the findings and their significance. When making claims based on data, the author needs to point to specific data from the study to ensure that these claims are supported by actual evidence. From this section it is important to tie the results back to the introduction section through the discussion.

The most important component of a discussion section is the analysis of the results in relation to each individual hypothesis that was made. This is the author's opportunity to discuss and explain the study findings. Any trends, patterns or relationships as well as unexpected results should be identified and explained. The author may often need to refer to the literature review chapter in this discussion as they try to position the research in the context of existing research. Here, the author will discuss how the new findings contradict, support, or extend the research covered previously in the literature review. Points of similarity should be highlighted if the findings support another prior study. On the other hand, if the results contradict previous research, any differences should be highlighted and explained as well.

11.2.8 The conclusion

This section concludes the research study and discusses its implications. The **conclusion** section should tie in closely with the contributions and results. The conclusion section should do more than just summarize the findings – it should illustrate the significance of the findings. However, it should not contain any new discussion and should be based entirely on what was covered in the discussion section. The conclusion section is also where the author will highlight any unresolved issues or new questions that arose from the results of the current study and which are beyond its scope, for example, the implications of the study on future research or future practice. Recommendations for improvements or the retention of current practices could be made based on the discussion section. The write up of the conclusion section is also the last opportunity for an author to showcase the strength of the research and how well the research has been executed. It is important that the author revisits the research aims and confirms in the conclusion section that these aims have been achieved, and if not, why.

Conversation box

Todd [student]:   Professor, is it possible to combine my results, discussion and conclusions into one chapter in my project?

Professor: Technically there is no restriction to this. In other words, it is fine for you to do that. The only problem, which is why you don't see this being done in most studies, is that when these elements are combined, this chapter can become too rich and heavy in content. And you also need to say that there are implications, limitations and suggestions for future research. So, it is better to cut all these components into two chapters for clarity and to make them more digestible for the reader.

The conclusion section also features discussion of the **limitations** of a study and suggestions for future research. It is important in any research work to recognize that there are always some limitations that may impede application of the results to different circumstances. Failure to recognize limitations reflects an inability to set the boundaries of your study and represents a deficiency. It should also be noted that it is difficult to argue that one's research does not have limitations, as we know that even the greatest scientific works have their limitations. It is worthwhile to note that limits on generalizability should be raised in regard to how the implications can be translated. Both Calder et al. (1981) and Mook (1983) provide good discussions around designing one's research to match with the desired applicability.

Normally, you have both theoretical and managerial **implications**. Theoretical implications cover mainly the contributions of the research. Therefore, when you write theoretical implications, it is essential to make sure these are aligned with the research objectives. Managerial implications are often a by-product of what are tested. How would managers use your findings? The advice is to try to relate this to the outcome and independent variables. The outcome variables are what managers should seek to achieve, such as lower turnover or higher profitability. Managerial implications should link, based on the relationships found in the research, to advise managers on how to make adjustments to the independent causal factor in order to work towards the desired and better outcome.

The extent of each of two implications will depend on the nature of the project and its intention in the first place. Not all research has strong managerial implications – studies have found that the link between academic quality and practical implications is not always positive (Baldridge et al., 2004). Conversely, not all good practice-oriented research has the right rigour (Vermeulen, 2005, 2007). The ideal state is for researchers to connect to the people who are practicing to ensure that a research project can have both rigour and relevance.

There are often questions raised as to what extent implications are needed in a research paper that is published in a research-oriented journal. If we go back to the need for our research to inform practice, then implications for practice are necessary regardless of how research-oriented your work might be. The writing of these implications is by no means easy. Bartunek and Rynes (2010) provide an extensive discussion of this aspect of implications, and also some suggestions of how to do this well.

There is always a lack of documentation in research work on the limitations of research. This is mainly due to the ambiguous nature of limitations – how much and what type of limitations should be highlighted? If a study has too many limitations, all the findings are void or suspected. However, failing to highlight limitations may give the impression that the author seeks to conceal the weaknesses of the research. So, a balance needs to be struck as to what needs to be highlighted – a judgement call. It must also be remembered that anything that is not covered within the scope of the current research can be but need not always be a limitation of your study. For example, the intentional choice to draw implications for firms in high technology industries would not be part of a limitation when the investigation has been conducted in high technology industries (see Mook (1983) for a discussion). On the other hand, if the implications drawn are more generic yet the sample used has come only from high technology industries, there would be a need to highlight this potential limitation. This situation, however, is not ideal, as perhaps what you are trying to imply stretches beyond what your research really covers.

It is important to note that any research should minimize limitations. As a rule of thumb, limitations should only occur when you had no choice in being unable to perform a step or procedure. Any step or procedure that you did not perform as a result of choice rather than being imposed upon should not be classified as a legitimate limitation. Classifying such failure to perform this step or procedure as a limitation would constitute a research flaw. For example, generating a minimum sample size for analysis even though the data collection process allows for a larger sample to be accessed would be a limiting choice. This is undesirable and can hardly be considered a legitimate limitation that is beyond a researcher's control. There is also a tendency to use extensive time and high costs as reasons for not performing certain steps or procedures in research. While these can be legitimate reasons, they are no substitute for good research rigour. Thus, it is important to ensure that the marginal benefits from more investments in time and costs for the current research are low before time and costs are stated as limitations.

Suggestions for future research are also derived from research objectives and findings. Potentially, these can be related to limitations of the study as well. As this section covers materials that are not included in your study, there is a tendency to list too many suggestions. It is important to note that these suggestions should be closely related to your work, and not normally outside your study scope due to constraints or aspects of research that you did not address, i.e. your limitations, rather than a broader suggestion in the field.

11.2.9 Acknowledgements

When a research study is financially sponsored by an institution, the researcher is expected to acknowledge their support. Acknowledgements are required for persons who have helped in the publication process, including research assistants for data collection or analysis, and colleagues who have made substantial comments on earlier versions of a research output. In most theses and projects, students will also acknowledge others who form part of their research environment, such as supervisors, family members and colleagues. In publications, upon acceptance, authors also acknowledge the advice of editors, anonymous reviewers and others who have helped to make the research a better piece of work and get it published.

11.3 WRITING STYLES

Conversation box

Katherine [student]:   Professor, given that there are different writing styles, which one should I use?

Professor: Writing styles are created by writers and so there are many different forms. There is no one single writing style that is considered the 'correct' way to express your research. In fact, the writing style does not only depend on individual preference; in many cases it also depends on the audience and venue you are targeting.

There are various output avenues, as discussed in Chapters 1 and 2. There are the typical research theses or projects, journals – which can be sub-divided into academic-oriented and practitioner-oriented, and other periodicals such as magazines and local publications. Some of these outlets require more formal structural reporting – no flowery language, just reporting on what the research is about, the facts and what the research found. Others are more particular, expecting the research output to be more managerial savvy. Managerial audiences do not want to be bothered with academic jargon. You will have to translate your research into manager-appropriate language to generate interest among managers. As outlets often have their own targeted audience in mind, adhering to the requirements of the research outlets is essential for you to get your work published. But regardless of whatever outlet you may be targeting, you will always need to get your message across to the audience as clearly as possible. To do that, there are some fundamental writing style guidelines that may be useful.

An important principle of good writing is attracting the attention of the reader. As with all writing, academic writing is directed at a specific audience. Good **writing styles** that convey the message in a crisp way, whether it is directly from the author or as a third-party description of another author's work, is essential to capture the attention of any reader. For me, writing in a way as if I am 'talking' to the audience, which is you, will be best. As qualitative studies tend to involve a lot of description of observations and weaving together of themes, the challenge of writing for qualitative studies can be more onerous, yet more essential (Sutton, 1997). Gioia et al. (2012), Pratt (2009) and Tracy (2010) provide good advice on better writing in qualitative research generally, while Golden-Biddle and Locke (1993) focus on ethnographic research and Siggelkow (2007) covers case study research.

This section will cover some basics of good writing and what constitutes unclear and bad writing. The key aspects that will be touched on are language, **structure and flow of writing**, and the **formats** of writing.

11.3.1 Language

While **language** may be determined to some extent by writing styles, there are some elements of language usage that are generic to good and clear writing. In the past there has been resistance to allowing authors to use the first-person in writing, the belief being that objectivity in research is important and the use of the first-person can lead an author to consciously or subconsciously instil some subjectivity into their research reporting. Writing as the third party and using the passive voice was encouraged instead. Over time, however, this view has changed, with the belief that authors need to take ownership of their work. As such, it makes sense for authors to use the first-person pronoun 'I'. These days, in most academic disciplines using the first person in writing is becoming common.

Jargon has been defined as those words 'that succinctly conveyed a concept to a professional audience, that were in frequent usage in an educational setting, and for which there were more general usage words or phrases available' (Brown et al., 1978: 334). Every field has its jargon. Very often, these jargon words function as a shorthand to allow us to quickly explain things in a field. Sometimes, however, we have to ask the question 'are we using jargon because it is easier, or are we using jargon because we want to portray that we are an expert?'

In reality, jargon has been found to make it difficult to convey messages (e.g. Joiner et al., 2002) and in particular when it relates to practitioners (Steffens et al., 2014). Jargon, by definition, suggests there are alternative ways to describe the same concept represented by the jargon. In other words, it is possible to avoid jargon and as far as possible this should be done, given the downsides it creates in **communication**.

Conversation box

Kieran [student]: Professor, how far should I avoid the use of jargon? I'm asking because it's quite widespread in my area and I find it hard not to use it without leaving myself with a lot of explaining to do.

Professor: Kieran, while there is no guideline as to how much jargon one can use, you should ask yourself a few questions. First, is the jargon employed to impress your reader? Second, is the jargon used to signal expertise in a disciplinary area? Third, is the jargon employed to communicate succinctly with colleagues? It is recommended that only jargon that serves its purposes and that does not hinder communication should be retained. And even when this happens, it is important for the authors to provide sufficient definition, background information, contextualization and other forms of explanations to the audience so that the message is properly conveyed.

It is important to recognize that very often some of your audience includes people with different backgrounds. Therefore, not using jargon is likely to be very helpful for this group. Your work can also generate more and wider interest as a result when it does not give the impression that the content is not designed for a non-expert in the field. In addition, while writing for people with different backgrounds is challenging, it is good practice and always a good test of your grasp of your work to communicate to a wider group.

When it comes to clearly conveying messages, it is always advisable to use repetition and parallel construction (Bem, 2003). As we write, sometimes we feel that we have used the same word several times, so we seek the thesaurus to find synonyms to replace our commonly used word. However, while it is easy to see why a reader might be irritated when coming across the same words quite a few times when going through your work, that would not be a reason to start swapping the specific terminologies of your subject matter with other similar words. As illustrated in our discussion of literature search, similar but different words may mean quite different things to search databases, resulting in different search outcomes. While it is understandable that different researchers use different words of the same meaning, it is essential that you should not confuse the reader with the use of different words in one research paper or project. While this means that you may have to repeat a term several times, even within a sentence, it is still better than to replace it with a synonym or a pronoun. Repetition in fact helps the reader to keep track of what you are saying. Synonyms may allow the text to appear to be more interesting, but they can often distract the reader.

The tense (past or present) has to be consistent within each aspect of the research output. You would usually use past tense when you report on the literature and all prior work done by others. You would also use past tense when you describe the activities that led to your research, for example how you have conducted your literature search and how data were collected. Past tense would normally be used if you are describing the analysis you have done. Present tense is used when you are reporting the results. Discussion and conclusions relating to the results are also generally described with the use of present tense. Again, these are guidelines and some journals, for example, do specify their expectations when it comes to writing with different tenses.

Another example of the need for cautious use of language would be in relation to gender bias. Gender language bias can occur without us intentionally introducing it. For example, the use of 'Chairman' may seem fine to some of us but takes no account of the fact that not all chairpersons are male. It is always wise to bear this potential gender-biased language in mind. Try to use plurals or a neutral word, or otherwise involve each gender when appropriate.

11.3.2 Structure and flow

In terms of structure, it is essential to organize your work by using primary, secondary and, if necessary, tertiary headings for substantial blocks of ideas. This way of structuring will ensure that there is clarity as to the importance of each idea, as well as indicating how ideas surface over time. Organizing material in this way will also allow a good flow that reduces the chance of fragmenting your work into small blocks of text and ideas.

As highlighted earlier, the starting part of any piece of work is critical for pitching to the audience. Therefore, it is essential for your introduction section to provide an excellent overview of the research and to briefly summarize the key questions. It is also important to ensure that the conclusions of the research are properly aligned to the introduction section. To that end, the conclusion of your work should include, among other things, a summary of the issues that the research had sought to address, and whether these have been resolved.

Conversation box

Lei [Honours student]:   Professor, as English is not my first language, I find myself more worried about the wrong use of words than the phrasing of the sentences.

Professor: Lei, we must all aim for perfection in both the usage of grammar and spelling. But try not to be too obsessed with these as it can lead to the tendency to copy word for word from the original sources of information. This leads to potential plagiarism. What is important is your ability to demonstrate clearly your understanding of the subject and your ability to organize information to answer a specific research question. You can then go on to take care of grammar and spelling.

Authors must remember that each and every paragraph and even every sentence in a study must present a single focus. Since it is the job of the author to provide clear and complete explanations to the readers, a good piece of writing should not make readers have to think hard to understand the ideas and logic put forward. This means that the author's thoughts and thought processes should be clearly and completely explained. To ensure that the flow in the text is neat, you should try to organize your paragraphs such that each paragraph illustrates a point. The key ideas for each paragraph should link together to provide a coherent story of your work. A paragraph that contains multiple ideas is likely to be confusing. At the same time, it will not link well with the next paragraph, as the reader would have been led in all directions by the paragraph with multiple ideas. In addition, avoid excessively long paragraphs as they lose the attention of the reader, but make sure no paragraph contains only one sentence.

The flow of your work is also dependent on your writing. It is important that you write in clear English. This may sound strange as we often treat writing clearly as a given. Clear writing also involves writing in simple English – which is actually easier said than done. To be able to convert jargon and business English into plain English is a major writing challenge. Simple and clear writing also leads to concise writing, which is probably the ultimate aim of any presentation of research output.

We often try to pack as much information as possible into a sentence. However, when we face the difficulty of trying to put all this information into one sentence, some of us will be tempted to use footnotes. After all, footnotes can help us clarify information that cannot otherwise be compressed into a sentence or a paragraph. I have run into this use of footnotes in books and more so in theses and projects. I can recall having seen a page of a thesis more than half dominated by footnotes! That certainly does not help with the reading, especially when the footnotes tend to be presented in smaller fonts. While it is not wrong to use footnotes, excessive use is not advisable. The tendency to use footnotes is often the result of an inability to communicate concisely. We know that readers are less likely to read footnotes, so why do we include them? Putting the extra information in the appendices may do the trick, but for journals, which tend to have limited space, even the appendix solution is sometimes not viable. In this case, we will be forced to balance what is relevant and what is not, and what is more relevant versus what is less. But if some information is important, then it definitely does not make any sense to put it in a footnote; you need to integrate this information into the main text.

11.3.3 Writing format

First and foremost, it is essential to eliminate spelling mistakes and grammatical errors. As mentioned above, writing clearly is a necessary condition for good presentation of the research. Readers will find it difficult to read and absorb texts with grammatical errors, let alone spelling mistakes. Journal editors and reviewers are unlikely to tolerate a paper submission that contains spelling mistakes and grammatical errors. These days, your computer software is likely to have grammar and spell-checking functions to help you identify spelling mistakes, passive voice, incorrect tenses, over-used words and other problems. However, use your own judgement rather than the software developer's judgement when it comes to what is clear and elegant.

Conversation box

Josephine [Masters student]: I have emailed the draft of my thesis to my supervisor so he can give me some feedback.

Terence [Masters student]: My supervisor has asked me to submit a hard copy draft, so I will have to go to the library to print it off. It seems that your supervisor does not mind the e-version while mine insists that she is better off reading a printed version of the draft.

If you are a new researcher, then it is likely that you live in the e-era. We have envisaged a paperless world to run our lives. Computer screens also get bigger, making reading easier. But if you have a conversation with a more experienced researcher, the advice you are likely to get is that you are often safer with a printed version of your research paper. The reason is that you are more likely to spot errors on a printed version than on the screen. While this may not always be true, especially for a more meticulous researcher or reader, reading a hard copy of a journal article before it is submitted is common practice even among experienced researchers. Mistakes that are more obvious on the printed page often slip by on the screen.

We tend to be repetitive when we write. How many times have you written a sentence and then find yourself writing a second one to clarify the first? If the first sentence is not clear enough, then it will be fine to use only the second sentence. Strunk and White (2000) touch on how we can omit needless words in our writing.

When we list items, there is a tendency for us to include 'etc.' at the end of a short list to let the reader know there could be more in the list. While this is understandable and more economical than including a huge list of items, it is better to write 'such as' and follow this by a small illustrative list. Otherwise, the full list or mention of all of the most relevant specific items is always preferred. Abbreviations should also be used with care – only if they are part of common usage and reduce your word count substantially. You want your readers to focus on your ideas, rather than trying to remember what your terms mean. If you must use an abbreviated term, spell out the term when you first use it. Finally, you should avoid using ambiguous stress terms such as 'quite' and 'somewhat', which are subject to individual interpretation. The logic of your discussion should show clearly how important a point is.

Holbrook (1986) provides some basic suggestions on organizing writing, including: making the paper interesting by using active verbs and avoiding a dull writing style; avoiding lengthy sentences; making sure that the length of the paper reflects the contribution; avoiding chopping a cohesive study into parts thinking that there will be more papers coming out from the same story; using clear headings and sub-headings; and accepting comments and criticisms positively and seeking to improve the paper from these. Bem (2003) provides an excellent guide on how to write empirical journal articles.

11.4 WRITING UP FOR JOURNAL SUBMISSION

Bergh (2002) advises on the risks of submitting prematurely to journals. Some authors even submit their work to top journals for comments and feedback. While it is the responsibility of the reviewers to give feedback, there are only so many reviewers who have the time to deal with the substantial number of submissions that flow through each journal. As such, more often than not the feedback on papers that are prematurely submitted tends to be broad and less helpful (Bergh, 2002). This potentially wastes precious time for editors, reviewers and authors. Therefore, authors should exercise due diligence in their work and only send good versions of their papers to journals for review. As top journals tend to emphasize transparency of reporting (Aytug et al., 2012), it will make sense to be more precise when it comes to writing for submission for top journals.

If you are writing for a journal, it is likely that you will encounter reviewers' comments for you to deal with. It is worth noting that bias in the review process can be unavoidable (Pfeffer, 2007) but this is not generally intentional. Agarwal et al. (2006) and Seibert (2006) discuss how authors can best handle the revision process when they have been offered a revise-and-resubmit. Feldman (2005) provides a lot of good advice on the dos and don'ts in the publishing journey, from time of submission to the revision process through to acceptance. Ketchen (2002) also provides some tips for authors in terms of handling the submission and reviewing process.

Both Bem (2003) and Feldman (2004) provide some tips for organizing various parts of a paper submission, including the title, abstract, introduction, theory, method, results, discussion, organization and referencing.

11.5 OTHER ADVICE ON WRITING UP

11.5.1 Read and appreciate why good publications almost always have good writing

You will have noticed that some top journal publications are in fact easier to read and understand than those published in lower-tier journals. This holds true probably about 85 per cent of the time. Clear writing is a necessary condition for good publications. Authors are expected to write in plain language, making their important discovery more accessible to the general reader. Very often as you read such publications, you get the feeling that they are easy to understand – to the extent of thinking that this is just common sense, so what's so special about this article? This feeling is common, but don't just put that publication away. Read the article again and ask yourself why it is appearing in a top journal? Usually, top journals in each field are aimed at by the best researchers. Writing concisely on complex scientific discoveries (within the limited space allocated by the best journals) using plain language is as hard as doing the research itself. Each submitted paper undergoes review by between two to four other established researchers in the same area. This process is typically done over three to four rounds and rejection can occur at any one of these rounds. Thus, the chances of weaker papers falling through the cracks to get published in top journals are minimized, leading to a greater probability that an article in a top journal will provide some value to you.

A good exercise is to read three papers published in the same research area, one each from three journals which are rated as different tiers. You should compare not just the content, but more importantly the clarity and disposition in the writing to get an appreciation of good writing that builds on research rigour.

11.5.2 Don't just read, write something, and keep rewriting later

Like you, I spend time reading lots of articles. The snowballing effect of reading is large. That is, as we read one article, we will be directed to another due to one interesting citation in the first article. So, we read on. Over time, we find that our reading list has ballooned until we don't even know when to stop. In fact, the more we read, the more likely we are to forget how to start writing, most likely a result of information overload. We should always avoid this cognitive trap by jotting down some of the ideas we have grasped from some of the papers we have read thus far. Reading and writing should be concurrent. So just write something – you can decide later whether it will be useful.

Rewriting is a virtue. For good journal submissions, I rewrite many times before they are submitted. Every rewrite is a result of a critical review of the previous version of the paper. Rewriting one's own work is not easy, as ambiguities and explanatory gaps are less noticeable, attention to detail is harder and restructuring is more likely required (Bem, 2003). Whenever I review my own paper, I try to read it as if it's not mine. This is not an easy task. Very often you find yourself knowing what you will read in the next line – not surprising, as you are the author! Staying away from the work for a few days may help. This self-reviewing step is critical, as it helps you to think through some of the issues your reader might have with your work, for example lack of clarity or that the sentences are not seamlessly connected, and you can make adjustments to pre-empt these potential issues.

It is important to always bear in mind who your target audience are. Your target audience can be purely academics, mainly practitioners or managers, or a mixture of both. While the question of 'so what?' will still hold in all these cases of audience mix, the requirements for the implications will actually be very dependent on the target group. For example, if your target group is a group of managers, it is important to write in managerial terms with illustrations that are more easily accessible. Jargon should be avoided or kept to a bare minimum. Further, the type of managers that you are targeting may also affect your pitching of the article. For example, you have conducted a study on how alliances can enhance a firm's performance. If your target audience is business managers, they would expect your study to discuss the broad implications of engaging in alliances. However, if your target audience is operations managers, they would expect you to highlight the functional aspects of alliances that will help firm performance. Johanson (2007) advises that the adoption of the reader's perspective is important for better writing. For example, pre-empting what the reader might ask will ensure that the work always has the answer immediately when the reader starts to ask questions after reading a section.

11.5.3 Keeping research notes

It is important to keep a close eye on the actual research process to facilitate writing up. This can be helped by keeping **research notes** or recording on tape when you actually perform the activities. Some of the things that are easily forgotten and deserve to be recorded include, but are not limited to:

- What decisions were made in order to narrow down the scope of the study?
- How did you arrive at the hypotheses?
- What issues were considered in choosing the sampling procedure and actually arriving at your final sample?
- How were the cases selected?
- Why did you select the variables that you did?
- How were the measurements developed if they were not from established scales?

Without constant writing or note keeping, we will run into problems that relate to recollection or retrospective accounts. Recollection or retrospective accounts are circumstances where respondents or informants have been asked to recall an activity or situation that they have encountered in the past (Golden, 1992, 1997; Schwenk, 1985). Due to the time lag between the actual incident and the time this request has been made, the recollection of the respondent or informant may not be complete. This might even be more challenging when it comes to recalling decision processes (Schwenk, 1985). As such, it is ideal for us to keep research notes all the time or put all decisions and processes down in writing.

11.5.4 Maintaining a reference list

It is important to keep a list of articles that you have read, even if you eventually find that some of them are not as relevant after reading. The articles you read reflect the routes of thought you have taken in your research process, especially with regards to the literature review and hypotheses development stages. You should also file them into folders (either hard copies in a cabinet, or soft copies on computer) based on sub-topics. You should have a record of the key issues in each article to allow you to refer back to them easily. The classification of topics for filing can be based on the concepts of the study, theories or geographical coverage (for area-specific type studies), depending on your preference, your own organization of the project, and how the literature review or results are to be organized.

11.5.5 Always seek to communicate your ideas

Many research students have the wrong perception that research is about sitting in front of the computer, writing an original piece of work and submitting it for publication. They do not realize that an important part of research success is actually the process of communicating their ideas. There are various ways in which research ideas can be communicated, such as formal or informal presentation to colleagues, roundtable discussions and seminar presentations. The essence of communication is not just to reach out to a potential audience; more importantly, communicating ideas often does help us crystallize our thinking.

KEY TERMS

- Abstract
- Communication
- Conclusion
- Discussion
- Flow of writing
- Hypotheses development
- Implication
- Introduction
- Jargon
- Language
- Limitations

- Literature review
- Methodology
- Reference list
- Research notes
- Results
- Rewriting
- Structure of writing
- Summary
- Writing format
- Writing style

SUMMARY

- A typical research study contains sections covering the following: (1) summary or abstract; (2) introduction; (3) background and literature review; (4) industry or location context (if research topic is highly industry- or location-specific); (5) development of theory and propositions or hypotheses development; (6) methodology; (7) results; (8) discussion; (9) conclusions; (10) references; and (11) tables, figures and appendices. Very often there is also an acknowledgement section.
- The summary or abstract presents the entirety of the research.
- A study may sometimes include an industry or location section if the study is industry- or location-specific.

- The limitations must be related to what are covered within the boundary of the study.
- While some jargon is largely unavoidable, it must be managed to ensure the readability of the research by a larger audience.
- The use of past and present tense must be consistent within a particular aspect of research output.
- Footnotes should be avoided as far as possible as they are less likely to attract the reader's attention.
- Spelling and grammatical errors should always be eliminated.
- Rewriting is essential to make the writing clearer.
- It is good practice to keep research notes, maintain a reference list and always seek to communicate your ideas.

QUESTIONS

1. What does a study's abstract section usually contain?
2. What should an introduction section of a study seek to achieve?
3. Discuss the pros and cons of using first-person language in research outputs.
4. What is jargon?
5. What are some of the things to look out for in terms of language when writing up?
6. What are some tips for rewriting?
7. What are some good practices when it comes to preparing for writing up?

ADDITIONAL READINGS

Amis, J.A. and Silk, M.L. (2008) 'The philosophy and politics of quality in qualitative organizational research', *Organizational Research Methods*, 11 (3): 456–80.

Arnaudet, M.L. and Barrett, M.E. (1984) *Approaches to Academic Reading and Writing.* Englewood Cliffs, NJ: Prentice Hall.

Bailey, S. (2011) *Academic Writing: A Handbook for International Students* (3rd edition). New York, NY: Routledge.

Bedeian, A.G., Sturman, M.C. and Streiner, D.L. (2009) 'Decimal dust, significant digits, and the search for stars', *Organizational Research Methods*, 12 (4): 687–94.

Behrens, L. and Rosen, L.J. (2011) *A Sequence for Academic Writing* (5th edition). New York: Pearson Education.

Cunliffe, A.L. (2011) 'Crafting qualitative research: Morgan and Smircich 30 years on', *Organizational Research Methods*, 14 (4): 647–73.

Duncan, W.J. (1974) 'Transferring management theory to practice', *Academy of Management Journal*, 17 (4): 724–38.

Edwards, J.R. and Berry, J.W. (2010) 'The presence of something or the absence of nothing: Increasing theoretical precision in management research', *Organizational Research Methods*, 13 (4): 668–89.

Evans, D.G. (1995) *How to Write a Better Thesis or Report*. Melbourne: Melbourne University Press.

Evans, D.G., Gruba, P. and Zobel, J. (2011) *How to Write a Better Thesis* (3rd edition). Parkville: Melbourne University Press.

Goldfarb, B. and King, A.A. (2016) 'Scientific apophenia in strategic management research: Significance tests and mistaken inference', *Strategic Management Journal*, 37 (1): 167–76.

Hartley, J. (2008) *Academic Writing and Publishing: A Practical Handbook*. Oxford: Routledge.

Heppner, P.P. and Heppner, M.J. (2004) *Writing and Publishing Your Thesis, Dissertation and Research: A Guide for Students in the Helping Professions*. Belmont, CA: Brooks/Cole.

Hogue, A. (2008) *First Steps in Academic Writing*. White Plains, NY: Pearson/Longman.

Kilduff, M. (2007) 'Editor's comments: The top ten reasons why your paper might not be sent out for review', *Academy of Management Review*, 32 (3): 700–2.

Kirkman, B.L. and Chen, G. (2011) 'Maximizing your data or data slicing? Recommendations for managing multiple submissions from the same dataset', *Management and Organization Review*, 7 (3): 433–46.

Kirton, B. (2012) *Brilliant Academic Writing*. New York: Pearson.

Leki, I. (1998) *Academic Writing: Exploring Processes and Strategies* (2nd edition). Cambridge: Cambridge University Press.

Lewis, M.W. (2000) 'Exploring paradox: Toward a more comprehensive guide', *Academy of Management Review*, 25 (4): 760–76.

Locke, L.F., Spirduso, W.W. and Silverman, S.J. (2013) *Proposals that Work: A Guide for Planning Dissertations and Grant Proposals* (6th edition). Thousand Oaks, CA: Sage Publishing.

Maxwell, S.E. and Cole, D.A. (1995) 'Tips for writing (and reading) methodological articles', *Psychological Bulletin*, 118 (2): 193–8.

Murray, R. (2011) *How to Write a Thesis* (3rd edition). Maidenhead: Open University Press.

Oliver, P. (2008) *Writing Your Thesis* (2nd edition). London: Sage Publishing.

Oshima, A. and Hogue, A. (2007) *Introduction to Academic Writing*. White Plains, NY: Pearson/Longman.

Pierce, J.R. and Aguinis, H. (2013) 'The too-much-of-a-good-thing effect in management', *Journal of Management*, 39 (2): 313–38.

Poole, M.S. and Van de Ven, A.H. (1989) 'Using paradox to build management and organization theories', *Academy of Management Review*, 14 (4): 562–78.

Richardson, L. (2000) 'Evaluating ethnography', *Qualitative Inquiry*, 6 (2): 253–5.

Rose, M. and Kiniry, M. (1998) *Critical Strategies for Academic Thinking and Writing* (3rd edition). Boston, MA: Bedford Books of St Martin's Press.

Rudestam, K.E. and Newton, R.R. (2007) *Surviving Your Dissertation: A Comprehensive Guide to Content and Process* (3rd edition). Thousand Oaks, CA: Sage Publishing.

Sadler, D.R. (2006) *Up the Publication Road: A Guide to Publishing in Scholarly Journals for Academics, Researchers and Graduate Students*. HERDSA Green Guide No. 2 (2nd edition). Brisbane: The University of Queensland, Teaching and Educational Development Institute.

Shrivastava, P. (1987) 'Rigor and practical usefulness of research in strategic management', *Strategic Management Journal*, 8(1): 77–92.

Soles, D. (2010) *The Essentials of Academic Writing* (2nd edition). New York, NY: Cengage Learning.

Swales, J.M. and Freak, C.B. (2012) *Academic Writing for Graduate Students: Essential Tasks and Skills* (3rd edition). Ann Arbor, MI: University of Michigan Press.

Sword, H. (2012) *Stylish Academic Writing.* Cambridge, MA: Harvard University Press.

Tushman, M. and O'Reilly III, C. (2007) 'Research and relevance: Implications of Pasteur's quadrant for doctoral programs and faculty development', *Academy of Management Journal*, 50 (4): 769–74.

Weiss, C.H. and Bucuvalas, M.J. (1980) 'Truth tests and utility tests: Decision-makers' frames of reference for social science research', *American Sociological Review*, 45 (2): 302–13.

Whetten, D.A. (1989) 'What constitutes a theoretical contribution?', *Academy of Management Review*, 14 (4): 490–95.

White, B. (2011) *Mapping Your Thesis: The Comprehensive Manual of Theory and Techniques for Masters and Doctoral Research.* Camberwell, Victoria: ACER Press.

REFERENCES

Agarwal, R., Echambadi, R., Franco, A.M. and Sarkar, M.B. (2006) 'Reap rewards: Maximizing benefits from reviewer comments', *Academy of Management Journal*, *49* (2): 191–6.

Aguinis, H., Werner, S., Abbott, J.L., Angert, C., Park, J.H. and Kohlhausen, D. (2010) 'Customer-centric science: Reporting significant research results with rigor, relevance, and practical impact in mind,' *Organizational Research Methods*, *13* (3): 515–39.

Angelova, M. and Riazantseva, A. (1999) '"If you don't tell me, how can I know?" A case study of four international students learning to write the U.S. way', *Written Communication*, *16* (4): 491–525.

Aytug, Z.G., Rothstein, H.R., Zhou, W. and Kern, M.C. (2012) 'Revealed or concealed? Transparency of procedures, decisions, and judgment calls in meta-analyses', *Organizational Research Methods*, *15* (1): 103–33.

Baldridge, D.C., Floyd, S.W. and Markóczy, L. (2004) 'Are managers from Mars and academicians from Venus? Toward an understanding of the relationship between academic quality and practical relevance', *Strategic Management Journal*, *25* (11): 1063–74.

Bartunek, J.M. and Rynes, S.L. (2010) 'The construction and contributions of "implications for practice": What's in them and what might they offer?', *Academy of Management Learning and Education*, *9* (1): 100–17.

Bem, D.J. (2003) 'Writing the empirical journal article', in J.M. Darley, M.P. Zanna and H.L. Roediger III (eds) *The Compleat Academic: A Career Guide* (2nd edition). Washington, DC: American Psychological Association. pp. 171–201.

Bergh, D. (2002) 'Deriving greater benefit from the reviewing process', *Academy of Management Journal*, *45* (4): 633–6.

Brown, R.D., Braskamp, L.A. and Newman, D.L. (1978) 'Evaluator credibility as a function of report style: Do jargon and data make a difference?', *Evaluation Quarterly*, *2* (2): 331–41.

Calder, B.J., Phillips, L.W. and Tybout, A.M. (1981) 'Designing research for application', *Journal of Consumer Research*, *8* (2): 197–207.

Cortina, J.M. and Folger, R.G. (1998) 'When is it acceptable to accept a null hypothesis: no way, Jose?', *Organizational Research Methods*, *1* (3): 334–50.

Feldman, D.C. (2004) 'The devil is in the details: Converting good research into publishable articles', *Journal of Management*, *30* (1): 1–6.

Feldman, D.C. (2005) 'Conversing with editors: Strategies for authors and reviewers', *Journal of Management*, *31* (5): 649–58.

Gioia, D.A., Corley, K.G. and Hamilton, A.L. (2012) 'Seeking qualitative rigor in inductive research: Notes on the Gioia methodology', *Organizational Research Methods*, *16* (1): 15–31.

Golden, B.R. (1992) 'The past is the past – or is it? The use of retrospective accounts as indicators of past strategy', *Academy of Management Journal*, *35* (4): 848–60.

Golden, B.R. (1997) 'Further remarks on retrospective accounts in organizational and strategic management research', *Academy of Management Journal*, *40* (5): 1243–52.

Golden-Biddle, K. and Locke, K. (1993) 'Appealing work: An investigation of how ethnographic texts convince', *Organization Science*, *4* (4): 595–616.

Holbrook, M.B. (1986) 'A note on sadomasochism in the review process: I hate when that happens', *Journal of Marketing*, *50* (3): 104–8.

Johanson, L.M. (2007) 'Sitting in your reader's chair: Attending to your academic sensemakers', *Journal of Management Inquiry*, *16* (3): 290–4.

Joiner, T.A., Leveson, L. and Langfield-Smith, K. (2002) 'Technical language, advice understandability, and perceptions of expertise and trustworthiness: The case of the financial planner', *Australian Journal of Management*, *27* (1): 25–43.

Kerr, N.L. (1998) 'HARKing: Hypothesizing after the results are known', *Personality and Social Psychology Review*, *2* (3): 196–217.

Ketchen, D.J. Jr. (2002) 'Some candid thoughts on the publication process', *Journal of Management*, *28* (5): 585–90.

Leung, K. (2011) 'Presenting post hoc hypotheses as a priori: Ethical and theoretical issues', *Management and Organization Review*, *7* (3): 471–9.

Mook, D.G. (1983) 'In defense of external invalidity', *American Psychologist*, *38* (4): 379–87.

Pfeffer, J. (2007) 'A modest proposal: how we might change the process and product of managerial research', *Academy of Management Journal*, *50* (6): 1334–45.

Pratt, M.G. (2009) 'From the editors. For the lack of a boilerplate: Tips on writing up (and reviewing) qualitative research', *Academy of Management Journal*, *52* (5): 856–62.

Rynes, S. and Gephart, R.P. Jr. (2004) 'From the editors: Qualitative research and the "Academy of Management Journal"', *Academy of Management Journal*, *47* (4): 454–62.

Schwenk, C.R. (1985) 'The use of participant recollection in the modeling of organizational decision processes', *Academy of Management Review*, *10* (3): 496–503.

Seibert, S.E. (2006) 'Anatomy of an R&R (or, reviewers are an author's best friends ...)', *Academy of Management Journal*, *49* (2): 203–7.

Siggelkow, N. (2007) 'Persuasion with case studies', *Academy of Management Journal*, *50* (1): 20–4.

Stanley, T.D. (2005) 'Beyond publication bias', *Journal of Economic Surveys*, *19* (3): 309–45.

Steffens, P.R., Weeks, C.S., Davidsson, P. and Isaak, L. (2014) 'Shouting from the ivory tower: A marketing approach to improve communication of academic research to entrepreneurs', *Entrepreneurship Theory and Practice*, *38* (2): 399–426.

Strunk, W. Jr. and White, E.B. (2000) *The Elements of Style* (4th edition). Englewood Cliffs, NJ: Longman.

Sutton, R.I. (1997) 'The virtues of closet qualitative research', *Organization Science*, *8* (1): 97–106.

Tracy, S.J. (2010) 'Qualitative quality: Eight "big-tent" criteria for excellent qualitative research', *Qualitative Inquiry, 16* (10): 837–51.

Vermeulen, F. (2005) 'On rigor and relevance: Fostering dialectic progress in management research', *Academy of Management Journal, 48* (6): 978–82.

Vermeulen, F. (2007) '"I shall not remain insignificant": Adding a second loop to matter more', *Academy of Management Journal, 50* (4): 754–61.

Zha, D., Melewar, T. C., Foroudi, P. and Jin, Z. (2020) 'An assessment of brand experience knowledge literature: Using bibliometric data to identify future research direction', *International Journal of Management Reviews*, doi.org/10.1111/ijmr.12226

Zupic, I. and Cater, T. (2015) 'Bibliometric methods in management and organization', *Organizational Research Methods, 18* (3): 429–72.

Index

NOTE: Page numbers in *italic* type refer to figures and tables.